So, you want to learn COPTIC?
A guide to Bohairic Grammar

So, you want to learn COPTIC?
A guide to Bohairic Grammar

Sameh Younan

**St. Mary, St. Bakhomious, and St. Shenouda
Coptic Orthodox Church Kirawee**

Cover illustrations:
Proceeding clockwise from top left:
Coptic Psalmody book opened to the relevant section according to the liturgical cycle
Monument at the site of the 'tree of St.Mary', Matariya, Cairo.
Beginning of the Gospel of Saint Mark, Coptic Manuscript 1, Institut Catholique, Paris reproduced from Cannuyer, Christian "Coptic Egypt- the Christians of the Nile" Thames and Hudson Limited, London 2001 pg.79
Fresco of the Annunciation- Church of Saint Mary, The Syrian Monastery, Wadi Natrun
Christ and the apostles in the storm- Bibliotèque Nationale Paris, Ms Copte 13, fol.21v reproduced from Huber, Robert "The Bible through the ages", pg.231 Readers Digest, New York 1996
Spine:
First page of the Theotokia of the 5th day from *Hymns for the entire year*, Coptic and Arabic hymnal, 13th century, Coptic Museum, Cairo. Reproduced from Cannuyer, Christian "Coptic Egypt- the Christians of the Nile" Thames and Hudson Limited, London 2001 pg.60

National library of Australia
Cataloguing-in-Publication Entry

Younan, Sameh.
So, you want to learn Coptic? : A guide to Bohairic grammar.

Bibliography.
Includes index.
ISBN 0 9757949 0 6 (Hb)- ISBN 0-9757949-1-4 (Pb).

1. Bohairic dialect - Grammar. I. St. Mary, St. Bakhomious and St. Shenouda Coptic Orthodox Church. II. Title.

493.25

Copyright©2005

This publication is copyright. Other than for the purposes of and subject to the conditions prescribed under the Copyright Act, no part of it may in any form or by any means (electronic, mechanical, micro copying, photocopying, recording or otherwise) be reproduced, stored in a retrieval system or transmitted without prior permission. Enquiries should be addressed to the publishers.

Publisher:
St.Mary, St.Bakhomious, St.Shenouda Coptic Orthodox Church Kirrawee, Sydney, Australia.
For further copies of this book, contact www.learncoptic.com

Acknowledgements

A long time ago, I used to think it only took one person to write a book. Six years later, I've found myself deeply indebted to several people without whom this book would not have been possible.

Firstly, I would like to offer my thanks to God, who has given me many wonderful gifts, one of which was the motivation to complete this book.

Secondly, I would like to thank my parents for raising me and their tremendous love throughout all my life. Many important things in my life would have not been possible without them, not the least of which was this book which depended to a large part on my father's translations to the printer in Egypt. I would also like to thank my sister Nancy and her husband Rafik for their helpful advice, as well as their son Jeremy (he's promised to buy the book as soon as he's learnt to read). I also owe my gratitude to the rest of my family for their continual support and reassurance in helping this book make its way from an idea in my head to words in print.

His Holiness has shown a great love to our Coptic culture, this has manifested itself in a renewed interest in the Coptic language. His Grace Bishop Daniel has continued to promote this renewed interest, as evidenced by his unwavering support in the establishment of the Masters of Coptic Studies course at Macquarie University. He has been extremely supportive and encouraging for the publication of this book and for that I am very grateful.

Sincere gratitude is especially due to the fathers of the Church which published this book; Father Tadros El Bakhoumi for inspiring us all with his love of the Coptic language and continual encouragement and support in all aspects of my life, as well as Father Sharobim for his enthusiasm and assistance with many aspects of the publication.

Sydney is very fortunate to have an academic of the caliber of Dr.Heike Behlmer to direct the afore mentioned Masters of Coptic Studies. She has been very supportive of the Coptic community in Sydney, and has given me a great deal of time, advice and assistance with this book even though I am not officially one of her students. For that I am extremely grateful. Eitan Grossman of the Hebrew University also provided many helpful comments. His support of the Bohairic dialect is greatly valued and admired.

I owe a special commendation to the others who proof read the manuscript: Dr.Christian Balanza and his wife Sara made the effort to spend hours proof reading the manuscript not once but twice, and in doing so screened out errors from nearly every page. Upcoming doctor, basketball star and musician Mark Dimitri somehow found the time to also the review book. Pharmacist in making Christeen Hanna managed to read every chapter, complete all the exercises, and point out a whole series of mistakes which would have made the book look really silly all in the first few weeks of her second year of Pharmacy, and Barbara Samuel who has demonstrated a remarkable ability to pick out subtle inconsistencies and to give this book a more professional polish. Special thanks go to another pharmacist, Lily Michael who spent an enormous amount of time and effort in providing some expert corrections to the Coptic text, as well as to Fady Bebawy who gave some much needed feedback.

If you've enjoyed looking at the front cover, then you will also join me in my appreciation of graphic artist Sylvia Gindy who apart from designing the cover also provided free professional advice regarding different aspects of publication.

I would also like to thank my cousin Shenouda Makarie for his encouragement along every step of the way of the development of this book.

Of course I can't forget my fellow registrars at St.George and Sutherland hospitals for their free survey advice regarding the choice of the cover.

Finally, I would again like to thank Father Tadros El Bakhoumi for planting the seed that has resulted in this fruit.

CONTENTS

Foreword   *1*

Preface   *3*

1.   ***Learning to Read*** 11
- **1.1.**   **The Coptic alphabet** 11
- **1.2.**   **Vowels** 13
- **1.3.**   **Consonants** 14
  - The jenkem 16
  - 1.3.i. Consonants with varying pronunciations 17
  - How do you know if a word is of Greek origin? 23
  - Back to ⲧ and ⲥ 24
- **1.4.**   **Some more vowel rules** 24
  - Double vowels 24
  - Repeating vowels 25

2.   ***Nouns*** *27*
- **2.1.**   **The Articles** 27
  - 2.1.i. The Definite article (saying 'The' in Coptic) 27
  - Singular nouns 27
  - Plural nouns 29
  - The vocative 30
  - 2.1.ii. The indefinite article 31
  - 2.1.iii. Possessive articles- My, your and his 32
  - 2.1.iv. 'This and that'- The demonstrative articles 34
  - Near demonstrative article 34
  - Far demonstrative article 34
- **2.2.**   **Substituting for nouns- pronouns** 35
  - 2.2.i. Personal pronouns 35
  - 2.2.ii. Demonstrative pronoun 36
  - Far demonstrative pronoun 36
- **2.3.**   **Writing abbreviations** 37
- **2.4.**   **Describing nouns** 38
  - 2.4.i. Attributive construction 38
  - 2.4.ii. The possessive construction 39
  - 2.4.iii. Other ways of describing nouns 40
  - Every 40
  - Inflected adjectives 41

3.	*Making our first sentences* *47*
3.1.	**Subject + Predicate** 48
3.2.	**Subject + Copula+ Predicate** 48
3.3.	**Pronoun + copula** 49
4.	*Learning to count- numbers in Coptic* *53*
4.1.	**Numbers 1-10** 53
4.1.i.	How many? 53
4.1.ii.	Finding your place 55
4.2.	**10-100** 55
4.3.	**Numbers 100-900** 56
4.4.	**1000 and beyond** 57
5.	*Introducing Verbs* *61*
5.1.	**The first present** 61
5.1.i.	Intransitive verbs 62
	The postponed subject indicator 65
	Being Negative 66
	Using nouns or names in the first present 66
5.1.ii.	The Qualitative 66
	Where to use the qualitative 67
	Some exceptional qualitative verbs 68
5.1.iii.	Those "in between words"- prepositions 69
	Simple 70
	Compound 70
	Greek prepositions 71
5.1.iv.	Transitive verbs 73
5.1.v.	Who or which: introducing the relative converter ... 79
	Antecedent as subject 80
	When the antecedent is not the subject 85
	Addressing the adjective gap- making adjectives from the qualitative 87
	1) Nouns starting with the definite article 88
	2) When the noun starts with an indefinite article 88
	The relative substantive- making nouns from the relative converter 90
5.2.	**The past perfect tense** 91
	The presubject form 93
5.2.i.	Negative of the past perfect 94

5.3.	Forms derived from the infinitive	96
5.3.i.	The pronominal form	96
5.3.ii.	The construct form	98
5.3.iii.	The qualitative	101
	The passive voice	103
5.4.	**The relative past tense converter**	**104**
5.4.i.	Negative past relative	106
5.5.	**Prepositional pronominal form**	**107**
5.6.	**Construct-a-verbs: Compound verbs**	**111**
5.7.	**The indirect object**	**113**
5.8.	**Doing unto one's self- the reflexive**	**115**
5.9.	**The first future**	**118**
5.9.i.	The Negative first future	120
5.9.ii.	Relative first future	121
6.	***Linking Clauses***	***123***
6.1.	**Conjunctions**	**123**
6.1.i.	First position conjunctions	123
6.1.ii.	All about ⲭⲉ	125
6.1.iii.	Enclitic conjunctions	126
6.2.	**The subjunctive**	**129**
6.2.i.	Setting limits- using the 'limitative'	132
6.2.ii.	The Negative subjunctive	136
7.	***Now and then again- some More past and present tenses***	***139***
7.1.	**Dealing with imperfection- the imperfect tense**	**139**
7.1.i.	More than perfect -the pluperfect	142
7.1.ii.	The relative imperfect	144
7.2.	**A matter of circumstance- the circumstantial tense**	**144**
7.2.i.	Circumstantial conversion of the past perfect	149
7.2.ii.	Circumstantial conversion of the future tense	149
8.	***Verbs with their own rules***	***153***
8.1.	**Some unusual verbs**	**153**
	ⲭⲱ (to say)	153

Pronominal form 153
The construct form 154
Past infinitive 154
–ⲡⲁⲛⲥ̄ ⲡⲁⲛ– 156
ⲟⲩⲉⲧ– 157

8.2. The impersonal verbs **158**
8.2.i. Subject is 'it' 158
8.2.ii. No subject at all 160

8.3. Not quite a verb, not quite an adjective- the adjective verbs **162**

9. *Adverbs* *165*

9.1. Adverbs of time and place: **165**
9.1.i. Telling the time 166
The hour 166
Periods of the day 166
The day 168
Months of the Coptic Calendar 169

9.2. Adverbs of manner: **171**

9.3. Adverbs of situation **173**

9.4. Making Comparisons **175**
9.4.i. When things are the same 176
9.4.ii. More than 176

10. *More tenses* *179*

10.1. In the habit- the habitual tense **179**
10.1.i. Negative habitual 181
Relative conversion of habitual 182

10.2. Back to the future- the emphatic future tense **183**
10.2.i. Negative emphatic future 188

10.3. The imperfect future **189**
10.3.i. 1) Was about to… 189
2) It would have… 190

10.4. Giving orders- the imperative **192**
10.4.i. Verbs which take an ⲁ- 193
10.4.ii. Verbs which take ⲙⲁ- 194
10.4.iii. The negative imperative 197

10.4.iv.	A Milder imperative- The 'Optative'	199
10.5.	**When or if- The conditional**	**201**
10.5.i.	Negative of the conditional	203
11.	***More on the Infinitive***	***207***
11.1.	**Making things happen- the causative**	**207**
11.1.i.	Negative of the causative	209
11.2.	**Verbal substantive- making nouns from verbs**	**210**
11.3.	**Being able- the potential infinitive**	**213**
11.3.i.	Not being able- the negative potential	215
11.4.	**Not yet**	**217**
11.5.	**When one verb leads to another**	**218**
12.	***Anyone for Seconds? - The second tense***	***221***
12.1.	**Second present**	**221**
12.2.	**The second future tense**	**223**
12.3.	**The second past tense**	**225**
13.	***Asking questions- the interrogative***	***227***
13.1.	**Change of intonation**	**227**
13.2.	**Using the interrogative particle**	**227**
13.3.	**Using the interrogative pronouns**	**229**
14.	***Making conversation***	***235***
14.1.	**Getting acquainted**	**235**
14.1.i.	Jobs for the boys	236
14.1.ii.	What have you been doing?	236
14.2.	**Interjections**	**238**
14.2.i.	Non inflected interjections	239
14.2.ii.	Inflected interjections	239
15.	***Different ways of Having things***	***243***
15.1.	**Possessive articles**	**243**
15.2.	**Possessive construction**	**243**
15.3.	**Using the existential οτοn**	**244**
15.4.	**Possessive pronouns**	**247**

| 15.5. | The Possessed nouns | 249 |

16.   *Appendicies* *255*

Appendix 1 : Verb tables 255

Appendix 2 :Useful prefixes 259

Appendix 3 :Where do compound prepositions come from? 263

Appendix 4 -:variations in the pronominal suffix 267

Appendix 5- Answers 271

Glossary   285

References 307

Index   *309*

FOREWORD

By His Grace Bishop Daniel, Bishop of Sydney and Affiliated regions.

How does one begin to explain the importance of Coptic to the life of the Church?

As a monk living in St.Anthony's monastery, I would share in the midnight praises, chanting the hymns in the same words and spirit as the fathers of the Church, whose written expression of their spiritual rejoicing have touched the hearts of many in the generations that followed. I would read the inscriptions on the precious icons illuminated by the candles lit through the humble petitions of the believers who venerated them. I would search through the ancient Coptic manuscripts in the library, whose ageing pages have borne the gaze of my fore fathers over hundreds of years.

Some would have no doubt been sceptical when the prophet Isaiah proclaimed "blessed is My people Egypt". For how could a powerful pagan nation, who revered their own human kings as gods, and who oppressed and enslaved the true people of God, ever become God's people? Yet God's people they became, as the rubble at Tel Basta has become a monument to the shattering of the idol statue before the face of the infant Christ, so did the Egyptian culture become ever transformed, bearing an eternal witness to the joy of the new Christians who had discovered freedom from the slavery of sin and the path to salvation. That phase of Egyptian life is now called Coptic, which has survived in some form in spite of neglect and even the concerted efforts of many to destroy it. It has passed from generation to generation, with the choices each generation making determining whether it would survive into the next.

Now it is our turn.

As a Bishop presiding over a region many thousands of kilometres removed from Egypt, it gives me great pleasure to see the efforts of this generation. Under the leadership of His Holiness Pope Shenouda, Coptic has continued to be taught in our Coptic schools and Theological College thanks to the dedicated efforts of our Church Fathers, teachers and lecturers. A more recent development has truly amazed all those who have come to cherish the Coptic language. Who would have thought that Macquarie University, a major Sydney university, would undertake to establish a course completely dedicated to the study of Coptic, at a time when many other faculties are undergoing considerable cut backs?

So, You want to learn Coptic?

The book you are now holding is a significant step in the revival of Coptic, written in an engaging and friendly style; it will make Coptic accessible to many who have not had the opportunity nor the means to understand the depths of their heritage.

There are some who have difficulty coming to grips with the Coptic culture, and in some ways find it even to be foreign. But perhaps through education and illumination, they will for themselves discover its hidden treasures.

Daniel
With the Grace of God
Bishop of Sydney & Affiliated Regions,
Singapore, Thailand & Japan

PREFACE

Sameh Younan's book "So you want to learn Coptic" is an introduction to Bohairic Coptic. Bohairic is a regional form (commonly called "dialect") which dominated the Egyptian-Coptic language after the most important dialect of the First Millennium CE, Sahidic Coptic, had lost its productive impetus. There is a rich literature in Bohairic Coptic preserving much of the fascinating heritage of Egyptian Christianity: Biblical translations, martyrdoms and other saints' lives, sermons and liturgical texts. Moreover, Bohairic Coptic is still of vital importance today as the liturgical language of the Coptic Church. Sameh Younan's goal is to provide an introduction to Bohairic Coptic especially for those with little previous familiarity with formal English grammar, who may be daunted by the terminology used in traditional grammars of the Coptic language. He achieves this by using a didactic approach which will certainly lower the threshold of worry for those wanting to learn Bohairic by self-study. The author is to be congratulated on his effort, which is certain to find a large resonance among readers interested in studying the wealth of Bohairic Coptic literature in the original.

Dr Heike Behlmer
Lecturer in Coptic Studies
Macquarie University, Sydney

INTRODUCTION

What is Coptic anyway?

If you've ever been in the position of looking for a job, you've probably heard the saying "it's not what you know, but who you know." Something similar applies to asking "what is Coptic?", because the answer really does depend on who you ask almost as much as on what it actually is. An Egyptologist will tell you that Coptic is the last phase in the development of the language of Ancient Egypt, which had started with those familiar hieroglyphics. A New Testament scholar will tell you that Coptic was one of the first languages into which the New Testament was translated. Now it comes time to ask an indigenous Orthodox Christian coming from Egypt- other wise known as a Copt. Even here, you'll find the answer still depends on which Copt you ask. Say you speak to a typical tertiary educated Copt (i.e. either an engineer or a pharmacist). He could tell you it's the language used for those really long hymns - the ones no one understands. However, ask a few more Copts, dig a little deeper, and you will start to get quite a different answer. They will start to tell you that the Coptic language is part of their heritage and roots, and that it would be wonderful if Copts could speak it but it's a shame that scarcely anybody can. 'Heritage'? 'Roots'? These are big words, but what exactly do they mean, and if this language really is so important, what happened to it? For these answers we would turn to the history books, or at least to the paragraph below.

The history and development of Coptic

Few subjects in school brought a lump to my throat as did year seven history. It was with great pride that I learnt about one of the greatest civilisations of all time; the pyramids, the sphinx, ridiculously large statues, Cleopatra, Aida, the setting for numerous Hollywood blockbusters; what other ancient civilisation had produced so many household names? (Apart from Greek, Roman and Chinese but let's not think about those). As every child in year seven knows, the Egyptians used to write in Hieroglyphics. All the Egyptian monuments are inscribed with hundreds of Hieroglyphics. Hieroglyphics was the written script of the language spoken by the Egyptians at that time, starting at about 3000 BC. As attractive as Hieroglyphics was to look at, it actually took quite a lot of effort to write. Each Hieroglyphic character represented a common object, they could represent the sound of the object, or an idea associated with the object. As you could imagine, this could lead to a lot of characters, in fact, Ancient Egyptian writing used more than 2000 characters. Now that's a lot to remember. No one knew this more than the pagan priests of the time, so they developed another script which simplified the hieroglyphics so that they wouldn't take as long to draw. This parallel script was called hieratic.

Meanwhile, Hieroglyphics became exported to the Sea Faring Phoenicians (modern day Lebanese). They took the Hieroglyphic script, simplified it, and eventually passed it on to the Greeks who used it as the basis of their alphabet (which eventually became the basis for the English Alphabet).

By the 5th century BC, even Hieratic was considered too laborious to write, so a new simpler and less attractive script was devised, which cut out about 90% of the hieroglyphics. This leaner and meaner script was called Demotic.

Times were changing on the international scene, as a new superpower began to emerge. Lead by Alexander the Great, Greek culture swept the world, and Egypt was no exception. Egypt was conquered by Greece in 313 BC, and became heavily influenced by Greek culture. The Greeks brought with them their alphabet which had originally come from Egypt, and which they were now about to give back to the Egyptians. Greek was very much the 'in culture', you had to be Greek to be seen. A crisis started to hit Egyptian pagan priests. Sales of magic amulets were an important revenue raiser, however sales had plummeted after people had stopped being able to read Demotic, as all the rich important people could only read Greek. The pagan priests at the time then decided to transliterate the spoken Egyptian language into Greek letters, adding some Demotic letters for sounds that didn't have a Greek equivalent. This new script was a hit, and started to spread to other applications.

At around 1300 BC, Egypt had a brief phase of Monotheism under the rule of Akhenaton, when they had worshipped the sun. Egypt was now to return to Monotheism, not to worship the sun, but to worship the "sun of righteousness"[*], the Lord Jesus Christ. After Saint Mark had completed his preaching mission, a growing number of Greek speaking, non Demotic reading missionaries came to Egypt to preach to the illiterate but spiritually hungry Egyptian speaking peasants. To meet them half way, the missionaries wrote their Greek texts into the Egyptian language using Greek letters. Unlike the pagan priests, they initially didn't use any Demotic letters, but later started to add them to the Greek alphabet, ending up with the script which we now call Coptic.

Coptic therefore became linked hand in hand with the Christianity of Egypt. It was the language which the common people of Egypt spoke. The Bible and other church writings were translated into Coptic, hymns were written in Coptic, and Abbots wrote to their monks in Coptic. The martyrs of Egypt, the Popes and the saints, spoke in Coptic, prayed and chanted in Coptic. Coptic was impossible to separate from Christianity in Egypt. It is therefore no surprise that by far the most prolific of Coptic writers was one of the great saints of the Church. St.Shenouda the Archimandrite of the

---

[*] Malachi 4:2

white monastery took Coptic to new literary heights using his considerable rhetorical and linguistic skill.

Egypt was conquered by the Arabs in 642 AD. The Arab leaders began to force the Copts who worked in important government positions to learn Arabic. At times, persecution became more direct and violent, with Coptic being actively prohibited. Meanwhile, Coptic liturgical texts began to appear written along side Arabic translations. It was clear that Arabic had begun to proliferate in the Church. Young people no longer saw a need to learn this old language. One can imagine a youth with an attitude telling their parents "get with the times, this is the 1500's, we've got to look to the future, we can't be stuck with the boring old past."

Slowly but surely, the Coptic language began to wither as a spoken language, probably dying by the 17th century. For the Egyptologist, the last enduring flame of the Ancient Egyptian language had been extinguished. For the Early Christian scholar, the real action was already over 1000 years before. For the Copts, an integral organ of their community had died.

Somewhat of a revival occurred in the 19th century under the leadership of Pope Cyril IV. He began a movement to educate the clergy in different Church teachings, which included Coptic language education. As part of this revival, Erian Moftah was appointed to standardise the pronunciation of Coptic. With this intention, he consulted the current Greek pronunciation, presuming that it had retained the original pronunciation of many of the Coptic letters. Perhaps unknown to Moftah, was the fact that Greek had itself undergone some changes in pronunciation under the reign of the Turks.

You mean there's more than one?

At this point it should be understood that when we talk about 'Coptic' we really need to be aware of the particular *dialect* to which we are referring. What do I mean by dialect? Let's take English as an example. Compare the variations in language which an Englishman, an American and an Australian would speak. The accents are different, some words may differ in meaning, and there may be some minor changes in spelling (e.g. swapping 'z's for 's's). By and large however, there would be no difficulty in the speakers of each understanding each other. Each of these variations is called a dialect. Whereas though there is scarcely little difference in written form between the English dialects, the variations in Coptic dialect are much larger. For example, one dialect has an extra letter, variations in spelling are the rule rather than the exception, and there are many words which are peculiar to only one dialect. It is likely that the Copts speaking the more different dialects would have had great difficulty understanding each other.

There were 5 major dialects used, but there were as many as 12 altogether, including the less common ones. The dialect which was spoken by a particular Copt depended largely on where he lived. Starting north in the Nile Delta, where Alexandria and Cairo are today, we find Bohairic. Travelling south we come to Fayum, where

Fayumic was spoken, followed by Lycopolitan of Asyut, then the Akhmin of middle Egypt which had Akhminic, and finally Sahidic of Upper Egypt. It was this dialect which became the mostly widely used, the dialect which Saint Shenouda used for his writings and indeed the dialect in which the official Church translation of the Bible was made. The Nile Delta however had the rich heritage of the Wadi Natrun monasteries, which kept the Bohairic dialect alive even as Arabic became more and more dominant. When the Church moved its official headquarters from Alexandria to Cairo, Bohairic became the official dialect of the Church, and it is this dialect which would be recognised by Copts today as being 'Coptic.' This creates a bit of a dilemma at times, because although Bohairic is the dialect which most Copts would be interested in, Sahidic is the one in which those Egyptologists and New Testament scholars have greater interest, especially when a large number of Gnostic texts were found in this dialect in the Nag Hammadi. As a result, the greater part of the Grammatical aids and published texts of the Western world are in Sahidic. In Egypt however, as you would imagine, nearly all Coptic resources are in Bohairic.

Where are we now?

In the 21st century, Coptic remains an unspoken language. Liturgy books are frequently published with either no Coptic or Coptic transliterated into a modern language. On the other hand, there continues to be an interest in learning Coptic among certain members of the community. New advances in technology, in particular the internet, have allowed access to resources which were otherwise inaccessible to all but the most devoted academics. In the West, those very same Egyptologists and Early Christian scholars have devoted a great deal of time to the research and publication of Coptic resources, notable examples being Crum's "Coptic Dictionary", Stern's "Koptisch Grammatik:" and more recently, Layton's "A Coptic Grammar." Meanwhile, the Coptic Orthodox Church has had a revival under the leadership of her last two patriarchs, Pope Cyril VI and Pope Shenouda III. The Copts in the Diaspora have been able to provide a wealth of resources under the freedom and prosperity of their newly adopted homes, and with that a new interest in Coptic by youths keen to discover their identity.

What is Coptic? In the book of Acts, we read that the handkerchief of St.Paul, a plain ordinary piece of cloth, was able to provide healing to those who touched it in faith[†]. Its mere presence before the Saint was enough to impart this blessing; the grace of Saint Paul could not be separated from the garments in which he lived. Coptic is the handkerchief which wiped the brow of the suffering martyrs who endured towards their heavenly reward; it is the relic bearing the everlasting impression of the lives of those

---

† Acts 19:12

who lived and breathed it, and it is the handkerchief infused with the fragrance of the sweet smelling aroma of the sacrifice of the first Christians of the Church.

Coptic is our link to the fathers of our Church, and is hence an invaluable treasure of our past. I pray that it will continue to be so for our present and our future.

So, You want to learn Coptic?

Abbreviations

AmBal= Balestri et. H. Hyvernat "Acta Martyrum" vol 1 Paris 1907

AmHyv= Hyvernat, Henri "Les Actes des Martyr de L'Egypte

adj= adjective

adv= adverb

art= article

comp= compound

conj= conjunction

dem= demonstrative

f= feminine noun

Gk= word of Greek origin

Heb= Hebrew

hom. vat ii= De vis, Henris "Homélies Coptes de la vaticane" vol. II Hauniae 1929

imp= imperative

infl.= inflected

interj= interjection

interrog.=interrogative

m= masculine noun

no= number

Obj=object

P= person

part=particle

p.noun=pronoun

pfx=prefix

pl= plural

Poss = possessive

poss. noun = possessed noun

prep= preposition

pronom=pronominal

prop.noun= proper noun

q= qualitative form

rfx= reflexive verb

s= singular

S.Pachomii vita=Lefort.L "S.Pachomii Vita- Bohairice scripta) Paris 1925

SinArch= Leipoldt, Iohannes "Sinuthii Archimandritae vita et opera omnia" Otto Harrassowitz 1906

v.i= intransitive verb

v.t= transitive verb

v= see

vb= verb

Note: - two references are given for each Psalm. The first in bold refers to the Septuagint reference, while the second refers to that of the Masoretic texts.

1. LEARNING TO READ

The first step in learning any language is learning to pronounce the letters. It would obviously be easier to learn a language like French or German which uses the same letters as English than it would be to learn Hebrew or Chinese. Coptic falls somewhere in between. Although it does not use a Latin based alphabet, many of the letters will look quite familiar and some will also share the same pronunciation in Coptic as they do in English.

Note that the pronunciation guide presented here is based on the modern ecclesiastical pronunciation. Recent research pioneered by Emil Maher (now Father Shenouda Maher) has suggested that the original Bohairic dialect may have been pronounced differently to the current pronunciation. That form of pronunciation is called *Old Bohairic*.

A brief reference will be made to the Old Bohairc pronunciation, however the major emphasis will be put on the modern pronunciation.

1.1. The Coptic alphabet

Coptic was the final stage of development of the ancient Egyptian language spoken since the time of the Pharaohs. Its earliest written form was Hieroglyphics. This later evolved to Hieratic then subsequently to Demotic. At some stage around the beginning of the first Millennium, the Coptic script was transcribed into the Greek alphabet. Hence the first 24 letters are imported directly from Greek.

After the 5th Greek letter, a Coptic letter ⲋ was added. This does not appear in any words and only ever appears as a number.

In the Bohairic dialect, another 7 letters of Demotic origin were added to the end of the alphabet to make up for sounds that have no equivalent in Greek, leaving a total of 32 letters. The letters are shown in the table below, with more explanation about each in the sections that follow.

So, You want to learn Coptic?

Letter	Name	Pronun.	Letter	Name	Pronun.
Ⲁ ⲁ	Alpha	a	Ⲡ ⲡ	Pe	p
Ⲃ ⲃ	Vita	b, v	Ⲣ ⲣ	Ro	r
Ⲅ ⲅ	Gamma	g, gh, n	Ⲥ ⲥ	Seema	s
Ⲇ ⲇ	Delta	d, th	Ⲧ ⲧ	Tav	t
Ⲉ ⲉ	Eey	e	Ⲩ ⲩ	Epsilon	i
Ⲋ ⲋ	So-ou	-	Ⲫ ⲫ	Phi	f
Ⲍ ⲍ	Zeeta	z	Ⲭ ⲭ	Key	k, sh, kh
Ⲏ ⲏ	Eeta	ee	Ⲯ ⲯ	Epsi	eps
Ⲑ ⲑ	Theta	th, t	Ⲱ ⲱ	Omega	au
Ⲓ ⲓ	Yota	i	Ϣ ϣ	Shai	sh
Ⲕ ⲕ	Kappa	k	Ϥ ϥ	Fai	f
Ⲗ ⲗ	Lola	l	Ϧ ϧ	Khai	kh
Ⲙ ⲙ	Mey	m	Ϩ ϩ	Hori	h
Ⲛ ⲛ	Ney	n	Ϫ ϫ	Jenja	j, g
Ⲝ ⲝ	Exi	x	Ϭ ϭ	Cheema	ch
Ⲟ ⲟ	O	o	Ϯ ϯ	Ti	ti

Learning to read

1.2. Vowels

What is a vowel? If you cast your mind back to Kindergarten, you'll remember the English vowels being a, e, i, o, u. Ever wondered why they were called vowels? I never did till I started learning Coptic. According to people "in the know", vowels are letters you say without closing any part of your mouth. Try it. The other letters are consonants, that require you to close part of your mouth while pronouncing the letter. You'll notice that there are scarcely any words that don't have any vowels (I can't think of any myself, but I'm sure that if I said that then somebody would find one). In fact, you can scarcely say more than two consonants in a row without needing a vowel.

Anyway, naturally Coptic also has vowels whose names and pronunciation are shown in the table below:

Ⲁ ⲁ	**Alpha**, "a" as in "art"
Ⲉ ⲉ	**Ey**, "e" as in "let"
Ⲏ ⲏ	**Eeta** "ee" as in "feet"
Ⲓ ⲓ, Ⲩ ⲩ	**Iota, Epsilon** both "i" as in "sit"
Ⲟ ⲟ	**O** "o" as in "stop"
ⲟⲩ	"ou" as in "soup"
Ⲱ ⲱ	**Omega** "au" as in "baud"

Two things are worth noticing here, the first is that the ⲓ and ⲩ are both pronounced the same. The second is that the same ⲩ appears twice in the table. The first time on its own, then two vowels down as a part of the combination vowel ⲟⲩ. The combination vowel has a different pronunciation to what you'd get if you simply added the combination of both the ⲟ and the ⲩ. ⲩ is pronounced differently again if its preceded by ⲉ or ⲁ. The different sounds ⲩ makes when combined with different letters are summarised in the table below:

ⲁⲩ	"av" is "have"
ⲉⲩ	"ev" as in "bev"
ⲟⲩ	"ou" as in "soup"
ⲩ	"i" if not preceded by any of the above

So, You want to learn Coptic?

Old Bohairic variations

Most of the vowels have a similar pronunciation, however ⲉ seems to have been pronounced more like ⲁ, as 'a' in 'fat' or 'far.'

1.3. Consonants

As English readers, we should be grateful that some of the Coptic consonants look and sound so similar to their English counterparts. Some of these are shown with some of the other more common consonants below.

Ⲙ ⲙ	**Mey**, pronounced 'm' as in 'man'
Ⲛ ⲛ	**Ney**, pronounced 'n' as in 'net'
Ⲕ ⲕ	**Kappa**, pronounced 'k' as in 'kite'
Ⲧ ⲧ	**Tav** "t" pronounced as in 'net'[‡]
Ⲥ ⲥ	**Seema**, pronounced "s" as in 'sit'[§]
Ⲡ ⲡ	**Pe**, pronounced "p" as in 'put'
Ⲣ ⲣ	**Ro**, pronounced 'r' as in 'rat'
Ϣ ϣ	**Sh**, pronounced 'sh' as in 'shut.'
Ϭ ϭ	**Chima**, pronounced 'tch' as in 'church'
Ⲍ ⲍ	**Zeeta**, pronounced 'z' as in 'zoo'

Old Bohairic variations: According to Old Bohairic proponents, ⲡ was pronounced as 'b' and ⲧ was usually pronounced as 'd', as in 'duck', though sometimes as 't' as in 'tide.' Some examples:

[‡] There is a case where the pronunciation of these letters varies which shall be discussed later on in this chapter.
[§] as above

Learning to read

ⲙⲉⲛ	men
ⲧⲉⲛ	ten
ⲧⲟⲡⲟⲥ	topos
ⲡⲟⲩ	pou
ⲕⲁⲧⲁ	kata

Now try to pronounce the following words:

Exercise 1.1

ⲛⲁⲛ	
ⲛⲁⲓ	
ⲙⲏⲧ	
ⲡⲁⲓ	
ⲙⲁⲩ	
ⲧⲁⲓ	
ⲙⲟϣⲓ	
ϩⲱⲛ	
ⲧⲱⲛ	

Now we'll look at some more consonants that have only one pronunciation:

Ⲍ ⲍ	"x"
Ⲕ ⲕ	"kh" ('ch' as in German 'Buch')
Ⲯ ⲯ	"ebs"
Ⲫ ⲫ	"ph" as in phone**

** Some people consider this letter to be also pronounced as 'v.' They say it is pronounced as 'ph' in all words of Greek origin as well as Coptic proper nouns, and as 'v' in all Coptic words apart from proper nouns.

So, You want to learn Coptic?

Ϥ ϥ	"f" as in fan
Ϩ ϩ	"h" as in "hat"
Ϯ ϯ	"ti" as in "tick"
ⲗ ⲗ	"l" as in lake

The jenkem

Now seems like a good time to introduce the jenkem. The jenkem is a little stroke that seems to appear all over the place. It looks like this: `

You'll see it appear in front of both consonants and vowels. When you see it come over a consonant, it is pronounced like an 'e' before the consonant.

E.g. ⲙⲙⲟⲛ is pronounced "emmon."

If it comes before a vowel, it places a stress on the vowel.

E.g. when pronouncing ⲁⲛⲟⲕ, you put a gap between the ⲁ and the rest of the word, so it's pronounced 'a-nok'.

Old Bohairic variations: According to the Old Bohairic pronunciation, ⲡ was pronounced as 'b.' Also, ⲫ was pronounced as 'ph' or as 'b.'

Some more examples:

ϣⲁⲣⲟⲛ	sharon
ϣⲁⲓ	shai
ϥⲁⲓ	fai
ⲡⲁⲧⲏⲣ	pateer
ϭⲓⲧϥ	chitf

Now try the following words:
Exercise 1.2

ⲍⲏⲗⲟⲥ	
ⲍⲩⲣⲟⲥ	

⳯ⲩⲗⲟⲛ	
ⲉⲟϯ	
ⲯⲁⲗⲓⲛ	
ϭⲉⲛ	
ϭⲁ	
ϯϣⲟⲩⲣⲏ	

How do you feel so far? You've now mastered 24 out of the 35 letters. By now you should be able to pronounce most words with little difficulty. Admittedly the letters to follow are a little more complicated, but you're well on the way to being able to read Coptic.

1.3.i. *Consonants with varying pronunciations*

Unfortunately, some consonants change their pronunciation depending on the letters around them. Before you start complaining, remember that English also has letters which change their pronunciation, and for no apparent reason. Consider 'g' for instance, sometimes it's a hard 'g', some times it's like 'j', and sometimes it's pronounced as 'f' if followed by an 'h.' At least Coptic rules have some consistency. Anyway, to start with, let's look at the first of these letters:

Ⲃ ⲃ Vita

This letter has two pronunciations: 'b' and 'v'
In names of places and people (proper nouns), it's always 'b'
In words which are not names, it's 'v' if followed by a vowel, but 'b' if it's followed by a consonant.

For example, ⲃⲱⲕ is not a name, the ⲃ is followed by a vowel, so the word is pronounced 'vauk'.

Ⲁⲃⲣⲁⲁⲙ on the other hand is a name, so the ⲃ is pronounced as 'b', and the word is abra-am.

Now how can you tell if a word is a proper noun? It's not as hard as you might think, as most of the proper nouns you'll come across will be recognisable as being similar to those in English, as with the Ⲁⲃⲣⲁⲁⲙ example above.

So, You want to learn Coptic?

Now try the following words:

Exercise 1.3

ϩⲱⲃ	
ⲃⲁⲗ	
ⲛⲟⲃⲓ	
ⲛ̀ⲛⲟⲩⲃ	
ⲃⲱϩⲉⲙ	
ⲗⲱⲃϣ	
ⲉ̀ⲃⲟⲗ	
ⲛⲓⲃⲉⲛ	

Old Bohairic variation: Ⲃ is considered to be pronounced as either 'b' or 'w.'

Ⲇ ⲇ Delta

Delta is pronounced as a hard 'th' as in "this" in all common nouns, but is pronounced as 'd' in proper nouns.

Examples:

ⲇⲉ	the
ⲓⲇⲱⲗⲉⲛ	ithaulen
ⲇⲟⲝⲁ	thoxa
ⲇⲓⲕⲉⲟⲥ	thikeos
ⲇⲁⲩⲓⲇ	david

Old Bohairic variation: Those who use the Old Bohairic pronunciation always pronounce Ⲇ as 'd.'

Exercise 1.4

ⲆⲨⲚⲀⲘⲒⲤ	
ⲆⲈⲖⲦⲀ	
ⲆⲒⲀⲔⲞⲚⲞⲤ	
ⲆⲒⲆⲞⲨ	
ⲆⲎⲘⲞⲤ	

Ⲑ ⲑ Theeta

Theeta is usually pronounced as a soft 'th' as in 'thin', but is pronounced as 't' if it comes after ⲱ, ⲥ, or ⲧ.

Old Bohairic variation: ⲑ is always pronounced as 't' in the old Bohairic pronunciation.

Examples:

ⲰⲐⲈϨ	eshteh
ⲐⲘⲀⲨ	ethmav
ⲐⲰⲰ	thaush
ⲰⲐⲞⲢⲦⲈⲢ	eshtorter
ⲘⲀⲦⲐⲈⲞⲚ	matteon

Exercise 1.5

ⲰⲐⲞⲨⲒⲦ	
ⲐⲈⲞⲤ	
ⲤⲐⲞⲒ	
ⲚⲐⲞⲔ	
ⲂⲎⲐⲖⲈⲈⲘ	
ⲐⲀⲘⲒⲞ	

So, You want to learn Coptic?

Ϧ ⳉ Ghama

Ghama has three separate pronunciations, which are as 'gh', 'g' and 'n.'

If it is followed by ⲱ, ⲟ or ⲁ, it's pronounced as 'gh.' There really isn't a corresponding letter for this sound in English, but think of the pronunciation as being similar to the sound you make when you gargle your throat.

If it's followed by ⲏ, ⲓ, ⲩ or ⲉ, it's pronounced as a hard 'g', as in 'get.'

If it's followed by ⳉ, ⲕ, ⲍ or ⲭ it's pronounced as 'n.'

If it's followed by any other consonant, it's pronounced as 'gh.'

I can hear you thinking from here: "how in the world am I going to remember all those?" In times like these it's always useful to make up a mnemonic. It works for me.

Let's first look at the first case where it's pronounced as 'gh.'

Now look at the letters ⲱ ⲟ ⲁ, if you pretend that the letters are English and that they're forming a word, you'll find that the word sounds like 'woah', as in the sound you'd make while falling down the slope of a roller coaster.

Similarly, if you look at the letters ⲏ ⲓ ⲩ ⲉ, you'd find that it looks like 'hive', as in 'bee hive.'

The next trick is to remember which sound each of these sets makes. This isn't so hard, all you need is an example that's easy to remember. One of the really common words you'll find is ⲁⳉⲓⲟⲥ (agios). Using this example you can see that the when the ⳉ comes before an ⲓ it's pronounced as 'g.' That way you know that it's pronounced as 'g' after all the other ⲏ ⲓ ⲩ ⲉ letters and that therefore it's the ⲱ ⲟ ⲁ letters that make it pronounced as 'gh.'

So much for the vowels. Now you need a way to remember how to pronounce ⳉ if followed by all other consonants.

You can remember the letters ⳉ ⲕ ⲍ ⲭ as 'gkxx.' As an example word, think of ⲁⳉⳉⲉⲗⲟⲥ, pronounced 'angelos.'

All that is left to remember is that ⳉ is pronounced the same way after consonants as it is after the ⲱ ⲟ ⲁ letters.

Learning to read

Some examples:

ⳅⲁⲣ	ghar
ⲁⳅⲓⲟⲥ	agios
ⳅⲉⲛⲛⲏⲧⲓⲥ	gennetis
ⳅⲏ	gee

Exercise 1.6

ⳅⲁⲙⲟⲥ	
ⳅⲟⳅⳅⳍⲗⲏ	
ⳅⲉⲛⲟⲥ	
ⲁⳅⲓⲁⲍⲓⲛ	

Old Bohairic variation: ⳅ is pronounced as g, gh or n.

ⳈⳈ Jenja

The good news about learning the ⲱ ⲟ ⲁ and ⲏ ⲓ ⳉ ⲉ mnemonics, is that they are also used for two other letters apart from ⳅ.

The first is for Ⳉ:

When followed by the ⲱ ⲟ ⲁ letters, its pronounced as 'g' as in 'get.'

When followed by ⲏ ⲓ ⳉ ⲉ letters, it's pronounced as 'j' as in jet.

Examples:

Ⳉⲉ	je
Ⳉⲁⲙⲏ	gamee
ⳈⲁⳈⲓ	gaji
Ⳉⲓⲙⲓ	jimi

Exercise 1.7

ⳈⲁⲡⲟⳈⲓ	

So, You want to learn Coptic?

ⲭⲏⲕ	
ⲡⲉϫⲁϥ	
ⲡⲉϫⲉ	
ⲕⲟⲩϫⲓ	
ⲡⲉϫⲱⲟⲩ	

Old Bohairic pronunciation: In the Old Bohairic pronunciation, ϫ is pronounced as 'dj', as in 'age.'

ⲭ ⲭ Key

Key is another one of those letters that has three pronunciations. This time the pronunciation depends on whether the word is of Greek or Coptic origin.

In words of Coptic origin, it's always pronounced 'k' as in 'kitchen.'

In words of Greek origin, it's pronounced as 'sh' if followed by the ⲏ ⲓ ⲩ ⲉ letters,

and 'kh' if followed by the ⲱ ⲟ ⲁ letters or a consonant.

A good example word to remember is ⲭⲉⲣⲉ which has the pronunciation of 'shere' as in

ⲭⲉⲣⲉ ⲛⲉ Ⲙⲁⲣⲓⲁ.

Examples:

ⲭⲏ (Coptic)	kee
ⲭⲣⲓⲥⲧⲟⲥ (Greek)	ekhristos
ⲃⲉⲭⲉ (Coptic)	veke
ⲭⲟⲣⲟⲥ (Greek)	khoros
ⲁⲣⲭⲱⲛ (Greek)	arkhaun

Exercise 1.8

Ⲙⲓⲭⲁⲏⲗ (Greek)	

Learning to read

ϫⲣⲱⲙ (Coptic)	
ϫⲁⲣⲓⲥⲙⲁ (Greek)	
ϫⲗⲟⲙ (Coptic)	
ϫⲏⲙⲓ (Coptic)	
ϫⲣⲓⲥⲧⲓⲁⲛⲟⲥ (Greek)	
ϫⲁⲣⲓⲍⲉⲥⲑⲉ (Greek)	

Old Bohairic: was usually pronounced as 'k', and may have been pronounced as 'kh' or 'sh' in Greek words.

You've now mastered the most common pronunciations in Coptic. Now just a few more details to polish off.

How do you know if a word is of Greek origin?

That's an obvious question which many people ask. Basically, you eventually learn through experience. However, here are some basic rules of thumb:
The word will generally be of Greek origin if it contains one of the following letters:

ⲍ ⲇ ⲅ ⲯ ⲋ ⲩ (as a vowel)

The word is of Coptic origin it contains one of the following letters:

ϣ ϥ ϧ ϫ ϭ ϯ

You may be wondering why I haven't included the 7th letter of Demotic origin, the ϩ in this list. There are in fact many Greek words that contain the ϩ, even though it is a letter of Egyptian origin. The reason for this is that there is a little stroke in Greek that looks like this: ʽ

As you can see, it looks like an apostrophe. It is called a 'rough breathing', and when it appears at the front of a word in Greek it's pronounced as 'h.'
Now when these words came to Coptic, they couldn't find a rough breathing to take, so they borrowed the ϩ instead. Hence some words of Greek origin use the ϩ.

Another discriminating feature is that verbs ending with any of the following syllables are generally of Greek origin:

−ⲓⲛ −ⲉⲓⲛ −ⲁⲛ −ⲥⲑⲉ −ⲓⲧⲉ −ⲥⲟⲛ −ⲱⲙⲉⲛ −ⲟⲩⲛ −ⲟⲓⲛ

Back to ⲧ and ⲥ

It was previously mentioned that the pronunciation of ⲧ and ⲥ sometimes varies. This occurs in words of Greek origin.

In words of Greek origin, ⲧ is pronounced 'd' as in 'dog' if it comes after a ⲛ and

ⲥ is pronounced 'z' if it comes before ⲙ.

Examples:

ⲡⲁⲛⲧⲟⲕⲣⲁⲧⲱⲣ	pandokrator
ⲁⲥⲡⲁⲥⲙⲟⲥ	aspazmos
ⲡⲗⲁⲥⲙⲁ	plazma
ⲡⲁⲛⲧⲱⲥ	pandaus

1.4. Some more vowel rules

At the beginning of a sentence

When the letter ⲓ begins a sentence and is followed by another vowel, it's pronounced as 'y.'

E.g. ⲓⲱⲧ is 'yaut'

Double vowels

ⲱⲓ

When the two letters ⲱⲓ come together, the combination is pronounced as 'oi' as in 'oil.'

E.g. ⲱⲓⲕ is pronounced 'oik.'

The following three double vowel rules apply only to Greek words.

ⲁⲓ

This combination is pronounced as 'e' in words of Greek origin.

E.g. ⲁⲓⲙⲁ— ema

Ⲇⲁⲓⲙⲟⲛ— themon

ⲕⲁⲓⲣⲟⲥ— keros

ⲉⲓ

ⲉⲓ is pronounced as 'i' in words of Greek origin.

ⲉⲡⲉⲓⲇⲏ— epithee

ⲉⲓⲣⲓⲛⲏ— irinee

Note that the ⲉ is very commonly left out altogether.

ⲟⲓ

ⲟⲓ is pronounced as ⲓ in words of Greek origin

ⲁⲣⲓⲛⲟⲓⲛ- arinin

ⲙⲉⲧⲁⲛⲟⲓⲁ - metania

ⲗⲟⲓⲡⲟⲛ - lipon

Repeating vowels

If a vowel is repeated to appear twice in a row in a word, a stress is made on the second vowel.

E.g. Ⲁⲃⲣⲁⲁⲙ is pronounced as 'Abra-am'

You've done it! You've now learnt all the rules for pronouncing Coptic. You may still not be able to read it fluently, but this will come with time. Practice reading every word you come across, refer back to the rules if you're unsure of a particular pronunciation. Eventually, you'll start to recognise words as opposed to recognising letters. By that stage, reading Coptic will have become second nature.

So, You want to learn Coptic?

2. NOUNS

2.1. The Articles

Now that you've learnt to read, the next step is to understand what you're reading. Here is where grammar and vocabulary come in. Learning what different words mean is the first step, putting them together requires an understanding of grammar.

The first important thing to learn is that different words belong to different classifications. Some words are nouns, some are verbs, some are prepositions. In fact, there are many different categories to which words can belong. These categories are known as "parts of speech."

The first part of speech we'll look at is the *noun*. Nouns are basic naming words. E.g. 'cat', 'dog', 'aircraft carrier' etc.

In many cases, nouns are introduced by little words called 'articles.' These are little words which frequently come before the nouns. Learning these will be our first step in learning Coptic grammar.

2.1.i. The Definite article (saying 'The' in Coptic)

Singular nouns

Ever wondered what the difference between 'the' and 'a' is? I.e. what is the difference between saying "the bird is singing" as opposed to "a bird is singing"?

The difference is that when you use 'the', you're referring to a particular bird, and everyone knows which bird you're talking about. When you use 'a bird', you could be referring to any bird at all rather than a particular one.

For this reason, 'the' is referred to as the 'definite' article, and 'a' is referred to as the 'indefinite' article.

Like English, Coptic also has definite and indefinite articles. Unlike English however, Coptic has more than one way of saying 'the.'

The way you use 'the' depends on what is referred to as the *gender* of the noun. If you've studied French or German at school, or are familiar with Arabic, you'll realise that different nouns are defined as being either masculine or feminine. There's no reason why a particular object should be masculine or feminine, but that's just the way it is. The only way you can know the gender is by learning it for each noun.

Coptic actually has three different masculine definite articles and three different feminine definite articles.

So, You want to learn Coptic?

The masculine definite articles are: **Ⲡⲓ** ⲡ̅ Ⲫ

The feminine definite articles are: Ϯ Ⲧ̅ Ⲑ

Before we go further, some basic ground rules need to be laid down:

Rule 1:

Ⲡⲓ is the exact equivalent of Ϯ

ⲡ̅ is the exact equivalent of Ⲧ̅

Ⲫ is the exact equivalent of Ⲑ

Rule 2:

Each set of articles can be divided into two groups. For the male set, the first group has **Ⲡⲓ** on its own, and the second has ⲡ̅ and Ⲫ together. Likewise, for the feminine set, Ϯ sits on its own, and Ⲧ̅ sits with Ⲑ.

Rule 3:

ⲡ̅ is very closely related to Ⲫ, and they have almost exactly the same grammatical use. The only difference is that Ⲫ is used before nouns starting with Ⲃ Ⲓ Ⲗ Ⲙ Ⲛ Ⲟ Ⲣ, and ⲡ̅ is used before all other nouns. The Ⲃ Ⲓ Ⲗ Ⲙ Ⲛ Ⲟ Ⲣ letters are affectionately known as the *vilminor letters*, which we'll find frequently effect the choice of letters for the spelling of words we'll come across throughout the book. A similar story applies to the feminine articles, here Ⲑ is used before the vilminor letters, and Ⲧ̅ is used before the non vilminor letters.

Now **Ⲡⲓ** and Ϯ are referred to as strong articles, but ⲡ̅/Ⲫ and Ⲧ̅ Ⲑ are referred to as a weak article. This is because **Ⲡⲓ** and Ϯ are used in more specific situations than their counterparts. For example, if you're referring to a specific father, you would say **ⲠⲒⲰⲦ**, because you're making a special effort to point out a particular father. If on the other hand, you were to say **ⲪⲒⲰⲦ**, you would be understood to be referring to the father who is already well known, or is already considered to be one of a kind. Hence ⲫⲓⲱⲧ would be understood to refer to *God* the Father, and likewise ⲡϣⲏⲣⲓ is understood to refer to the son Jesus Christ.

The use of these articles is summarised in the following table:

	Masculine	Female
strong	ⲡⲓ	ϯ
weak- non vilminor	ⲡ	ⲧ̇
weak- vilminor	ⲫ	ⲑ

Don't worry too much if you don't quite understand the difference about the weak and strong articles. In the end, they all just translate as 'the'.

Plural nouns

This is all fine, except for one thing. And that is these articles only apply for the *singular* form of the noun. That is, one of those articles would be appropriate for saying 'the' in 'the dog', but it would not be appropriate for saying 'the' in 'the *dogs.*' The feature of the noun which describes whether it's in the singular or plural is called it's *number*.

There are two definite articles for denoting the plural in Coptic. Unlike the singular definite articles, they are not dependent on the gender of the noun.

They are ⲛⲓ and ⲛⲉⲛ

ⲛⲓ is used in the vast majority of cases.

ⲛⲉⲛ is only used in sentences with constructions involving the word "of", the sentence taking the form of:

ⲛⲉⲛ (noun1) of (noun 2)

We shall will be formally introduced to the 'of' construction in **(2.4.i)**, and **(2.4.ii)** but for now we'll just take a brief example of its use to contrast the use of ⲛⲓ as opposed to ⲛⲉⲛ.

E.g. Saying "the hands" on its own would be ⲛⲓϫⲓϫ

However, "the hands of Aaron" is ⲛⲉⲛϫⲓϫ ⲛⲁ̇ⲁⲣⲱⲛ

Most nouns can be expressed in the plural without any change to the actual form of the noun. E.g. while in English the plural form of 'hand' is 'hands', in Coptic the plural form of ⲭⲓϫ is still ⲭⲓϫ.' The only thing that tells you if it's plural or not is the article in front.

The exceptions

Having said all that, there are actually a few nouns which take a different form in the plural than they do in the singular. Some of them are shown in the table below:

ϯⲫⲉ	The Heaven	ⲛⲓⲫⲏⲟⲩⲓ	The heavens
ⲡⲓⲁⲗⲟⲩ	The child	ⲛⲓⲁⲗⲱⲟⲩⲓ	The children
ⲡⲓⲥⲟⲛ	The brother	ⲛⲓⲥⲛⲏⲟⲩ	The brothers
ϯⲥⲱⲛⲓ	The sister	ⲛⲓⲥⲱⲛⲓ	The sisters
ⲫⲓⲱⲧ	The father	ⲛⲓⲟϯ	The fathers, parents
ϯⲥϩⲓⲙⲓ	The woman	ⲛⲓϩⲓⲟⲙⲓ	The women
ϩⲱⲃ	thing, work	ϩⲃⲏⲟⲩⲓ	things, works
ⲡⲃⲱⲕ	The slave/servant	ⲛⲓⲉⲃⲓⲁⲓⲕ	The slaves/servants

The vocative

I remember looking through the criteria for a course I was trying to get into, and finding that they were looking for "a sense of vocation" in the applicant. I couldn't quite understand what they meant, till I was told that 'vocation' means 'a calling.' So they were looking for a 'sense of calling.' Now I don't know if I had that sense of calling, but Coptic at least has a way of describing "a calling" which is called the 'vocative.' The vocative is used to call upon someone, usually in the context of asking for their help. Now here things become familiar, as the construction used for the definite article is also often used as the vocative.

For example, Ⲡϭⲟⲓⲥ doesn't just mean *"the Lord"*, but in some cases it means *'O Lord.'* It's usually easy to tell when the construction is being used for the definite article or for the vocative, as translating it as 'the' when it was intended for the vocative just doesn't make sense.

If this paragraph in particular seems a little hard to understand, don't worry. Just come back to it after you've gone a bit further into the book, by then you'll have come across many examples where it's clear that the definite article can only be translated as the vocative. We will need to learn a bit more grammar though before we come to those examples.

To make things a little easier, there is a letter specifically used for the vocative which is ⲱ, this is conveniently translated as 'O' as in ⲱ Ⲙⲁⲣⲓⲁ *"O' Mary."*

2.1.ii. The indefinite article

Next we'll look at saying 'a.' That is in saying 'a bag' instead of 'the bag.' Remember that this is called the 'indefinite article' whereas 'the' is called the 'definite' article. The Coptic word for 'a' is ⲟⲩ

Unlike the definite article, the indefinite article is independent of gender, so it doesn't change regardless of whether the noun is masculine or feminine.
E.g.

'A man' = ⲟⲩⲣⲱⲙⲓ

'A woman' = ⲟⲩⲥϩⲓⲙⲓ

Coptic differs again from English in that it has a *plural* form of the indefinite article. There is no direct English translation for this, but the closest approximation is 'some.' The plural indefinite article is ϩⲁⲛ which also attaches directly to the noun.
E.g.

(Some) men = ϩⲁⲛⲣⲱⲙⲓ

(Some) women = ϩⲁⲛϩⲓⲟⲙⲓ

ϩⲁⲛ is also combined with the word ⲟⲩⲟⲛ to give the special construction ϩⲁⲛⲟⲩⲟⲛ, which means 'some' as in 'some people.'

Vocab			
ⲓⲱⲧ	father (m)	ϣⲏⲣⲓ	son (m)
ⲙⲁⲩ	mother (f)	ϣⲉⲣⲓ	daughter (f)

Exercise 2.1
Translate the following into English:

a) Ⲫⲓⲱⲧ
b) ⲟⲩⲙⲁⲩ
c) ⲡϣⲏⲣⲓ

d) ϯϣⲉⲣⲓ
e) ϩⲁⲛⲓⲟϯ
f) ϩⲁⲛⲥⲛⲏⲟⲩ

2.1.iii. Possessive articles- My, your and his

In the earlier sections, we talked about the definite and indefinite articles. Now we will do the *possessive* articles. These articles refer to people and are used to indicate possession. Like the definite and indefinite articles, they attach directly to the noun with no gap in between.

Masculine object	Feminine object	Plural object	
ⲡⲁ	ⲧⲁ	ⲛⲁ	My
ⲡⲉⲕ	ⲧⲉⲕ	ⲛⲉⲕ	Your (masculine)
ⲡⲉ	ⲧⲉ	ⲛⲉ	(feminine)
ⲡⲉⲧⲉⲛ	ⲧⲉⲧⲉⲛ	ⲛⲉⲧⲉⲛ	(plural)
ⲡⲉϥ	ⲧⲉϥ	ⲛⲉϥ	His
ⲡⲉⲥ	ⲧⲉⲥ	ⲛⲉⲥ	Her
ⲡⲉⲛ	ⲧⲉⲛ	ⲛⲉⲛ	Our
ⲡⲟⲩ	ⲧⲟⲩ	ⲛⲟⲩ	Their

Note that whether the pronoun starts with a ⲡ or ⲧ for singular objects depends on the gender of the *object*, not the subject.

So for example if you were to say 'his mother', you would base the decision on the gender of 'mother', so it would be ⲧⲉϥⲙⲁⲩ.

People often get mixed up at this very point, so let's work through an example. Say you want to say "his mother."

Looking at the table above, you'd have three choices, ⲡⲉϥ Ⲧⲉϥ Ⲛⲉϥ

Ⲛⲉϥ only applies to plural words, so you can strike that off the list.

That leaves ⲡⲉϥ and Ⲧⲉϥ.

Your next step now is to think of the gender of the noun. ⲙⲁⲩ is a feminine word. So you pick the possessive article in the feminine object column which in this case is Ⲧⲉϥ.

Let's look at another example. Suppose you wanted to say "your father" while speaking to a feminine. To start with, we have a choice of ⲡⲉⲕ Ⲧⲉⲕ ⲡⲉ and Ⲧⲉ. (After scratching out the plural ones).

Now the first step is to look at the gender of the word for father, which is ⲓⲱⲧ. ⲓⲱⲧ is a masculine word, so you pick the possessive articles in the masculine object column which leaves you a choice of ⲡⲉⲕ and ⲡⲉ.

Since you're speaking to a feminine, you pick the ⲡⲉ, leaving you with: ⲡⲉⲓⲱⲧ

Vocab			
ⲥⲱⲙⲁ	body (m)	ⲉⲛⲧⲟⲗⲏ	commandment (f)
ⲥⲛⲟϥ	blood (m)	ϫⲱⲙ	book (m)
ϣⲟⲩⲣⲏ	censer (f)	ϣⲫⲏⲣ	friend (m)
ⲱⲓⲕ	bread (m)	ⲁⲫⲟⲧ	cup, chalice (f)
ⲁⲫⲉ	head (f)	ϫⲓϫ	hand (f)
ⲥⲱⲧⲏⲣ	Saviour (m)	ϣⲫⲉⲣⲓ	friend (f)

Exercise 2.2

a) ⲡⲁⲥⲱⲙⲁ *(Luke 22:19)*

b) ⲡⲉϥⲥⲛⲟϥ *(Acts 20:28)*

c) ⲡⲉⲛⲓⲱⲧ *(James 2:28)*

d) ⲡⲉⲛⲥⲱⲧⲏⲣ *(2 Peter 3:2)*

So, You want to learn Coptic?

e) ⲧⲉⲧⲉⲛⲁⲫⲉ (Acts 18:6)

f) ⲡⲉⲧⲉⲛⲛⲁϩϯ (1 Peter 1:7)

g) ⲡⲉⲛⲁϩϯ (Luke 7:50)

h) ⲧⲉϫⲓϫ (Acts 4:28)

Fill in the blanks:

i) ____ϣⲏⲣⲓ   your son (speaking to a female)

j) ____ⲓⲱⲧ   her father

k) ____ⲙⲁⲩ your mother (speaking to a group of people)

2.1.iv. 'This and that'- The demonstrative articles

Two commonly used words for introducing nouns are 'this' and 'that.' They are used to 'point' to a particular noun, or to 'demonstrate' it. Hence they are called the 'demonstrative.' When we point at something relatively close, we would say 'this', so 'this' is called the 'near demonstrative.' When you point to something further away, you would say 'that', which is called the 'far demonstrative.'

There are two broad groups of the 'demonstrative' in Coptic. The first which we shall look at here is the 'demonstrative article' and the second is the 'demonstrative pronoun', which we'll take a look at in **(2.2.ii)**.

Near demonstrative article

There are three near demonstrative articles in Coptic used as follows:

	masculine	feminine	plural
Demonstrative article	ⲡⲁⲓ	ⲧⲁⲓ	ⲛⲁⲓ

The demonstrative article comes straight before the noun in the same way that the other articles do.

So for example, let's work through how you would write 'this censer.'

The Coptic word for 'censer' is ϣⲟⲩⲣⲏ.

As it is a feminine word, you would chose ⲧⲁⲓ as the demonstrative article. You would then place it before ϣⲟⲩⲣⲏ to produce: ⲧⲁⲓϣⲟⲩⲣⲏ

Far demonstrative article

The far demonstrative, or the word for 'that' is ⲉⲧⲉ ⲙⲙⲁⲩ. It's different to the other articles we have learnt in that:

a) it comes after the noun

b) the noun still takes a definite article before it.

E.g **ⲡⲓⲥⲏⲟⲩ ⲉⲧⲉ ⲙⲙⲁⲩ** *(Matthew 14:1)*
"that time"

2.2. Substituting for nouns- pronouns

2.2.i. Personal pronouns

Occasionally, you may need to refer to a noun without mentioning its name. Instead of using the noun itself, you use what is called a 'pronoun.'

Personal pronouns are words used to substitute for names of people. Say you were to describe an action that somebody is doing; you could either use their name as for example "Peter is walking" or you could indirectly refer to Peter by saying "He is walking."

You would use the second case if it was already understood that Peter was the person being talked about. So here 'He' is the personal pronoun used to substitute for the noun 'Peter.' As 'Peter' is a person, 'He' becomes an example of a *personal* pronoun. Some other personal pronouns are: I, You, He/ She, they and we.

Coptic also has personal pronouns. The ones in the table below are called independent personal pronouns, because they can stand alone in the sentence. There are also *dependent* personal pronouns which we shall come across in **(5.1.i.)**

English	Coptic
I	ⲁⲛⲟⲕ
You (masculine)	ⲛⲑⲟⲕ
You (feminine)	ⲛⲑⲟ
You (plural)	ⲛⲑⲱⲧⲉⲛ
He	ⲛⲑⲟϥ
She	ⲛⲑⲟⲥ
We	ⲁⲛⲟⲛ
They	ⲛⲑⲱⲟⲩ

So, You want to learn Coptic?

2.2.ii. *Demonstrative pronoun*

Compare the sentences 'I saw this man', with 'I saw this.'
As discussed above, the word 'this' is referred to as the demonstrative. However, each of the two sentences in the line above illustrate a different type of demonstrative.

In the first case, the word 'this' comes before the word 'man' and hence as discussed in **(2.1.iv)** is the article.

In the second case, the word 'this' is not preceding a noun but is actually *replacing*, or substituting for the noun, so it is a pronoun. Hence in the second case it's used as the *demonstrative pronoun*.

In English, the demonstrative pronoun and the demonstrative article are the same word, which is simply 'this', however in Coptic, they are a bit different as we can compare in the table below:

	masculine	feminine	plural
Demonstrative pronoun	ⲫⲁⲓ	ⲑⲁⲓ	ⲛⲁⲓ
Demonstrative article	ⲡⲁⲓ	ⲧⲁⲓ	ⲛⲁⲓ

As an example, consider the sentence below where the 'this' does not come directly before the noun and hence the demonstrative pronoun is used.

E.g. ⲫⲁⲓ ⲡⲉ ⲡ̄ϣⲏⲣⲓ ⲙ̄ⲫϯ

"this is the son of God"

Note, there is a special set construction in Coptic as below:

ⲡⲁⲓⲁⲫⲟⲧ ⲫⲁⲓ

Here you can see the **ⲡⲁⲓ** before **ⲁⲫⲟⲧ** meaning 'this', but then there's also the demonstrative pronoun following it (ⲫⲁⲓ), if this were translated literally, it would mean: *"this chalice this"*
which wouldn't make sense.

However, in Coptic this construction has the sense of adding emphasis to the word 'this', so it actually means *"this very chalice"*.

Far demonstrative pronoun

In the above we have been dealing with the word 'this.' 'This' is actually called the 'near demonstrative.' In English, we also use a word for the *far* demonstrative. Any ideas what it could be?

It is actually the word 'that.' Coptic has three words for 'that' as shown below:

	masculine	feminine	plural
far demonstrative	ⲫⲏ	ⲑⲏ	ⲛⲏ

2.3. Writing abbreviations

There was no printing in the days of Coptic, manuscripts were copied by hand, which as you could imagine could be quite a time consuming process. To make things a little easier, some abbreviations were agreed upon, the most common of which are shown in the table below:

original	abbreviation	English
Ⲓⲏⲥⲟⲩⲥ	Ⲓⲏ̄ⲥ	Jesus
Ⲡⲓⲭⲣⲓⲥⲧⲟⲥ	Ⲡⲭ̄ⲥ̄	Christ
Ⲫⲛⲟⲩϯ	Ⲫϯ	God
ⲡⲛⲉⲩⲙⲁ	ⲡⲛ̄ⲁ	spirit
ⲉⲑⲟⲩⲁⲃ	ⲉⲑ̄ⲩ	Holy
ⲡ̅ϭⲟⲓⲥ	Ⲡⲟ̄ⲥ̄	Lord
ⲓⲉⲣⲟⲥⲁⲗⲏⲙ	Ⲓⲗ̄ⲏⲙ	Jerusalem
ⲑⲉⲟⲥ	ⲑ̄ⲥ̄	God (Gk)
Ⲩⲓⲟⲥ	ⲩ̄ⲥ̄	Son (Gk)
ⲁⲗⲗⲏⲗⲟⲩⲓⲁ	ⲁ̄ⲗ̄	Hallelujah (Heb)
ⲥⲧⲁⲩⲣⲟⲥ	⳨	Cross (Gk)
ⲙⲁⲣⲧⲩⲣⲟⲥ	⳦	Martyr (Gk)
ⲓⲥⲣⲁⲏⲗ	Ⲓⲥ̄ⲗ	Israel

The abbreviations for "Jesus" and "Christ" are the same in the New Testament Greek. In fact, they appear so often in early Greek manuscripts, that some people say there must have been a very early decision within the Church to use these abbreviations, perhaps even at the council of Jerusalem.

2.4. Describing nouns

How would you go about describing different types of nouns? For example, if you were to think about having bricks, we could have big bricks or small bricks, stone bricks or mud bricks, round bricks or square bricks. Some of the words we use to describe these different types of bricks are called *adjectives*, which are basically *describing* words, or words that qualify a noun or pronoun. You'll also notice that some nouns are used to describe other nouns. For example, in 'mud brick', both 'mud' and 'brick' are nouns, but here 'mud' is used to describe the brick.

There are two different constructions for describing nouns:

    a)   the attributive construction
    b)   the inflected adjectives

2.4.i. Attributive construction

An attribute is a characteristic you can give to something. There is a special construction in Coptic which is used to express an attribute.

Consider this example:

ⲡⲓⲣⲱⲙⲓ ⲛ̀ⲁⲡⲁⲥ

ⲡⲓⲣⲱⲙⲓ means 'the man'

ⲁⲡⲁⲥ is an adjective meaning 'old.'

What then is the little letter ⲛ̀ before ⲁⲡⲁⲥ?

ⲛ̀ is the 'attributive construction.' The ⲛ̀ is used to tell you something about the "the man." In this case it's telling you that the man is old. Here ⲁⲡⲁⲥ is an adjective.

However, the ⲛ̀ can also be used in between two nouns, when one noun tells you something about the other.

E.g. ϯϣⲟⲩⲣⲏ ⲛ̀ⲛⲟⲩⲃ

"the golden censor"

Notice here that there are two nouns at either side of the ⲛ̀? This tells us that the second noun gives some characteristic to the first noun, which is that the censor is golden.

Now consider this example:

ⲡⲓⲣⲱⲙⲓ ⲙ̀ⲃⲉⲣⲓ

"the new man"

Making our first sentences

You would probably guess that the ⲙ here is the attributive construction, but why is it ⲙ in this case and not ⲛ̄?

Here a simple rule applies:

ⲙ is used if the word it follows starts with one of the following letters:

ⲙ ⲡ ⲃ ⲫ ⲯ

For any other word not starting with one of those letters, ⲛ̄ is used instead.

Things are slightly different for the adjective ⲛⲓϣϯ which means 'great'. It likes to swap places with the noun in the attributive construction, so that the article which belongs to the noun actually comes before the ⲛⲓϣϯ, and the ⲛ̄/ⲙ comes before the noun.

E.g. ⲡⲓⲛⲓϣϯ ⲛ̄ⲁⲣⲭⲏⲁⲅⲅⲉⲗⲟⲥ
"the great archangel"

2.4.ii. *The possessive construction*

Similar to the attributive construction is the possessive construction, which is used to state the idea of 'possession', that is when something belongs to someone. For example, consider this sentence: ⲡϩⲓ ⲙ̄ⲡⲓⲣⲱⲙⲓ

Let's look at each word.

ⲡϩⲓ is 'the house'

ⲣⲱⲙⲓ is 'man'

Here the possessive construction is used to give the idea of possession, so the sentence means "the house belonging to the man" or "the house of the man."

Also, another example:

ⲡⲟⲩⲣⲟ ⲛ̄ϯⲃⲁⲕⲓ means "the king of the city."

Notice that the second noun in the attributive construction doesn't take an article, whereas the second noun in the possessive construction does.

Now, when the possessive construction is used, an alternative to ⲛ̄/ⲙ can be used. This alternative is ⲛ̄ⲧⲉ.

ⲛ̄ⲧⲉ can be used in any case, but is especially used when the first noun is preceded by an indefinite article ('a')

So You want to Learn Coptic?

E.g. **ⲟⲩϣⲉⲣⲓ ⲛ̀ⲧⲉ ϯⲥ̀ϩⲓⲙⲓ**
"a daughter of the woman"

Note that **ⲛ̀ⲧⲉ** can only be used as the possessive construction to describe possession, and cannot be used when describing an attribute.

Vocab			
ⲃⲉⲣⲓ	new (adjective)	ⲥⲁⲃⲏ	wise (feminine)
ⲁⲡⲁⲥ	old (adjective)	ⲑ̀ⲣⲟⲛⲟⲥ	throne (m)
ϩ̀ⲙⲟⲩ	salt (m)	ⲟⲩⲱⲓⲛⲓ	light (m)
ⲕⲟⲥⲙⲟⲥ	world (m)	ⲓⲟⲩⲇⲁⲓ	Jew (m)
ⲉⲡⲁⲅⲅⲉⲗⲓⲁ	promise (f)	ⲛⲓϣϯ	great (adj.)
ⲥⲁⲃⲉ	wise (masculine)	ⲙⲏϣ	multitude (m)
ⲃⲁⲕⲓ	city (f)		

Exercise 2.3

a) **Ⲟⲩⲣⲱⲙⲓ ⲙ̀ⲃⲉⲣⲓ** *(Colossians 3:10)*

b) **Ⲡⲓⲣⲱⲙⲓ ⲛ̀ⲁⲡⲁⲥ** *(Colossians 3:9)*

c) **Ϯⲛⲓϣϯ ⲙ̀ⲃⲁⲕⲓ** *(Jonah 3:2)*

d) **ⲟⲩⲛⲟⲩϯ ⲛ̀ⲟⲩⲱⲧ** *(Nicene Creed)*

e) **ⲡ̀ⲑ̀ⲣⲟⲛⲟⲥ ⲛ̀ⲧⲉ Ⲫϯ** *(Matthew 23:22)*

f) **ⲟⲩⲙⲏϣ ⲛ̀ⲣⲱⲙⲓ ⲛ̀ⲥⲁⲃⲉ ⲛⲉⲙ ⲟⲩⲙⲏϣ ⲛ̀ϩⲓⲟⲙⲓ ⲛ̀ⲥⲁⲃⲏ** *(hom vatt ii pg.79)*

2.4.iii.   *Other ways of describing nouns*

There are some special constructions which are able to describe nouns without using the attributive and possessive constructions:

Every

Firstly, there is a special adjective that simply comes after the noun and does not need the attributive construction.

Making our first sentences

This adjective is **ⲚⲒⲂⲈⲚ** which means 'every'. It always comes after the noun. So, for an example, we'll it use it with the word **ϨⲰⲂ**, which means 'thing'

E.g. **ϨⲰⲂ ⲚⲒⲂⲈⲚ**
"everything."

ⲚⲒⲂⲈⲚ is often combined with the word **ⲞⲨⲞⲚ**. On its own, **ⲞⲨⲞⲚ** means 'someone' or 'something', when combined with **ⲚⲒⲂⲈⲚ**, you get

ⲞⲨⲞⲚ ⲚⲒⲂⲈⲚ
Which means *'everyone.'*

Inflected adjectives

The next type of adjectives which don't use the attributive construction are called the *inflected* adjectives. These are shown in the following table:

These modifiers also have the special property of changing their ending, based on whether the noun is masculine or feminine, and whether it's in the singular or plural. For this reason, they get the 'inflected' in their name, as the modifier changes its ending or 'inflects' depending on which noun comes before it.

Before we move on, we'll need to talk a little more about grammar. If you look through an English grammar book, you'll find all kinds of references to 'first person', 'second person' and 'third person.'

What do all these refer to? Basically, the first person refers to the words 'I' and

ⲘⲘⲀⲨⲀⲦ⸗	only, alone
ⲦⲎⲢ⸗	all
ϨⲰ⸗	also
ⲘⲘⲒⲚ ⲘⲘⲞ⸗	own

'we', the second person refers to 'you', and the third refers to 'he', 'she' or 'they.' Another important term to know is 'number.' Now most people would know what a number is, but it has a special meaning when used grammatically. Number is used to indicate whether something is in the singular or the plural. So for example, the number of the word 'dog' is 'singular', whereas the number of the word 'pencils' is 'plural.'
The table below summarises these two ideas:

	singular	plural
first person	I	we
second person	you (for both masculine and feminine)	you
third person	he, she	they

Therefore if a book is writing about a particular character, it's written in the third person. If someone is writing a book about himself, he's writing in the first person. Computer games have also borrowed these terms, so a shoot 'em up game where you can see the character you're controlling is described as having a third person perspective, whereas one where you can't see the character apart from his gun is called a 'first person' perspective shooter (because they're pretending the one holding the gun is you).

Taking an example from the table, 'he' would be described as 'third person singular masculine', and 'you' (m) as second person singular masculine.

Now we'll return to our inflected modifiers in the table below:

ⲙ̀ⲙⲁⲩⲁⲧ⸗

This word means 'alone' or 'only.' It can also be used to give the meaning of "…self" as in 'himself' or 'herself.'

We'll borrow from the 'person' table above to create the table below:

ⲙ̀ⲙⲁⲩⲁⲧ	first person singular
ⲙ̀ⲙⲁⲩⲁⲧⲕ	second person singular masculine
ⲙ̀ⲙⲁⲩⲁϯ	second person singular feminine
ⲙ̀ⲙⲁⲩⲁⲧϥ	third person singular masculine
ⲙ̀ⲙⲁⲩⲁⲧⲥ	third person singular feminine
ⲙ̀ⲙⲁⲩⲁⲧⲉⲛ	first person plural
ⲙ̀ⲙⲁⲩⲁⲧⲉⲛ ⲑⲏⲛⲟⲩ	second person plural
ⲙ̀ⲙⲁⲩⲁⲧⲟⲩ	third person plural

ⲙ̀ⲙⲁⲩⲁⲧ⸗ follows the noun it describes, with the suffix agreeing with the noun in gender, person, and number.

E.g. ⲛ̀ⲑⲟⲕ ⲙ̀ⲙⲁⲩⲁⲧⲕ

"you only"

ⲫⲓⲱⲧ ⲙ̅ⲙⲁⲩⲁⲧϥ

"the father only"

ⲧⲏⲣ⳱

    ⲧⲏⲣ⳱ also comes after the word it's describing, and has the meaning of 'all.' Its different forms are also shown below: Note that the second person plural form is the same as that of third person plural.

ⲧⲏⲣⲧ	first person singular
ⲧⲏⲣⲕ	second person singular masculine
ⲧⲏⲣⲓ	second person singular feminine
ⲧⲏⲣϥ	third person singular masculine
ⲧⲏⲣⲥ	third person singular feminine
ⲧⲏⲣⲉⲛ	first person plural
ⲧⲏⲣⲟⲩ	second person plural
ⲧⲏⲣⲟⲩ	third person plural

E.g. ⲡⲉⲛϩⲏⲧ ⲧⲏⲣϥ

"all our heart"

ϩⲱ⳱

    The third inflected modifier ϩⲱ⳱ means 'also', unlike ⲙ̅ⲙⲁⲩⲁⲧ⳱ and ⲧⲏⲣ⳱ it doesn't have to come after a noun.

ϩⲱ	first person singular
ϩⲱⲕ	second person singular masculine
ϩⲱⲓ	second person singular feminine
ϩⲱϥ	third person singular masculine
ϩⲱⲥ	third person singular feminine

So You want to Learn Coptic?

ϩⲱⲛ	first person plural
ϩⲱⲧⲉⲛ	second person plural
ϩⲱⲟⲩ	third person plural

ⲁⲛⲟⲕ ϩⲱ
"I also"

ⲁⲛⲟⲛ ϩⲱⲛ (Acts 14:14)
"we also"

ⲙⲙⲓⲛ ⲙⲙⲟ⸗

Our fourth inflected modifier is ⲙⲙⲓⲛ ⲙⲙⲟ⸗. It comes after a noun which is itself preceded by a possessive article, and agrees with the article in person and number.

E.g. ⲡⲉϥⲥⲛⲟϥ ⲙⲙⲓⲛ ⲙⲙⲟϥ (Acts 20:28)
"his own blood"

ⲡⲉⲕⲉⲑⲛⲟⲥ ⲙⲙⲓⲛ ⲙⲙⲟⲕ (John 18:35)
"Your own people"

Not another one...

A neat little article is ⲕⲉ which comes directly before the noun. It actually has two different meanings. In the first case, it can mean 'other' ;

E.g. ⲕⲉⲣⲱⲙⲓ
"another man"

"Other men" would be:

ϩⲁⲛⲕⲉⲣⲱⲙⲓ

The word for "one" is ⲟⲩⲁⲓ, so to say "another one" is therefore:

ⲕⲉⲟⲩⲁⲓ

And in the second case, ⲕⲉ can take the meaning of "also."

E.g. ⲡⲓⲕⲉⲣⲱⲙⲓ

Making our first sentences

"also the man"

Vocab			
ϩⲏⲧ	heart (m)	ⲁⲛⲁⲥⲧⲁⲥⲓⲥ	resurrection (f)
ⲓⲟⲩⲇⲁⲓ	Jew (m)	Ⲓⲱⲁⲛⲛⲏⲥ	John (prop.noun)
ⲗⲁⲟⲥ	people, nation (m)	ⲉⲕⲕ̀ⲗⲏⲥⲓⲁ	Church (f)
ⲓⲟⲩⲇⲉⲁ	Judea (f)	ⲉⲑⲛⲟⲥ	nation, people (Gk,f)

Exercise 2.4

a) Ⲡⲭ̄ⲥ̄ ϩⲱϥ   *(1 Peter 2:21)*

b) ⲛ̀ⲓⲟⲩⲇⲁⲓ ⲙ̀ⲙⲁⲩⲁⲧⲟⲩ   *(Acts 11:19)*

c) ⲛ̀ⲑⲟ ϩⲱⲓ   *(Luke 2:35)*

d) ⲗⲁⲟⲥ ⲛⲓⲃⲉⲛ   *(Revelation 11:9)*

e) ϯⲓⲟⲩⲇⲉⲁ ⲧⲏⲣⲥ   *(Acts 1:8)*

f) ⲣⲱⲙⲓ ⲛⲓⲃⲉⲛ   *(Acts 22:15)*

g) ⲛ̀ⲑⲱⲧⲉⲛ ϩⲱⲧⲉⲛ   *(Acts 7:51)*

h) ⲧⲉⲛⲁⲛⲁⲥⲧⲁⲥⲓⲥ ⲧⲏⲣⲉⲛ   *(Litany of the Gospel, Divine Liturgy)*

i) Ⲓⲱⲁⲛⲛⲏⲥ ⲙ̀ⲙⲁⲩⲁⲧϥ   *(Acts 18:25)*

j) ϯⲉⲕⲕ̀ⲗⲏⲥⲓⲁ̀ ⲧⲏⲣⲥ   *(Acts 5:11)*

So You want to Learn Coptic?

3. MAKING OUR FIRST SENTENCES

We now already have the tools for making very basic sentences. These sentences are called "nominal sentences" or "non verbal sentences."

Before looking at these, we'll have to learn some important English terms. The first of these are the *subject* and the *predicate*.

In general, sentences can be split into two parts. The first refers to what the sentence is all about, and is called the subject. The second part, which tells you something about the subject, is called the predicate. For an example, consider the sentence:

"They built a sandcastle."

The subject of the sentence is 'they.' The rest of the sentence (the predicate) tells us something about 'they', which is that they built a sandcastle. This is summarised in the table below.

"they"	built a sandcastle"
what the sentence is about	statement made about the subject
SUBJECT	PREDICATE

The next term we'll learn is the *copula*. The copula is basically a word which is used as a connection between the subject and the predicate. In English, this is most often translated as 'is.' For example, in the sentence:

"Peter is a father"

The subject of the sentence is "Peter", the predicate is "a father", and the Copula is that little 'is' after Peter.

There are three types of Copula, each type used according to the gender of the subject and whether it's in the singular or plural form.

ⲡⲉ	"is" or "am" for a masculine subject
ⲧⲉ	"is" or "am" for a feminine subject
ⲛⲉ	"are" for a subject which is in the plural

We will need these terms as we look at three different patterns of nominal sentences below. They are constructed as follows:

Subject + predicate
Subject + copula + predicate
Predicate + copula

3.1. Subject + Predicate

The first nominal sentences we'll look at are simply composed of a subject and a predicate. For an example, look at the sentence below:

ⲁⲛⲟⲕ ⲟⲩⲡⲣⲟⲫⲏⲧⲏⲥ *(Revelation 2:20)*

"I am a prophet"

Note that the subject is ⲁⲛⲟⲕ, and the predicate is ⲡⲣⲟⲫⲏⲧⲏⲥ. Though a literal English translation would come out as only "I a prophet", in Coptic this structure is recognised as meaning "I *am* a prophet." That is, the "am" is understood by the context of the sentence.

Here is another example:

ⲛ̅ⲑⲟⲕ ⲡⲭ̅ⲥ̅ *(Matthew 16:16)*

"You are the Christ"

Here the word ⲛ̅ⲑⲟⲕ, is the *subject* of the sentence, since that's what the sentence is about. The predicate is the statement made about the subject, which is that He is ⲡⲭ̅ⲥ̅ (the Christ).

Once again we see that no Coptic equivalent for 'are' is used.

3.2. Subject + Copula + Predicate

We noted that no copulas were used for the subject + predicate constructions above, the fact is however that copulas can actually be used in between the subject and predicate.
Examples:

ⲁⲛⲟⲕ ⲡⲉ ⲅⲁⲃⲣⲓⲏⲗ *(Luke 1:19)*

"I am Gabriel"

ⲁⲛⲟⲕ ⲡⲉ ϯⲁⲛⲁⲥⲧⲁⲥⲓⲥ *(John 11:25)*

"I am the resurrection"

Unfortunately, there doesn't seem to be any rule to tell us when the copula should be used.
Did you notice that in the above sentences, the order of the nouns and the verb is exactly the same as you'd see in English? This is the case when the definite article is used before the predicate. However, if an indefinite article comes before the noun, then the copula comes *after* the noun.

E.g. **Ⲓⲱⲥⲏϥ ⲟⲩϩⲁⲙϣⲉ ⲡⲉ**
"Joseph is a carpenter"

We introduced the demonstrative pronoun in **(2.2.ii)**. Demonstrative pronouns can also be used to form nominal sentences. Those sentences always contain the copula. Once again, if the predicate is preceded by a definite article, then the copula comes in between the demonstrative pronoun and the predicate:

E.g **ⲫⲁⲓ ⲡⲉ ⲡⲁⲛⲟⲩϯ** *(Exodus 15:2)*
"This is my God"

If on the other hand the predicate is preceded by an indefinite article, then the copula goes to the end of the sentence.

E.g. **ⲫⲁⲓ ⲟⲩϣⲏⲣⲓ ⲡⲉ**
"this is a son"

3.3. Pronoun + copula

This type is a little more tricky. It only uses a predicate and the copula. What happens to the subject? In these cases, the subject is only implied without actually being written.

So for example, **ⲁⲛⲟⲕ ⲡⲉ** on its own does not mean 'I am' but actually means 'It is I.' The subject here isn't actually written in the Coptic, but is implied to be 'it.' The predicate, which is telling you something about the subject 'it' is **ⲁⲛⲟⲕ**, telling you that 'it' is I.'

This particular construction comes up now and then. When Christ came to the apostles walking on water, He reassured them saying **ⲁⲛⲟⲕ ⲡⲉ**, and in the Divine Liturgy, the expression translated as 'It is You' or 'You are He' (around whom the angels stand) is **ⲛⲑⲟⲕ ⲡⲉ**.

Confusion Corner

You would have noticed that the copulas ⲡⲉ, ⲧⲉ and ⲛⲉ are identical to the possessive articles used for 'you' when speaking to a female **(2.1.iii)**.

How do you tell which is which? One easy way is to remember that the copula will always be separate from the noun, whereas the possessive article will always be attached to it. However, this explanation is a bit artificial since separating words in Coptic is a relatively new invention. The Copts didn't seem to believe in conventions like having spaces between words. Maybe it was to save paper,(or should I say to save 'papyri'). In any case all their words were linked together without spaces.

The best way to recognise the difference is to have a good understanding of the grammar. Basically, if there is a copula before a noun in the sentence, the noun would already have to have an article between it and the copula. The copula cannot come directly before a noun which doesn't already have an article. To clarify, think of this example:

ⲛ̀ⲑⲟϥ ⲡⲉ ⲡⲉϣⲏⲣⲓ

Notice that the ⲡⲉ occurs twice. The first ⲡⲉ is the copula, and the second is the article which comes between the copula and the noun ϣⲏⲣⲓ.

Vocab			
ⲡⲁⲣⲑⲉⲛⲟⲥ	Virgin (Gk,f)	ⲉⲣⲫⲉⲓ	sanctuary, temple (m)
ⲭⲣⲏⲥⲧⲓⲁⲛⲟⲥ	Christian (m)	ϫ̀ⲣⲟϫ	seed (m)
ϩⲁⲡ	judgment (m)	ⲥⲁⲓⲏ	beautiful person (f)
ⲙⲏⲓ	truth, justice, righteousness (f)	ⲥⲁϫⲓ	word (m)
ⲗⲁⲥ	tongue (m)	ⲓⲟⲩⲇⲁⲓ	Jew (m, prop.noun)
ⲕⲁϣ	pen (m)	ⲥⲁϧ	teacher, scribe (m)
ϩⲁⲙϣⲉ	Carpenter (m)	ⲑⲉⲟⲧⲟⲕⲟⲥ	Mother of God (Gk,f)

Exercise 3.1

a) Ⲫⲁⲓ ⲡⲉ ⲡⲁⲥⲱⲙⲁ *(Luke 22:19)*

b) ⲁⲛⲟⲛ ϩⲁⲛⲭⲣⲏⲥⲧⲓⲁⲛⲟⲥ *(AmBal pg.1)*

c) ⲡⲓϫⲣⲟϫ ⲡⲉ ⲡⲓⲥⲁϫⲓ ⲛ̀ⲧⲉ Ⲫⲛⲟⲩϯ *(Luke 8:11)*

d) ⲁⲛⲟⲕ ⲡⲉ Ⲡⲓⲭ̅ⲥ̅ *(Matthew 24:5)*

e) Ν̀ⲑⲟⲕ ⲡⲉ Ⲡⲭ̅ⲥ̅ *(Mark 8:29)*

f) ⲁ̀ⲛⲟⲛ ϩⲁⲛⲓⲟⲩⲇⲁⲓ *(Galatians 2:15)*

g) ⲛⲉⲛⲥⲱⲙⲁ ϩⲁⲛⲉⲣⲫⲉⲓ ⲛ̀ⲧⲉ Ⲫϯ ⲙ̀ⲡⲓⲥ̅ⲗ̅ ⲛⲉ *(hom vatt ii pg.75)*

h) Ⲛⲓϩⲁⲡ ⲛ̀ⲧⲉ Ⲡϭⲟⲓⲥ ϩⲁⲛϩⲁⲡ ⲙ̀ⲙⲏⲓ ⲛⲉ *(Psalm **18:10** 19:9)*

i) ⲡⲁⲗⲁⲥ ⲟⲩⲕⲁϣ ⲡⲉ ⲛ̀ⲧⲉ ⲟⲩⲥⲁϧ *(Psalm **44:2** 45:1)*

j) Ν̀ⲑⲟⲕ ⲡⲉ ⲡⲁⲛⲟⲩϯ *(Psalm **117:28** 118:28)*

k) Ν̀ⲑⲟ ⲟⲩⲥ̀ϩⲓⲙⲓ ⲛ̀ⲥⲁⲓⲏ *(Gnesis 12:11)*

l) ⲁ̀ⲛⲟⲛ ϩⲁⲛϣⲏⲣⲓ ⲛ̀ⲧⲉ ϯⲉⲡⲁⲅⲅⲉⲗⲓⲁ *(Galatians 4:28)*

m) Ν̀ⲑⲱⲧⲉⲛ ⲡⲉ Ⲫⲟⲩⲱⲓⲛⲓ ⲙ̀ⲡⲓⲕⲟⲥⲙⲟⲥ *(Matthew 5:14)*

n) Ν̀ⲑⲱⲧⲉⲛ ⲡⲉ ⲡ̀ϩⲙⲟⲩ ⲙ̀ⲡⲓⲕⲁϩⲓ *(Matthew 5:13)*

o) Ⲫⲁⲓ ⲡⲉ ⲡ̀ⲟⲩⲣⲟ ⲛ̀ⲧⲉ ⲛⲓⲓⲟⲩⲇⲁⲓ *(Matthew 27:37)*

Practice text 1

ⲥⲁϫⲓ ⲛⲉⲙⲁⲛ *pg.64*

Ⲱ ⲧⲉⲛⲙⲁⲩ ⲧ̀ⲁ̀ⲅⲓⲁ̀ Ⲙⲁⲣⲓⲁ ϯⲡⲁⲣⲑⲉⲛⲟⲥ ⲁ̀ⲛⲟⲛ ⲛⲉ ⲛⲉϣⲏⲣⲓ ⲟⲩⲟϩ ⲛ̀ⲑⲟ ⲧⲉ ⲧⲉⲛⲙⲁⲩ. Ⲁ̀ⲛⲟⲛ ⲛⲉ ⲛⲓϣⲏⲣⲓ ⲙ̀ⲡⲉϣⲏⲣⲓ ⲙ̀ⲙⲉⲛⲣⲓⲧ. Ⲛ̀ⲑⲟϥ ⲡⲉ Ⲡⲉⲛⲟ̅ⲥ̅ ⲟⲩⲟϩ ⲁ̀ⲛⲟⲛ ⲛⲉ ⲛⲉϥⲉ̀ⲃⲓⲁⲓⲕ. Ⲛ̀ⲑⲟϥ ⲡⲉ ⲡⲉⲛⲓⲱⲧ ⲟⲩⲟϩ ⲁ̀ⲛⲟⲛ ⲛⲉ ⲛⲉϥϣⲏⲣⲓ

Vocab			
ⲁⲅⲓⲁ	saint (f, Gk)	ⲡⲁⲣⲑⲉⲛⲟⲥ	virgin (f, Gk)
ⲙⲉⲛⲣⲓⲧ	beloved (adj.)	ⲟⲩⲟϩ	and (conj)

4. LEARNING TO COUNT- NUMBERS IN COPTIC

4.1. Numbers 1-10

You can't have a language without having numbers, and Coptic is no exception. Coptic differs from English in that the characters used to represent the numbers are actually derived from the same characters used to give the alphabet. In fact, the numerical sequence largely follows that of the alphabet. However, the characters are then given a different name from the original letter, and some are given both a masculine and feminine form.

Let's first take a look at the numbers one to ten.

		masculine	female
one	ⲁ̄	ⲟⲩⲁⲓ	ⲟⲩⲓ
two	ⲃ̄	ⲥⲛⲁⲩ	ⲥⲛⲟⲩϯ
three	ⲅ̄	ϣⲟⲙⲧ	ϣⲟⲙϯ
four	ⲇ̄	ϥⲧⲟⲩ	ϥⲧⲟⲩⲉ̀
five	ⲉ̄	ϯⲟⲩ	ϯⲉ̀
six	ⲋ̄	ⲥⲟⲟⲩ	ⲥⲟ
seven	ⲍ̄	ϣⲁϣϥ	ϣⲁϣϥⲓ
eight	ⲏ̄	ϣⲙⲏⲛ	ϣⲙⲏⲛⲓ
nine	ⲑ̄	ⲯⲓⲧ	ⲯⲓϯ
ten	ⲓ̄	ⲙⲏⲧ	ⲙⲏϯ

So you'll notice in the table above that numbers 1-10 are simply represented as the first 10 letters of the alphabet with strokes over their heads. This also explains the mysterious ⲋ̄, which hasn't been used in any of the words up till now even though it appears in the alphabet.

4.1.i. How many?

You may be wondering why the numbers have both masculine and feminine forms. This is because Coptic numbers can be used with the attributive construction

(2.4.i) to describe how many of something in particular there are. Now, the gender of the noun at issue determines which gender of the number will be used. To see if you really understand, let's ask how would you write 'three sons.'

First, the word for son is ϣHpi, which is a masculine word. So you would use ϣoµτ as opposed to ϣoµϯ for 'three'. You would then write ϣoµτ ɴϣHpi using the attributive construction. On the other hand, if you were to say *'three daughters'*, you would use ϣoµϯ as daughter' is a feminine word to give ϣoµϯ ɴϣepi.

Now, to say *'the* three sons', you would still use the singular definite article, which in this case is the masculine definite article. In fact, the plural definite article is never used with numbers using the attributive construction.

πιϣoµτ ɴϣHpi

Likewise, to say *'the three daughters'*, you would use the feminine definite article:

ϯϣoµϯ ɴϣepi

This pattern continues for most of the other numbers.

E.g. πιϥτoυ ɴϣHpi

"the four brothers"

ϣaϣϥ ɴcoπ

"seven times"

This pattern works well for numbers 3 and up, but there is a separate way for numbers 1 and 2. When saying "one of something", the attributive construction is still used, but this time the noun comes before the number, and instead of oυai or oυi as you'd expect, the noun is followed instead by oυωτ. So, *"one man"* is written as

oυpωµi ɴoυωτ and *"one people"* as oυγeɴoc ɴoυωτ *(Genesis 34:16)*

If you were to say "two of something", you would also place the noun first, but this time you wouldn't use the attributive construction at all.

Examples: pωµi cɴaυ

"two men"

cϩiµi cɴoυϯ *(Genesis 4:19)*

"two wives"

λeπτoɴ cɴaυ *(Luke 21:2)*

"two mites"

4.1.ii. Finding your place

Let's pretend you have just attended a race, and the time has come to list the finishing places of the contestants. Let's start with the winner.

There is a special word in Coptic for 'first' used for describing nouns which is 'ϣopπ'. It is also used with the attributive construction.

E.g. ⲡⲓϣopπ ⲙ̄ⲙⲁⲣⲧⲩⲣⲟⲥ
"The first martyr"

ϣopπ can also be used as a noun, as in *'the first'* - ⲡⲓϣopπ.

An alternative to saying 'the first' is ϩⲟⲩⲓⲧ which may be used both as a noun and as an adjective. As a noun, ⲡⲓϩⲟⲩⲓⲧ is used for masculine words and ϯϩⲟⲩⲓϯ for feminine words. The plural form also has a different form and is ⲛⲓϩⲟⲩⲁϯ

However, for other places apart from 'the first', there is a special generic construction which uses the word ⲙⲁϩ (which itself means 'place'). The construction takes the following form:

ⲡⲓⲙⲁϩ + number

E.g. So, *"the third"*

is ⲡⲓⲙⲁϩ ϣⲟⲙⲧ

As in ⲁⲃⲃⲁ ϣⲉⲛⲟⲩϯ ⲙ̄ⲙⲁϩ ϣⲟⲙⲧ
"Pope Shenouda the third"

Lucky last is written as ⲡⲓϧⲁⲉ *"the last"* when referring to singular masculine, and

ⲛⲓϧⲁⲉⲩ "the last" when referring to nouns in the plural.

4.2.   10-100

Whereas English makes all its numbers out of a combination of only ten digits, Coptic continues to move down the alphabet as it gets letters for the higher numbers. You'll notice in the following table that now only the numbers 'ten' and 'twenty' have feminine and masculine forms.

So You want to Learn Coptic?

ten	ⲓ̅	ⲙⲏⲧ	ⲙⲏϯ
twenty	ⲕ̅	ϫⲟⲩⲧ	ϫⲱϯ
thirty	ⲗ̅	ⲙⲁⲡ	
forty	ⲙ̅	ϩⲙⲉ	
fifty	ⲛ̅	ⲧⲉⲃⲓ	
sixty	ⲝ̅	ⲥⲉ	
seventy	ⲟ̅	ϣⲃⲉ	
eighty	ⲡ̅	ϧⲁⲙⲛⲉ	
ninety	ϥ̅	ⲡⲓⲥⲧⲁⲩ	
100	ⲣ̅	ϣⲉ	

These are combined with the 1-9 digits to create the numbers in between. The masculine and feminine forms continue only for the numbers 10 and 20 and numbers between 10 and 20 which end in 1,2, 8 or 9.

E.g. ⲡⲓⲙⲏⲧ ⲥ̀ⲛⲁⲩ ⲙ̀ⲙⲁⲑⲏⲧⲏⲥ

"the 12 disciples"

4.3. Numbers 100-900

In the table below you can see that ϣⲉ is used for the number 100 and that it is also used with other multiples of 100:

100	ⲣ̅	ϣⲉ
200	ⲥ̅	ⲥ̀ⲛⲁⲩ ϣⲉ
300	ⲧ̅	ϣⲟⲙⲧ ϣⲉ
400	ⲩ̅	ϥⲧⲟⲩ ϣⲉ
500	ⲫ̅	ϯⲟⲩ ϣⲉ

Learning to count

600	x̄	ⲥⲟⲟⲩ ϣⲉ
700	ψ̄	ϣⲁϣϥ ϣⲉ
800	ω̄	ϣⲙⲏⲛ ϣⲉ
900	ϣ̄	ⲯⲓⲧ ϣⲉ

The numbers coming in between the numbers of 100 are formed by combing them with the numbers made from multiples of 10 from the previous table. The attributive construction is sometimes used to link the two sets together:
Examples:

ϣⲉ ⲥⲉ ⲧⲓⲟⲩ ⲛ̀ⲣⲟⲙⲡⲓ (ρ̄ⲍ̄ⲉ̄)
"165 years"

ⲯⲓⲧ ϣⲉ ⲥⲉ ⲯⲓⲧ ⲛ̀ⲣⲟⲙⲡⲓ (ϣ̄ⲍ̄ⲑ̄) *(Genesis 5:27)*
"969 years"

ϣⲉ ϧⲙⲛⲉ is 180

ϣⲉ ϣⲃⲉ (ρ̄ⲟ̄) is 170

ϣⲁϣϥ ϣⲉ ⲛ̀ϩⲙⲉ (ψ̄ⲙ̄) is 740

4.4. 1000 and beyond

Coptic finally begins to recycle the characters used for its numbers after 1000. The old ⲁ returns, this time with two strokes above it, to represent the number 1000.

Two strokes above the ⲃ gives the number 2000, and two strokes above a ⲅ gives 3000, and so on for all the other numbers. Note that apart from the first stroke which all numbers have, each subsequent stroke adds an other three zeros to the number, so three strokes with an ⲁ gives 1,000,000. The strokes may be split up to come above or beneath the character.

1000	ⲁ̿	ϣⲟ
10,000	ⲃ̿	ⲙⲏⲧ ⲛ̀ϣⲟ
100,000	ⲣ̿	ϣⲉ ⲛ̀ ϣⲟ
1,000,000	ⲁ̿	ϣⲟ ⲛ̀ ϣⲟ

So You want to Learn Coptic?

Vocab			
ⲣⲟⲙⲡⲓ	year (f)	**ⲡⲣⲉⲥⲃⲩⲧⲉⲣⲟⲥ**	priest (m)
ⲙⲁϩⲓ	cubit (m)		

Exercise 4.1

a) $\overline{\text{ⲣⲍⲉ}}$ ⲛ̀ⲣⲟⲙⲡⲓ   *(Genesis 5:15)*

b) ϣⲁϣϥ ϣⲉ ⲙⲁⲡ ⲛ̀ⲣⲟⲙⲡⲓ   *(Genesis 5:16)*

c) $\overline{\text{ⲓⲃ}}$ ⲛ̀ⲥⲟⲛ   *(Genesis 42:13)*

d) ⲡⲓ$\overline{\text{ⲕⲇ}}$ ⲙ̀ⲡⲣⲉⲥⲃⲩⲧⲉⲣⲟⲥ   *(Revelation 19:4)*

e) $\overline{\text{ⲅ}}$ ⲙ̀ⲙⲁϩⲓ   *(Exodus 26:16)*

f) $\overline{\text{ⲩ}}$ ⲛ̀ⲣⲟⲙⲡⲓ   *(Acts 7:6)*

g) $\overline{\text{ⲙⲋ}}$ ⲛ̀ϣⲟ ⲛⲉⲙ $\overline{\text{ⲯⲗ}}$ *(Numbers 26:7)*

Practice text 2

One of the hymns chanted in the presence of a Bishop is

ϯⲙⲏⲧ ⲥ̀ⲛⲟⲩϯ ⲛ̀ⲁⲣⲏⲧⲏ *("The twelve virtues")*.

This hymn describes the twelve virtues of the Holy Spirit which we pray will be with the Bishop. The hymn makes good use of the ranking constructions we learnt above. The relevant section of the hymn is shown below:

ϯϩⲟⲩⲓϯ ⲧⲉ ϯⲁⲅⲁⲡⲏ   ϯⲇⲓⲕⲉⲟⲥⲩⲛⲏ

ϯⲙⲁϩ ⲥ̀ⲛⲟⲩϯ ⲧⲉ ϯϩⲉⲗⲡⲓⲥ   ϯⲙⲁϩ ⲯⲓⲧ ⲧⲉ

ϯⲙⲁϩ ϣⲟⲙϯ ⲧⲉ ϯⲡⲓⲥⲧⲟⲥ   ϯⲙⲉⲧⲣⲉⲙⲣⲁⲩϣ

ϯⲙⲁϩ ϥⲧⲟⲉ ⲧⲉ ⲡⲓⲧⲟⲩⲃⲟ   ϯⲙⲁϩ ⲙⲏⲧ ⲧⲉ ϯϩⲩⲡⲟⲙⲟⲛⲏ

ϯⲙⲁϩ ϯⲉ ⲧⲉ ϯⲡⲁⲣⲑⲉⲛⲓⲁ   ϯⲙⲁϩ ⲙⲏⲧ ⲟⲩⲓ ⲧⲉ

ϯⲙⲁϩ ⲥⲟ ⲧⲉ ϯϩⲓⲣⲏⲛⲏ   ϯⲙⲉⲧⲣⲉϥϣⲱⲟⲩ ⲛ̀ϩⲏⲧ

ϯⲙⲁϩ ϣⲁϣϥⲓ ⲧⲉ ϯⲥⲟⲫⲓⲁ   ϯⲙⲁϩ ⲙⲏⲧ ⲥ̀ⲛⲟⲩϯ ⲧⲉ

ϯⲙⲁϩ ϣ̀ⲙⲏⲛⲓ ⲧⲉ   ϯⲉⲅⲕⲣⲁⲧⲓⲁ

Vocab			
ⲁⲅⲁⲡⲏ	love (Gk,f)	ⲡⲓⲥⲧⲟⲥ	faith (Gk,f)
ⲉⲅⲕⲣⲁⲧⲓⲁ	asceticism (Gk,f)	ⲥⲟⲫⲓⲁ	wisdom (Gk,f)
ⲇⲓⲕⲉⲟⲥⲩⲛⲏ	righteousness (Gk)	ⲧⲟⲩⲃⲟ	purity (f)
ⲙⲉⲧⲣⲉⲙⲣⲁⲩϣ	meekness (Gk,f)	ϩⲉⲗⲡⲓⲥ	hope (Gk,f)
ⲙⲉⲧⲣⲉϥϣⲱⲟⲩ ⲛ̀ϩⲏⲧ	long suffering (Gk,f)	ϩⲓⲣⲏⲛⲏ	peace (Gk,f)
ⲡⲁⲣⲑⲉⲛⲓⲁ	virginity (Gk)	ϩⲩⲡⲟⲙⲟⲛⲏ	patience (Gk,f)

So You want to Learn Coptic?

5. INTRODUCING VERBS

5.1. The first present

From the Coptic point of view, the sentences introduced in chapter 3 didn't really use a verb. While the copula in English is considered to be a form of the verb 'to be', in Coptic the copula doesn't actually fit under the normal definition of a verb.

So what exactly is a verb? A verb represents an action, so for example *building* is the verb in "I am building" and *reading* is the verb in "Mark is reading a book."

To help us find its place in the sentence, we'll bring back the example we looked at in **(3.)**

	"they	built a sandcastle"
	what the sentence is about	statement made about the subject
	SUBJECT	PREDICATE

The verb in the sentence above is 'built', which is part of the predicate. Looking more closely at the sentence, we can see that the action of the subject (they) was directed towards something (the sandcastle). The sandcastle is thus called the *object* of this sentence, as the action of the verb is directed towards it. So in another example, "Jack hit the ball"
"Jack" is the subject, "hit" is the verb, and "ball" is the object.

So if we look at our sample sentence again, we find we can divide it into the following parts of speech:

	"they	built	a sandcastle"
		VERB	OBJECT
	what the sentence is about	statement made about the subject	
	SUBJECT	PREDICATE	

Now there are two major types of verbs in Coptic: *transitive* and *intransitive*. Transitive verbs are those that take an object. E.g. "to hit" is a transitive verb because you can hit an object such as a ball. "I sit" on the other hand is an intransitive verb because you can't "sit something."

Both transitive and intransitive verbs have what are called different *tenses*. What exactly is meant by 'tense'? To help answer this question, consider the following sentences:
"I am making", "I made", I will make."

You will notice that there are similar words representing the same verb in each of these, but that the form of the verb is not quite the same. This is because they refer to different *times* in which the verb is performed. In other words, the form of the verb

So You want to Learn Coptic?

changes according to the tense. The first tense refers to the present, the second to the past and the third to the future.

5.1.i. *Intransitive verbs*

Now let's take a look at an example of an intransitive verb in what is called the "first present tense."

Consider the phrase "I am walking", this tells you that "I am walking" at this very moment, hence it represents the present tense. There may still be this question nagging at the back of your mind. "but, why is this tense called the *first* present?" Well, later on we'll discover that there are also a *second* present (**12.1**) and a *third* present tense (**7.2**), but for now, we'll concentrate on the first present.

"To walk" is the base form of the verb, from which other verbs are derived. It is called "the infinitive."

The infinitive in Coptic is ⲙⲟϣⲓ. Certain letters are then added in front of the infinitive to indicate different subjects as you can see in the table below. These letters represent the *dependent personal pronoun*. They're called pronouns because they indicate the subject, and they're dependent because they have to be attached to the verb, that is they can't stand on their own.

ϯⲙⲟϣⲓ	I am walking
ⲭⲙⲟϣⲓ	You are walking (m)
ⲧⲉⲙⲟϣⲓ	You are walking (f)
ϥⲙⲟϣⲓ	He is walking
ⲥⲙⲟϣⲓ	She is walking
ⲧⲉⲛⲙⲟϣⲓ	We are walking
ⲧⲉⲧⲉⲛⲙⲟϣⲓ	You are walking (pl)
ⲥⲉⲙⲟϣⲓ	They are walking

Introducing verbs

Here is another example, this time with the verb **ⲥⲁϫⲓ** (to speak).

ϯⲥⲁϫⲓ	I am speaking
ⲕ̀ⲥⲁϫⲓ	You are speaking (m)
ⲧⲉⲥⲁϫⲓ	You are speaking (f)
ⲧⲉⲧⲉⲛⲥⲁϫⲓ	You are speaking (plural)
ϥ̀ⲥⲁϫⲓ	He is speaking
ⲥ̀ⲥⲁϫⲓ	She is speaking
ⲧⲉⲛⲥⲁϫⲓ	We are speaking
ⲥⲉⲥⲁϫⲓ	They are speaking

Now a more general term for the letters that appear before the verb is the *subject prefix*. Did you notice how the subject prefix for you (m) changed from ϫ to ⲕ̀? A simple rule guides the choice, which is that words starting with one of the *vilminor* letters **(2.1.i)** use ϫ, and those starting with any other letter use ⲕ̀.

Hang on…didn't we already have different words for representing the subject like **ⲁⲛⲟⲕ**, **ⲛ̀ⲑⲟϥ** etc? Confused? You've come to the right place. See confusion corner below:

63

So You want to Learn Coptic?

Confusion Corner
Dependent vs. .independent personal pronouns
(*Reference Plumley pg. 56*)

In **(3.1)** we talked about the independent personal pronouns like ⲁⲛⲟⲕ, ⲛⲑⲟϥ, ⲁⲛⲟⲛ which had meanings like 'I, he and we.'

In the section above, we introduced the dependent personal pronouns, like ϯ, ϥ and ⲧⲉⲛ, which also have the meanings of 'I, he and we.'
So how do you know which to use?

The dependent personal pronouns are used most of the time, with the independent personal pronoun being used only in the following cases:

e. In the simple subject + predicate type sentences E.g. ⲛⲑⲟⲕ ⲡⲁϣⲏⲣⲓ

f. when the sentence is based around the copula. E.g. ⲁⲛⲟⲕ ⲡⲉ Ⲡⲉⲧⲣⲟⲥ

g. The independent personal pronoun may be used in addition to the dependent for added emphasis E.g. ⲁⲛⲟⲕ ϯⲭⲱ ⲙ̄ⲙⲟⲥ
" I say to you"

h. The independent personal pronoun sometimes also comes after another part of speech with which it shares the same number and gender to emphasise its meaning. E.g. ⲧⲁϩⲓⲣⲏⲛⲏ ⲁⲛⲟⲕ. Even though this phrase would seem to be translated as 'my peace I', the actual meaning is a little different. As the personal pronoun is used here to emphasise the meaning of the possessive article, which in this case means 'my' the combination comes out as: *"my own peace"*

Personal pronouns which look like other things

Take a look at the word for 'we' in the first present tense table above and the word for 'our' in the table for the possessive articles **(2.1.iii)**. You'll notice that they both use the word ⲧⲉⲛ.

Now take a look at the word for 'you' plural, and that for 'your' plural female object. They both share the same Coptic word ⲧⲉⲧⲉⲛ.

So how would you know which meaning to choose if you saw either ⲧⲉⲛ or ⲧⲉⲧⲉⲛ in a text?

Technically, if it comes before a noun, you would translate it as the

Introducing verbs

> possessive article, and if it comes before a verb, you translate it as the first present tense. Practically, you'd use which ever makes more sense.
>
> For example, if you were to see ⲧⲉⲛⲛⲁⲩ, knowing ⲛⲁⲩ means 'see', you'd translate the expression to mean 'we see' as saying 'our see' wouldn't make sense.
>
> You'll also notice that the first person personal pronoun ϯ is identical to one of the female definite articles **(2.1.i)**. Here's it's easy to tell them apart. The article will only ever appear before a noun, whereas the pronoun will only come before a verb.

The postponed subject indicator

Have you ever been postponed? I have. All the time in fact. One of the characteristics of modern day Egyptians is that they are often postponed.

In keeping with the spirit, Coptic has its own special postponed subject indicator which is ⲛ̀ϫⲉ. In what we have seen so far, the subject has been coming before the verb. However, when ⲛ̀ϫⲉ is used, the subject comes late, that is it comes after the verb. As an example consider the following sentence:

ⲡⲓⲣⲱⲙⲓ ϥϩⲉⲙⲥⲓ

"the man is sitting"

As you can see here, the subject ⲡⲓⲣⲱⲙⲓ comes before the verb. An alternate way to give the same meaning using ⲛ̀ϫⲉ is ϥϩⲉⲙⲥⲓ ⲛ̀ϫⲉ ⲡⲓⲣⲱⲙⲓ, so that now the subject comes after the verb. ⲛ̀ϫⲉ usually remains untranslated, however if you really wanted to translate it, you would say "who is."

People often ask why Coptic has ⲛ̀ϫⲉ at all, that is why couldn't the Copts have simply always placed the subject in front of the verb. A possible reason was to preserve the word order from the Greek originals from which the Coptic was translated. You see, Greek word order doesn't always come in the sequence we're used to in English, and the subject often comes after the verb. So, it's possible that the Coptic scribes who wanted to translate from Greek introduced ⲛ̀ϫⲉ to retain the Greek word order as much as possible.

Being Negative

Suppose you wanted to say "he is *not* speaking" or "they are *not* speaking." There are two ways by which you could do this. The first involves a convenient word in Coptic called ⲁⲛ. This word simply follows the verb to puts the sentence into the negative.

E.g. ⲕⲥⲁϫⲓ ⲁⲛ

"you are not speaking"

The other method is almost the same, but also involves placing the prefix ⲛ̀ before the verb. So in this example, we get:

ⲛ̀ⲕⲥⲁϫⲓ ⲁⲛ

Which also means *"you are not speaking."*

Using nouns or names in the first present

Up to this point, we've only seen the dependent personal pronoun come before the verb. You can also place a noun or a name before the verb in the sentence. In these cases, the dependent personal pronoun usually still appears in between the subject and the verb:

E.g. ⲫⲓⲱⲧ ϥⲙⲉⲓ *(John 5:20)*

Although this sentence would be literally translated as "the Father He loves", the meaning would be understood as just "the Father loves."

However, the dependent personal pronoun isn't always used. For example, the following phrase is also from the Gospel of John, with exactly the same meaning as the previous example, but it doesn't use the ϥ.

ⲫⲓⲱⲧ ⲙⲉⲓ *(John 3:35)*

5.1.ii. The Qualitative

There is a special form of Coptic verb called the qualitative. It is a bit hard to come to terms with, but basically it expresses a state or a quality which has come about as a result of the completed action of a verb.

To clarify, compare the words 'to multiply' and 'to be abundant.' Notice how the first word expresses the action itself, whereas the second expresses the *result* of that action having been completed?

Also, compare the following phrases; "to turn white" and "to be white." In these examples, the first phrase corresponds to the infinitive while the second corresponds to the qualitative. In the following table, there are some more examples of the infinitive and qualitative forms of some intransitive verbs.

Introducing verbs

Infinitive	Qualitative	Infinitive	Qualitative
ⲁⲓⲁⲓ	ⲟⲓ	ⲥⲙⲟⲩ	ⲥⲙⲁⲣⲱⲟⲩⲧ
to grow, multiply	to be abundant	to bless	to be blessed
ⲓⲃⲓ	ⲟⲃⲓ	ⲧⲁⲓⲟ	ⲧⲁⲓⲏⲟⲩⲧ
to become thirsty	to be thirsty	to honour	to be honoured
ⲓⲛⲓ	ⲟⲛⲓ	ⲧⲟⲩⲃⲟ	ⲧⲟⲩⲃⲏⲟⲩⲧ
to liken	to be like	to purify	to be purified
ⲕⲉⲛⲓ	ⲕⲉⲛⲓⲱⲟⲩⲧ	ϧⲱⲛⲧ	ϧⲉⲛⲧ
to become fat	to be fat	to approach, come near	to be near
ⲙⲟⲩ	ⲙⲱⲟⲩⲧ	ϩⲉⲓ	ϩⲓⲱⲟⲩⲧ
to die	to be dead	to fall	to be fallen
ⲛⲁϩϯ	ⲛϩⲟⲧ	ϩⲕⲟ	ϩⲟⲕⲉⲣ
to believe	to be believing	to hunger	to be hungry
ⲟⲩⲃⲁϣ,	ⲟⲩⲟⲃϣ	ϫⲱⲓⲗⲓ	ϫⲁⲗⲏⲟⲩⲧ
to become white	to be white	to lodge	to be lodging
ⲟⲩⲟⲡ††	ⲟⲩⲁⲃ	ϭⲓⲥⲓ	ϭⲟⲥⲓ
to become holy	to be holy	to exalt	to be exalted

Where to use the qualitative

Most qualitative verbs may be used in the present tense as in the following examples:

ⲥⲉⲙⲟⲩ *"they die"*

ⲥⲉⲙⲱⲟⲩⲧ *"they are dead"*

ϥⲓⲃⲓ *"he is becoming thirsty"*

---

†† The infinitive ⲟⲩⲟⲡ seems to have been replaced by ⲧⲟⲩⲃⲟ in Bohairic. However, ⲟⲩⲟⲡ continues to remain in Sahidic, suggesting that the qualitative ⲟⲩⲁⲃ was originally derived from it.

ϥⲟⲃⲓ *"he is thirsty"*

ⲫⲁⲓ ϥϫⲁⲗⲏⲟⲩⲧ *"this (he) is lodging"* (Acts 10:5)

The qualitative may also be used in the *imperfect* past tense **(7.1)**, but not in the *perfect* past tense **(5.2)**. We will meet both later.

Some exceptional qualitative verbs

In the above examples we saw that both the infinitive and qualitative can be used for the present tense. For the following verbs however, *only* the qualitative form can be used in the present tense, whereas the infinitive can be used for the past tense but not the present.

Infinitive		Qualitative	
ⲃⲱⲕ	to go	ⲃⲏⲕ	to be gone
ⲓ̀	to come	ⲛⲏⲟⲩ	to be coming
ⲫⲱⲧ	to run, flee	ⲫⲏⲧ	to be running, fleeing
ϩⲉⲓ	to fall	ϩⲓⲟⲩⲧ	to be fallen

So for an example, to say "he is coming" (which is in the present tense), you can only use the qualitative form so you'd say ϥⲛⲏⲟⲩ. However, to say "he came" (past tense), you'd have to use the infinitive form.

Vocab			
ⲉⲙⲁϣⲱ	very (adv)	ⲣⲓⲙⲓ	to cry (v.i)
ⲉⲣⲛⲏⲥⲧⲉⲩⲓⲛ	to fast (Gk)	ⲫⲁⲣⲓⲥⲉⲟⲥ	Pharisee (Gk,m)
ⲕⲁϯ	to understand (v.t)	ϣⲱⲙ	summer (m)
ⲛⲉⲙ	and (conj.)	ϧⲉⲛ	in (prep.)
ⲛⲉϫⲓ	womb (f)	ϩⲟϯ	fear (f)
ⲟⲩⲧⲁϩ	fruit (m)		

Exercise 5.1

a) ⲧⲉⲣⲓⲙⲓ (John 20:13)

b) ⲧⲉϭⲟⲥⲓ (Sunday Theotokia Midnight praises)

c) ϥϭⲉⲛⲧ ⲛ̀ϫⲉ Ⲡ̅ⲟ̅ⲥ̅ (Psalm *33:19* 34:18)

d) ϯϩⲟϯ ⲛ̀ⲧⲉ Ⲡϭⲟⲓⲥ ⲉ̀ⲧⲟⲩⲃⲏⲟⲩⲧ (Psalm **18:10** 19:9)

e) ⲁ̀ⲛⲟⲛ ⲛⲉⲙ ⲛⲓⲫⲁⲣⲓⲥⲉⲟⲥ ⲧⲉⲛⲉⲣⲛⲏⲥⲧⲉⲩⲓⲛ (Matthew 9:14)

f) ⲧⲉⲥⲙⲁⲣⲱⲟⲩⲧ ⲛ̀ⲑⲟ ϧⲉⲛ ⲛⲓϩⲓⲟ̀ⲙⲓ ⲟⲩⲟϩ ϥ̀ⲥ̀ⲙⲁⲣⲱⲟⲩⲧ ⲛ̀ϫⲉ ⲡ̀ⲟⲩⲧⲁϩ ⲛ̀ⲧⲉ ⲧⲉⲛⲉϫⲓ (Luke 1:42)

g) ⲥⲉⲛⲏⲟⲩ ⲛ̀ϫⲉ ϩⲁⲛⲉ̀ϩⲟⲟⲩ (Acts 21:6)

h) ⲥⲉⲕⲁϯ ϧⲉⲛ ⲡⲟⲩϩⲏⲧ (Matthew 13:15)

i) ϥϭⲉⲛⲧ ⲛ̀ϫⲉ ⲡⲓϣⲱⲙ (Matthew 24:32)

5.1.iii. *Those "in between words"- prepositions*

So far we've talked about nouns and verbs. Now let's look at another type of part of speech. Take a look at the sentence below:
"The man walks on the street."
When we break it down, we can see that:
'The' is the definite article
'Walk' is the verb
'Street' is the noun

And "On" is the... What is "on"?

'On' fits into the same category as other words such as "to", "in" and "from." These words go before nouns to indicate their relation to other words in the sentence. These words are called **Prepositions**

There are two basic types of prepositions in Coptic:
1) Simple
2) Compound

Compound prepositions are made from smaller words which have been linked together. In fact, many of them involve simple prepositions in their make up. You can refer to **(Appendix 3-where do compound prepositions come from)** to see how they're constructed. Simple prepositions are the base elements so to speak, and cannot be broken down any further. The most common simple and complex prepositions are shown in the tables below:

Simple

ⲉ̀	to, for, in regard to	ϧⲉⲛ	in
ⲛ̀	in, from, with	ⲉⲑⲃⲉ	because of
ⲛⲉⲙ	and, with	ϣⲁ	to, toward, till
ϩⲓ	on	ϩⲱⲥ	like, as
ϩⲁ	to, under	ⲓⲥϫⲉⲛ	from, since
ⲟⲩⲧⲉ	between, among	ⲙⲉⲛⲉⲛⲥⲁ	after
ϧⲁ	below		

Compound

ϩⲓϫⲉⲛ	on, above	ⲉ̀ⲃⲟⲗ	away from
ⲛ̀ⲥⲁ	behind	ⲉ̀ϧⲟⲩⲛ	inside
ⲉϫⲉⲛ	upon, on behalf of	ϩⲓⲧⲉⲛ	through
ⲉ̀ⲡϣⲱⲓ	upwards	ⲉ̀ϩⲣⲉⲛ	facing, in front of
ⲉ̀ⲡⲉⲥⲏⲧ	downward		

Nominal sentences can be built around these prepositions without them needing a Coptic equivalent for the word 'is.'

E.g. ⲡⲓⲣⲱⲙⲓ ϩⲓϫⲉⲛ ⲡⲓⲙⲱⲓⲧ

This sentence is understood to mean *"the man is on the road"*, without the need for the copula to come before the preposition. The same applies for the next example:

†ⲥϩⲓⲙⲓ ϧⲉⲛ ⲡⲏⲓ

"the woman is inside the house."

Greek prepositions

Apart from the above 'pure' Coptic prepositions, there are also prepositions directly imported from Greek. The most common of these are:

ⲕⲁⲧⲁ	according to
ⲡⲁⲣⲁ	against, opposite, behind
ⲭⲱⲣⲓⲥ	without
ϩⲱⲥ	as

These retain the same word order as you'd expect in English:

ⲟⲩⲣⲱⲙⲓ ⲕⲁⲧⲁ ⲡⲁϩⲏⲧ *(Acts 13:22)*

"a man according to my heart"

It's worth noting that a noun that follows ⲭⲱⲣⲓⲥ loses its article:

E.g. ⲡⲓⲕⲁϩⲓ ⲭⲱⲣⲓⲥ ⲥⲉⲛϯ *(Luke 6:49)*

"the land without foundation"

Vocab			
ⲁⲡⲟⲥⲧⲟⲗⲟⲥ	Apostle, messenger, (m)	ⲡⲩⲗⲏ	gate (Gk,f)
ⲁϣⲁⲓ	Abundance	ⲥⲉⲛϯ	foundation (f)
ⲃⲁⲗ	eye (m)	ⲥⲛⲟϥ	blood (m)
ⲃⲏⲙⲁ	platform, step (Gk,m)	ⲧⲟⲧⲥ	chair (m)
ⲉⲕⲕⲗⲏⲥⲓⲁ	Church (Gk,f)	ⲧⲣⲁⲡⲉⲍⲁ	table (f)
ⲉⲣⲫⲉⲓ	sanctuary (m)	ⲭⲉⲣⲟⲩⲃⲓⲙ	Cherubim (Gk,m)
ⲉⲩⲭⲏ	prayer (Gk,f)	ⲱⲟⲩ	glory (f)
ⲑⲙⲏⲓ	righteous person (m)	ϥⲁⲓ	to raise, carry (v.t)
ⲙⲉⲧⲥⲁⲓⲉ	beauty	ϧⲣⲱⲟⲩ	voice (m)

So You want to Learn Coptic?

| ⲡⲉⲧⲣⲁ | rock (Gk,f) | ϫⲟⲙ | power (f) |

Exercise 5.2

a) ⲉϫⲉⲛ ⲟⲩⲡⲉⲧⲣⲁ   *(Luke 8:6)*

b) ϧⲉⲛ ⲫⲣⲁⲛ ⲙ̀ⲫⲓⲱⲧ

c) ϩⲓϫⲉⲛ ⲡ̀ⲕⲁϩⲓ ⲧⲏⲣϥ   *(Psalm 8:1 8:1)*

d) ⲕ̀ⲣⲁϣⲓ ⲉϫⲉⲛ ϩⲁⲛϣⲏⲣⲓ   *(hom vatt ii pg.239)*

e) ⲛⲉⲛⲃⲁⲗ ⲙ̀Ⲡ̅Ⲟ̅Ⲥ̅ ⲉϫⲉⲛ ⲛⲓⲑⲙⲏⲓ   *(Psalm **33:16** 34:16)*

f) ϩⲓⲧⲉⲛ ⲛⲓⲉⲩⲭⲏ ⲛ̀ⲧⲉ ⲙⲁⲣⲕⲟⲥ ⲡⲓⲁⲡⲟⲥⲧⲟⲗⲟⲥ

g) ⲉ̄ ⲛ̀ϣⲟ ⲛ̀ⲣⲱⲙⲓ ⲭⲱⲣⲓⲥ ⲁⲗⲟⲩ ⲛⲉⲙ ⲥ̀ϩⲓⲙⲓ   *(Matthew 14:21)*

h) ⲁϥϩⲉⲙⲥⲓ ϩⲓ ⲡⲓⲃⲏⲙⲁ   *(John 19:13)*

i) Ⲡ̄ϭⲟⲓⲥ ϥ̀ϩⲉⲙⲥⲓ ϩⲓϫⲉⲛ ⲛⲓⲭⲉⲣⲟⲩⲃⲓⲙ

j) ϥⲁⲓ ⲛ̀ⲛⲉⲧⲉⲛⲡⲩⲗⲏ ⲉ̀ⲡ̀ϣⲱⲓ   *(Psalm **23:7** 24:7)*

k) ⲡ̀ϧ̀ⲣⲱⲟⲩ ⲙ̀Ⲡ̅Ⲟ̅Ⲥ̅ ϩⲓϫⲉⲛ ⲛⲓⲙⲱⲟⲩ ⲡ̀ϧ̀ⲣⲱⲟⲩ ⲙ̀Ⲡ̅Ⲟ̅Ⲥ̅ ϧⲉⲛ ⲟⲩϫⲟⲙ ⲡ̀ϧ̀ⲣⲱⲟⲩ ⲙ̀Ⲡ̅Ⲟ̅Ⲥ̅ ϧⲉⲛ ⲟⲩⲛⲓϣϯ ⲙ̀ⲙⲉⲧⲥⲁⲓⲉ̀   *(Psalm **28:3** 29:3)*

l) ⲉⲑⲃⲉ ⲡⲉⲕⲣⲁⲛ ⲡ̀ϭⲟⲓⲥ   *(Pslam **142:11** 143:11))*

m) ⲡⲓⲥ̀ⲛⲟϥ ⲉϥⲛⲏⲟⲩ ⲉ̀ⲡⲉⲥⲏⲧ ϩⲓϫⲉⲛ ⲡⲓⲕⲁϩⲓ   *(Luke 22:44)*

n) ⲭⲱⲣⲓⲥ ϭⲟ ⲛⲉⲙ ϯⲥⲟ   *(Sunday Theotokia, 7th section)*

Introducing verbs

> **Confusion corner**
> Reference: (Matter pg.241)
>
> **The many meanings of the 'simple' preposition ϧⲁ**
>
> ϧⲁ is a little word which is used in many different places and always seems to have a different meaning each time.
> It's various uses and meanings can be summarised as follows:
> - to mean "under"
> - to mean "towards the direction of"
> - used in "apposition", that is it comes in between two nouns to tell you that they both refer to each other. E.g. ⲁⲛⲟⲕ ϧⲁ ⲡⲓⲣⲉϥⲉⲣⲛⲟⲃⲓ *"I the sinner"*
> - to mean "for the sake of" or "concerning"
> - to mean 'against', as in the sense of talking against someone.

5.1.iv. Transitive verbs

The verbs we met above are all examples of *intransitive* verbs, which are verbs that don't take an object. We'll now look at transitive verbs, which are verbs that do take an object.

In order to deal with transitive verbs, you have to understand a special letter construction called the 'object marker.'
This is basically a letter that sits before the object. Consider the following example:
"I understand the truth"
For a word for word translation in Coptic, you'd have:

†ⲕⲁ† †ⲙⲉⲑⲙⲏⲓ

However, this would not be enough in Coptic. Here the object is ⲙⲉⲑⲙⲏⲓ, and it requires an object marker before it. The object marker in this case, using this particular verb and object, is ⲛ̅.

So, the correct way of writing this sentence is:

†ⲕⲁ† ⲛ̅†ⲙⲉⲑⲙⲏⲓ

(You'll notice that the ⲛ̅ was used earlier in the attributive construction in **(2.4.i)**, but here it means something quite different). As mentioned, the object marker is not constant. For instance, ⲙ is used as the object marker instead of ⲛ̅ when the object begins with one of the following letters.

73

So You want to Learn Coptic?

ⲙ ⲡ ⲃ ⲯ ⲫ

E.g. ϯⲕⲁϯ ⲙ̀ⲡⲓⲥⲁϫⲓ

"I understand the word"

Now suppose you wanted to say "He created Him" or "He created them." In these cases, the object is actually a pronoun rather than a noun. Here you need to use a special pronoun form for the object marker. The pronoun form for ⲙ̀ / ⲛ̀ depends on the person and number of the object, as shown in the following table:

	object being indicated
ⲙ̀ⲙⲟⲓ	me
ⲙ̀ⲙⲟⲕ	you (masculine)
ⲙ̀ⲙⲟ	you (feminine)
ⲙ̀ⲙⲟϥ	him (masculine)
ⲙ̀ⲙⲟⲥ	her (feminine)
ⲙ̀ⲙⲟⲛ	us
ⲙ̀ⲙⲱⲧⲉⲛ	you (plural)
ⲙ̀ⲙⲱⲟⲩ	them

So, "I understand him" becomes

ϯⲕⲁϯ ⲙ̀ⲙⲟϥ

Some other verbs which take ⲙ̀/ⲛ̀ as their object marker are shown below:

| ⲧⲱⲃϩ | ⲙ̀/ⲛ̀ | to pray to |
| ϫⲓⲙⲓ | ⲛ̀ (ⲙ̀) ⲙⲟ | to find |

E.g. ⲧⲉⲛⲧⲱⲃϩ ⲙ̀ⲙⲟⲕ ϧⲉⲛ ⲡⲉϥⲣⲁⲛ *(Absolution of ninth hour prayer, Liturgy of the hours)*
"we pray to you in His name."

While ⲙ̀ and ⲛ̀ are the most commonly used object markers, they are not the only ones. The most commonly used after them is ⲉ̀.

Introducing verbs

When is ⲉ̀ used as opposed to ⲙ̀ / ⲛ̀? The choice of the object marker depends completely on the verb, that is certain verbs take certain object markers. It so happens that the verbs of perception (those which have something to do with the senses) most commonly take ⲉ̀ as their object marker, as shown in the table below:

verb	object marker	
ⲛⲁⲩ	ⲉ̀ ⲉⲣⲟ⳽	to see
ⲥⲱⲧⲉⲙ	ⲉ̀ ⲉⲣⲟ⳽	to hear
	ⲛ̀ⲥⲁ ⲛ̀ⲥⲱ⳽	to obey
ϣⲱⲗⲉⲙ	ⲉ̀ ⲉⲣⲟ⳽	to smell

So, "I see the man" is ϯⲛⲁⲩ ⲉ̀ⲡⲓⲣⲱⲙⲓ

And "he sees the woman" is ϥⲛⲁⲩ ⲉ̀ϯⲥϩⲓⲙⲓ

You'll notice in the table above that the meaning of ⲥⲱⲧⲉⲙ changes depending on which object marker it uses. This is an important point, because it means that the meaning of the verb depends on the object marker that it takes.

There is also a pronoun form for ⲉ̀, which is as formed as follows:

	Object being indicated
ⲉ̀ⲣⲟⲓ	me
ⲉ̀ⲣⲟⲕ	you (m)
ⲉ̀ⲣⲟ	you (f)
ⲉ̀ⲣⲟϥ	him
ⲉ̀ⲣⲟⲥ	her
ⲉ̀ⲣⲟⲛ	us
ⲉ̀ⲣⲱⲧⲉⲛ	you (plural)
ⲉ̀ⲣⲱⲟⲩ	them

So for example, *we see them"*, would be: **ⲧⲉⲛⲛⲁⲩ ⲉⲣⲱⲟⲩ**. The table below shows some other verbs which take ⲉ̀ (ⲉ̀ⲣⲟ⸗) as their object marker:

Vocab		
infinitive	**object marker**	**translation**
ⲉ̀ⲙⲓ	ⲉ̀ ⲉⲣⲟ⸗	to know, understand
ⲕⲁϯ	ⲉ̀ ⲉⲣⲟ⸗	to understand
ϩⲱⲥ	ⲉ̀ ⲉⲣⲟ⸗	to praise
ⲥ̀ⲙⲟⲩ	ⲉ̀ ⲉⲣⲟ⸗	to bless
ϯϩⲟ	ⲉ̀ ⲉⲣⲟ⸗	to ask

Now if the verb is already using a preposition, then the preposition functions as the object marker.

E.g. **ⲧⲉⲛⲥⲱⲧⲉⲙ ⲛ̀ⲥⲁ ⲛⲓⲉⲛⲧⲟⲗⲏ**

"We obey the commandments"

Here you can see that the preposition **ⲛ̀ⲥⲁ** functions as the object marker

As mentioned above, the same verb can sometimes use different object markers/prepositions. In these cases, the meaning of the verb often changes.

For example, **ⲧⲉⲛⲥⲱⲧⲉⲙ ⲉ̀ⲧⲉϥⲥ̀ⲙⲏ**

is *"we hear His word"*.

Whereas **ⲧⲉⲛⲥⲱⲧⲉⲙ ⲛ̀ⲥⲁ ⲧⲉϥⲥ̀ⲙⲏ**

is *"we obey His word"*

As you can see, verbs are quite complicated. And this is only the start! So let's take a moment to summarise what we've learnt so far:

a) The two major categories of verbs are **transitive** and **intransitive**. Transitive verbs take an object whereas intransitive verbs don't.

b) Transitive verbs require an object marker or a preposition between the object and the verb. The object marker is usually ⲉ̀ or ⲛ̀ (ⲙ̀), but it can also be a different preposition. The meaning of the verb may change depending on which object marker or preposition is used.

Some examples of verbs whose meaning changes depending on the preposition they use are shown in the table below:

Vocab

ⲕⲱϯ		ⲫⲱⲧ	
	ⲉ̀	to surround, seek, visit	ϣⲁ	to flee, run to
	ⲛ̄- ⲙ̀ⲙⲟ⸗	to turn self, return	ⲛ̀ⲥⲁ	to pursue
	ⲛ̀ⲥⲁ	to seek		
ⲙⲟϣⲓ		ⲱϣ		
	ϣⲁ	to walk to	ⲉ̀	to cry to, to cry for, to read to
	ⲛ̀ⲥⲁ	to walk behind	ⲉ̀ⲃⲟⲗ	to cry out
ⲥⲁϫⲓ		ϭⲓ		
	ⲉ̀	to speak, talk to	ⲛ̄- ⲙ̀ⲙⲟ⸗	to take, receive
	ⲛⲉⲙ	to speak with	ⲛⲉⲙ	to touch
	ⲉ̀/ ⲉⲑⲃⲉ/ ϧⲁ	to speak about		
	ⲛ̀ⲥⲁ/ ⲟⲩⲃⲏ/ ⲟⲩⲃⲉ	to speak against		

It's well worth noting that some verbs always appear with a particular preposition. In some of those cases, a word for word translation of the verb with the preposition doesn't give you the true intended meaning of the combination.

E.g. In ϫⲱⲕ ⲉ̀ⲃⲟⲗ, ⲉ̀ⲃⲟⲗ on its own would be translated as 'away', however, when it appears with ϫⲱⲕ, the combination means "to complete" or "to perfect" so that the

So You want to Learn Coptic?

ⲉⲃⲟⲗ doesn't seem to contribute to the final meaning of the verb. Another example is ϥⲁⲓ ϧⲁ, which doesn't mean "to carry under", but simply "to carry".

> **Confusion corner**
> Note that when the object marker ⲉ̀ is followed by the indefinite article, the combination is contracted to form ⲉⲩ.
> For example:
> ⲉ̀ ⲟⲩⲥⲱⲧⲏⲣⲓⲁ is contracted to ⲉⲩⲥⲱⲧⲏⲣⲓⲁ

Vocab			
ⲉⲣⲉⲧⲓⲛ ⲛ̀(ⲙ)	to ask, inquire (v.t Gk)	ⲛⲱⲟⲩ	them (ind. obj) **(5.7)**
ⲕⲟⲥⲙⲟⲥ	world (Gk,m)	ⲟⲩⲱϣⲧ ⲛ̀(ⲙ)	to worship, kneel unto (v.t)
ⲙⲏⲓⲛⲓ	sign, wonder (m)	ⲟⲩⲉⲓⲛⲓⲛ	Greek person (m)
ⲙⲟⲩϯ ⲉ̀ⲣⲟ⸗	to call (v.t)	ⲥⲟⲫⲓⲁ	wisdom (Gk,f)

Exercise 5.3

a) ϯϯϩⲟ ⲉ̀ⲣⲱⲧⲉⲛ (Ephesians 4:1)

b) ⲛⲓⲟⲩⲇⲁⲓ ⲥⲉⲉⲣⲉⲧⲓⲛ ⲛ̀ϩⲁⲛⲙⲏⲓⲛⲓ ⲟⲩⲟϩ ⲛⲓⲟⲩⲉⲓⲛⲓⲛ ⲥⲉⲕⲱϯ ⲛ̀ⲥⲁ ϯⲥⲟⲫⲓⲁ (1 Corinth 1:22)

c) ⲡⲓⲕⲟⲥⲙⲟⲥ ⲙⲟⲥϯ ⲙ̀ⲙⲱⲧⲉⲛ (John 15:18)

d) ⲥⲉⲥⲱⲧⲉⲙ ⲉ̀ⲡⲓⲥⲁϫⲓ ⲛ̀ⲧⲉ Ⲫⲛⲟⲩϯ (Luke 8:21)

e) ϥϯⲥⲃⲱ ⲙ̀ⲡⲓⲙⲱⲓⲧ ⲛ̀ⲧⲉ Ⲫⲛⲟⲩϯ (Matthew 22:16)

f) ⲥⲉϯⲱⲟⲩ ⲛⲱⲟⲩ ⲛ̀ϫⲉ ⲛⲓⲣⲱⲙⲓ (Matthew 6:2)

g) Ⲛⲓⲫⲏⲟⲩⲓ ⲥⲉⲥⲁϫⲓ ⲙ̀ⲡⲱⲟⲩ ⲙ̀Ⲫⲛⲟⲩϯ (Psalm **18:2** 19:1)

h) ⲛ̀ϥⲕⲁϯ ⲉ̀ⲣⲟϥ ⲁⲛ (Matthew 13:19)

i) ϥⲙⲟⲩϯ ⲉⲣⲟ   *(John 11:28)*

j) ⲥⲉⲟⲩⲱϣϯ ⲛ̀ⲟⲩⲛⲟⲩϯ ⲛ̀ⲟⲩⲱⲧ

> **Practice text 3**
> *Psalm (**95:1-5** 96:1-5)*
> This psalm from the ninth hour of the liturgy of the hours provides a good opportunity to practice some of the skills you've learnt so far:
>
> ϩⲱⲥ ⲉ̀Ⲡϭⲟⲓⲥ ϧⲉⲛ ⲟⲩϩⲱⲥ ⲙ̀ⲃⲉⲣⲓ ϩⲱⲥ ⲉ̀Ⲡ̅ⲟ̅ⲥ̅ ⲡⲕⲁϩⲓ ⲧⲏⲣϥ
>
> ϩⲱⲥ ⲉ̀Ⲡ̅ⲟ̅ⲥ̅ ⲥ̀ⲙⲟⲩ ⲉ̀ⲡⲉϥⲣⲁⲛ ϩⲓϣⲉⲛⲛⲟⲩϥⲓ ⲙ̀ⲡⲉϥⲟⲩϫⲁⲓ ⲛ̀ⲉϩⲟⲟⲩ
>
> ϧⲁⲧϩⲏ ⲛ̀ⲉϩⲟⲟⲩ
>
> ⲥⲁϫⲓ ⲙ̀ⲡⲉϥⲱⲟⲩ ϧⲉⲛ ⲛⲓⲉⲑⲛⲟⲥ ⲛⲉⲙ ⲛⲉϥϣⲫⲏⲣⲓ ϧⲉⲛ ⲛⲓⲗⲁⲟⲥ
>
> ⲧⲏⲣⲟⲩ
>
> ϫⲉ ⲟⲩⲛⲓϣϯ ⲡⲉ Ⲡϭⲟⲓⲥ ⲟⲩⲟϩ ϥ̀ⲥ̀ⲙⲁⲣⲱⲟⲩⲧ ⲉ̀ⲙⲁϣⲱ ϥ̀ⲟⲓ ⲛ̀ϩⲟϯ
>
> ⲉ̀ϫⲉⲛ ⲛⲓⲛⲟⲩϯ ⲧⲏⲣⲟⲩ
>
> ϫⲉ ⲛⲓⲛⲟⲩϯ ⲧⲏⲣⲟⲩ ⲛ̀ⲧⲉ ⲛⲓⲉⲑⲛⲟⲥ ϩⲁⲛⲇⲉⲙⲱⲛ ⲛⲉ
>
> | Vocab | | | |
> |---|---|---|---|
> | ⲇⲉⲙⲱⲛ | demon (m) | ϣⲫⲏⲣⲓ | wonder, amazement (f) |
> | ⲉ̀ⲙⲁϣⲱ | very (adverb) | ϩⲓϣⲉⲛⲛⲟⲩϥⲓ | to preach, proclaim (v.i) |
> | ⲛ̀ⲉϩⲟⲟⲩ ϧⲁⲧϩⲏ ⲛ̀ⲉϩⲟⲟⲩ | day by day (adv) | ϩⲟϯ | fear (f) |
> | ⲟⲩϫⲁⲓ | salvation, health (m) | | |

5.1.v. Who or which: introducing the relative converter

There is a very commonly used device in Coptic called the *relative converter*. Basically, it's a little construction used in a sentence to give the meaning of 'who', 'whose' or 'which', as for instance, you'd use in a sentence like "the man who is crying."

Now the form of the relative pronoun changes depending on the other words around it and the situation in which it is used. One of the factors that determines the

form is the *antecedent*. "What is the antecedent?" I hear you ask. The antecedent is the first noun that appears in a sentence, as illustrated in the following examples:
"the man who saw the duck"
and "the house which he built."

In the first example, the antecedent is "the man." In this case, "the man" also happens to be the subject of the sentence, as he's the one who saw the duck.

In the second example, the antecedent is "the house." In this case however, 'the house' is not the subject, rather the subject is 'he.'

The relative converter used partly depends on whether the antecedent is the subject, or whether the antecedent is different to the subject. In the sections below, we'll look at how the relative converter changes depending on whether the antecedent is the same as or different to the subject.

Antecedent as subject

When the antecedent is the same as the subject, the relative converter used will either be ⲉⲧ, ⲉ—, ⲉ̀ⲧⲉ or ⲉ̀ⲣⲉ

The first of these which we'll consider is ⲉⲧ. It usually comes before the verb, and is used when the subject has a definite article before it.

E.g. ⲡⲓⲣⲱⲙⲓ ⲉⲧⲣⲓⲙⲓ

"the man who is crying"

ϯⲥ̀ϩⲓⲙⲓ ⲉⲧⲱϣ ⲙ̀ⲡⲓϫⲱⲙ

"the woman who reads the book"

ⲡ̀ϣⲏⲣⲓ ⲉⲧⲥⲱⲧⲉⲙ ⲉ̀ϯⲥ̀ⲙⲏ ⲙ̀ⲡⲉϥⲓⲱⲧ

"the son who hears the voice of his father"

ⲉⲧ is also often used before prepositions such as ϧⲉⲛ when there is no verb in the sentence.

E.g. ⲡⲉⲛⲓⲱⲧ ⲉⲧϧⲉⲛ ⲛⲓⲫⲏⲟⲩⲓ

"Our father who is in the Heavens"

Note that ⲉⲧ changes to ⲉⲑ when the verb it precedes starts with one of the vilminor letters **(2.1.i)**.

The ⲉ— construction is also used as a relative converter. It's chosen when the subject of the sentence has an *indefinite* article. The stroke after the ⲉ tells you that the letter which follows the ⲉ will change depending on whether the noun is masculine or feminine, or whether it's in the plural.

ⲉϥ–	masculine noun
ⲉⲥ–	feminine noun
ⲉⲩ–	plural noun

So a masculine noun would take ⲉϥ before the verb.

E.g ⲟⲩⲣⲱⲙⲓ ⲉϥⲣⲓⲙⲓ

"a man who is crying"

In the examples above, the relative converter has been coming before the verb. Sometimes however the relative converter comes before the subject. Those forms are ⲉⲧⲉ and ⲉⲣⲉ and are known as the *pre-subject* forms.

ⲉⲧⲉ is the pre-subject form for ⲉⲧ-.

E.g. ⲉⲧⲉ ⲡⲓⲣⲱⲙⲓ ⲣⲓⲙⲓ

"the man who is crying"

....and ⲉⲣⲉ is the presubject form for ⲉ–

ⲉⲣⲉ ⲟⲩⲣⲱⲙⲓ ⲣⲓⲙⲓ

'*a man who is crying*'

While this should mean that ⲉⲧⲉ is used for nouns with a definite article, and ⲉⲣⲉ for those with an indefinite article, the reality is that ⲉⲧⲉ and ⲉⲣⲉ are often used interchangeably. As they are used before a noun, their translation often comes out to mean "whose."

E.g. ⲉ̀ⲣⲉ ⲧⲉϥϫⲓϫ ⲛⲟⲩⲓⲛⲁⲙ ϣⲟⲩⲱⲟⲩ *(Luke 6:8)*

"whose right hand is withered"

So You want to Learn Coptic?

Confusion corner
What was that again?

The range of relative converter may seem a bit overwhelming, so hopefully you'll find this flow chart makes the choice a bit easier.

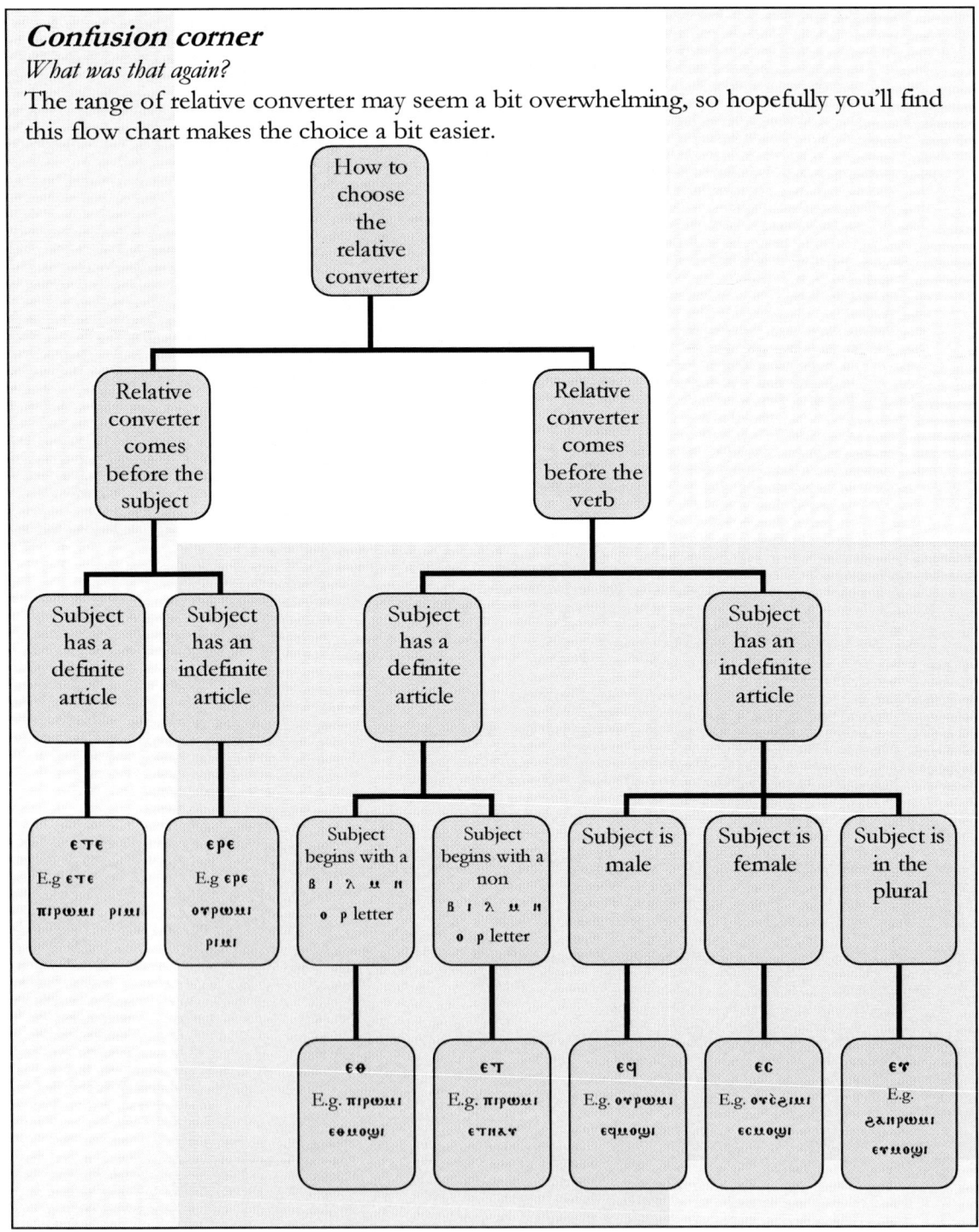

Introducing verbs

In the examples above, 'real' verbs were used, but what if the sentence uses the copula (i.e. ⲡⲉ or ⲧⲉ) rather than a verb? In these cases, the relative pronoun used is ⲉ̀.

Now, the relative pronoun cannot be combined directly with the copula, so it comes before the subject, so for example, in the sentence:

"A man whose name is Joseph", the copula is ⲡⲉ. So the ⲉ̀ comes before the subject which is ⲣⲁⲛ (name). Now the ⲉ̀ also comes before what ever articles were before the noun, which in this case is ⲡⲉϥ (his).

So, the end result is:

ⲟⲩⲣⲱⲙⲓ ⲉ̀ ⲡⲉϥⲣⲁⲛ ⲡⲉ Ⲓⲱⲥⲏⲫ
"a man whose name is Joseph"

You'll notice here that the ⲉ̀ doesn't have any letters added to it, as it is not directly attached to a verb.

Both ⲉⲧⲉ and ⲉⲣⲉ can also take a copula and sandwich a noun between them to mean "which is" or "who is."

E.g ⲉ̀ⲧⲉ Ⲓⲏⲥ ⲡⲉ ⲡ̀ϣⲏⲣⲓ ⲛ̀Ⲓⲱⲥⲏϥ *(John 1:45)*
"who is Jesus the son of Joseph"

ⲉ̀ⲧⲉ ⲡⲁϣⲏⲣⲓ ⲙ̀ⲙⲉⲛⲣⲓⲧ ⲡⲉ *(1 Corinth 4:17)*
"who is my beloved son"

ⲉⲧⲉ and ⲉⲣⲉ can also take the meaning of "which is" without even using the copula:

E.g. ⲉ̀ⲧⲉ ⲧ̀ϩⲉⲣⲉⲥⲓⲥ ⲛ̀ⲧⲉ ⲛⲓⲥⲁⲇⲇⲟⲩⲕⲉⲟⲥ *(Acts 7:14)*
"which is the sect of the Sadducees"

Sometimes you will see ⲉ̀ⲧⲉ followed by ⲫⲁⲓ ⲡⲉ to form ⲉ̀ⲧⲉ ⲫⲁⲓ ⲡⲉ. This is a set expression meaning "which is this"

E.g. ⲉ̀ⲧⲉ ⲫⲁⲓ ⲡⲉ ⲡⲓⲙⲱⲟⲩ ⲛⲉⲙ ⲡⲓⲥ̀ⲛⲟϥ ⲉ̀ⲧⲉ ⲛⲓⲭⲣⲓⲥⲧⲓⲁⲛⲟⲥ ϭⲓ ⲉ̀ⲃⲟⲗ *(hom vatt ii pg.66)*
"which is the water and the blood which the Christians take of"

ⲉⲧⲉ (and less commonly ⲉⲣⲉ) can also come after ⲫⲁⲓ and ⲛⲏ to form ⲫⲁⲓ ⲉⲧⲉ/ⲉⲣⲉ and ⲛⲏ ⲉⲧⲉ, which mean "that which" and "those which" respectively.

E.g. ⲫⲁⲓ ⲉⲧⲉ ⲛⲓⲡⲣⲟⲫⲏⲧⲏⲥ ⲧⲏⲣⲟⲩ *(Acts 10:43)*
"this which all the prophets"

Vocab			
ⲉⲣⲡⲣⲉⲡⲉⲓ	to be fitting,(v.i)	ⲥⲏⲟⲩ	time (m)
ⲏⲓ	house (m)	ⲭⲁⲕⲓ	darkness (m)
ⲙⲟϩ, ⲙⲉϩ (q)	to fill (v.t)	ϣⲓϯ	to leap, gush, vomit (v.t)
ⲛⲏⲥⲟⲥ	island (f)	ϣⲱⲟⲩⲓ, ϣⲟⲩⲱⲟⲩ (q)	to dry, to be dried, withered (q)
ⲛϧⲏⲧ⸗	inside (prep. Pronom) **(5.5)**	ϣⲱⲡ	to accept, receive, buy (v.t)
ⲟⲩⲓⲛⲁⲙ	right hand (m)	ϣϣⲏⲛ	tree (m)
ⲟⲩⲧⲁϩ	fruit (m)	ϩⲟⲩⲓⲧ	first (adj)
ⲣⲉⲙⲣⲁⲩϣ	gentle person (m)	ϫⲱⲛⲧ	anger (m)
ⲥⲁⲓⲉ̀	beautiful (adj)		

Exercise 5.4:

a) ⲛⲓϧⲉⲗⲗⲟⲓ ⲉ̀ⲧⲉ ⲉ̀ϧⲟⲩⲛ ⲙ̀ⲡⲓⲏⲓ *(Ezekiel 9:6)*

b) ⲟⲩⲟⲛ ⲛⲓⲃⲉⲛ ⲉⲧⲥⲱⲧⲉⲙ ⲉ̀ⲛⲁⲥⲁϫⲓ ⲛⲁⲓ *(Matthew 7:26)*

c) Ⲡ̅ⲟ̅ⲥ̅ ⲉⲧϣⲟⲡ ⲛ̀ⲛⲓⲣⲉⲙⲣⲁⲩϣ *(Psalm **146:6** 147:6)*

d) ϣϣⲏⲛ ⲛⲓⲃⲉⲛ ⲉ̀ⲧⲉ ⲡⲉϥⲟⲩⲧⲁϩ ⲛ̀ϧⲏⲧϥ *(Genesis 1:29)*

e) ⲟⲩⲁⲓ ⲉ̀ⲡⲉϥⲣⲁⲛ ⲡⲉ ⲧⲓⲧⲟⲥ *(Acts 18:7)*

f) ⲟⲩⲥ̀ϩⲓⲙⲓ ⲉ̀ⲣⲉ ⲡⲉⲥⲥⲛⲟϥ ϣⲁⲧ ⲉ̀ⲃⲟⲗ *(Matthew 9:20)*

g) ⲡⲓϩⲟⲩⲓⲧ ⲛ̀ⲧⲉ ϯⲛⲏⲥⲟⲥ ⲉ̀ⲡⲉϥⲣⲁⲛ ⲡⲉ ⲡⲟⲩⲡⲗⲓⲟⲥ *(Acts 28:7)*

h) ⲉ̀ⲣⲉ ⲛⲟⲩϩⲓ̀ ⲟⲓ ⲛ̀ⲥⲁⲓⲉ̀ (Hom vatt ii pg.239)

When the antecedent is not the subject

The relative pronouns above only applied when the antecedent was the same as the subject. Things become a little trickier when the subject is different to the antecedent; here the relative pronoun actually changes depending on the subject of the sentence, which becomes represented in the form of the relative converter, giving the forms shown in the table below:

ⲉϯ	which I
ⲉⲧⲉⲕ	which you (m)
ⲉⲧⲉ	which you (f)
ⲉⲧⲉϥ	which he
ⲉⲧⲉⲥ	which she
ⲉⲧⲉⲛ	which we
ⲉⲧⲉⲧⲉⲛ	which you (pl)
ⲉⲧⲟⲩ	which they
ⲉⲧⲉ	pre subject form

When this type of relative converter is used, another word is added which we normally wouldn't use in an equivalent English translation. To have a better idea of what I'm trying to say, read the following example:

ⲡⲓϩⲁⲡ ⲉⲧⲉⲕϯ ⲙ̀ⲙⲟϥ ⲉ̀ⲡⲉⲕϣⲫⲏⲣ (Romans 2:1)

In the example above, ϩⲁⲡ means 'judgement' ϯ is the verb 'to give' and ϣⲫⲏⲣ is 'friend' or 'companion', so a word by word translation would come out as: *"the judgment which you give it to your friend."*

Now in English, we would have left out the 'it' after 'give', which is translated from the ⲙ̀ⲙⲟϥ in the Coptic sentence. In this particular case, ⲙ̀ⲙⲟϥ serves the role of the *resumptive morph*, which Coptic insists on including after the verb when this particular type of relative pronoun is used. The form of the resumptive morph comes from the pronoun form of the object marker **(5.1.iv)**, and takes the same gender and number as the antecedent. So in the above example, ⲙ̀ⲙⲟϥ was chosen as the resumptive morph as the object marker for the verb ϯ is ⲙ̀, and the antecedent is ϩⲁⲡ which is a singular masculine word.

Vocab			
ⲙⲉⲧⲣⲉϥϯⲥⲃⲱ	teaching	ⲥⲧⲩⲗⲏ	pillar, column (Gk,f)
ⲙⲏⲓⲛⲓ	wonder, sign miracle (m)	ϣⲉⲙϣⲓ	to serve, worship (v.t)
ⲛⲱⲧⲉⲛ	to you (indirect obj) **(5.7)**		

Exercise 5.5

a) ⲛⲁⲓⲙⲏⲓⲛⲓ ⲉ̀ⲧⲉⲕⲓⲣⲓ ⲙ̀ⲙⲱⲟⲩ *(John 3:2)*

b) ⲛⲓⲥⲧⲩⲗⲏ ⲧⲏⲣⲟⲩ ⲉ̀ⲧⲟⲩϣⲉⲙϣⲓ ⲙ̀ⲙⲱⲟⲩ *(hom vatt ii pg71)*

c) ⲉⲧⲉ ⲛⲁⲓ ⲛⲏⲉⲧⲉⲛⲥⲁϫⲓ ⲙ̀ⲙⲱⲟⲩ ϧⲉⲛ ϩⲁⲛⲙⲉⲧⲣⲉϥϯⲥⲃⲱ
(1 Corinthians 2:13)

d) ⲫⲁⲓ ⲉ̀ⲧⲉⲧⲉⲛⲛⲁⲩ ⲉ̀ⲣⲟϥ ⲟⲩⲟϩ ⲧⲉⲧⲉⲛⲥⲱⲟⲩⲛ ⲙ̀ⲙⲟϥ *(Acts 3:16)*

e) ⲫⲁⲓ ⲡⲉ Ⲓⲏⲥ Ⲡⲭⲥ ⲫⲁⲓ[φ] ⲁⲛⲟⲕ ⲉϯϩⲓⲱⲓϣ ⲙ̀ⲙⲟϥ ⲛⲱⲧⲉⲛ *(Acts 17:3)*

[φ] Here the ⲫⲁⲓ is used to emphasise the first ⲫⲁⲓ in the sentence, as was discussed on pg.**36**

Introducing verbs

> ### Practice text 4
> Many of the hymns of the liturgy change with the liturgical season. The following example is chanted following the prayer of the absolution of the ministers during the weekdays of the Holy Great Fasting.
>
> Ⲛⲑⲟ ⲧⲉ ϯϣⲟⲩⲣⲏ ⲛ̀ⲛⲟⲩⲃ ⲛ̀ⲕⲁⲑⲁⲣⲟⲥ ⲉⲧϥⲁⲓ ϧⲁ ⲡⲓϫⲉⲃⲥ
>
> ⲛ̀ⲭⲣⲱⲙ ⲉⲧⲥ̀ⲙⲁⲣⲱⲟⲩⲧ
>
> | *Vocab* | | | |
> |---|---|---|---|
> | ⲆⲒⲔⲈⲞⲤⲨⲚⲎ | righteousness (Gk) | ⲭⲣⲱⲙ | fire (Gk,m) |
> | ⲔⲀⲐⲀⲢⲞⲤ | pure (adj, Gk) | ϫⲉⲃⲥ | coal (m, f,) |

The negative relative

The relative converter can also be used in the negative. Once again, the form changes depending on whether there is a definite or indefinite antecedent. It essentially combines the pre subject from (either ⲈⲦⲈ or Ⲉ̀ depending on the antecedent) with the Ⲛ̀...ⲀⲚ construction from page **(66)**.

For a definite antecedent, the following construction is used:

ⲈⲦⲈ + Ⲛ̀ + verb + ⲀⲚ

E.g. ⲞⲨϨⲰⲞⲨⲦ ⲚⲈⲘ ⲞⲨⲤ̀ϨⲒⲘⲒ ⲈⲂⲞⲖ ϦⲈⲚ ⲚⲒⲦⲈⲂⲚⲰⲞⲨⲒ̀ ⲈⲦⲈ Ⲛ̀ⲤⲈⲞⲨⲀⲂ

ⲀⲚ *(Genesis 7:2)*

"a male and a female from the beasts which are not pure"

Whereas for an indefinite antecedent, this construction is used:

a) Ⲉ̀ + noun + Ⲛ̀ + verb + ⲀⲚ

Addressing the adjective gap- making adjectives from the qualitative

While some adjectives were mentioned in **(2.4)**, Coptic doesn't actually have many dedicated adjectives in their own right. To meet this lack, Coptic uses the qualitative form of the infinitive **(5.1.ii)** and combines it with the relative converter **(5.1.v)** to make a whole new series of words which can be used as adjectives.

For example, let's take the verb ⲞⲨⲞⲠ- "to become Holy."

The qualitative form for this verb is **ⲟⲩⲁⲃ** - "to be Holy."

Now there are two types of relative pronouns which can be used with the qualitative. As can be seen in the table below, the choice depends on whether the noun which is being described is preceded by a definite or an indefinite article. Notice that these are the same as two of the relative pronouns which we looked at in **(5.1.v.)**

| ⲉⲧ (ⲉⲑ) | for nouns starting with a definite article |
| ⲉ⸗ | for nouns starting with an indefinite article |

1) Nouns starting with the definite article

As with the infinitive form, the qualitative is preceded by the relative converter **ⲉⲧ (ⲉⲑ)** when the subject has a definite article.

Now with this type of adjective, the attribute construction is not used, so no **ⲙ** (**ⲛ̀**) is required before the adjective. Let's work through an example to write 'the Holy Spirit.'

The first step is to write the noun:

Ⲡⲓⲡ̀ⲛⲉⲩⲙⲁ *"the spirit"*

The next step is to find the correct qualitative verb. As discussed above, the qualitative form for Holy is **ⲟⲩⲁⲃ**.

The third step is to pick the write relative converter to go before the qualitative. As the verb here begins with an **ⲟ**, which is one of those special vilminor letters mentioned above, an **ⲉⲑ** is used instead of **ⲉⲧ**.

So "the Holy Spirit" is written as:

Ⲡⲓⲡ̀ⲛⲉⲩⲙⲁ ⲉⲑⲟⲩⲁⲃ

2) When the noun starts with an indefinite article

Again, as with the infinitive form, the qualitative is preceded by the **ⲉ⸗** construction when the subject of the verb uses an indefinite article:

Introducing verbs

ⲉϥ–	masculine noun
ⲉⲥ–	feminine noun
ⲉⲩ–	plural noun

So, to say "*a Holy man*", you would see that man is a masculine word, so you would use ⲉϥ before the qualitative, which gives you:

ⲟⲩⲣⲱⲙⲓ ⲉϥⲟⲩⲁⲃ

The table below shows some verbs with both their infinitive and qualitative forms.

Infinitive		Qualitative	
ⲁϣⲁⲓ	to increase, multiply	ⲟϣ	to be abundant
ⲑⲱⲗⲉⲃ	to defile, pollute	ⲑⲟⲗⲉⲃ	to be defiled
ⲑⲱϩⲉⲙ	to knock, summon, invite	ⲑⲁϩⲉⲙ	to be summoned
ⲣⲱⲧ	to bud, grow	ⲣⲏⲧ	budding, growing
ⲥⲙⲟⲩ	to bless	ⲥⲙⲁⲣⲱⲟⲩⲧ	to be blessed
ϣⲱⲡ	to accept, buy	ϣⲏⲡ	acceptable
–	–	ϩⲱⲟⲩ	to be evil

Vocab			
ⲑⲩⲥⲓⲁ	offering (f)	ⲥⲏⲟⲩ	time (m)
ⲙⲏϣ	multitude (m)	ϣϣⲏⲛ	tree (m)
ⲟⲩⲱⲙ	to eat (v.t)		

Exercise 5.6

a) ⲛⲓⲥⲁϫⲓ ⲛ̀ⲧⲉ Π̄ⲟ̄ⲥ̄ ϩⲁⲛⲥⲁϫⲓ ⲉⲩⲟⲩⲁⲃ ⲛⲉ (*Psalm 11:7 12:6*)

b) ϩⲁⲛⲡ̀ⲛⲉⲩⲙⲁ ⲉⲩϩⲱⲟⲩ (*Luke 7:21*)

c) ϧⲉⲛ ϩⲁⲛϫⲓϫ ⲉⲩⲑⲟⲗⲉⲃ ⲥⲉⲟⲩⲱⲙ ⲙ̀ⲡⲓⲱⲓⲕ (*Mark 7:5*)

So You want to Learn Coptic?

d) Ⲡⲁⲩⲗⲟⲥ ⲫⲃⲱⲕ ⲙⲠⲉⲛϭⲟⲓⲥ Ⲓⲏ̅ⲥ̅ Ⲡⲭ̅ⲥ̅ ⲡⲓⲁⲡⲟⲥⲧⲟⲗⲟⲥ

ⲉⲑⲟⲩⲁⲃ *(Introduction to the reading of the Pauline epistle, Divine Liturgy)*

e) ⲟⲩⲥⲛⲟⲩ ⲉϥϣⲏⲡ

f) an acceptable sacrifice

g) the growing tree

h) the numerous multitude

The relative substantive- making nouns from the relative converter

The relative converters that we've been dealing with are actually pronouns, because they refer to nouns but aren't actually nouns themselves. They can however be converted to nouns. This is done by combining the far demonstratives that we mentioned in **(2.2.ii)** (ⲫⲏ, ⲑⲏ and ⲛⲏ) with the relative converters to form composites called the *relative substantives*. The term substantive means that part of that expression refers to the phrase as 'having substance', or in other words, being a noun.

To make it a bit clearer, you're adding the relative converter meaning 'who' or 'which' with the far demonstrative 'that', to give the nouns 'that who' or 'that which'. E.g.

ⲫⲏ + ⲉⲧ = ⲫⲏⲉⲧ

This expression ⲫⲏⲉⲧ is called the relative substantives, which is then combined with the qualitative form of the relevant verb to give us a new noun. E.g.

ⲫⲏ = 'that'

ⲉⲑⲟⲩⲁⲃ = 'which is Holy'

ⲫⲏ + ⲉⲑⲟⲩⲁⲃ = ⲫⲏⲉⲑⲟⲩⲁⲃ
"that which is Holy" = "the Saint"

ⲛⲏ = 'those'

ⲉⲑⲙⲱⲟⲩⲧ = "who are dead"

ⲛⲏ + ⲉⲑⲙⲱⲟⲩⲧ = ⲛⲏⲉⲑⲙⲱⲟⲩⲧ = *"those who are dead"* = *"the dead"*

Introducing verbs

An alternative relative substantive is ⲡⲉⲧ which is formed by adding the definite article ⲡ̅ to the relative pronoun ⲉⲧ.

E.g. ⲡ̅ϭⲟⲓⲥ ⲡⲉⲧ ϯⲥⲟⲫⲓⲁ *(Proverbs 2:6)*
"The Lord is the one who gives wisdom"

The ⲡⲉⲧ is also called the articulated relative because it's really made by adding the article (hence the 'articulated' part of the name) to the relative converter.

Vocab			
ϫⲉⲛⲉⲁ	race, generation, family (f)	ⲥⲱⲛϩ	to be bound (v.i)
ⲓⲁⲕⲱⲃ	Jacob (prop. noun)	ϣⲁϥⲉ	desert, wilderness (m)
ⲙⲟⲩϯ	to call, pronounce (v.t)	ϧⲣⲱⲟⲩ	voice (m)
ⲧⲉⲃⲛⲏ	beast (m)	ϩⲟ	face (m)
ⲧⲉⲃⲛⲱⲟⲩⲓ	beasts (pl)	ϩⲱⲟⲩⲧ	male, husband (m)

Exercise 5.7

a) ⲡ̅ϧⲣⲱⲟⲩ ⲙ̅ⲡⲉⲧⲱϣ ⲉⲃⲟⲗ ϩⲓ ⲡϣⲁϥⲉ *(Mark 1:3)*

b) ⲛⲏ ⲉⲧⲉⲧⲉⲛⲛⲁⲩ ⲉⲣⲱⲟⲩ *(Luke 7:22)*

c) ⲛⲁⲓ ⲛⲉ ⲛⲏ ⲉⲧⲥⲱⲧⲉⲙ *(Luke 8:14)*

d) ⲁⲛⲟⲕ ⲡⲉⲧⲥⲱⲛϩ ϧⲉⲛ Π̅ⲟ̅ⲥ̅ *(Ephesians 4:1)*

e) ⲑⲏ ⲉⲧⲟⲩⲙⲟⲩϯ ⲉⲣⲟⲥ ϫⲉ ϯⲙⲁⲅⲇⲁⲗⲓⲛⲏ *(Luke 8:2)*

f) ⲑⲁⲓ ⲧⲉ ϯϫⲉⲛⲉⲁ ⲛ̅ⲧⲉ ⲛⲏⲉⲧⲕⲱϯ ⲛ̅ⲥⲁ Π̅ϭⲟⲓⲥ ⲉⲧⲕⲱϯ ⲛ̅ⲥⲁ ⲡϩⲟ ⲙ̅Ⲫϯ ⲛ̅ⲓⲁⲕⲱⲃ *(Psalm 23:6 24:6)*

5.2. The past perfect tense

Up till now, we have only talked about describing an action that is currently being performed. But how do you describe an action that occurred in the past?

Your reply might be "Use the past tense", but which past tense do you use? "You mean there's more than one?" I hear you ask,
Well yes. Consider the following sentences.

91

So You want to Learn Coptic?

"He was running"
"He ran."

What's the difference between them? In the first case, as far as we know, the man is still running. Something may have later happened while he was running, or he may have been running and stopped, but it's not clear from the sentence. As far as we're concerned, the man is still in a suspended state of running. However, in the second sentence, it is clear that the man has stopped running. The action is complete, or to put it another way, the action is perfect. For this reason, a completed action in the past is described in the perfect tense.

Hence the second sentence is an example of the use of the *perfect* tense, and the first sentence was an example of what is called the *imperfect* tense.

So how do you use the perfect tense in Coptic? Basically, the letter ⲁ is placed first, followed by a subject prefix, which is finally followed by the verb itself. Let's use our old friend ⲙⲟϣⲓ as an example:

ⲁⲓⲙⲟϣⲓ	I walked
ⲁⲕⲙⲟϣⲓ	You walked (m)
ⲁⲣⲉⲙⲟϣⲓ	You walked (f)
ⲁⲣⲉⲧⲉⲛⲙⲟϣⲓ	You walked (plural)
ⲁϥⲙⲟϣⲓ	He walked
ⲁⲥⲙⲟϣⲓ	She walked
ⲁⲛⲙⲟϣⲓ	We walked
ⲁⲩⲙⲟϣⲓ	They walked
ⲁ	pre subject form

You can see that each form takes an ⲁ at the beginning, which is then followed by the subject prefix coming in between the verb ⲙⲟϣⲓ. Bear in mind that the subject prefixes for the past perfect are not all the same as those used with the first present (**5.1**).

Introducing verbs

The presubject form

What's this presubject form at the bottom of the above table? This is an alternative way to write the sentence when a noun rather than a pronoun is used for the subject.

For example, in **ⲁϥⲣⲓⲙⲓ**, only the pronoun (he) is present but the subject noun is not indicated. That is it says "he cried" but it doesn't specify who cried.

However, in **ⲡⲓⲣⲱⲙⲓ ⲁϥⲣⲓⲙⲓ**, the subject noun is indicated (**ⲣⲱⲙⲓ**). That is, we know it is the man who cried.

In these cases, the **ⲁ** can be split off from the verb and placed before the subject. So the sentence becomes: **ⲁ ⲡⲓⲣⲱⲙⲓ ⲣⲓⲙⲓ**

This **ⲁ** at the front is therefore known as the pre subject form. You'll come to see that different tenses also have their own presubject forms which can also be used in this way.

Vocab			
ⲓⲛⲓ	to bring (v.t)	ⲧⲥⲟ	to give to drink (v.t)
ⲓⲉⲣⲟⲩⲥⲁⲗⲏⲙ	Jerusalem (prop noun)	ⲧⲱⲟⲩ	mountain (m)
ⲕⲁϩⲓ	earth, land (m)	ⲭⲁⲕⲓ	darkness (m)
ⲗⲁⲟⲥ	people, nation (m)	ϣⲓⲛⲓ ⲉ	to visit (v.t)
ⲙⲓⲥⲓ	to give birth to (v.t)	ⲛⲥⲁ	to inquire for, seek after
ⲙⲱⲟⲩ	water (m)	ϣⲫⲏⲣ	friend, companion (m)
ⲛⲁϩϯ	to believe (v.t)	ϭⲱⲧⲉⲃ	to kill (v.t)
ⲟⲩⲟϩ	and (conj.6.1)	ϩⲟϫϩⲉϫ	distress, need, trouble (m)
ⲟⲩⲱⲣⲡ	to send (v.i)	ϩⲱⲗⲉⲙ	to rob (v.t)
ⲡⲉⲧⲣⲁ	rock (Gk,m)	ϭⲱⲣⲉⲙ	to make sign, beckon (v.i)
Ⲥⲁⲣⲣⲁ	Sarah (prop. noun)		

So You want to Learn Coptic?

Exercise 5.8

a) ⲁ Ⲓⲏⲥ ⲟⲩⲱⲣⲡ ⲙ̀ⲙⲁⲑⲏⲧⲏⲥ ⲃ̄ *(Matthew 21:1)*

b) ⲁⲛⲟⲛ ϩⲱⲛ ⲁⲛⲛⲁϩϯ ⲉ̀Ⲡⲭ̄ⲥ̄ Ⲓⲏⲥ *(Galatians 2:16)*

c) ⲁ ⲟⲩⲭⲁⲕⲓ ϣⲱⲡⲓ ϩⲓϫⲉⲛ ⲡⲕⲁϩⲓ ⲧⲏⲣϥ *(Luke 23:44)*

d) ⲁϥϩⲱⲗⲉⲙ ⲙ̀ⲡⲉϥⲏⲓ *(Matthew 12:29)*

e) ⲁϥϭⲱⲣⲉⲙ ⲉ̀ⲣⲱⲟⲩ *(Luke 1:22)*

f) ⲁⲩϭⲱⲣⲉⲙ ⲉ̀ⲛⲟⲩϣⲫⲏⲣ *(Luke 5:7)*

g) ⲓⲉⲣⲟⲩⲥⲁⲗⲏⲙ ⲁⲥϧⲱⲧⲉⲃ ⲛ̀ⲛⲓⲡⲣⲟⲫⲏⲧⲏⲥ *(Matthew 23:37)*

h) ⲁ Ⲫⲓⲱⲧ ϫⲟⲩϣⲧ ⲉ̀ⲃⲟⲗϧⲉⲛ ⲧ̀ⲫⲉ ⲉ̀ϫⲉⲛ ⲛⲏ ⲉⲧϣⲟⲡ ϩⲓϫⲉⲛ ⲡⲓⲕⲁϩⲓ *(Doxology for feast of the Annunciation)*

i) ⲁϥⲓⲛⲓ ⲛ̀ⲟⲩⲙⲱⲟⲩ ⲉ̀ⲃⲟⲗϧⲉⲛ ⲟⲩⲡⲉⲧⲣⲁ ⲁϥⲧ̀ⲥⲟ ⲙ̀ⲡⲉϥⲗⲁⲟⲥ *(Adam Psali, Second hoas, midnight praises)*

j) ⲁ Ⲡ̀ϭⲟⲓⲥ ϣⲓⲛⲓ ⲉ̀ⲥⲁⲣⲣⲁ *(Genesis 21:1)*

k) ⲁⲥⲙⲓⲥⲓ ⲛ̀ϫⲉ ⲥⲁⲣⲣⲁ ⲛ̀ⲟⲩϣⲏⲣⲓ *(Genesis 21:2)*

l) ⲁ ⲛⲓⲑ̀ⲙⲏⲓ ⲱϣ ⲉ̀ⲃⲟⲗ ⲟⲩⲟϩ ⲁ Ⲡ̀ϭⲟⲓⲥ ⲥⲱⲧⲉⲙ ⲉ̀ⲣⲱⲟⲩ ⲟⲩⲟϩ ⲁϥⲛⲁϩⲙⲟⲩ ⲉ̀ⲃⲟⲗϧⲉⲛ ⲛⲟⲩϩⲟϫϩⲉϫ ⲧⲏⲣⲟⲩ *(Psalm **33:18** 34:17)*

5.2.i. Negative of the past perfect

Our old friend ⲁⲛ isn't used for negative of the past perfect. Instead, the verb prefix takes on a completely different form as shown in the table below:

ⲙ̀ⲡⲓ–	I did not
ⲙ̀ⲡⲉⲕ–	You (masculine singular) did not
ⲙ̀ⲡⲉ–	You (feminine singular) did not
ⲙ̀ⲡⲉϥ–	He did not
ⲙ̀ⲡⲉⲥ–	She did not

Introducing verbs

ⲙ̀ⲡⲉⲛ–	We did not
ⲙ̀ⲡⲉⲧⲉⲛ–	You did not (plural)
ⲙ̀ⲡⲟⲩ–	They did not
ⲙ̀ⲡⲉ	presubject form

The prefix above is attached to the front of the verb. So, to say for example "we did not rejoice", you would take the prefix for "we did not" which is ⲙ̀ⲡⲉⲛ, then attach it to the verb ⲣⲁϣⲓ *"to rejoice"*, to give ⲙ̀ⲡⲉⲛⲣⲁϣⲓ

There is also a presubject form as can be seen in the table above, which comes before the subject, as we saw with the past perfect affirmative in (**5.2**).

E.g. ⲙ̀ⲡⲉ ⲛⲓⲗⲁⲟⲥ ⲣⲁϣⲓ

"the people did not rejoice"

Vocab			
ⲉⲣϩⲏⲃⲓ	to weep, lament (v.i)	ⲥⲱⲟⲩⲛ	to know (v.t)
ⲙⲉⲑⲛⲟⲩϯ	Divinity (f)	ⲭⲣⲱⲙ	fire (m)
ⲟⲩⲛⲟⲩ	hour (f)	ϩⲟⲛϩⲉⲛ	commandment (m)
ⲡⲣⲉⲧⲱⲣⲓⲟⲛ	Praetorium (m)	ϫⲱ	to sing, praise (v.t)
ⲣⲱⲕϩ	to burn (v.t)	ϭⲟⲥϫⲉⲥ	to dance (v.i)

Exercise 5.9

a) ⲁⲛⲉⲣϩⲏⲃⲓ ⲟⲩⲟϩ ⲙ̀ⲡⲉⲧⲉⲛⲣⲓⲙⲓ *(Luke 7:32)*

b) ⲙ̀ⲡⲉ ⲡⲓⲭⲣⲱⲙ ⲛ̀ⲧⲉ ⲧⲉϥⲙⲉⲑⲛⲟⲩϯ ⲣⲱⲕϩ ⲛ̀ⲑⲛⲉⲭⲓ ⲛ̀ϯⲡⲁⲣⲑⲉⲛⲟⲥ
(Theotokia of the fifth day)

c) ⲛⲏ ⲉ̀ⲧⲉ ⲙ̀ⲡⲟⲩⲥⲟⲩⲉⲛ Ⲫϯ *(2 Thessalonians 1:8)*

d) ⲁⲛϫⲱ ⲉ̀ⲣⲱⲧⲉⲛ ⲟⲩⲟϩ ⲙ̀ⲡⲉⲧⲉⲛϭⲟⲥϫⲉⲥ ⲁⲛⲣⲓⲙⲓ ⲟⲩⲟϩ
ⲙ̀ⲡⲉⲧⲉⲛⲛⲉϩⲡⲓ *(Matthew 11:17)*

e) ⲙ̀ⲡⲟⲩⲓ̀ ⲉ̀ϧⲟⲩⲛ ⲉ̀ⲡⲓⲡⲣⲉⲧⲱⲣⲓⲟⲛ *(John 18:28)*

5.3. Forms derived from the infinitive

Transitive verbs have various ways in which they indicate the object. The four major forms are:
a) the infinitive or Absolute form (what we've already met)
b) the pronominal form
c) the construct or prenominal form
d) the qualitative (which we have met before with intransitive verbs)

It must be noted that the pronominal and construct forms are not used in the present tense, they are **only** used for the perfect tense and the future tense (which we will meet in **(5.9)**).

Those middle two sound fairly complicated, so let's go take a closer look at them.

5.3.i. The pronominal form

In this form, the infinitive changes spelling to a word that looks quite similar to the infinitive but is not quite the same. This new word is called a 'stem', because it then has different endings attached to the stem, like branches to the stem of a plant. These ending are pronouns which tell you the person, gender and number of the object, that is they give you the pronoun of who the verb is directed to. So the stem itself never changes, but the letters attached to the stem change according to the object.

Let's work through the following example to make it a bit clearer. Consider the verb ϥⲁⲓ *"to carry."*

The above form is the infinitive, or the dictionary form of the verb.
Suppose you wanted to say "I carried him". From what we'd learnt before, you'd say

ⲁⲓϥⲁⲓ ⲙ̄ⲙⲟϥ

Now let's try to write the same thing using the pronominal form, which is made up of the stem plus the pronoun (hence the name *pronom*inal). For ϥⲁⲓ, the stem happens to be ϥⲓⲧ⸗

The ⲁⲓ at the front remains the same as before giving ⲁⲓϥⲓⲧ⸗

Now all that remains is to add the object pronoun at the end. These object pronouns are also called the personal suffixes. The suffixes for this particular verb are shown in the table below:

Introducing verbs

I carried me	ⲁⲓϥⲓ⸗ⲧ
I carried you (m)	ⲁⲓϥⲓⲧ⸗ⲕ
I carried you (f)	ⲁⲓϥⲓϯ
I carried you (pl)	ⲁⲓϥⲓ−ⲑⲏⲛⲟⲩ
I carried him/it	ⲁⲓϥⲓⲧ⸗ϥ
I carried her/it	ⲁⲓϥⲓⲧ⸗ⲥ
I carried us	ⲁϥⲓⲧ⸗ⲉⲛ
I carried them	ⲁⲓϥⲓⲧ⸗ⲟⲩ

So in this example, we would use ⲁⲓϥⲓⲧϥ

Notice how there is a ⸗ after the stem? This sign is specifically used after the stem of the pronominal form. If you see it in a dictionary, it lets you know that it is coming after the pronominal form of the verb.

Now the suffixes are not the same for every verb. We'll show the endings of two more verbs below, one ending with a vowel and the other with a consonant, as these represent the most common cases. The two verbs we'll use are ⲧⲁⲙⲟ *"to tell"*, pronominal form ⲧⲁⲙⲟ⸗ and ⲃⲱⲗ *"to untie"*, pronominal form ⲃⲟⲗ⸗.

1ˢᵗ person singular	ⲧⲁⲙⲟ⸗ⲓ	ⲃⲟⲗ⸗ⲧ
2ⁿᵈ person singular masc.	ⲧⲁⲙⲟ⸗ⲕ	ⲃⲟⲗ⸗ⲕ
2ⁿᵈ person singular fem.	ⲧⲁⲙⲟ⸗	ⲃⲟⲗ⸗ⲓ
3ʳᵈ person singular masc.	ⲧⲁⲙⲟ⸗ϥ	ⲃⲟⲗ⸗ϥ
3ʳᵈ person singular fem.	ⲧⲁⲙⲟ⸗ⲥ	ⲃⲟⲗ⸗ⲥ
1ˢᵗ person plural	ⲧⲁⲙⲟ⸗ⲛ	ⲃⲟⲗ⸗ⲧⲉⲛ
2ⁿᵈ person plural	ⲧⲁⲙⲱⲧⲉⲛ/ⲧⲁⲙⲉ−ⲑⲏⲛⲟⲩ	ⲃⲉⲗ−ⲑⲏⲛⲟⲩ
3ʳᵈ person plural	ⲧⲁⲙⲱ⸗ⲟⲩ	ⲃⲟⲗ⸗ⲟⲩ

If you compare the two columns above, you'll notice that there are different endings for the 1st person singular, the 2nd person singular feminine and the first person plural forms. For more detail as to which form the suffix takes, and other variations for the above, see **Appendix 4**.

The vocab box below includes some verbs with their pronominal forms:

Vocab			
ⲓⲟⲙ	sea (m)	ⲱⲟⲩ	glory (m)
ⲇⲓⲁⲃⲟⲗⲟⲥ	devil (m)	ϧⲙⲟⲙ	fever, heat (m)
ⲑⲁⲙⲓⲟ ⲑⲁⲙⲓⲟ⳱	to create (v.t)	ϩⲱⲃⲥ ϩⲟⲃⲥ⳱	to cover (v.t)
ⲟⲩⲛⲟϥ	joy, delight (m)	ϭⲓ ϭⲓⲧ⳱	
ⲡⲁⲣⲁⲇⲓⲥⲟⲥ	paradise (Gk,m)	ⲉ̀	to receive, take
ⲭⲱ ⲭⲁ⳱	to place, leave (v.t)	ⲛⲉⲙ	to touch
ⲱⲗⲓ ⲟⲗ⳱	to take, lift up		

Exercise 5.10

a) ⲁϥⲟⲗϥ ⲛ̀ϫⲉ ⲡⲓⲇⲓⲁⲃⲟⲗⲟⲥ ⲉϫⲉⲛ ⲟⲩⲧⲱⲟⲩ   (Matthew 4:8)

b) ⲁϥϭⲓⲧⲟⲩ ⲉϫⲉⲛ ⲟⲩⲧⲱⲟⲩ (Matthew 17:1)

c) ⲁϥϭⲓ ⲛⲉⲙ ⲧⲉⲥϫⲓϫ ⲟⲩⲟϩ ⲁϥⲭⲁⲥ ⲛ̀ϫⲉ ⲡⲓϧⲙⲟⲙ (Matthew 8:15)

d) ⲁϥⲑⲁⲙⲓⲟⲥ ϧⲉⲛ ⲟⲩⲱⲟⲩ ⲕⲁⲧⲁ ⲡ̀ⲥⲁϫⲓ ⲙ̀Ⲡ̅ⲟ̅ⲥ̅ (Sunday Theotokia section 1)

e) ⲁϥϩⲟⲃⲥⲟⲩ ⲛ̀ϫⲉ ⲫⲓⲟⲙ (Exodus 15:10)

f) ⲁϥⲑⲁⲙⲓⲟⲛ ⲟⲩⲟϩ ⲁϥⲭⲁⲛ ϧⲉⲛ ⲡⲓⲡⲁⲣⲁⲇⲓⲥⲟⲥ ⲛ̀ⲧⲉ ⲡ̀ⲟⲩⲛⲟϥ
(Anaphora, liturgy of St.Basil)

g) Ⲓ̅ⲏ̅ⲥ̅ Ⲡ̅ⲭ̅ⲥ̅ ⲡ̀ϣⲏⲣⲓ ⲙ̀Ⲫⲛⲟⲩϯ ⲁⲥⲙⲁⲥϥ ⲛ̀ϫⲉ ϯⲡⲁⲣⲑⲉⲛⲟⲥ (Psalm response, Liturgy of the feast of the Nativity)

5.3.ii. *The construct form*

The next form of the infinitive is the construct form, which is also sometimes called the prenominal form. 'Pre' means 'before', and 'nominal' means 'noun', so this just really means "the form that comes before a noun", so whereas the stem was attached to a pronoun for the pronominal form, the construct form is actually attached to a noun. The stem for the pronominal form is usually different in appearance to that of the construct form, although with some verbs they are often the same. The more astute of you may ask how does this form differ in use from the infinitive form. After all, the infinitive form also comes before a noun. The essential difference is that the construct form doesn't use an object marker, whereas the infinitive always needs to have one.

Let's take an example to show how the construct form is used. In the case of the verb ϥⲁⲓ which we used above, the construct form is ϥⲓ— (that minus sign (-) next to the stem is the convention used to show that one is talking about the construct form.)

For an example of how to use the construct form, let's say "I carried the book." In this simple expression, we need to indicate the subject, the tense, the verb and the object.

The tense is the perfect tense, which is represented by ⲁ

The subject is 'I', indicated by ⲓ (5.2)

The construct stem is ϥⲓ—

The book is ⲡⲓϫⲱⲙ

Put them altogether and we get ⲁⲓϥⲓ ⲡⲓϫⲱⲙ

Notice that there is no object marker after the construct form, whereas if you were to use the infinitive form, you would get ⲁⲓϥⲁⲓ ⲙ̄ⲡⲓϫⲱⲙ where you can see an object marker is used.

Let's take another example, this time with the verb ⲥⲟⲃϯ (to prepare).

The infinitive form is ⲥⲟⲃϯ

The prenominal from is ⲥⲉⲃⲧⲉ-

and the pronominal form is ⲥⲉⲃⲧⲱⲧ⸗

So, to say "he prepared your way" using the infinitive, you would say ⲁϥⲥⲟⲃϯ ⲙ̄ⲡⲉⲕⲙⲱⲓⲧ with the prefix ⲁϥ being placed before the infinitive form, and the object marker ⲙ̄ appearing before ⲡⲉⲕⲙⲱⲓⲧ.

So You want to Learn Coptic?

To say the same thing using the construct form, you would say ⲁϥⲥⲉⲃⲧⲉ ⲡⲉⲕⲙⲱⲓⲧ, and to say *"he prepares it"* using the pronominal form you would write ⲁϥⲥⲉⲃⲧⲱⲧϥ.

The table below shows the verb forms for some of the more common Coptic verbs. Some verbs which were shown earlier have made a reappearance, this time with their construct form. You'll notice that there is also a column for the qualitative form, which will be discussed further down:

infinitive	construct	pronominal	qualitative	
ⲓⲛⲓ	ⲉⲛ–	ⲉⲛ⸗	–	to bring
ⲓⲣⲓ	ⲉⲣ–	ⲁⲓ⸗	ⲟⲓ	to make, do
ⲓϣⲓ	ⲉϣ–	ⲁϣ⸗	ⲁϣⲓ	to hang, suspend, crucify
ⲙⲉⲓ	ⲙⲉⲛⲣⲉ–	ⲙⲉⲛⲣⲓⲧ⸗	–	to love
ⲙⲓⲥⲓ	ⲙⲉⲥ–	ⲙⲁⲥ⸗	ⲙⲟⲥⲓ	to give birth to
ⲙⲟⲥϯ	ⲙⲉⲥⲧⲉ–	ⲙⲉⲥⲧⲱ⸗	–	to hate
ⲣⲓⲕⲓ	ⲣⲉⲕ–	ⲣⲁⲕ⸗	ⲣⲁⲕⲓ	to bend, lean, tilt
ⲣⲱⲧ	ⲣⲉⲧ–	ⲣⲟⲧ⸗	ⲣⲏⲧ	to bud
ⲥⲟⲃϯ	ⲥⲉⲃⲧⲉ–	ⲥⲉⲃⲧⲱⲧ⸗	ⲥⲉⲃⲧⲱⲧ	to prepare
ⲧⲁⲙⲟ	ⲧⲁⲙⲉ–	ⲧⲁⲙⲟ⸗	–	to tell, inform
ⲭⲱ	ⲭⲁ–	ⲭⲁ⸗	ⲭⲏ	to place, leave
ⲱⲗⲓ	ⲉⲗ–	ⲟⲗ⸗	ⲟⲗ (ⲏⲗ)	to take, carry
ϩⲓⲟⲩⲓ	ϩⲓ–	ϩⲓⲧ⸗	ϩⲱⲟⲩⲓ	to throw, strike
ϥⲁⲓ	ϥⲓ–	ϥⲓⲧ⸗	–	to carry
ϫⲓⲙⲓ	ϫⲉⲙ–	ϫⲉⲙ⸗	–	to find
ϭⲓ	ϭⲓ–	ϭⲓⲧ⸗	ϭⲏⲟⲩ	to take
ϯ	ϯ–	ϯⲏⲓ⸗		to give

Introducing verbs

Vocab			
ⲁⲛⲟⲙⲓⲁ	iniquity (f)	ⲑⲙⲏⲓ	righteousness (m)
ⲃⲁⲗ	eye (m)	ⲟⲩⲧⲁϩ	fruit (m)
ⲇⲉⲙⲱⲛ	demon (m)	ⲥⲟⲛⲓ	thief (m)
ⲇⲏⲛⲁⲣⲓⲟⲛ	denarius (Roman coin)	ⲭⲱⲟⲩ	generation (m)

Exercise 5.11

a) ⲁⲩϯ ⲟⲩⲧⲁϩ *(Matthew 13:8)*

b) ⲁⲕⲙⲉⲛⲣⲉ ⲑⲙⲏⲓ ⲟⲩⲟϩ ⲁⲕⲙⲉⲥⲧⲉ ϯⲁⲛⲟⲙⲓⲁ *(Psalm 44:8 45:7)*

c) ⲁⲩⲧⲁⲙⲉ ⲓⲱⲁⲛⲛⲏⲥ ⲛ̀ϫⲉ ⲛⲉϥⲙⲁⲑⲏⲧⲏⲥ *(Luke 7:18)*

d) ⲁϥⲣⲉⲕ ⲛⲓⲫⲏⲟⲩⲓ ⲛ̀ⲧⲉ ⲛⲓⲫⲏⲟⲩⲓ *(Doxology for Feast of the Annunciation)*

e) ⲡⲓⲡ̅ⲛ̅ⲉⲩⲙⲁ ⲁϥⲟⲗϥ ⲉ̀ⲡ̀ϣⲁϥⲉ *(Luke 4:1)*

f) ⲁⲩⲱ ⲕⲉⲥⲟⲛⲓ[#] ⲥ̀ⲛⲁⲩ ⲛⲉⲙⲁϥ *(Matthew 27:38)*

g) ⲁϥⲉⲛ ⲇⲏⲛⲁⲣⲓⲟⲛ ⲃ̅ ⲉⲃⲟⲗ *(Luke 10:35)*

h) ⲁⲓⲙⲉⲥⲧⲉ ⲡⲓⲭⲱⲟⲩ ⲉ̀ⲧⲉ ⲙ̀ⲙⲁⲩ^{§§} *(Hebrews 3:10)*

i) ⲁⲩⲉⲗ ⲓⲏⲥⲟⲩⲥ ⲉ̀ϧⲟⲩⲛ *(Matthew 27:27)*

j) ⲁⲛϩⲓ ⲇⲉⲙⲱⲛ ⲉ̀ⲃⲟⲗ *(Matthew 7:22)*

5.3.iii.   The qualitative

You'll notice a fourth column has been added for the qualitative form. As explained in **(5.1.ii)** when we were talking about the intransitive verbs, this form describes a state or quality which has come about as a result of the completed action of a verb.

[#] hint: see page 44

^{§§} hint: see **(2.1.iv)**

So for the example of the infinitive ⲣⲱⲧ *'to bud'*, the qualitative ⲣⲏⲧ means 'budding' or 'planted.'

The qualitative is also used for most transitive verbs, so for ϩⲓ *'to throw'*, the qualitative ϩⲱⲟⲩⲓ means "to be thrown."

The qualitative is not used in the same tenses as the prenominal and pronoun forms, so the qualitative is not used for the perfect tense. The qualitative is however used for the present tense as well as the imperfect (which we'll meet in **(7.1)**. When used in the present, it takes an object marker just like the infinitive.

We'll illustrate this with an example using the verb ϫⲱⲓⲗⲓ which means to "reside in, dwell" and whose qualitative form ϫⲁⲗⲏⲟⲩⲧ means "to be located, dwelling."

ⲡⲉⲧⲣⲟⲥ ϥϫⲁⲗⲏⲟⲩⲧ ⲉⲡⲁⲓⲙⲁ *(Acts 10:18)*
"Peter is dwelling in this place"

In this example, you can see that the object marker ⲉ̀ has been used with the qualitative.

For our next example, we'll use the qualitative form of the verb ⲭⲱ. Now the qualitative of this verb is actually quite important. The infinitive means "to place", or "to leave." The qualitative therefore means "to be placed," or to be in a particular place, which we often translate in English simply as 'is.' 'Is' is quite a common word in English, and you'll find that ⲭⲏ is used to mean this quite a lot.

E.g. ϥⲭⲏ ⲙ̀ⲡⲁⲓⲙⲁ ⲁⲛ *(Matthew 28:6)*
"he is not here"

As in the example above, the object marker often ends up being translated as 'in' when the qualitative is used in this way.

ⲭⲏ can also use the prepositions from **(5.1.iii)** in place of the object marker, as with the example below where the preposition ϧⲉⲛ is used.

E.g. ⲥⲉⲭⲏ ϧⲉⲛ ⲡⲓⲕⲟⲥⲙⲟⲥ *(John 17:11)*
"they are in the world"

Introducing verbs

The qualitative form of the infinitive ⲓⲣⲓ *"to make"* is also important. Its qualitative form is ⲟⲓ which means "to be." If you can't make the link in meaning between the infinitive and the qualitative, think of it this way. If the infinitive is "to make," then the resultant action of "being made" is to then "exist", or "to be." Hence:

ϥⲟⲓ ⲛ̀ϣⲫⲏⲣ ⲉⲛⲉϥϩ̀ⲃⲏⲟⲩⲓ ⲉⲧϩⲱⲟⲩ *(2 John 1:11)*

means *"he is a partaker of his evil deeds."*

Vocab			
ⲁⲣⲭⲓⲉⲣⲉⲩⲥ	high priest (Gk,m)	ⲛⲟⲩⲛⲓ	root (f)
ⲕⲉⲗⲉⲃⲓⲛ	axe (m)	ⲥⲟⲓ	wooden beam (m,f)
ⲙⲉⲑⲣⲉ	witness, testimony (m)	ϣⲫⲏⲣ	partaker, companion (m)

Exercise 5.12

a) ⲡⲓⲁⲣⲭⲓⲉⲣⲉⲩⲥ ⲟⲓ ⲙ̀ⲙⲉⲑⲣⲉ *(Acts 22:5)*

b) ⲡⲓⲕⲉⲗⲉⲃⲓⲛ ϥⲭⲏ ϧⲁ ⲑ̀ⲛⲟⲩⲛⲓ *(Matthew 3:10)*

c) ⲁⲛⲟⲛ ⲧⲏⲣⲉⲛ ⲧⲉⲛⲟⲓ ⲙ̀ⲙⲉⲑⲣⲉ *(Acts 2:32)*

d) ⲡⲓⲥⲟⲓ ϥⲭⲏ ϧⲉⲛ ⲡⲉⲕⲃⲁⲗ *(Matthew 7:4)*

The passive voice

Let's consider a typical day to day scenario. Say you accidentally crashed your dad's car, and the time has come to own up. The most honest and direct way of admitting to your crime would be to say "I crashed the car." However, if you were to be a little more subtle and cunning, you could say "the car was smashed." That is, you're shifting attention away from who smashed the car to the car itself. This construction where the object and action are high lighted is called the *passive* voice. One of the real advantages of the passive voice is that you often don't need to reveal what the subject is at all. Anyway, the passive voice for the past tense has exactly the same form as used for the perfect tense for 'they' (represented by the letters ⲁⲩ). So how can you tell if the verb is in the passive form or not? It's a matter of looking at the context.

Consider the following example,

Ⲓⲏⲥ Ⲡⲭ̅ⲥ̅ ⲁⲩⲙⲁⲥϥ ϧⲉⲛ Ⲃⲏⲑⲗⲉⲉⲙ.

From what has been said, there would be two different ways of translating this sentence. One would be "Jesus Christ they bore Him in Bethlehem", the other would be

"Jesus Christ was born in Bethlehem." Seeing as the first doesn't make any sense, it would have to be the second.

Also, if no indication were given of who 'they' could be referring to, then you would have to assume that the passive voice was being referred to. The passive tense can also be used with the present tense, and is again identical to the third person plural form which is **ⲥⲉ**.

E.g. **ⲥⲉⲙⲟⲩϯ ⲉ̀ⲣⲟ** *(Sunday Theotokia)*
"you are called"

5.4. The relative past tense converter

We met the relative converter when we looked at the present tense earlier in **(5.1.v)**. Not to be left out, there is also a relative converter used with the past tense. As with the present tense, the form of the relative converter changes depending on whether the antecedent is preceded by a definite or indefinite article.

In the case of an indefinite antecedent, the relative converter is **ⲉ̀**, which is placed before the verb and its subject prefix.

E.g. **ⲟⲩⲣⲱⲙⲓ ⲉ̀ⲁϥⲕⲱⲧ ⲛ̀ⲟⲩⲏⲓ** *(Luke 6:49)*
"a man who built a house"

In the case of a definite antecedent, the relative converter used depends on the person, gender and number of the verb, as shown in the table below:

ⲉⲧⲁⲓ	which, when I
ⲉⲧⲁⲕ	which, when you (m)
ⲉⲧⲁⲣⲉ	which, when you (f)
ⲉⲧⲁϥ	which, when he
ⲉⲧⲁⲥ	which, when she
ⲉⲧⲁⲛ	which, when we
ⲉⲧⲁⲣⲉⲧⲉⲛ	which, when you (pl)
ⲉⲧⲁⲩ	which they

Introducing verbs

ⲉⲧⲁ	pre subject form

(Be wary however, that `ⲉ–` is sometimes used instead with a definite antecedent.)

The relative converter is then placed in front of the relevant verb. The verb can be in the infinitive, construct or pronominal form. You'll recall from **(5.1.v)** that the relative converter could be translated to mean "who", "that", "which" or "whose" depending on the context, as in the following example:

ⲁⲓϫⲓⲙⲓ ⲙ̄ⲡⲁⲉⲥⲱⲟⲩ ⲉⲧⲁϥⲧⲁⲕⲟ *(Luke 15:3)*
"I found my sheep which was lost"

The relative converter of the past tense can still take all those meanings, but it can also take the additional meaning of 'when' as for when an action has been completed. An example in English would be, 'when I saw him, I talked to him.' Here the completed action is 'saw', which is followed by another action 'talked.'

E.g. ⲉⲧⲁϥⲥⲟⲩⲧⲉⲛ ⲧⲉϥϫⲓϫ ⲉ̀ⲃⲟⲗ *(Matthew 8:3)*
"when he stretched out his hand…"

As with the present relative converter, the past relative converter can also be combined with the far demonstrative pronoun **(2.1.iv)**.

E.g. ⲫⲏⲉⲧⲁϥϫⲓⲙⲓ ⲛ̀ϩⲙⲟⲧ *(Acts 7:46)*
"the one who found grace"

You may remember the resumptive morph which we met with the present relative converter in **(5.1.v)**. This is also required with the past tense when the antecedent is not the same as the subject;

E.g. ⲡⲓⲙⲁ ⲉⲧⲁⲩⲭⲁϥ ⲙ̀ⲙⲟϥ *(Mark 16:6)*
"the place where they put him"

In the example above, ⲙⲁ is the antecedent, which is not the subject of the sentence (being 'they' in this case). So you need a resumptive morph to refer back to ⲙⲁ, which in this case is ⲙ̀ⲙⲟϥ.

If the verb is in the pronominal form, the personal suffix is used as the resumptive morph.

E.g. ⲡⲓⲙⲁⲥⲓ ⲉⲧⲁϥⲑⲁⲙⲓⲟϥ *(Genesis 13:8)*
"The calf which he made (prepared)"

So You want to Learn Coptic?

Here the ⁻ϥ at the end of ⲑⲁⲙⲓⲟ⸗ acts as the resumptive morph referring to ⲙⲁⲥⲓ. Remember, the resumptive morph is only used when the antecedent is not the same as the subject of the verb. So when the antecedent is the same as the subject, no resumptive morph is needed.

E.g. I̅H̅C̅ ⲉⲧⲁϥϭⲓⲱⲙⲥ   *(Luke 3:21)*
"Jesus who received baptism (was baptised)"

5.4.i. Negative past relative

The negative form of the past relative is formed by placing an `ⲉⲧⲉ before the negative form of the past perfect **(5.2.i)**:

E.g. Ⲟⲩⲙⲁⲕⲁⲣⲓⲟⲥ ⲡⲉ ⲡⲓⲣⲱⲙⲓ ⲉⲧⲉ ⲙⲡⲉϥϣⲉ ϧⲉⲛ ⲡ̅ⲥⲟϭⲛⲓ ⲛ̅ⲧⲉ ⲛⲓⲁⲥⲉⲃⲏⲥ *(Psalm 1:1 1:1)*
"blessed is the man who did not walk in the council of the ungodly"

ⲉⲧⲉ ⲙ̅ⲡⲉ ϯϭⲣⲟⲙⲡⲓ ϫⲉⲙ ⲙⲁⲛ̅ⲙ̅ⲧⲟⲛ ⲛ̅ⲛⲉⲥϭⲁⲗⲁⲩϫ *(Genesis 8:9)*
"when the dove did not find a place of rest for her feet"

Vocab			
ⲅⲁⲗⲓⲗⲉⲁ	Galilee (prop.noun)	ⲥⲟⲩⲧⲱⲛ	to stretch, straighten (v.t)
ⲕⲁⲛⲁ	Canna (prop.noun)	ϣⲱ	sand (m)
ⲕⲱⲧ	to build (v.t)	ϩⲉⲓ	to fall
ⲙⲁⲕⲁⲣⲓⲟⲥ	blessed one (m)	ϩⲟⲛϩⲉⲛ	commandment (m)
ⲙⲁⲛ̅ⲙ̅ⲧⲟⲛ	place of rest (m)	ϭⲁⲗⲁⲩϫ	feet (m)
ⲙⲁⲥⲓ	calf (m)	ϭⲓⲥⲃⲱ	to learn (v.t)
ⲥⲁϧ	teacher, scribe (m)	ϭⲓⲥⲓ ϭⲁⲥ⁻ ϭⲁⲥ⸗	to lift, exalt (v.t)
ⲥⲓⲟⲩ	star (m)	ϭⲓⲱⲙⲥ	to be baptised

Exercise 5.13

a) ⲁⲓⲛⲁⲩ ⲉⲟⲩⲥⲓⲟⲩ ⲉⲁϥϩⲉⲓ *(Revelation 9:1)*

Introducing verbs

b) ⲥⲁϧ ⲛⲓⲃⲉⲛ ⲉⲁϥϭⲓⲥⲃⲱ ⲉϯⲙⲉⲧⲟⲩⲣⲟ ⲛ̀ⲧⲉ ⲛⲓⲫⲏⲟⲩⲓ *(Matthew 13:52)*

c) ϩⲱⲃ ⲛⲓⲃⲉⲛ ⲉⲧⲁϥⲥⲁϫⲓ ⲙ̀ⲙⲱⲟⲩ ⲛ̀ϫⲉ Ⲫϯ *(Acts 3:21)*

d) ⲛⲓⲣⲱⲙⲓ ⲉⲧⲁϥⲟⲩⲟⲣⲡⲟⲩ ⲛ̀ϫⲉ ⲕⲟⲣⲛⲏⲗⲓⲟⲥ ⲉⲁⲩϣⲓⲛⲓ ⲛ̀ⲥⲁ ⲡ̀ⲏⲓ ⲛ̀ⲥⲓⲙⲱⲛ *(Acts 10:17)*

e) ⲛⲓⲣⲱⲙⲓ ⲉⲧⲁⲕϭⲁⲥⲟⲩ ϧⲉⲛ ⲧⲉⲕⲙⲉⲧⲟⲩⲣⲟ ⲙ̀ⲡⲟⲩⲥⲱⲧⲉⲙ ⲛ̀ⲥⲁ ⲡⲉⲕϩⲟⲛϩⲉⲛ *(hom vat ii pg.81)*

f) ⲫⲁⲓ ⲡⲉ ⲡⲓϩⲟⲩⲓⲧ ⲙ̀ⲙⲏⲓⲛⲓ ⲉⲧⲁϥⲁⲓϥ ⲛ̀ϫⲉ Ⲓⲏ̅ⲥ̅ ϧⲉⲛ ϯⲕⲁⲛⲁ ⲛ̀ⲧⲉ ϯⲅⲁⲗⲓⲗⲉⲁ *(John 2:11)*

g) ⲛⲓⲥⲁϫⲓ ⲉⲧⲁⲕⲧⲏⲓⲧⲟⲩ ⲛⲏⲓ ⲁⲓⲧⲏⲓⲧⲟⲩ ⲛⲱⲟⲩ *(John 17:8)*

h) ⲫⲏ ⲉⲧⲁⲣⲉⲧⲉⲛϭⲓⲧϥ ⲛ̀ⲧⲉ Ⲫϯ *(1 Corinthians 6:19)*

i) ⲫⲁⲓ ⲉⲧⲁϥⲕⲱⲧ ⲙ̀ⲡⲉϥⲏⲓ ϩⲓϫⲉⲛ ⲡⲓϣⲱ *(Matthew 7:26)*

Practice text 5

This hymn, familiar to many Copts, is chanted before the reading of the Acts during the ordinary year days.

Ⲭⲉⲣⲉ ⲛⲉ Ⲙⲁⲣⲓⲁ ϯϭⲣⲟⲙⲡⲓ ⲉⲑⲛⲉⲥⲱⲥ ⲑⲏⲉⲧⲁⲥⲙⲓⲥⲓ ⲛⲁⲛ ⲙ̀Ⲫϯ ⲡⲓⲗⲟⲅⲟⲥ. ⲕ̀ⲥ̀ⲙⲁⲣⲱⲟⲩⲧ ⲁⲗⲏⲑⲱⲥ ⲛⲉⲙ ⲡⲉⲕⲓⲱⲧ ⲛ̀ⲁⲅⲁⲑⲟⲥ ⲛⲉⲙ ⲡⲓⲡ̀ⲛⲉⲩⲙⲁ ⲉⲑⲟⲩⲁⲃ ϫⲉ ⲁⲕⲓ̀ ⲁⲕⲥⲱϯ ⲙ̀ⲙⲟⲛ.

Vocab			
ⲁⲅⲁⲑⲟⲥ	good, righteous (Gk, adj)	ⲉⲑⲛⲉⲥⲱⲥ	beautiful
ⲁⲗⲏⲑⲱⲥ	truly (adv) **(9.2)**	ⲗⲟⲅⲟⲥ	word (Gk,m)

5.5. Prepositional pronominal form

Now that we've learnt about the construct and pronominal form of the transitive verbs, it's time to take another look at the simple prepositions of **(5.1.iii)**, which also

So You want to Learn Coptic?

have construct and pronoun forms. As a reminder, these prepositions come before the noun, as with the ϧⲉⲛ in the following example:

ⲛⲓⲁⲡⲟⲥⲧⲟⲗⲟⲥ ϧⲉⲛ ⲓ̅ⲗ̅ⲏ̅ⲙ̅   *(Acts 2:43)*
"The apostles in Jerusalem"

You may recall that another name used for the construct form is the prenoun form, as it's the form that comes before the noun. Hence, the simple prepositions we've looked at could be considered to be in their prenoun form. Now these prepositions also have a pronoun forms. We've actually already met the pronoun forms of ⲉ̀ and ⲛ̀ when we considered their role as object markers in **(5.1.iv)**. As for example:

ⲥ̀ⲙⲟⲩ ⲉ̀ⲣⲟϥ
"bless him"

The other simple prepositions which were mentioned also have pronominal forms, as can be seen in the following table:

Prenoun form	Pronoun form	
ⲉ̀	ⲉⲣⲟ⸗	to, for, in regard to
ⲉⲑⲃⲉ	ⲉⲑⲃⲏⲧ⸗	about, concerning
ⲛⲉⲙ	ⲛⲉⲙ⸗	with
ⲛ̀ⲥⲁ	ⲛ̀ⲥⲱ⸗	against, behind, before, following after
ⲟⲩⲃⲉ	ⲟⲩⲃⲏ⸗	against
ⲟⲩⲧⲉ	ⲟⲩⲧⲱ⸗	in between
ϣⲁ	ϣⲁⲣⲟ⸗	to
ϧⲁ	ϧⲁⲣⲟ⸗	under, about, regarding
ϧⲁϫⲉⲛ	ϧⲁϫⲱ⸗	before
ϧⲉⲛ	ⲛ̀ϧⲏⲧ⸗	in
ϩⲁ	ϩⲁⲣⲟ⸗	to, toward
ϩⲓ	ϩⲓⲱⲧ⸗	on

Once again, we call upon the personal suffixes which were used with the transitive verbs **(5.3.i)** to latch unto the end of these prepositions. These suffixes have

Introducing verbs

the role of indicating who the preposition is directed to. Some examples of the conjugations of these prepositions are shown in the tables below:

ⲉⲣⲟ⳼		ⲛ̀ϧⲏⲧ⳼	
ⲉⲣⲟⲓ	to me	ⲛ̀ϧⲏⲧ	in me
ⲉⲣⲟⲕ	to you (m)	ⲛ̀ϧⲏⲧⲕ	in you
ⲉⲣⲟ	to you (f)	ⲛ̀ϧⲏϯ	in you (f)
ⲉⲣⲟϥ	to him	ⲛ̀ϧⲏⲧϥ	in him
ⲉⲣⲟⲥ	to her	ⲛ̀ϧⲏⲧⲥ	in her
ⲉⲣⲟⲛ	to us	ⲛ̀ϧⲏⲧⲉⲛ	in us
ⲉⲣⲱⲧⲉⲛ	to you (pl)	ϧⲉⲛ ⲑⲏⲛⲟⲩ	in you (pl)
ⲉⲣⲱⲟⲩ	to them	ⲛ̀ϧⲏⲧⲟⲩ	in them

The same endings are used for ϣⲁⲣⲟ⳼ and ϩⲁⲣⲟ⳼

ⲛⲉⲙⲏⲓ	with me	ⲉϫⲱⲓ	upon me
ⲛⲉⲙⲁⲕ	with you (m)	ⲉϫⲱⲕ	upon you (m)
ⲛⲉⲙⲉ	with you (f)	ⲉϫⲱ	upon you (f)
ⲛⲉⲙⲁϥ	with him	ⲉϫⲱϥ	upon him
ⲛⲉⲙⲁⲥ	with her	ⲉϫⲱⲥ	upon her
ⲛⲉⲙⲁⲛ	with us	ⲉϫⲱⲛ	upon us
ⲛⲉⲙⲱⲧⲉⲛ	with you (pl)	ⲉϫⲉⲛ ⲑⲏⲛⲟⲩ	upon you (pl)
ⲛⲉⲙⲱⲟⲩ	with them	ⲉϫⲱⲟⲩ	upon them

Now when we studied the relative pronouns in **(5.1.v)** we saw how the pronoun forms of the object markers could be used as the resumptive morph. The pronoun forms of these prepositions can also be used as resumptive morphs, as in the following example where the pronoun from of ⲛ̀ⲥⲁ refers back to Ⲓⲏⲥ:

109

ⲁⲛⲟⲕ ⲡⲉ Ⲓⲏⲥ ⲫⲏ ⲛ̀ⲑⲟⲕ ⲉ̀ⲧⲉⲕϭⲟϫⲓ ⲛ̀ⲥⲱϥ (Acts 9:5)

"I am Jesus, He whom you are persecuting"

Vocab			
ⲉⲣⲡⲣⲟⲫⲏⲧⲉⲩⲓⲛ	to prophesy (v.i)	ⲟⲩⲱⲣⲡ ⲟⲩⲉⲣⲡ− ⲟⲩⲟⲣⲡ⸍	to send (v.t)
Ⲓⲱⲍⲓⲁⲥ	Josiah (prop.noun)	ⲥⲉⲣⲁⲫⲓⲙ	Seraphim (m)
ⲙⲁⲛⲉⲣϣⲱⲟⲩϣⲓ	altar (m)	ⲉ̀ⲗⲓ	anything, nothing, at all (pnoun)
Ⲙⲱⲩ̀ⲥⲏⲥ	Moses (prop.noun)	ϩⲱϯ ⲛ̀ⲧ⸍, ⲛ̀ⲧⲉ	'it is necessary that' subj **(8.2.ii)**
ⲛⲁⲓ	to have mercy (v.t)	ϭⲟϫⲓ	to run (v.i)
ⲛⲟⲙⲟⲥ	law (m)		ⲛ̀ⲥⲁ to run after, persecute

Exercise 5.14:

a) ⲉ̀ⲧⲁϥⲓ̀ ϩⲁⲣⲟⲥ ⲙ̀ⲡⲉϥϫⲉⲙ ⲉ̀ⲗⲓ ϩⲓⲱⲧⲥ (Matthew 21:19)

b) Ⲓⲱⲁⲛⲛⲏⲥ ⲡⲓⲣⲉϥϯⲱⲙⲥ ⲁϥⲟⲩⲟⲣⲡⲧⲉⲛ ϩⲁⲣⲟⲕ (Luke 7:20)

c) ⲁϥⲟⲩⲱⲣⲡ ϩⲁⲣⲟⲓ ⲛ̀ⲟⲩⲁⲓ ⲛ̀ⲛⲓⲥⲉⲣⲁⲫⲓⲙ (Isaiah 6:6)

d) ϩⲱϯ ⲛ̀ⲧⲟⲩϫⲱⲕ ⲉ̀ⲃⲟⲗ ⲛ̀ϫⲉ ϩⲱⲃ ⲛⲓⲃⲉⲛ ⲉⲧⲥ̀ϧⲏⲟⲩⲧ ϧⲉⲛ ⲫ̀ⲛⲟⲙⲟⲥ ⲙ̀ⲙⲱⲩ̀ⲥⲏⲥ ⲛⲉⲙ ⲛⲓⲡ̀ⲣⲟⲫⲏⲧⲏⲥ ⲛⲉⲙ ⲛⲓⲯⲁⲗⲙⲟⲥ ⲉⲑⲃⲏⲧ (Luke 24:44)

e) ⲫⲁⲓ ⲡⲉ Ⲓⲱⲍⲓⲁⲥ ⲫⲏ ⲉⲧⲁ ⲡⲓⲡ̀ⲣⲟⲫⲏⲧⲏⲥ ⲉⲣⲡⲣⲟⲫⲏⲧⲉⲩⲓⲛ ϩⲁⲣⲟϥ ϩⲓϫⲉⲛ ⲡⲓⲙⲁⲛⲉⲣϣⲱⲟⲩϣⲓ (hom vatt ii pg.66)

f) ⲛⲁⲓ ϧⲁⲣⲟⲛ Ⲓⲏⲥ ⲡ̀ϣⲏⲣⲓ ⲛ̀Ⲇⲁⲩⲓⲇ (Matthew 20:30)

g) ⲟⲩⲧⲁϩ ⲉ̀ⲣⲉ ⲡⲉϥⲭ̀ⲣⲟϫ ⲛ̀ϧⲏⲧϥ (Genesis 1:11)

h) ⲫⲏ ⲉⲧⲁ Ⲙⲱⲩⲥⲏⲥ ⲥ̀ϧⲁⲓ ⲉⲑⲃⲏⲧϥ ϩⲓ ⲡⲓⲛⲟⲙⲟⲥ ⲛⲉⲙ ⲛⲓ̀ⲡⲣⲟⲫⲏⲧⲏⲥ *(John 1:45)*

5.6. Construct-a-verbs: Compound verbs

Not content with the already considerable number of verbs in its arsenal, Coptic has the ability to combine the construct form of a verb **(5.3.ii)** with a wide variety of nouns to form a whole new series of verbs. This new verb has a modified meaning when compared to the construct stem from which it came.

E.g. ϩⲓ (construct form of ϩⲓⲟⲩⲓ – *"to cast"*) + ⲱⲓϣ *"cry"*

= ϩⲓⲱⲓϣ which is translated as to *"cast a cry"* or *"to preach"*

Even though compound verbs use the construct form as part of their make up, the verb that results has a different meaning to what you would get if you used the construct form on its own without forming it into the compound verb.

For example, if we were to use the construct form of the infinitive above as opposed to the compound verb, we would need to include an article, whether it be the:

definite article: - ϩⲓⲡⲓⲱⲓϣ

or the indefinite article- ϩⲓ ϩⲁⲛⲱⲓϣ

or a possessive article E.g. ϩⲓ ⲡⲉϥⲱⲓϣ etc.

The meaning here would just be to "throw the cry" or "throw cries" or to "throw his cry" but it would *not* be 'preach' since this is an exclusive meaning of the compound verb.

Some verbs tend to be associated with many compound verbs. One of the most prolific is the verb ϯ which means "to give." Now the construct form of ϯ happens to be just the same as the infinitive. Some examples of its use in different compound verbs are shown below:

ϯⲁⲥⲟ	to give compassion or to be compassionate
ϯⲛⲟⲙϯ	to give strength or to strengthen
ϯⲥⲃⲱ	to give teaching or to teach
ϯⲱⲙⲥ	to give baptism or to baptise

ϯⲱⲟⲩ	to give glory or to glorify
ϯϩⲁⲡ	to give judgement or to judge

The verb **ⲓⲣⲓ** "to make, do," tends to be used to make compound verbs even more than **ϯ**. Its construct form is **ⲉⲣ**-.

Now many, many compound verbs are formed from **ⲉⲣ**. In particular, many Greek nouns have a habit of being used with **ⲉⲣ** to turn them into verbs. A small sample is shown below:

ⲉⲣⲁⲅⲓⲁⲍⲓⲛ	to sanctify	ⲉⲣⲫⲙⲉⲩⲓ	to remember
ⲉⲣⲛⲓϣϯ	to be great	ⲉⲣⲡⲓⲣⲁⲍⲓⲛ	to tempt
ⲉⲣⲟⲩⲱⲓⲛⲓ	to shine	ⲉⲣⲟⲩⲱ	to answer
ⲉⲣϩⲉⲗⲡⲓⲥ	to hope	ⲉⲣⲡⲣⲟⲥⲉⲩⲭⲉⲥⲑⲉ	to pray
ⲉⲣϩⲟⲩⲟ	to increase	ⲉⲣⲛⲟⲃⲓ	to sin

Here are another two examples:

ϭⲓ is the verb *"to take "* whose construct form is also **ϭⲓ**-.

ϭⲓⲥⲁⲣⲝ	to incarnate
ϭⲓⲥⲃⲱ	to learn

The next verb is **ϣⲱⲡ**, *"to receive, accept, buy"* whose construct form is **ϣⲉⲡ**-

ϣⲉⲡϩⲙⲟⲧ	to accept grace (thank)
ϣⲉⲡϭⲓⲥⲓ	to suffer

Compound verbs take the same subject prefixes as the verbs we've already met. Here are a couple of examples:

ⲁϥϣⲉⲡϩⲙⲟⲧ
"he gave thanks"

Introducing verbs

ⲁⲕⲉⲣϩⲉⲗⲡⲓⲥ
"you hoped"

Vocab			
ⲉⲱⲛ	age, eon (Gk,m)	ϫⲉⲙⲛⲟⲩϯ	to find comfort (v.i)
ϩⲓⲱⲛⲓ	to throw stones (v.t)		

Exercise 5.15

a) ⲁⲩϩⲓⲱⲛⲓ ⲉⲣⲱⲟⲩ *(Mark 12:5)*

b) ⲁⲓⲉⲣⲫⲙⲉⲩⲓ ⲙⲡⲉⲕⲣⲁⲛ ⲟⲩⲟϩ ⲁⲓϫⲉⲙⲛⲟⲩϯ ⲡⲟⲩⲣⲟ ⲛⲛⲓⲉⲱⲛ Ⲫϯ ⲛ̀ⲧⲉ ⲛⲓⲛⲟⲩϯ *(Sunday Theotokia, Midnight praises)*

c) ⲁϥⲉⲣⲫⲙⲉⲩⲓ ⲛ̀ϫⲉ ⲡⲉⲧⲣⲟⲥ ⲙ̀ⲡⲓⲥⲁϫⲓ *(Matthew 26:75)*

d) ⲉⲧⲁϥϭⲓ ⲛ̀ⲟⲩⲱⲓⲕ ⲁϥϣⲉⲡϩ̀ⲙⲟⲧ *(Luke 22:19)*

e) ⲁⲩϩⲓⲱⲓϣ ⲙ̀ⲡⲓⲥⲁϫⲓ ⲛ̀ⲧⲉ Ⲫϯ *(Acts 13:5)*

5.7. The indirect object

Consider the sentence: "He gave the book to him."

The subject of the sentence is 'He.' But what's the object? There are actually two objects in the sentence. The first is 'book', and the second is 'him.' As the 'book' is 'directly' affected by the action of giving, it is called the '*direct* object.' 'Him' is 'indirectly' affected by the 'giving', so is called 'the *indirect* object.' Coptic has a special range of pronouns to represent the indirect object, which are as follows:

ⲛⲏⲓ	to me
ⲛⲁⲕ	to you (masculine)
ⲛⲉ	to you (feminine)
ⲛⲁϥ	to him
ⲛⲁⲥ	to her
ⲛⲁⲛ	to us

So You want to Learn Coptic?

ⲛⲱⲧⲉⲛ	to you (plural)
ⲛⲱⲟⲩ	to them

Unlike English, the indirect object in Coptic often comes before the direct object in the sentence, E.g.:

ⲁϥϯ ⲛⲁϥ ⲙ̀ⲡⲓϫⲱⲙ

"he gave the book to him"

and again;

ⲁϥϣⲱⲡⲓ ⲛⲏⲓ ⲉ̀ⲟⲩⲥⲱⲧⲏⲣⲓⲁ

"he became to me a salvation"

The greeting ⲭⲉⲣⲉ- "hail" is commonly used with the indirect object:

ⲭⲉⲣⲉ ⲛⲁⲕ

"hail to you" (to a male)

ⲭⲉⲣⲉ ⲛⲉ Ⲙⲁⲣⲓⲁ

"hail to you O Mary"

ⲭⲉⲣⲉ ⲛⲏⲓ

"hail to me"

Certain verbs exclusively use the indirect object, as with ⲛⲁⲓ *"to have mercy"*

E.g. ⲛⲁⲓ ⲛⲁⲛ

"Have mercy upon us"

Vocab			
ⲃⲉⲗⲗⲉ	blind person (m)	ⲡⲁⲣⲁⲕⲗⲏⲧⲟⲛ	comforter (Gk,m)
ⲓⲛⲓ ⲉⲛ— ⲉⲛ⸗	to bring (v.t)	ⲣⲁϣⲓ	gladness, joy (m)
ⲉⲣⲟⲩⲱ	to answer (v.t)	ⲥⲁⲣⲣⲁ	Sarah (prop.noun)
ⲙⲟⲩϯ	to call, name (v.t)	ⲫⲱⲛϩ	to turn (v.t)
ⲛⲉϩⲡⲓ	weeping (m)	ϩⲩⲙⲛⲟⲥ	hymn (Gk,m)

Introducing verbs

ⲟⲩⲱⲣⲡ	to send (v.t)		

Exercise 5.16

a) ⲁⲩⲓⲛⲓ ⲛⲁϥ ⲛⲟⲩⲃⲉⲗⲗⲉ   (Mark 8:22)

b) ⲧⲉⲛⲟⲩⲱⲣⲡ ⲛⲁⲕ ⲙ̀ⲡⲓϩⲩⲙⲛⲟⲥ   (Doxology for Feast of Nairuz)

c) ⲁϥϯ ⲛ̀ⲥⲁⲣⲣⲁ ⲧⲉϥⲥ̀ϩⲓⲙⲓ ⲛⲁϥ   (Genesis 20:14)

d) ⲁϥⲟⲩⲱⲣⲡ ⲛⲁⲛ ⲙ̀ⲡⲓⲡⲁⲣⲁⲕⲗⲏⲧⲟⲛ   (Verses of the cymbals)

e) Ⲁ ⲡ̀ϭⲟⲓⲥ ⲥⲱⲧⲉⲙ ⲟⲩⲟϩ ⲁϥⲛⲁⲓ ⲛⲏⲓ ⲁϥⲫⲱⲛϩ ⲙ̀ⲡⲁⲛⲉϩⲡⲓ ⲉⲩⲣⲁϣⲓ ⲛⲏⲓ*** (Hymn for Communion, Joyous Saturday Divine Liturgy)

f) ⲁⲓⲙⲟⲩϯ ⲉ̀ⲣⲱⲧⲉⲛ ⲟⲩⲟϩ ⲙ̀ⲡⲉⲧⲉⲛⲉⲣⲟⲩⲱ ⲛⲏⲓ   (Isaiah 65:12)

5.8. Doing unto one's self- the reflexive

People often do things to themselves, in these cases, the person doing an action is also the person who is receiving the action. There's a special form of verb called the 'reflexive' which is used to represent this case, where the subject is the same as the object. In English, this is where the "….self" form is used, as in 'myself', 'himself' etc.

For example, in "he washed himself", the subject of the sentence is 'he', and the object is also 'he.' Coptic verbs can also be used in the reflexive. To take another example, let's consider how you'd say 'he prepared himself.'

You could use either the pronominal form or the infinitive form. We'll use the pronominal form ⲥⲉⲃⲧⲱⲧ⸗ here:

To say 'he prepared', you would add the 'ⲁ' to indicate the perfect past and the appropriate personal suffix from **(5.3.i)** to indicate the 'he.' In this case it's 'ϥ', so you get ⲁϥⲥⲉⲃⲧⲱⲧ⸗.

*** Hint: see confusion corner page **78**

Now, to say 'he prepared *himself*', you simply add an 'ϥ' to the end to indicate that 'he' is the object, and you end up with ⲁϥⲥⲉⲃⲧⲱⲧϥ.

Using the infinitive form, you'd say ⲁϥⲥⲟⲃϯ ⲙⲙⲟϥ.

So in either of these cases, how can you tell if this phrase is saying "he prepared *him*" as opposed to 'he prepared *himself*?" In these cases, you need to rely on the other words in the sentence; that is if no mention of any other 'he' is made, then you can assume the 'ϥ' refers to 'himself.'

Another example of a verb which can be used in the reflexive sense is ⲕⲱϯ, whose infinitive, construct, and pronominal forms are shown below:

ⲕⲱϯ ⲕⲉⲧ⁻ ⲕⲟⲧ⸗

Now ⲕⲱϯ has a number of meanings, which are to *"to seek, surround, repeat"* or *"to return."*

E.g. ⲁϥⲕⲟⲧϥ *"he returned himself"*

ⲕⲱϯ can also be used to indicate a repeat of action.

E.g. ⲁϥⲕⲟⲧϥ ⲁϥⲣⲓⲙⲓ means *"he wept again"*

More examples of verbs which can be used in the reflexive are given in the table below. Two meanings are given for each verb, the first refers to the reflexive use and the second to when the non reflexive form is used.

			Reflexive	**Non reflexive**
ⲟⲩⲱⲛϩ	—	ⲟⲩⲟⲛϩ⸗	to reveal one's self	to announce, appear
ⲧⲁⲗⲟ	ⲧⲁⲗⲉ⁻	ⲧⲁⲗⲟ⸗	to lift up, mount one's self	to lift, raise
ⲧⲱⲟⲩⲛ	ⲧⲉⲛ⁻	ⲧⲱⲛ⸗	to raise one's self	to raise

Now there are some verbs which can *only* be used in the reflexive form. These are combined with a specific preposition.

For example, the reflexive verb ⲓⲱⲥ takes ⲙⲙⲟ⸗ as its preposition and is written as ⲓⲱⲥ ⲙⲙⲟ⸗

with the combination meaning *"to hurry."*

So you can't just say ⲁⲛⲱⲥ for "I hurried", but you have to attach the ⲙ̅ⲙⲟ⸗ with its appropriate suffix, so that you're literally saying "I hurried myself", i.e:

ⲁⲛⲱⲥ ⲙ̅ⲙⲟⲓ

The verb ϣⲉ ⲛ⸗ *"to go"* is usually used in the reflexive, but it can also be used without it. When it is used in the reflexive, it uses the indirect object stem ⲛ⸗ **(5.7)** linked with the appropriate suffix. When using the reflexive, saying "I am going" would come out as ϯϣⲉ ⲛⲏⲓ. Likewise, to say "he is going" is ϥϣⲉ ⲛⲁϥ and "we are going" is ⲧⲉⲛ ϣⲉⲛⲁⲛ.

Another verb which only uses the reflexive is ⲟϩⲓ ⲉⲣⲁⲧ⸗ "to stand", which must be linked to the compound preposition ⲉⲣⲁⲧ⸗. **(See Appendix 3).**

So, to tell a male "you are standing" you would say: ⲕⲟϩⲓ ⲉⲣⲁⲧⲕ and to say "he stands" you would say ϥⲟϩⲓ ⲉⲣⲁⲧϥ.

Here are some more verbs which are only ever used in the reflexive form. They are all combined with the preposition ⲙ̅ⲙⲟ⸗.

| ⲙ̅ⲧⲟⲛ ⲙ̅ⲙⲟ⸗ | to rest | ⲟⲩⲛⲟϥ ⲙ̅ⲙⲟ⸗ | to rejoice |
| ⲓⲏⲥ ⲙ̅ⲙⲟ⸗ | to hasten | ⲭⲱⲗⲉⲙ ⲙ̅ⲙⲟ⸗ | to hurry |

Vocab			
ⲉϧⲟⲩⲛ	inside (adv) **(9.3)**	ⲥⲕⲩⲛⲏ	tabernacle, tent, dome (Gk,f)
ⲕⲩⲃⲱⲧⲟⲥ	ark (Gk,f)	ϩⲏⲅⲉⲩⲙⲱⲛ	governor (Gk,m)
ⲣⲁⲥⲟⲩⲓ	dream (f)		

Exercise 5.17

a) ⲁϥⲓⲏⲥ ⲙ̅ⲙⲟϥ ⲛ̅ϫⲉ ⲁⲃⲣⲁⲁⲙ ⲁϥϣⲉⲛⲁϥ ⲉϧⲟⲩⲛ ⲉϯⲥⲕⲩⲛⲏ
(Gen 18:6)

So You want to Learn Coptic?

b) ⲁϥϣⲉⲛⲁϥ ⲛ̀ϫⲉ Ⲛⲱⲉ ⲛⲉⲙ ⲧⲉϥⲥ̀ϩⲓⲙⲓ ⲛⲉⲙ ⲛⲉϥϣⲏⲣⲓ ⲛⲉⲙ ⲛⲓϩⲓⲟⲙⲓ ⲛ̀ⲧⲉ ⲛⲉϥϣⲏⲣⲓ ⲛⲉⲙⲁϥ ⲉ̀ϧⲟⲩⲛ ⲉ̀ϯⲕⲩⲃⲱⲧⲟⲥ *(Gen 7:7)*

c) ⲟⲩⲁⲅⲅⲉⲗⲟⲥ ⲛ̀ⲧⲉ Ⲡ̅ⲟ̅ⲥ̅ ⲁϥⲟⲩⲟⲛϩϥ ⲉ̀ⲓⲱⲥⲏϥ ϧⲉⲛ ⲟⲩⲣⲁⲥⲟⲩⲓ *(Matthew 2:19)*

d) ⲧⲟⲧⲉ ⲁⲩⲏⲥ ⲙ̀ⲙⲱⲟⲩ ⲛ̀ϫⲉ ⲛⲓϩⲩⲅⲉⲩⲙⲱⲛ *(First canticle, midnight praises)*

5.9. The first future

We've now looked at the past and present, so where else can we look to now but the future? There are actually a few different types of future tense, but we shall only look at the most common (and the simplest) at the moment. To form this tense, the letters ⲛⲁ are simply placed in between the subject pronouns used in the *present* tense (**5.1**) and the infinitive. We'll use the verb ⲣⲓⲙⲓ *"to cry"* as an example:

ϯⲛⲁ—	I will
ϥⲛⲁ—	He will
ⲥⲛⲁ—	she will
ⲭⲛⲁ—	you will (masculine)
ⲧⲉⲧⲉⲛⲛⲁ—	you will (plural)
ⲧⲉⲛⲁ— ⲧⲉⲣⲁ— (rare variant)	you will (feminine)
ⲧⲉⲛⲛⲁ—	we will
ⲥⲉⲛⲁ—	they will
-	pre noun as subject form

So for example, "he will cry" is ϥⲛⲁⲣⲓⲙⲓ and "they will cry" is ⲥⲉⲛⲁⲣⲓⲙⲓ.

As with the present tense, there is no pre noun as subject form. Unlike the present tense however, the future is able to use the construct and the pronominal forms which we saw used with the past perfect (**5.3**).

Introducing verbs

Vocab			
ⲃⲉⲭⲉ	reward (m)	ⲥⲱϯ	to save (v.t)
ⲉ̀ⲃⲓⲁⲓⲕ	servants, slaves (pl of ⲃⲱⲕ)	ⲭⲣⲱⲙ	fire (m)
ⲉ̀ϫⲱⲣϩ	evening (m)	ϣⲁϩ	flame (m)
ⲥⲓⲛⲓ	to pass by, to pass away (v.i)	ϫⲱⲣ ⲉ̀ⲃⲟⲗ	to scatter, disperse (v.t)
ⲥⲱⲟⲩⲛ ⲥⲟⲩⲉⲛ— ⲥⲟⲩⲱⲛ⸗	to know (v.t)	ϭⲓⲙ̀ⲡ̀ϣⲓϣ	vengeance (m)

Exercise 5.18

a) ⲫⲁⲓ ⲡⲉ ⲡⲁⲛⲟⲩϯ ϯⲛⲁϯⲱⲟⲩ ⲛⲁϥ ⲫϯ ⲙ̀ⲡⲁⲓⲱⲧ ϯⲛⲁϭⲁⲥϥ
 (*Exodus 15:2*)

b) Ⲡϭⲟⲓⲥ ⲛⲁⲥⲱϯ ⲛ̀ⲧⲯⲩⲭⲏ ⲛ̀ⲧⲉ ⲛⲉϥⲉ̀ⲃⲓⲁⲓⲕ (*Psalm 33:23* 34:22)

c) ⲡϭⲟⲓⲥ ⲛⲁϫⲉⲣ ⲛⲓⲥⲟϭⲛⲓ ⲛ̀ⲧⲉ ⲛⲓⲉⲑⲛⲟⲥ ⲉ̀ⲃⲟⲗ (*Psalm 32:10* 33:10)

d) ⲥⲉⲛⲁϩⲓⲧϥ ⲉ̀ⲡⲓⲭⲣⲱⲙ (*Matthew 3:10*)

e) ϥⲛⲁϭⲓ ⲙ̀ⲡⲉϥⲃⲉⲭⲉ (*John 4:36*)

f) ϥⲛⲁⲙⲟϣⲓ ϧⲉⲛ ⲡⲓⲉ̀ϫⲱⲣϩ (*John 11:10*)

g) ⲧ̀ⲫⲉ ⲛⲉⲙ ⲡ̀ⲕⲁϩⲓ ⲥⲉⲛⲁⲥⲓⲛⲓ (*Luke 21:33*)

h) ϧⲉⲛ ⲟⲩϣⲁϩ ⲛ̀ⲭⲣⲱⲙ ⲉϥⲛⲁϯ ⲛⲟⲩϭⲓⲙ̀ⲡ̀ϣⲓϣ ⲛ̀ⲛⲏ ⲉ̀ⲧⲉ ⲙ̀ⲡⲟⲩⲥⲟⲩⲉⲛ ⲫϯ (*2 Thessalonians 1:8*)

So You want to Learn Coptic?

> **Practice text 6**
> *(12ᵗʰ hour prayer of the Liturgy of the hours)*
>   The introduction to the compline (prayer before sleeping) of the Liturgy of the hours (or the Agpia) may be familiar in English to many Copts, but here it is in the original Coptic:
>
> Πιϩυμνος ⲛ̀ⲧⲉ ⲡⲓϩⲩⲛⲓⲙ ⲉⲧⲥ̀ⲙⲁⲣⲱⲟⲩⲧ ϯⲛⲁⲧⲏⲓϥ ⲙ̀Ⲡⲓⲭⲣⲓⲥⲧⲟⲥ
>
> ⲡⲁⲟⲩⲣⲟ ⲟⲩⲟϩ ⲡⲁⲛⲟⲩϯ ϯⲛⲁⲉⲣϩⲉⲗⲡⲓⲥ ⲉ̀ⲣⲟϥ
>
> | *Vocab* | | | |
> |---|---|---|---|
> | ϩⲩⲙⲛⲟⲥ | hymn (m) | ϩⲩⲛⲓⲙ | slumber (m) |

5.9.i. The Negative first future

The negative first future is used when you want to say that something *won't* happen. This tense is made up in much the same way as the first present negative (**5.1.i**). As with that case, an **ⲁⲛ** is simply added after the verb. You can also have an optional **ⲛ̀** placed before the verb with the **ⲁⲛ** remaining after the verb.

Vocab			
ⲃⲱⲗ ⲃⲉⲗ— ⲃⲟⲗ⸗		ⲟⲩⲇⲉ	nor (conj.) (**6.1**)
ⲉ̀ⲃⲟⲗ	to untie, undo (v.t)	ϩⲉⲙⲥⲓ	to sit (v.i)
ⲉ̀ⲙⲓ	to know (v.t)	ϯⲁⲥⲟ	to have compassion (v.i)

Exercise 5.19

a)   ϥⲛⲁϩⲉⲙⲥⲓ ⲁⲛ   *(Luke 14:28)*

b)   ⲛ̀ⲥⲉⲛⲁⲃⲟⲗϥ ⲉ̀ⲃⲟⲗ ⲁⲛ   *(Matthew 24:2)*

c)   ⲛ̀ϥⲛⲁⲉⲙⲓ ⲁⲛ ⲛ̀ⲑⲟϥ   *(Mark 4:27)*

d)   ⲥⲉⲛⲁⲉⲙⲓ ⲉ̀ⲣⲟϥ ⲁⲛ   *(Matthew 10:26)*

e)   /ⲛⲁⲃⲁⲗ ⲛⲁϯⲁⲥⲟ ⲁⲛ ⲟⲩⲇⲉ ⲛ̀ϯⲛⲁⲛⲁⲓ ⲛⲱⲟⲩ ⲁⲛ   *(Ezekiel 8:18)*

5.9.ii. *Relative first future*

The relative form of the first future is simply formed by adding a variant of ⲉⲧ to the beginning of the normal first future construction, as in the table below:

	Relative Future
1ˢᵗ person (s)	ⲉϯⲛⲁ–
2ⁿᵈ person (m)	ⲉⲧⲉⲕⲛⲁ–
2ⁿᵈ person (f)	ⲉⲧⲉⲣⲁ–
3ʳᵈ person (m)	ⲉⲧⲉϥⲛⲁ–
3ʳᵈ person (f)	ⲉⲧⲉⲥⲛⲁ–
1ˢᵗ person (pl)	ⲉⲧⲉⲛⲛⲁ–
2ⁿᵈ person (pl)	ⲉⲧⲉⲧⲉⲛⲛⲁ–
3ʳᵈ person (pl)	ⲉⲧⲟⲩⲛⲁ–
Pre subject form	ⲉⲧⲉ/ⲉⲣⲉ...ⲛⲁ

E.g. **ⲡⲓⲙⲱⲟⲩ ⲉ̇ϯⲛⲁⲧⲏⲓϥ ⲛⲁϥ**   *(John 4:14)*
"the water which I will give him"

The relative future also has the same pre subject relative form as the relative form which was used with the present tense **(5.1.v)**:

ⲉ̇ⲧⲉ ⲡⲉϥϣⲏⲣⲓ ⲛⲁⲉⲣⲉⲧⲓⲛ ⲙ̇ⲙⲟϥ ⲛ̇ⲟⲩⲱⲓⲕ   *(Matthew 7:9)*
"his son who will ask for bread"

When the antecedent (the first noun in the sentence) is not the same as the subject, the construction takes the same form as the first present **(5.1.v)**, with the only difference being that the **ⲛⲁ** comes between the prefix and the verb.

E.g. **ϧⲉⲛ ⲡⲓⲉ̇ϩⲟⲟⲩ ⲉⲧⲉⲕⲛⲁϭⲓ ⲛⲉⲙⲱⲟⲩ ϧⲉⲛ ⲟⲩⲙⲟⲩ ⲭ̇ⲛⲁⲙⲟⲩ**
(hom vatt ii pg.73)
"In the day that you touch them you will die (in death)"

So You want to Learn Coptic?

Vocab			
ⲙⲟⲩ	to die (v.i)	ϣⲓ	measure (m)
	death (m)		to measure (v.t)
ⲟⲩⲁϩⲥⲁϩⲛⲓ	to lay a command (v.i)	ϣⲟⲩⲟ, ϣⲟⲩⲓⲧ (q)	to empty flow out/ to be empty , vain (q)
ⲣⲱⲓⲥ	to watch over, be careful (v.i)	ϣⲱⲡ ϣⲉⲡ– ϣⲟⲡ⸌ ϣⲏⲡ	to accept, buy (v.t)
		ⲭⲱ ⲭⲉ– ⲭⲟⲧ⸌	to speak (v.t) **(8.1)**

Exercise 5.20

a) ϧⲉⲛ ⲡⲓϣⲓ ⲉⲧⲉⲧⲉⲛⲛⲁϣⲓ ⲙ̇ⲙⲟϥ *(Matthew 7:2)*

b) Ⲡϭⲟⲓⲥ ⲡⲉⲑⲛⲁϣⲟⲡⲧ ⲉ̇ⲣⲟϥ *(Psalm 3:4 3:3)*

c) ⲥⲁϫⲓ ⲛⲓⲃⲉⲛ ⲉⲧϣⲟⲩⲓⲧ ⲉ̇ⲧⲉ ⲛⲓⲣⲱⲙⲓ ⲛⲁⲭⲟⲧⲟⲩ *(Matthew 12:36)*

d) Ⲫⲏ ⲉ̇ⲧⲉⲕⲛⲁⲟⲩⲁϩⲥⲁϩⲛⲓ ⲙ̇ⲙⲟϥ ⲛⲁⲛ ⲧⲉⲛⲛⲁⲁⲓϥ *(AmBal p2)*

e) ⲁ̇ⲛⲟⲕ ⲡⲉ ⲉⲧⲣⲱⲓⲥ ⲉ̇ⲣⲟⲕ ϧⲉⲛ ⲡⲓⲙⲱⲓⲧ ⲛⲓⲃⲉⲛ ⲉ̇ⲧⲉⲕⲛⲁϩⲱⲗ ⲉ̇ⲣⲱⲟⲩ *(AmBal p6)*

6. LINKING CLAUSES

6.1. Conjunctions

Junctions are places where things join, meet or cross, such as roads or railway lines. Conjunctions are also used to join, but rather than joining roads, they're used to join words, phrases, sentences or clauses together. Clauses? What do we mean by clauses? A clause is a piece of writing which contains both a predicate **(3.1)** and a subject. For example, take a look at the following two sentences:
I saw. I wept.

Each of these is a clause, as each contains a subject and a predicate which tells you something about the subject. Now a clause may also be a sentence, but sometimes clauses can have a subject and predicate but still not make sense on their own. In these cases, they can be combined with other clauses to form a full sentence.

Now if the two clauses in the example above appeared after each other, the writing would sound disjointed. However, if you add a conjunction in between, then the writing flows a lot more smoothly. What are some examples of conjunctions? They are actually very common words that we all use many times every day e.g. and, but, then, so that, lest. etc.

Some examples of the different conjunctions you could use with the example above are shown below:

"I saw and I wept"
"I saw but I wept"
"I saw then I wept"
"I saw so that I wept."

As with English, Coptic also has many conjunctions of its own. Unlike English however, these are divided into two groups, first position conjunctions which come at the beginning of the clause, and enclitic conjunctions, which don't start the clause.

6.1.i. First position conjunctions

These clauses are fairly straight forward, because they come in the same position the clause as you'd expect in English.

ⲁⲗⲗⲁ	but	ⲛⲉⲙ	with, and (used to link nouns)
ⲉⲡⲓⲇⲏ	after, that, since, when	ⲟⲩⲇⲉ	nor

So You want to Learn Coptic?

ⲉⲑⲃⲉ	for the sake of, because	ⲟⲩⲟϩ	and, (used to link phrases)
ⲉⲧⲓ	after, during, and (Gk)	ⲧⲟⲧⲉ	then
ⲓⲉ	or	ϫⲉⲕⲁⲥ	so that, although
ⲓⲥϫⲉ	if	ϩⲓⲛⲁ	so that
ⲕⲁⲛ	even if	ϩⲟⲡⲱⲥ	so that
ⲙⲉⲛⲉⲛⲥⲁ	after	ϩⲱⲥⲧⲉ	and so
ⲙⲏⲡⲟⲧⲉ	lest	ϫⲉ	because, that, used to introduce speech

Vocab			
ⲁⲣⲭⲏⲁⲅⲅⲉⲗⲟⲥ	arch angel (m)	ⲥⲱⲛⲧ ⲥⲉⲛⲧ– ⲥⲟⲛⲧ⸗	to create, to renew (v.t)
ⲁⲣⲭⲱⲛ	chief, prince (m)	ϣⲱⲛϩ	to deprive (v.t)
ⲁⲫⲉ	head (f)	ϥⲱⲓ	hair (m)
ⲡⲁⲧⲣⲓⲁⲣⲭⲏⲥ	patriarch (m)	ϩⲏⲧ	heart (m)
ⲥⲁϩⲛⲓ	command (v.t)	ϩⲟⲛϩⲉⲛ	to command (v.t)

Exercise 6.1

a) **Ⲡⲉⲧⲣⲟⲥ ⲛⲉⲙ Ⲓⲱⲁⲛⲛⲏⲥ** *(Acts 3:11)*

b) **Ⲡ̅ⲟ̅ⲥ̅ ⲁϥϩⲟⲛϩⲉⲛ ⲟⲩⲟϩ ⲁⲩⲥⲱⲛⲧ** *(fourth hoas Midnight praises)*

c) **ⲟⲩⲇⲉ ⲁⲣⲭⲏⲁⲅⲅⲉⲗⲟⲥ ⲟⲩⲇⲉ ⲡⲁⲧⲣⲓⲁⲣⲭⲏⲥ ⲟⲩⲇⲉ ⲡⲣⲟⲫⲏⲧⲏⲥ**
(Prayer of reconciliation, Liturgy of St.Gregory)

d) **ⲧⲟⲧⲉ ⲁϥϩⲱⲥ ⲛ̇ϫⲉ Ⲙⲱⲓⲥⲏⲥ** *(Exodus 15:1)*

e) **ⲉⲡⲓⲇⲏ ⲟⲩⲥⲁϩⲛⲓ ⲡⲉ** *(Congregation of the saints, Liturgy of St.Basil)*

f) **ⲁⲣⲭⲱⲛ ⲓⲉ ⲣⲉϥϯϩⲁⲡ** *(Acts 7:35)*

Linking clauses

g) ⲓⲥϫⲉ ⲛ̄ⲑⲟⲕ ⲡⲉ ⲡ̄ϣⲏⲣⲓ ⲙ̄ⲫϯ ϩⲓⲧⲕ ⲉⲡⲉⲥⲏⲧ ⲉⲃⲟⲗ ⲧⲁⲓ *(Matthew 4:6)*

h) ϩⲱⲥⲧⲉ ⲛ̄ⲑⲟⲕ ⲟⲩⲃⲱⲕ ⲁⲛ ϫⲉ ⲁⲗⲗⲁ ⲟⲩϣⲏⲣⲓ *(Galatians 4:7)*

i) ⲙ̄ⲡⲉ ⲡⲓⲭⲣⲱⲙ ϭⲓ ⲛⲉⲙⲱⲟⲩ ⲟⲩⲇⲉ ⲟⲩϥⲱⲓ ⲛ̄ⲧⲉ ⲧⲟⲩⲁ̀ⲫⲉ ⲙ̄ⲡⲉϥϣⲱⲛϩ *(hom vatt ii pg.85)*

j) Ⲡϭⲟⲓⲥ ⲙ̄ⲡⲉϥϭⲓⲥⲓ ⲛ̄ϫⲉ ⲡⲁϩⲏⲧ ⲟⲩⲇⲉ ⲙ̄ⲡⲟⲩϭⲁⲥⲟⲩ ⲛ̄ϫⲉ ⲛⲁⲃⲁⲗ *(Psalm **130:1** 130:1)*

6.1.ii. All about ϫⲉ

ϫⲉ is such a special conjunction that it deserves its own subheading. It's one of those words that seems to pop up everywhere and to mean something different on each occasion. It actually has four different meanings which will be explained here:

a) Its first use is to introduce direct speech after the speaker has been introduced, in much the same way as inverted commas are used in English. The difference is that whereas in English inverted commas come on both sides of the quote, Coptic only has the ϫⲉ coming in front, with nothing to mark the end of the quote. Here, ϫⲉ is intimately related with the verb ϫⲱ, which means "to say" **(8.1)**. In these cases the ϫⲉ is not translated, but is only used as a marker that speech is about to start.

E.g. ϯϫⲱ ⲙ̄ⲙⲟⲥ ⲛⲱⲧⲉⲛ ϫⲉ ⲙⲉⲛⲣⲉ ⲛⲉⲧⲉⲛϫⲁϫⲓ *(Matthew 5:44)*
"I say to you love your enemies"

b) ϫⲉ is also used to introduce *indirect* speech. How can speech be indirect? Indirect speech is more like a report or reference of something which was thought or said rather than a quote of the actual words which were used. ϫⲉ is translated as 'that' in this situation:

E.g. ⲧⲉⲛⲛⲁϩϯ ϫⲉ ⲫⲁⲓ ⲡⲉ ϧⲉⲛ ⲟⲩⲙⲉⲑⲙⲏⲓ *(Consecration, Liturgy of St.Basil)*
"we believe that this is in truth"

c) ϫⲉ is also used to introduce a name, usually after the verb "to call."

E.g. ⲓⲱⲥⲏⲫ ⲫⲏ ⲉ̀ⲧⲟⲩⲙⲟⲩϯ ⲉⲣⲟϥ ϫⲉ ⲃⲁⲣⲥⲁⲃⲃⲁⲥ *(Acts 1:23)*
"Joseph who is called Barsabas"

d) The final use for ⲭⲉ is to introduce a causative clause, that is a clause which is used to give the reason or the cause for the main clause of the sentence. Here ⲭⲉ is translated as 'for' or 'because.'

E.g. ⲧⲉⲛⲟⲩⲱϣⲧ ⲙ̀ⲙⲟⲕ ⲱ ⲡⲓⲭ̀ⲣⲓⲥⲧⲟⲥ ⲛⲉⲙ ⲡⲉⲕⲓⲱⲧ ⲛ̀ⲁⲅⲁⲑⲟⲥ ⲛⲉⲙ ⲡⲓⲡ̀ⲛⲉⲩⲙⲁ ⲉⲑⲟⲩⲁⲃ ⲭⲉ ⲁⲕⲓ ⲁⲕⲥⲱϯ ⲙ̀ⲙⲟⲛ

"we worship You O' Christ with your good Father and the Holy Spirit for you came, you saved us".

6.1.iii.   *Enclitic conjunctions*

These conjunctions don't come at the beginning of the clause, which makes the clause a little more tricky to translate. Some examples of these are:

ⲅⲁⲣ	for, because
ⲇⲉ	but, and
ⲙⲉⲛ	indeed
ⲟⲛ	also

The idea of the conjunction not starting the clause may seem to be a little confusing, what exactly do I mean? This example will make it clearer:

ⲫⲁⲓ ⲅⲁⲣ ⲡⲉ ⲡⲁⲥⲱⲙⲁ   *(Consecration, Liturgy of St.Basil)*

The conjunction in this example is actually ⲅⲁⲣ, which means 'because' or 'for.' As you can see, it doesn't start the clause, but is the second word. In English, the translation of the clause is:
"for this is my body."

So in English, the conjunction comes at the beginning of the clause, but in Coptic ⲅⲁⲣ cannot begin the clause, the earliest position it can take is as the second word in the sentence. ⲅⲁⲣ and the other conjunctions like it which don't start the clause are called *enclitic* conjunctions.

Another common enclitic conjunction is ⲇⲉ, which if you're not concentrating may look like ⲭⲉ. ⲇⲉ is a tricky word, because it can mean either 'and' or 'but.' In order to tell which meaning it has in a particular sentence, you need to pay close attention to the context.

Linking clauses

The last enclitic conjunction we'll talk about here is ⲙⲉⲛ. On its own, it means "indeed."

E.g. ⲡⲓϩⲟⲩⲓⲧ ⲙⲉⲛ ⲛ̀ⲥⲁϫⲓ ⲁⲓⲁⲓϥ ⲉⲑⲃⲉ ϩⲱⲃ ⲛⲓⲃⲉⲛ *(Acts 1:1)*
"indeed the first word (account) I made concerning everything"

It can also be used with ⲇⲉ, where the ⲙⲉⲛ is used in the first clause of the sentence and ⲇⲉ is used in the second. This is used to contrast the two clauses, as if to say 'on the one hand....', 'but on the other....'

E.g. ⲓⲱⲁⲛⲛⲏⲥ ⲙⲉⲛ ⲁϥϯⲱⲙⲥ ϧⲉⲛ ⲟⲩⲙⲱⲟⲩ ⲛ̀ⲑⲱⲧⲉⲛ ⲇⲉ ⲥⲉⲛⲁⲉⲙⲥ ⲑⲏⲛⲟⲩ ϧⲉⲛ ⲟⲩⲡ̅ⲛ̅ⲁ̅ ⲉϥⲟⲩⲁⲃ *(Acts 1:5)*
"Indeed John baptised in water but you will be baptised in a Holy Spirit"

Vocab			
ⲉ̀ⲙⲓ	to know (v.i)	ⲛ̀ϣⲟⲣⲡ	first (adv)
ⲉⲣⲛⲏⲥⲧⲉⲩⲓⲛ	to fast (v.i, Gk)	ⲣⲉϥⲉⲣⲛⲟⲃⲓ	sinner (m)
ⲉⲑⲛⲟⲥ	nation (Gk,m)	ⲧⲁⲙⲟ ⲧⲁⲙⲉ- ⲧⲁⲙⲟ⸗	to inform, tell
ⲕⲁⲗⲩⲙⲙⲁ	Veil (Gk,m)	ⲧⲉⲛϩⲟⲩⲧ	to believe, to trust (v.i)
ⲙⲉⲑⲙⲏⲓ	truth (f)	ⲱⲙⲥ ⲉⲙⲥ- ⲟⲙⲥ⸗	to baptise (v.t)
ⲙⲉⲧⲁⲛⲟⲓⲁ	repentance (Gk,f)	ϩⲁⲛⲟⲩⲟⲛ	some
ⲡⲩⲗⲏ	gate (f)	ϩⲏⲧ	heart (m)

Exercise 6.2

a) ϯⲉⲙⲓ ⲅⲁⲣ ϧⲉⲛ ⲟⲩⲙⲉⲑⲙⲏⲓ ϫⲉ ⲁⲛⲟⲕ ⲟⲩⲣⲉϥⲉⲣⲛⲟⲃⲓ *(Doxology for Holy Great Fasting)*

b) Ⲉⲗⲓⲁⲥ ⲙⲉⲛ ⲁϥⲓ̀ ⲛ̀ϣⲟⲣⲡ *(Mark 9:13)*

c) ⲁⲛⲟⲕ ⲙⲉⲛ ϯⲱⲙⲥ ⲙ̀ⲙⲱⲧⲉⲛ ϧⲉⲛ ⲟⲩⲙⲱⲟⲩ ⲙ̀ⲙⲉⲧⲁⲛⲟⲓⲁ *(Doxology for Paramoun of Feast of Epiphany)*

d) ⲛ̀ⲑⲱⲟⲩ ⲇⲉ ⲥⲉⲉⲣⲛⲏⲥⲧⲉⲩⲓⲛ ⲁⲛ *(Matthew 9:14)*

e) ⲙ̀ⲡⲉⲕⲧⲁⲙⲟⲓ ϫⲉ ⲧⲁⲥϩⲓⲙⲓ ⲧⲉ   *(Genesis 12:18)*

f) ⲡⲓⲕⲁⲗⲩⲙⲙⲁ ⲟⲛ ϥ̀ⲭⲏ ⲉ̀ϫⲉⲛ ⲡⲟⲩϩⲏⲧ   *(2 Corinthians 3:15)*

g) ⲉⲧⲁϥⲓ̀ ⲇⲉ ⲉ̀ⲡⲉⲥⲏⲧ ⲉ̀ⲃⲟⲗ ϩⲓϫⲉⲛ ⲡⲓⲧⲱⲟⲩ   *(Matthew 8:1)*

h) ⲁⲩⲥⲱⲧⲉⲙ ⲇⲉ ⲛ̀ϫⲉ ⲛⲓⲁ̀ⲡⲟⲥⲧⲟⲗⲟⲥ ⲛⲉⲙ ⲛⲓⲥ̀ⲛⲏⲟⲩ ⲉⲧϣⲟⲡ ϧⲉⲛ ϯⲓⲟⲩⲇⲉⲁ ϫⲉ ⲁ ⲛⲓⲕⲉⲉⲑⲛⲟⲥ ϣⲉⲡ ⲡⲓⲥⲁϫⲓ ⲛ̀ⲧⲉ Ⲫϯ ⲉ̀ⲣⲱⲟⲩ   *(Acts 11:1)*

i) ⲛ̀ⲥⲉⲧⲉⲛϩⲟⲩⲧ ⲙ̀ⲙⲟϥ ⲁⲛ ϫⲉ ⲟⲩⲙⲁⲑⲏⲧⲏⲥ ⲡⲉ   *(Acts 9:26)*

Practice text 7
Doxology for Arch Angel Gabriel

ⲁ̅. ⲛ̀ⲑⲟⲕ ⲟⲩⲛⲓϣϯ ⲁ̀ⲗⲏⲑⲱⲥ ⲱ ⲡⲓϥⲁⲓϣⲉⲛⲛⲟⲩϥⲓ ⲛ̀ⲕⲁⲗⲱⲥ ϧⲉⲛ ⲛⲓⲧⲁⲝⲓⲥ ⲛ̀ⲁⲅⲅⲉⲗⲓⲕⲟⲛ ⲛⲉⲙ ⲛⲓⲧⲁⲅⲙⲁ ⲛ̀ⲉ̀ⲡⲟⲩⲣⲁⲛⲓⲟⲛ

ⲃ̅. ⲅⲁⲃⲣⲓⲏⲗ ⲡⲓϥⲁⲓϣⲉⲛⲛⲟⲩϥⲓ ⲡⲓⲛⲓϣϯ ϧⲉⲛ ⲛⲓⲁⲅⲅⲉⲗⲟⲥ ⲛⲉⲙ ⲛⲓⲧⲁⲅⲙⲁ ⲉ̅ⲑ̅ⲩ̅ ⲉⲧϭⲟⲥⲓ ⲉⲧϥⲁⲓ ϧⲁ ϯⲥⲏϥⲓ ⲛ̀ϣⲁϩ ⲛ̀ⲭⲣⲱⲙ

ⲅ̅. ⲁϥⲛⲁⲩ ⲅⲁⲣ ⲉ̀ⲡⲉⲕⲧⲁⲓⲟ ⲛ̀ϫⲉ ⲇⲁⲛⲓⲏⲗ ⲡⲓⲡ̀ⲣⲟⲫⲏⲧⲏⲥ ⲟⲩⲟϩ ⲁⲕⲧⲁⲙⲟϥ ⲉ̀ⲡⲓⲙⲩⲥⲧⲏⲣⲓⲟⲛ ⲛ̀ϯⲧ̀ⲣⲓⲁⲥ ⲛ̀ⲣⲉϥⲧⲁⲛϧⲟ

ⲇ̅. ⲟⲩⲟϩ ⲍⲁⲭⲁⲣⲓⲁⲥ ⲡⲓⲟⲩⲏⲃ ⲛ̀ⲑⲟⲕ ⲁⲕϩⲓϣⲉⲛⲛⲟⲩϥⲓ ⲛⲁϥ ϧⲉⲛ ⲡ̀ϫⲓⲛⲙⲓⲥⲓ ⲙ̀ⲡⲓⲡ̀ⲣⲟⲇⲣⲟⲙⲟⲥ Ⲓⲱⲁⲛⲛⲏⲥ ⲡⲓⲣⲉϥϯⲱⲙⲥ

ⲉ̅. ⲁⲕϩⲓϣⲉⲛⲛⲟⲩϥⲓ ⲟⲛ ⲛ̀ϯⲡⲁⲣⲑⲉⲛⲟⲥ ϫⲉ ⲭⲉⲣⲉ ⲑⲏ ⲉⲑⲙⲉϩ ⲛ̀ϩ̀ⲙⲟⲧ Ⲡ̅ⲟ̅ⲥ̅ ⲛⲉⲙⲉ ⲧⲉⲣⲁⲙⲓⲥⲓ ⲙ̀Ⲡⲓⲥⲱⲧⲏⲣ ⲙ̀ⲡⲓⲕⲟⲥⲙⲟⲥ ⲧⲏⲣϥ

ⲋ̅. ⲁⲣⲓⲡ̀ⲣⲉⲥⲃⲉⲩⲓⲛ ⲱ ⲡⲓⲁⲣⲭⲏⲁⲅⲅⲉⲗⲟⲥ ⲉ̅ⲑ̅ⲩ̅ ⲅⲁⲃⲣⲓⲏⲗ ⲡⲓϥⲁⲓϣⲉⲛⲛⲟⲩϥⲓ

Vocab			
ⲁⲅⲅⲉⲗⲓⲕⲟⲛ	angelic (Gk)	ⲧⲁⲙⲟ ⲧⲁⲙⲟ⁻ ⲧⲁⲙⲉ⳱	to inform, tell (v.t)
ⲁⲗⲏⲑⲱⲥ	truly (adv)	ⲧⲁⲝⲓⲥ	rank (Gk)
ⲕⲁⲗⲟⲥ	beautiful, fair, good (adj.)	⳨ⲣⲓⲁⲥ	Trinity (Gk)
ⲙⲩⲥⲧⲏⲣⲓⲟⲛ	sacrament, mystery (Gk,m)	ⲭⲣⲱⲙ	fire (m)
ⲟⲩⲏⲃ	priest (m)	ϣⲁϩ	flame, fire (m)
ⲡⲣⲟⲇⲣⲟⲙⲟⲥ	forerunner (Gk,m)	ϥⲁⲓϣⲉⲛⲛⲟⲩϥⲓ	announcer (m)
ⲣⲉϥⲧⲁⲛϩⲟ	life giver (m)	ϩⲓϣⲉⲛⲛⲟⲩϥⲓ	to announce (v.t)
ⲥⲏϥⲓ	sword (f)	ϫⲓⲛⲙⲓⲥⲓ	birth (m)
ⲧⲁⲅⲙⲁ	core, division (Gk,m)		

6.2. The subjunctive

The subjunctive is a special type of conjunction used either within or between clauses. It will usually come at some point following the first verb in the clause then immediately before the second verb.

Depending on the circumstances, it will either be translated as 'so that' or simply as 'and' but in some cases, it's really not translated at all. The different uses are explained further down. As can be seen in the table below, the subjunctive takes different endings depending on the subject of the verb.

	singular	plural
first person	ⲛ̀ⲧⲁ	ⲛ̀ⲧⲉⲛ
second person	ⲛ̀ⲧⲉⲕ (m) ⲛ̀ⲧⲉ (f)	ⲛ̀ⲧⲉⲧⲉⲛ
third person	ⲛ̀ⲧⲉϥ (m) ⲛ̀ⲧⲉⲥ (f)	ⲛ̀ⲧⲟⲩ/ ⲛ̀ⲥⲉ
before a noun	ⲛ̀ⲧⲉ	

So for example, ⲙⲟⲓ ⲛⲏⲓ ⲛ̀ⲧⲁⲥⲱ *(John 4:10)* means *"give me so that I drink"* or *"Give me to drink"*

The first verb is ⲙⲟⲓ (the imperative of which we'll meet in **(10.4)**), and the second verb is ⲥⲱ. As you can see, the subjunctive ⲛ̀ⲧⲁ comes before the second verb, and it is in the first person (because "me", or strictly speaking "I" is the subject of the second verb).

There are five major uses for the subjunctive:

a) To connect two verbs together where the first verb has the meaning of a wish, request, command or intention for the second verb to occur. In this context, it has the meaning of "so that" or "in order to."

E.g. ⲁⲛⲓ ⲛ̀ⲧⲉⲛⲟⲩⲱϣⲧ ⲙ̀ⲙⲟϥ *(Matthew 2:2)*
"we came to worship Him"

b) To connect verbs of the same tense together:

In these cases, ⲟⲩⲟϩ is also used with the subjunctive. Here, the subjunctive is actually left untranslated.

E.g. ⲟⲩⲟϩ ⲛ̀ⲥⲉⲁϣϥ ⲟⲩⲟϩ ⲛ̀ⲧⲉϥⲧⲱⲛϥ *(Luke 24:7)*
"and they will crucify him and he rise (himself)"

c) To follow the impersonal verb ϩⲱϯ *"it is necessary"*

ϩⲱϯ belongs to a category of verbs called the impersonal verbs which we shall meet in **(8.2)**. It's always used with the subjunctive as with the example below:

E.g. ϩⲱϯ ⲡⲉ ⲛ̀ⲧⲉⲥϫⲱⲕ ⲉ̀ⲃⲟⲗ ⲛ̀ϫⲉ ϯⲅⲣⲁⲫⲏ *(Acts 1:16)*
"it is necessary that the scriptures be fulfilled"

d) To follow the conditional ⲉ̀ϣⲱⲡ:

ⲉ̀ϣⲱⲡ is a special word belonging to the category of the conditional (**10.5**). The conditionals are used to start a clause meaning 'if' or 'when.' ⲉ̀ϣⲱⲡ is sometimes followed by the subjunctive as in the following example:

Linking clauses

E.g. ⲉϣⲱⲡ ⲅⲁⲣ ⲛ̀ⲧⲉⲧⲉⲛⲙⲉⲛⲣⲉ ⲛⲏ ⲉⲑⲙⲉⲓ ⲙ̀ⲙⲱⲧⲉⲛ ⲁϣ ⲡⲉ ⲡⲉⲧⲉⲛⲃⲉⲭⲉ (Matthew 5:46)

"for if you love those who love you what is your reward?"

e) After certain conjunctions as in the following:

ϩⲟⲡⲱⲥ - so that (Gk)

ⲙⲏⲡⲟⲧⲉ / ⲙⲏⲡⲱⲥ - lest, perhaps

ϩⲓⲛⲁ – so that

E.g. ϩⲟⲡⲱⲥ ⲛ̀ⲧⲉϥⲉⲣϩⲙⲟⲧ ⲛⲁⲛ ⲙ̀ⲡⲥⲱϯ ⲛ̀ⲛⲉⲛⲯⲩⲭⲏ *(introduction of Midnight praises)*

"So that He grants us the salvation for our souls"

ϩⲓⲛⲁ ⲛ̀ⲧⲉϥⲉⲣⲙⲉⲑⲣⲉ ϧⲁ ⲡⲓⲟⲩⲱⲓⲛⲓ *(John 1:8)*

"So that he bears witness to the light"

Practice text 8
Conclusion of Adam Theotokia, Midnight praises

Ⲉⲙⲙⲁⲛⲟⲩⲏⲗ Ⲡⲉⲛⲛⲟⲩϯ ϧⲉⲛ ⲧⲉⲛⲙⲏϯ ϯⲛⲟⲩ ϧⲉⲛ ⲡ̀ⲱⲟⲩ ⲛ̀ⲧⲉ ⲡⲉϥⲓⲱⲧ ⲛⲉⲙ ⲡⲓⲡ̀ⲛⲉⲩⲙⲁ ⲉⲑⲟⲩⲁⲃ ⲛ̀ⲧⲉϥⲥ̀ⲙⲟⲩ ⲉⲣⲟⲛ ⲧⲏⲣⲉⲛ ⲛ̀ⲧⲉϥⲧⲟⲩⲃⲟ ⲛ̀ⲛⲉⲛϩⲏⲧ ⲛ̀ⲧⲉϥⲧⲁⲗϭⲟ ⲛ̀ⲛⲓϣⲱⲛⲓ ⲛ̀ⲧⲉ ⲛⲉⲛⲯⲩⲭⲏ ⲛⲉⲙ ⲛⲉⲛⲥⲱⲙⲁ

ⲙⲏϯ		middle (f)	ⲯⲩⲭⲏ	soul (m)
ⲥⲱⲙⲁ		body (m)	ϣⲱⲛⲓ	sickness, disease (m)
ⲧⲁⲗϭⲟ ⲧⲁⲗϭⲉ- ⲧⲁⲗϭⲟ⸗		to heal (v.t)	ϯⲛⲟⲩ	now (adv)
ⲧⲟⲩⲃⲟ ⲧⲟⲩⲃⲉ- ⲧⲟⲩⲃⲟ⸗ ⲧⲟⲩⲃⲏⲟⲩⲧ (q)		to purify (v.t)		

6.2.i. Setting limits- using the 'limitative'

If you look back at the table of preposition we met way back in **(5.1.iii)** you'll find ϣⲁ which means 'to', 'toward' or 'till.' This preposition also has a special relationship with the subjunctive, in that they link together to form the *limitative* construction.

When is setting limits relevant to grammar? Consider this example "Jarred will study eight hours a day till he finishes his exams." Here we're talking about a verb (to study) which will continue till another event happens (finishing his exams). In that way, a *limit* has been set to the study (thank God!) hence the name "limitative." In other words, the limitative carries the meaning of what we commonly understand by the word 'until.'

This construction is simply made by adding the ϣⲁ before the subjunctive.

E.g. ϣⲁ + ⲛ̇ⲧⲉⲕⲓ = ϣⲁⲛⲧⲉⲕⲓ

"till you come"

There is also a shorter alternative formed by dropping the ⲛ̇ from the subjunctive, so the example above would become:

ϣⲁⲧⲉⲕⲓ

Which also means *"till you come"*

In the following table both the combined and shortened forms are written. Note that the combined form of the first person singular gives you a bit of a choice with two forms you can chose from:

		singular	plural
first person	combined	ϣⲁⲛⲧⲁ⁻ ϣⲁⲛϯ⁻	ϣⲁⲛⲧⲉⲛ⁻
	shortened	ϣⲁϯ⁻	ϣⲁⲧⲉⲛ⁻
second person	combined	ϣⲁⲛⲧⲉⲕ⁻ (m) ϣⲁⲛⲧⲉ⁻ (f)	ϣⲁⲛⲧⲉⲧⲉⲛ⁻
	shortened	ϣⲁⲧⲉⲕ⁻ (m) ϣⲁⲧⲉ⁻ (f)	ϣⲁⲧⲉⲧⲉⲛ⁻
third person	combined	ϣⲁⲛⲧⲉϥ⁻ (m) ϣⲁⲛⲧⲉⲥ⁻ (f)	ϣⲁⲛⲧⲟⲩ⁻
	shortened	ϣⲁⲧⲉϥ⁻ (m) ϣⲁⲧⲉⲥ⁻ (f)	ϣⲁⲧⲟⲩ⁻
before a noun	combined	ϣⲁⲛⲧⲉ	
	shortened	ϣⲁⲧⲉ	

Linking clauses

So, to take another example, we'll read this verse from the Gospel of Matthew:

ⲟⲩⲟϩ ⲙ̅ⲡⲉϥⲥⲟⲩⲱⲛⲥ ϣⲁⲧⲉⲥⲙⲓⲥⲓ ⲙ̅ⲡⲓϣⲏⲣⲓ *(Matthew 1:25)*
"and he did not know her till she gave birth to the son"

Vocab			
ⲁⲓⲁⲓ	to grow, increase (v.i)	ⲣⲱⲧ ⲣⲉⲧ— ⲣⲟⲩ⳱ ⲣⲏⲧ	to grow, spread, sprout, bring forth (v.t)
ⲁⲗⲏⲓ	to mount, go up (v.i)	ⲥⲓⲛⲓ	to pass by, to pass away (v.i)
ⲁⲙⲁϩⲓ	to prevail, rule, possess (v.i)	ⲥⲟⲗⲥⲉⲗ ⲥⲉⲗⲥⲉⲗ— ⲥⲉⲗⲥⲱⲗ⳱	to adorn (v.t)
ⲁⲛⲟⲙⲓⲁ	iniquity (f)	ⲥⲱϫⲡ	remainder (m)
ⲁϣⲁⲓ	to become many, multiply (v.i)	ⲧⲉⲛϩ	wing (m)
ⲃⲏⲃ	cave, hole, den (m)	ⲧⲟⲩϫⲟ ⲧⲟⲩϫⲉ— ⲧⲟⲩϫⲟ⳱ ⲧⲟⲩϫⲏⲟⲩⲧ	to make whole, save (v.t)
ⲉⲑⲛⲟⲥ	nation (Gk,m)	ⲫⲓⲣⲓ	to come forth, blossom
ⲉ̀ⲛⲧⲟⲗⲏ	commandment (f)	ⲭⲏⲙⲓ	Egypt (prop.noun)
ⲑⲱⲟⲩϯ ⲑⲟⲩⲉⲧ— ⲑⲟⲩⲱⲧ⳱ ⲑⲟⲩⲏⲧ	to gather (v.t)	ϣϣⲏⲛ	tree (m)
ⲑ̀ⲙⲏⲓ	righteous person (m)	ϧⲏⲓⲃⲓ	shadow (m)
ⲕⲱⲧ ⲕⲉⲧ—	to build (v.t)	ϩⲓⲛⲓ ϩⲉⲛ— ϩⲉⲛ⳱	to move self forward, to move

133

ⲕⲟⲧ⳿ ⲕⲏⲧ			backward
ⲙⲉⲓ ⲙⲉⲛⲣⲉ– ⲙⲉⲛⲣⲓⲧ⳿	to love (v.t)	ϩⲟ	face (m)
ⲙⲏϣ	multitude (m)	ϩⲱⲙⲓ ϩⲉⲙ– ϩⲟⲙ⳿ ϩⲟⲙⲓ	to tread, trample (v.t)
ⲙⲟⲩⲛϩⲱⲟⲩ	rain (m)	ϩⲱⲟⲩ	to rain (v.i)
ⲙ̀ϩⲁⲩ	tomb (m)	ϫⲟⲓ	ship, boat (m)
ⲛⲓϥⲓ	to breath, blow (v.i)	ϫⲟⲙϫⲉⲙ	to touch, grope (v.t)

Exercise 6.3

a) ϫⲉ ⲧⲉⲧⲉⲛⲕⲱⲧ ⲛ̀ⲛⲓⲙ̀ϩⲁⲩ ⲛ̀ⲧⲉ ⲛⲓⲡ̀ⲣⲟⲫⲏⲧⲏⲥ ⲟⲩⲟϩ ⲛ̀ⲧⲉⲧⲉⲛⲥⲟⲗⲥⲉⲗ ⲛ̀ⲛⲓⲃⲏⲃ ⲛ̀ⲧⲉ ⲛⲓⲑ̀ⲙⲏⲓ (Matthew 23:29)

b) ϩⲓⲛⲁ ⲛ̀ⲧⲉⲧⲉⲛⲉⲣϣⲏⲣⲓ ⲙ̀ⲡⲉⲧⲉⲛⲓⲱⲧ ⲉⲧϧⲉⲛ ⲛⲓⲫⲏⲟⲩⲓ (Matthew 5:45)

c) ⲟⲩⲟϩ ⲁϥⲑⲱⲟⲩϯ ϩⲁⲣⲟϥ ⲛ̀ϫⲉ ϩⲁⲛⲛⲓϣϯ ⲙ̀ⲙⲏϣ ϩⲱⲥⲧⲉ ⲛ̀ⲧⲉϥⲁⲗⲏⲓ ⲉ̀ⲡ̀ϫⲟⲓ (Matthew 13:2)

d) ⲁϥⲁⲓⲁⲓ ⲛ̀ϫⲉ ⲡⲓⲗⲁⲟⲥ ⲟⲩⲟϩ ⲁϥⲁⲙⲁϩⲓ ⲁϥⲁϣⲁⲓ ⲛ̀ϩ̀ⲣⲏⲓ ϧⲉⲛ ⲭⲏⲙⲓ ϣⲁⲛⲧⲉϥⲧⲱⲛϥ ⲛ̀ϫⲉ ⲕⲉⲟⲩⲣⲟ ⲉ̀ϫⲉⲛ ⲭⲏⲙⲓ (Acts 7:17-18)

e) ϩⲟⲡⲱⲥ ⲛ̀ⲥⲉⲕⲱϯ ⲛ̀ⲥⲁ Ⲡ̅ⲟ̅ⲥ̅ ⲛ̀ϫⲉ ⲡ̀ⲥⲱϫⲡ ⲛ̀ⲛⲓⲣⲱⲙⲓ ⲛⲉⲙ ⲛⲓⲉⲑⲛⲟⲥ ⲧⲏⲣⲟⲩ (Acts 15:17)

f) ⲁϥϩⲱⲟⲩ ⲛ̀ⲟⲩⲙⲟⲩⲛϩⲱⲟⲩ ϩⲓϫⲉⲛ ⲡ̀ϩⲟ ⲙ̀ⲡ̀ⲕⲁϩⲓ ϣⲁⲛⲧⲉϥⲣⲱⲧ ⲉ̀ⲡ̀ϣⲱⲓ ⲛ̀ⲧⲉϥϯ ⲙ̀ⲡⲉϥⲟⲩⲧⲁϩ (Epsali Adam for second Canticle, Midnight praises)

g) ⲁϥⲛⲓϥⲓ ⲛ̀ⲥⲁ ⲛⲓϣ̀ϣⲏⲛ ϣⲁ ⲛ̀ⲧⲟⲩⲫⲓⲣⲓ ⲉ̀ⲃⲟⲗ (Epsali Adam for second Canticle, Midnight Praises)

Linking clauses

h) ⲙⲏⲡⲱⲥ ⲛ̅ⲥⲉⲛⲁⲩ ⲛ̅ⲛⲟⲩⲃⲁⲗ ⲟⲩⲟϩ ⲛ̅ⲥⲉⲥⲱⲧⲉⲙ ϧⲉⲛ ⲛⲟⲩⲙⲁϣϫ ⲟⲩⲟϩ ⲛ̅ⲥⲉⲕⲁϯ ϧⲉⲛ ⲡⲟⲩϩⲏⲧ ⲛ̅ⲥⲉⲕⲟⲧⲟⲩ ⲛ̅ⲧⲁⲧⲟⲩϫⲱⲟⲩ *(Acts 28:27)*

i) ϩⲉⲛⲕ ⲉⲣⲟⲓ ⲛ̅ⲧⲁϫⲟⲙϫⲉⲙ ⲉⲣⲟⲕ ϫⲉ ⲛ̅ⲑⲟⲕ ⲡⲉ ⲡⲁϣⲏⲣⲓ *(Genesis 27:21)*

j) ⲙⲏⲡⲟⲧⲉ ⲛ̅ⲥⲉϩⲱⲙⲓ ⲉϫⲱⲟⲩ *(Matthew 7:6)*

k) ϯⲛⲁⲉⲣϩⲉⲗⲡⲓⲥ ϧⲁ ⲧϧⲏⲓⲃⲓ ⲛ̅ⲧⲉ ⲛⲉⲕⲧⲉⲛϩ ϣⲁⲧⲉⲥⲥⲓⲛⲓ ⲛ̅ϫⲉ ϯⲁⲛⲟⲙⲓⲁ *(Psalm 56:1 57:1)*

> **Confusion Corner**
>
> If you take a close look at the table in **pg 129**, you'll notice that the presubject form of the subjunctive is identical to the ⲛ̅ⲧⲉ of the possessive construction **(2.4.ii)**. This can easily lead to confusion because it's very easy to get into the habit of translating ⲛ̅ⲧⲉ as 'of', then running into difficulties when the ⲛ̅ⲧⲉ happens to belong to the subjunctive. Usually, just keeping the two meanings for ⲛ̅ⲧⲉ in the back of your mind is enough to avoid confusion, but if you get stuck and have to decide between the two, then you need to think of the different constructions for each:
>
> The attributive construction is always used between to nouns:
>
> Noun + ⲛ̅ⲧⲉ + noun
>
> While the subjunctive ⲛ̅ⲧⲉ also comes before a noun, you'll find that a verb will then always come after that noun.
>
> ⲛ̅ⲧⲉ + noun + verb
>
> E.g. ⲁϥⲉⲣⲫⲁϧⲣⲓ ⲉⲣⲟϥ ϩⲱⲥⲧⲉ ⲛ̅ⲧⲉ ⲡⲓⲉⲃⲟ ⲥⲁϫⲓ *(Matthew 12:22)*
> "He healed him so that the mute spoke"

So You want to Learn Coptic?

6.2.ii.   *The Negative subjunctive*

The subjunctive also has a negative form. It's made by throwing in the word ϣⲧⲉⲙ between the normal affirmative form we saw above and the verb which the subjunctive is referring to. For example,

"that he will come" would be ⲛ̀ⲧⲉϥⲓ̀

"that he will not come" is therefore ⲛ̀ⲧⲉϥϣⲧⲉⲙⲓ̀

The negative subjunctive is used in much the same situations as the affirmative subjunctive, as you'll see from the exercises below:

Vocab			
ⲅⲉⲉⲛⲁ	Gehana, Hades (m)	ⲡⲁⲣⲁⲡⲧⲱⲙⲁ	trespass (Gk,m)
ⲉⲃⲟ	mute person (m)	ⲣⲱϣⲓ ⲣⲁϣ− ⲣⲁϣⲧ⳱ ⲣⲁϣⲓ	to suffice, be sufficient (v.t)
ⲉⲣⲛⲟϥⲣⲓ	to be good (v.i)	ⲭⲁⲕⲓ	darkness (m)
ⲙⲉⲗⲟⲥ	limb, member, (Gk,m)	ⲧⲁⲕⲟ ⲧⲁⲕⲉ− ⲧⲁⲕⲟ⳱ ⲧⲁⲕⲏⲟⲩⲧ	to destroy, lose (v.t)
ⲛⲉⲙⲱⲧⲉⲛ	with you (pl) pron. form of prep. **(5.5)**	ⲧⲁϩⲟ ⲧⲁϩⲉ− ⲧⲁϩⲟ⳱ ⲧⲁϩⲏⲟⲩⲧ	to reach, attain (v.t)

Exercise 6.4

a) ⲙⲏⲡⲟⲧⲉ ⲛ̀ⲧⲉϥϣⲧⲉⲙ ⲣⲁϣⲧⲉⲛ ⲛⲉⲙⲱⲧⲉⲛ   (Matthew 25:9)

b) ⲥⲉⲣⲛⲟϥⲣⲓ ⲅⲁⲣ ⲛⲁⲕ ⲛ̀ⲧⲉ ⲟⲩⲁⲓ ⲛ̀ⲛⲉⲕⲙⲉⲗⲟⲥ ⲧⲁⲕⲟ ⲟⲩⲟϩ ⲛ̀ⲧⲉϣⲧⲉⲙ ⲡⲉⲕⲥⲱⲙⲁ ⲧⲏⲣϥ ϣⲉ ⲛⲁϥ ⲉ̀ϯⲅⲉⲉⲛⲁ (Matthew 5:30)

c) ϩⲓⲛⲁ ⲛ̀ⲧⲉϣⲧⲉⲙ ⲡⲓⲭⲁⲕⲓ ⲧⲁϩⲉⲑⲏⲛⲟⲩ   (John 12:35)

d) ⲉϣⲱⲡ ⲇⲉ ⲛ̀ⲧⲉⲧⲉⲛϣ̀ⲧⲉⲙⲭⲱ ⲉⲃⲟⲗ ⲛ̀ⲛⲓⲣⲱⲙⲓ ⲛ̀ⲛⲟⲩⲡⲁⲣⲁⲡⲧⲱⲙⲁ ⲟⲩⲇⲉ ⲡⲉⲧⲉⲛⲓⲱⲧ ϥ̀ⲛⲁⲭⲱ ⲛⲱⲧⲉⲛ ⲉⲃⲟⲗ ⲁⲛ ⲛ̀ⲛⲉⲧⲉⲛⲡⲁⲣⲁⲡⲧⲱⲙⲁ *(Matthew 6:15)*

e) ⲛⲁϣⲏⲣⲓ ⲛⲁⲓ ϯⲥϧⲁⲓ ⲙ̀ⲙⲱⲟⲩ ⲛⲱⲧⲉⲛ ϩⲓⲛⲁ ⲛ̀ⲧⲉⲧⲉⲛϣ̀ⲧⲉⲙⲉⲣⲛⲟⲃⲓ *(1 John 2:1)*

7. NOW AND THEN AGAIN- SOME MORE PAST AND PRESENT TENSES

We've already taken a look at the first present, the perfect past tense and the first future, but there are other types of past and future tenses which are used to give different meanings. In this chapter, we'll take a look at the past imperfect tense and at a rather common construction called circumstantial conversion.

7.1. Dealing with imperfection- the imperfect tense

The imperfect tense is another type of past tense. We spoke about the difference between it and the past perfect in **(5.2)**, but to highlight another example, consider the difference between "the man was walking" and "the man walked."

In the first case, the action isn't quite complete, for all you know, the man could still be walking now. In the second case however, it's clear that the man walked and is not walking any longer. Because the verb in the first sentence hasn't quite been completed, it's an example of what is called the *imperfect* tense.

Coptic also has an imperfect tense, which takes the following form:

ⲛⲁⲓ⁻	I was
ⲛⲁϥ⁻	He was
ⲛⲁⲥ⁻	she was
ⲛⲁⲕ⁻	you were
ⲛⲁⲣⲉ⁻	you were (f)
ⲛⲁⲛ⁻	we were
ⲛⲁⲡⲉⲧⲉⲛ⁻	you were (plural)
ⲛⲁⲩ⁻	they were
ⲛⲁⲣⲉ, ⲛⲉ	pre noun as subject form

The appropriate form in terms of number and gender is attached before the infinitive.

E. g. ⲛⲁⲓⲣⲓⲙⲓ

"I was crying"

ⲛⲁϥϩⲉⲙⲥⲓ

"he was sitting"

ⲛⲁⲛⲙⲟϣⲓ

"we were walking"

As you can see in the table above, there is also a presubject form for the imperfect, so to say "the man was walking", you could say:

ⲡⲓⲣⲱⲙⲓ ⲛⲁϥⲙⲟϣⲓ

or ⲛⲁⲣⲉ ⲡⲓⲣⲱⲙⲓ ⲙⲟϣⲓ

An optional ⲡⲉ may be attached to the end of the sentence, so the above becomes:

ⲛⲁⲣⲉ ⲡⲓⲣⲱⲙⲓ ⲙⲟϣⲓ ⲡⲉ

Sometimes ⲛⲉ is used as the presubject form instead of ⲛⲁⲣⲉ, as in the first sentence of the Gospel of John.

ϧⲉⲛ ⲟⲩⲁⲣⲭⲏ ⲛⲉ ⲡ̄ⲥⲁϫⲓ ⲡⲉ *(John 1:1)*

"in (a) beginning was the word"

The imperfect may also be used with the qualitative **(5.1.ii)**.

E.g. ⲛⲁϥⲟⲃⲓ

"he was thirsty"

ⲛⲁⲣⲉ ⲧⲉϥⲥⲉⲛϯ ⲅⲁⲣ ⲧⲁϫⲣⲏⲟⲩⲧ ⲡⲉ ϩⲓϫⲉⲛ ϯⲡⲉⲧⲣⲁ *(Matthew 7:25)*

"for his foundation was firm upon the rock"

Verbs aren't the only part of speech to which the imperfect can attach, as it can also attach to simple prepositions.

E.g. ⲛⲁⲓϧⲉⲛ ϯⲡⲟⲗⲓⲥ

"I was in the city"

Vocab			
ⲉⲣϣⲫⲏⲣⲓ	to be amazed, to wonder (v.i)	ⲧⲁϫⲣⲟ ⲧⲁϫⲣⲉ- ⲧⲁϫⲣⲟ⸗ ⲧⲁϫⲣⲏⲟⲩⲧ	to make firm, strong (v.t)
Ⲓⲱⲡⲡⲏ	Joppa (prop.noun)	ⲧⲱⲙⲧ	to be surprised, amazed (v.i)

ⲙⲟⲩⲙⲓ	well, spring (f)	ϣⲓⲛⲓ ϣⲉⲛ- ϣⲉⲛ⸗	to seek, ask (v.t)
ⲙ̀ⲙⲁⲩ	there (adverb) **(9.1)**	ⲉ̀	to visit
ⲙⲱⲟⲩ	water (m)	ⲛ̀ ⲛ̀ⲥⲁ	to inquire for, seek after
ⲡⲁⲣⲁⲃⲟⲗⲏ	parable (Gk,f)	ϣⲱⲛⲓ	to be sick, weak (v.i)
ⲥⲉⲛϯ	foundation (f)	ϭⲓⲥⲓ ϭⲟⲥⲓ	to tire, suffer (v.i)
ⲥⲱⲃⲓ	to laugh, deride, mock (v.t)	ϭⲓⲥⲓ ϭⲁⲥ- ϭⲁⲥ⸗ ϭⲟⲥⲓ	to exalt (v.t)

Exercise 7.1

a) ⲛⲁϥⲥⲁϫⲓ ⲛⲉⲙⲱⲟⲩ ⲛ̀ϩⲁⲛⲙⲏϣ ϧⲉⲛ ϩⲁⲛⲡⲁⲣⲁⲃⲟⲗⲏ (Matthew 13:3)

b) ⲛⲁⲩϣⲓⲛⲓ ⲙ̀ⲙⲟϥ ⲛ̀ϫⲉ ⲛⲉϥⲙⲁⲑⲏⲧⲏⲥ ⲉ̀ϯⲡⲁⲣⲁⲃⲟⲗⲏ (Mark 7:17)

c) ⲛⲁⲩⲥⲱⲃⲓ ⲙ̀ⲙⲟϥ ⲡⲉ (Matthew 9:24)

d) ⲛⲁⲩⲉⲣϣⲫⲏⲣⲓ ⲛ̀ϫⲉ ⲛⲓⲙⲏϣ (Matthew 9:33)

e) ⲛⲁⲥⲭⲏ ⲇⲉ ⲙ̀ⲙⲁⲩ ⲛ̀ϫⲉ ⲟⲩⲙⲟⲩⲙⲓ ⲙ̀ⲙⲱⲟⲩ ⲛ̀ⲧⲉ ⲓⲁⲕⲱⲃ (John 4:6)

f) ⲛⲁⲩⲥⲱⲟⲩⲛ ⲇⲉ ⲙ̀ⲙⲱⲟⲩ ϫⲉ ⲛⲁⲩⲭⲏ ⲛⲉⲙ ⲓⲏⲥ ⲡⲉ (Acts 4:13)

g) ⲛⲁⲩⲧⲱⲙⲧ ⲇⲉ ⲧⲏⲣⲟⲩ ⲡⲉ (Acts 2:12)

h) ⲁⲛⲟⲕ ⲛⲁⲓϧⲉⲛ ⲓⲱⲡⲡⲏ ϯⲡⲟⲗⲓⲥ (Acts 11:5)

Practice text 9
Letter to Philemon verses 10-11

One of the most moving Pauline epistles is the letter to Philemon. Here is a short section which highlights some of the different grammar we have learnt up till now.

ϯϯϩο ⲉⲣⲟⲕ ⲉⲑⲃⲉ ⲡⲁϣⲏⲣⲓ ⲫⲁⲓ ⲉ̀ⲧⲁⲓϫⲫⲟϥ ϧⲉⲛ ⲛⲁⲥⲛⲁⲩϩ

ⲟⲛⲏⲥⲓⲙⲟⲥ. ⲫⲁⲓ ⲉⲧⲉ ⲛⲁϥⲟⲓ ⲛ̀ⲁⲧϣⲁⲩ ⲛⲁⲕ ⲛ̀ⲟⲩⲥⲏⲟⲩ. ϯⲛⲟⲩ ⲇⲉ

ϥⲟⲓ ⲛ̀ϣⲁⲩ ⲛⲏⲓ ⲛⲉⲙⲁⲕ. ⲫⲁⲓ ⲉⲧⲁⲓⲟⲩⲟⲣⲡϥ ϩⲁⲣⲟⲕ

Vocab			
ⲁⲧϣⲁⲩ	worthless (adj.)	ϩⲁⲣⲟⲕ	to you (preposition)
ⲛ̀ⲟⲩⲥⲏⲟⲩ	for a time (adv)	ϫⲫⲟ ϫⲫⲉ- ϫⲫⲟ⸌	to beget, bring forth
ⲟⲩⲱⲣⲡ ⲟⲩⲉⲣⲡ- ⲟⲩⲟⲣⲡ⸌	to send (v.t)	ϣⲁⲩ	of value (adj.)
ⲟⲛⲏⲥⲓⲙⲟⲥ	Onesimus (prop.noun)	ϯⲛⲟⲩ	now (9.1)
ⲥⲛⲁⲩϩ	bond (m)		

7.1.i. More than perfect - the pluperfect

Take a look at the sentence:
"They had been walking in the park when it rained"
You can see here that two events are being described, the first being "walking in the park" and the second "rained."

The second event "rained" is in the perfect tense since it was already completed. The first event 'walking in the park' had occurred even before "it rained", hence it is even "more perfect" than the second event since it had already been completed before it.

Grammatically, "had been walking in the park" is in the *plu*perfect tense, being derived from the Latin *plus quam perfectum* meaning "more than perfect."

If the above is a little too complicated to understand, you can simply consider the plu perfect to be the equivalent of the English word *had*.

Now and then again

In Coptic, the pluperfect is formed by combining both the perfect and the imperfect past tenses together. This is basically done by wrapping the ⲛⲉ.....ⲡⲉ combination of the imperfect **(7.1)** around the perfect tense construction **(5.2)**. To clarify, take a look at the example below:

ⲡⲓⲣⲱⲙⲓ ⲁϥⲙⲟϣⲓ - "the man walked"

ⲡⲓⲣⲱⲙⲓ ⲛⲉ ⲁϥⲙⲟϣⲓ ⲡⲉ - "the man had walked"

Another example is shown below:

ⲟⲩⲙⲏϣ ⲇⲉ ⲉⲃⲟⲗ ϧⲉⲛ ⲛⲓⲓⲟⲩⲇⲁⲓ ⲛⲉ ⲁⲩⲓ ⲡⲉ ϩⲁ ⲙⲁⲣⲓⲁ ⲛⲉⲙ ⲙⲁⲣⲑⲁ ⲉⲑⲃⲉ ⲡⲟⲩⲥⲟⲛ *(John 11:19)*

"and a multitude from the Jews had come to Mary and Martha for the sake of their brother"

Here you can see the ⲁⲩⲓ which means 'they came'; around the ⲁⲩⲓ are the ⲛⲉ and ⲡⲉ, so the combination takes the meaning of "they had come."

Vocab			
ⲉⲛⲧⲟⲗⲏ	commandment (Gk,f)	ⲥⲑⲉⲣⲧⲉⲣ	trembling(m)
ⲕⲗⲁⲩⲇⲓⲟⲥ	Claudius (prop. noun)	ϧⲱⲛⲧ ϧⲉⲛⲧ— ϧⲟⲛⲧ⸌ ϧⲉⲛⲧ	to approach, come near (v.i)
ⲟⲩⲁϩⲥⲁϩⲛⲓ	to lay a command (v.t)	ϣⲁⲓ	feast (m)
ⲡⲁⲥⲭⲁ	Passover (prop.noun)		

Exercise 7.2

a) ⲛⲉ ⲁⲩϯ ⲉⲛⲧⲟⲗⲏ ⲡⲉ ⲛ̇ϫⲉ ⲛⲓⲁⲣⲭⲓⲉⲣⲉⲩⲥ ⲛⲉⲙ ⲛⲓⲫⲁⲣⲓⲥⲉⲟⲥ *(John 11:57)*

b) ⲟⲩⲟϩ ⲁⲩⲓ ⲉ̇ⲃⲟⲗ ⲁⲩⲫⲱⲧ ⲉ̇ⲃⲟⲗ ϩⲁ ⲡⲓⲙ̇ϩⲁⲩ ⲛⲉ ⲁ ⲟⲩⲥⲑⲉⲣⲧⲉⲣ ⲅⲁⲣ ⲧⲁϩⲱⲟⲩ ⲡⲉ *(Mark 16:8)*

c) ⲛⲉ ⲁϥⲟⲩⲁϩⲥⲁϩⲛⲓ ⲡⲉ ⲛ̇ϫⲉ ⲕⲗⲁⲩⲇⲓⲟⲥ *(Acts 18:2)*

d) ⲛⲉ ⲁϥϧⲱⲛⲧ ⲇⲉ ⲡⲉ ⲛ̇ϫⲉ ⲡⲓⲡⲁⲥⲭⲁ ⲡ̇ϣⲁⲓ ⲛ̇ⲧⲉ ⲛⲓⲓⲟⲩⲇⲁⲓ *(John 6:4)*

7.1.ii. The relative imperfect

We first talked about the relative in section **(5.1.v)**, and revisited it when talking about the past tense in **(5.4)** and the future tense in **(5.9.ii)**. The relative is also used with the imperfect tense. Here the relative converter is ⲉ̀ which is attached to the beginning of the imperfect form, to also give the meaning of 'who', 'which' or 'when.'

E.g. ⲫⲁⲓ ⲉ̀ⲛⲁϥⲟⲓ ⲙ̀ⲃⲉⲗⲗⲉ *(John 9:24)*
"this who was blind"

Vocab			
ⲉⲣⲅⲁⲥⲓⲁ	work, business (Gk,f)		

Exercise 7.3

a) ⲡⲓⲙⲁ ⲉ̀ⲛⲁϥϣⲟⲡ ⲛ̀ϧⲏⲧϥ ⲛ̀ϫⲉ ⲡⲉⲧⲣⲟⲥ *(Acts 1:13)*

b) ⲑⲁⲓ ⲉ̀ⲛⲁⲥϯ ⲛ̀ⲟⲩⲙⲏϣ ⲛ̀ⲉⲣⲅⲁⲥⲓⲁ *(Acts 16:16)*

7.2. A matter of circumstance - the circumstantial tense

In the sentence "He saw the man while he was crying", you'll notice that there are two verbs, the first being 'saw' and the second 'crying.'

A closer look will reveal that there are actually two clauses **(6.1)** to the sentence, which are "He saw the man" and "while he was crying." The first clause here is called the *main clause* because it would make sense if it were read on its own. The second is called the *dependent* or *subordinate* clause, because it would not make sense on its own, so it actually *depends* on the main clause to have meaning.

In this case, the dependent clause can be thought of as describing the *circumstance* in which the main clause occurred. This is where we come to the concept of *circumstantial conversion*. Coptic has a special form which converts the verb of a dependent clause to make it clear that it is describing the circumstance in which an associated main clause occurs. Most of the Coptic tenses can be converted in this way.

The table below shows the circumstantial conversion of the verb ⲣⲓⲙⲓ in the present tense. You can see that the forms we end up with are only a little different to what we would have got if we had simply attached an ⲉ̀ to the normal first present tense form. This circumstantial conversion of the present tense is also called the *third present*.

I, crying	ⲉⲓⲣⲓⲙⲓ
you, crying (m)	ⲉⲕⲣⲓⲙⲓ
you, crying (plural)	ⲉⲣⲉⲣⲓⲙⲓ
he, crying	ⲉϥⲣⲓⲙⲓ
she crying	ⲉⲥⲣⲓⲙⲓ
we, crying	ⲉⲛⲣⲓⲙⲓ
you, crying (plural)	ⲉⲣⲉⲧⲉⲛⲣⲓⲙⲓ
they, crying	ⲉⲩⲣⲓⲙⲓ
pre subject form	ⲉⲣⲉ

So, if you were just to say the "he is crying" it would be ϥⲣⲓⲙⲓ
But if you were to say 'I saw the man crying', 'crying' now becomes a dependent clause describing the main clause 'I saw the man.'

ⲁⲓⲛⲁⲩ ⲉ̀ⲡⲓⲣⲱⲙⲓ ⲉϥⲣⲓⲙⲓ

The circumstantial also has a presubject form which goes before the noun which is ⲉⲣⲉ (which you may remember is identical to the ⲉⲣⲉ of the relative converter **(5.1.v)**). As for the perfect tense, the pre subject form of the circumstantial converter goes before the subject with the infinitive following the subject.

So for the example above you could alternatively have said:

ⲁⲓⲛⲁⲩ ⲉⲣⲉ ⲡⲓⲣⲱⲙⲓ ⲣⲓⲙⲓ

A particular verb which should be introduced here is **ⲕⲏⲛ**, which requires a dependent clause to be used in the circumstantial when it itself is used in a main clause. It has two particular meanings.

The first use is to mean "to cease from," here it comes before another verb which is in the circumstantial form to say that that particular action has ceased.

E.g. **ⲁϥⲕⲏⲛ ⲉϥⲥⲁϫⲓ.**
"he ceased speaking"

So You want to Learn Coptic?

In the second case it has the meaning of 'already', where it has a similar construction .E.g. ⲀⲨⲔⲎⲚ ⲈⲨϬⲒ Ⲙ̄ⲠⲞⲨⲂⲈⲬⲈ *(Matthew 6:5)*
"they have already received their reward."

> **Confusion Corner**
> *Relative versus Circumstantial*
>
> The circumstantial bears more than a passing resemblance to the Ⲉ⁻ form of the relative converter introduced in **(5.1.v)**; we said that the relative converters of the male, female and plural indefinite antecedent forms were ⲈϤ, ⲈⲤ and ⲈⲨ respectively, which are identical to the respective forms of the circumstantial. The presubject form of the circumstantial ⲈⲢⲈ is also one of the pre subject forms of the relative.
>
> One clue you can use to tell which conversion is called for is remembering that the circumstantial occurs in the same sentence as another verb which will be in a different tense. Also, the Ⲉ⁻ form of the relative converter is usually only used with an indefinite antecedent, so if there is an indefinite antecedent, it's likely that the Ⲉ⁻ is actually referring to the relative. Another trick which may help is to substitute the words, 'who', 'which' or 'while' for the Ⲉ⁻ and to see which makes the most sense. If translating 'who' or 'which', makes more sense, then it's the relative, if 'while' makes more sense, then it's the circumstantial.

Vocab			
Ⲁⲣⲭⲓⲉⲣⲉⲩⲥ	High priest (m)	ⲛ̀ⲥⲱϥ	behind him **(5.5)**
ⲃⲁⲧⲟⲥ	bush (Gk,m)	ⲟⲩⲱⲙ	to eat (v.t)
ⲃⲉⲭⲉ	reward (m)	ⲟⲩⲱϣ	wish, desire, will (m)
ⲉⲣⲡ̅ⲣⲟⲥⲉⲩⲭⲉⲥⲑⲉ	to pray (v.t)	ⲥ̀ⲕⲉⲩⲟⲥ	vessel (m)
ⲉⲣⲯⲁⲗⲓⲛ	to chant psalms (v.t)	ⲥⲩⲛⲁⲅⲱⲅⲏ	synagogue (f)
ⲉⲩⲁⲅⲅⲉⲗⲓⲟⲛ	gospel (m)	ⲧⲱⲙⲧ	amazement, trance (m)
ⲕⲱϯ ⲉ̀	to surround, seek, visit (v.t)	ϩⲁⲣⲟϥ	to him (prep. pronoun form)
ⲙⲁⲣⲧⲩⲣⲟⲥ	martyr (m)	ϩⲓⲱⲓϣ	to preach (v.i)
ⲙⲉⲧⲁⲛⲟⲓⲁ	repentance (f)	ϩⲟⲛϩⲉⲛ	to command (v.t)
ⲙⲉⲧⲟⲩⲣⲟ	kingdom (f)	ϩⲟⲣⲁⲙⲁ	vision (Gk,m)
ⲙⲟϩ	to fill, burn (v.t)	ϫⲱ	to speak (v.i)
ⲙ̀ⲫⲣⲏϯ	like (adv)	ϯⲙⲓ	village (m)
ⲛⲉⲙⲱⲟⲩ	with them (prep. pronoun form) **(5.5)**	ϯⲥ̀ⲃⲱ	To teach (v.i)
ⲛⲟⲙⲟⲥ	law (m)	ϯⲱⲙⲥ	to baptise (v.t)

Exercise 7.4

a) ⲁⲩⲓ̀ ϩⲁⲣⲟϥ ⲉϥϯⲥ̀ⲃⲱ ⲛ̀ϫⲉ ⲛⲓⲁⲣⲭⲓⲉⲣⲉⲩⲥ ⲛ̀ⲧⲉ ⲡⲓⲗⲁⲟⲥ (Matthew 21:23)

b) ⲡⲓⲃⲁⲧⲟⲥ ⲉ̀ⲧⲁ Ⲙⲱⲩ̀ⲥⲏⲥ ⲛⲁⲩ ⲉ̀ⲣⲟϥ ⲉⲃⲟⲗ ϩⲓ ⲡ̀ϣⲁϥⲉ ⲉⲣⲉ ⲡⲓⲭ̀ⲣⲱⲙ ⲙⲟϩ ⲛ̀ϧⲏⲧϥ (*Theotokia of the fifth day*)

c) ⲁϥⲛⲁⲩ ⲉ̀ⲟⲩⲣⲱⲙⲓ ⲉϥϩⲉⲙⲥⲓ (Matthew 9:9)

So You want to Learn Coptic?

d) ⲁⲩⲙⲟϣⲓ ⲛ̀ⲥⲱϥ ⲛ̀ϫⲉ ⲃⲉⲗⲗⲉ ⲃ̅ ⲉⲩⲱϣ ⲉ̀ⲃⲟⲗ *(Matthew 9:27)*

e) ⲟⲩⲟϩ ⲛⲁϥⲕⲱϯ ⲡⲉ ⲛ̀ϫⲉ Ⲓⲏ̅ⲥ̅ ⲉ̀ⲛⲓⲃⲁⲕⲓ ⲧⲏⲣⲟⲩ ⲛⲉⲙ ⲛⲓϯⲙⲓ ⲉϥϯⲥⲃⲱ ⲛ̀ϧⲣⲏⲓ ϧⲉⲛ ⲛⲟⲩⲥⲩⲛⲁⲅⲱⲅⲏ ⲟⲩⲟϩ ⲉϥϩⲓⲱⲓϣ ⲙ̀ⲡⲓⲉⲩⲁⲅⲅⲉⲗⲓⲟⲛ ⲛ̀ⲧⲉ ϯⲙⲉⲧⲟⲩⲣⲟ *(Matthew 9:35)*

f) ⲟⲩⲟϩ ⲉϥⲟⲩⲱⲙ ⲛⲉⲙⲱⲟⲩ ⲁϥϩⲟⲛϩⲉⲛ ⲛⲱⲟⲩ *(Acts 1:4)*

g) ⲁ ⲡⲁⲓⲱⲧ ⲕⲏⲛ ⲉ̀ⲥϧⲁⲓ ⲙ̀ⲡⲉⲕⲣⲁⲛ *(AmHyv p2)*

h) ⲁ̀ⲛⲟⲕ ⲛⲁⲓϧⲉⲛ ⲓⲟⲡⲡⲏ ϯⲡⲟⲗⲓⲥ ⲉⲓⲉⲣⲡ̅ⲣⲟⲥⲉⲩⲭⲉⲥⲑⲉ ⲟⲩⲟϩ ⲁⲓⲛⲁⲩ ϧⲉⲛ ⲟⲩⲧⲱⲙⲧ ⲉ̀ⲟⲩϩⲟⲣⲁⲙⲁ ⲉϥⲛⲏⲟⲩ ⲉ̀ⲡⲉⲥⲏⲧ ⲛ̀ϫⲉ ⲟⲩⲥⲕⲉⲩⲟⲥ *(Acts 11:5)*

i) ⲁⲗⲗⲁ ⲉ̀ⲣⲉ ⲡⲉϥⲟⲩⲱϣ ϣⲱⲡⲓ ϧⲉⲛ ⲫ̀ⲛⲟⲙⲟⲥ ⲙ̀Ⲡ̅ⲟ̅ⲥ̅ *(Psalm 1:2 1:2)*

Practice text 10
Luke 8:1-3

It's now the time to have a passage from the Gospels. This particular section gives the chance to practice both the circumstantial and the relative.

Ⲟⲩⲟϩ ⲁⲥϣⲱⲡⲓ ⲙⲉⲛⲉⲛⲥⲁ ⲛⲁⲓ ⲟⲩⲟϩ ⲛ̀ⲑⲟϥ ⲛⲁϥⲙⲟϣⲓ ⲕⲁⲧⲁ ⲃⲁⲕⲓ ⲛⲉⲙ ϯⲙⲓ ⲉϥϩⲓⲱⲓϣ ⲟⲩⲟϩ ⲉϥϩⲓϣⲉⲛⲛⲟⲩϥⲓ ⲛ̀ϯⲙⲉⲧⲟⲩⲣⲟ ⲛ̀ⲧⲉ Ⲫϯ. Ⲟⲩⲟϩ ⲡⲓⲓ̅ⲃ̅ ⲉⲧⲛⲉⲙⲁϥ. ⲛⲉⲙ ϩⲁⲛⲕⲉϩⲓⲟⲙⲓ ⲛⲏ ⲉⲧⲁϥⲉⲣⲫⲁϩⲣⲓ ⲉ̀ⲣⲱⲟⲩ ⲉ̀ⲃⲟⲗ ϧⲉⲛ ϩⲁⲛⲡ̅ⲛ̅ⲁ̅ ⲉⲧϩⲱⲟⲩ ⲛⲉⲙ ϩⲁⲛϣⲱⲛⲓ.

Ⲙⲁⲣⲓⲁ ⲑⲏ ⲉ̀ⲧⲟⲩⲙⲟⲩϯ ⲉ̀ⲣⲟⲥ ϫⲉ ϯⲙⲁⲅⲇⲁⲗⲓⲛⲏ. ⲑⲏ ⲉ̀ⲧⲁϥⲓ ⲡⲓⲍ̅ ⲛ̀ⲇⲉⲙⲱⲛ ⲉ̀ⲃⲟⲗ ϩⲓⲱⲧⲥ.

Ⲛⲉⲙ ⲓⲱⲁⲛⲛⲁ ⲧ̀ⲥϩⲓⲙⲓ ⲛ̀ⲭⲟⲩⲍⲁ ⲡⲓⲉⲡⲓⲧⲣⲟⲡⲟⲥ ⲛ̀ⲧⲉ ⲏⲣⲱⲇⲏⲥ ⲛⲉⲙ ⲥⲟⲩⲥⲁⲛⲛⲁ ⲛⲉⲙ ϩⲁⲛⲕⲉⲭⲱⲟⲩⲛⲓ ⲉ̀ⲟϣ ⲛⲏ ⲉ̀ⲛⲁⲩϣⲉⲙϣⲓ ⲙ̀ⲙⲟϥ ⲉ̀ⲃⲟⲗ ϧⲉⲛ ⲛⲟⲩϩⲩⲡⲁⲣⲭⲟⲛⲧⲁ.

Vocab			
ⲉⲣⲫⲁϧⲣⲓ	to heal (v.t)	ϩⲓⲟⲩⲓ ϩⲓ- ϩⲓⲧ⸍	to throw, strike (v.t)
ⲉⲡⲓⲧⲣⲟⲡⲟⲥ	steward (m)	ϩⲱⲟⲩ	to be evil (v.i)
ⲛ̀ⲟⲩⲥⲏⲟⲩ	for a time (adv.) (9.1)	ϩⲩⲡⲁⲭⲟⲛⲧⲁ	possessions, property (Gk,m)
ⲭⲟⲩⲍⲁ	Chuza (prop. noun)	ϯⲛⲟⲩ	now (adv.) (9.1)
ϣⲱⲛⲓ	sickness, disease (m)		

7.2.i. Circumstantial conversion of the past perfect

The circumstantial is not only used with the present tense, but is in fact with many of the other tenses. The next tense we'll look at converting here is the past perfect. The conversion is achieved by adding the prefix ⲉ̀ before the relevant form of the past perfect (5.2) where it gives the meaning of 'when', 'as' and sometimes 'if.'

E.g ⲉ̀ⲁϥⲁⲙⲁϩⲓ ⲇⲉ ⲙ̀Ⲡⲉⲧⲣⲟⲥ ⲛⲉⲙ Ⲓⲱⲁⲛⲛⲏⲥ ⲁϥⲫⲱⲧ ϩⲁⲣⲱⲟⲩ ⲛ̀ϫⲉ ⲡⲓⲗⲁⲟⲥ ⲧⲏⲣϥ (Acts 3:11)

You can see that there are two separate verbs here using the past tense, the first being ⲁⲙⲁϩⲓ "to hold, grasp" and the second ⲫⲱⲧ "to run". ⲁⲙⲁϩⲓ is converted with the circumstantial by adding an ⲉ̀ to let you know that it is occurring at the same time as the second verb. So the verse is translated:

"And as he held Peter and John all the people ran before them."

7.2.ii. Circumstantial conversion of the future tense

Not to be left out, the first future tense (5.9) is also converted in much the same way. Once again, the ⲉ̀ is added to the normal first future construction. This new future tense is also known as the third future. When used in this way, the expression has the meaning of 'about to.' For example:

ⲉⲩⲛⲁϫⲱⲕ ⲇⲉ ⲉ̀ⲃⲟⲗ ⲛ̀ϫⲉ ⲡⲓⲍ̄ ⲛ̀ⲉϩⲟⲟⲩ (Acts 21:27)

So You want to Learn Coptic?

"And when the 7 days were about to finish"

Vocab			
ⲁⲅⲓⲟⲥ	saint (m)	ⲟⲩⲱⲛ, ⲟⲩⲏⲛ (q)	to open/ to be opened (q)
ⲉⲣⲫⲉⲓ	altar (m)	ⲡⲁⲣⲉⲙⲃⲟⲗⲏ	castle (f)
ⲑⲱⲕⲉⲙ	to draw out (v.t)	ⲣⲉϥⲁⲣⲉϩ	guard (m)
ⲕⲁⲧⲁⲡⲉⲧⲁⲥⲙⲁ	veil (Gk,m)	ⲣⲟ	mouth (m)
ⲗⲩⲇⲇⲁ	Lydda (prop. noun)	ⲣⲱⲟⲩ	mouths (pl)
ⲙⲁ	place (m)	ⲥⲏϥⲓ	sword (f)
ⲙⲏϯ	middle (f)	ⲥⲱⲛϩ	to bind (v.t)
ⲙⲉⲩⲓ	to think, suppose (v.i)	ϣⲁϣⲛⲓ	to win, gain (v.t)
ⲙⲟⲩⲛⲕ	to cease, perish (v.i)	ϧⲱⲧⲉⲃ ϧⲁⲧⲉⲃ- ϧⲟⲑⲃ	to kill (v.t)
ⲛⲉϩⲥⲓ	to awaken (v.i)	ϩⲟⲛϩⲉⲛ	to command (v.t)

Exercise 7.5

a) ⲉϥⲛⲁⲙⲟⲩⲛⲕ ⲇⲉ ⲛϫⲉ ⲡⲓⲣⲏ ⲁ ⲡⲓⲕⲁⲧⲁⲡⲉⲧⲁⲥⲙⲁ ⲛⲧⲉ ⲡⲓⲉⲣⲫⲉⲓ ⲫⲱϧ ϧⲉⲛ ⲧⲉϥⲙⲏϯ (*Luke 23:45*)

b) ⲡⲓⲓ̅ⲃ̅ ⲁϥⲟⲩⲟⲣⲡⲟⲩ ⲛϫⲉ Ⲓⲏ̅ⲥ̅ ⲉⲁϥϩⲟⲛϩⲉⲛ ⲛⲱⲟⲩ (*Matthew 10:5*)

c) ⲉⲩⲛⲁⲉⲛϥ ⲇⲉ ⲉϧⲟⲩⲛ ⲉϯⲡⲁⲣⲉⲙⲃⲟⲗⲏ (*Acts 21:37*)

d) Ⲁⲥϣⲱⲡⲓ ⲇⲉ ⲉⲣⲉ ⲡⲉⲧⲣⲟⲥ ⲛⲁⲥⲓⲛⲓ ⲉⲃⲟⲗ ϩⲓⲧⲉⲛ ⲛⲓⲥⲙⲏⲟⲩ ⲧⲏⲣⲟⲩ ⲁϥⲓ ϣⲁ ⲛⲓⲁⲅⲓⲟⲥ ϧⲉⲛ ⲗⲩⲇⲇⲁ (*Acts 9:32*)

Now and then again

e) ⲉⲁϥϣⲁϣⲛⲓ ⲇⲉ ⲉⲟⲩⲛⲓϣϯ ⲛ̀ⲛⲁⲓ ⲛ̀ⲧⲉ Ⲫϯ ⲁϥϣⲱⲡⲓ ⲛ̀ⲭⲣⲏⲥⲧⲓⲁⲛⲟⲥ *(S.Pachomii vita pg.1)*

f) ⲉⲧⲁϥⲛⲉϩⲥⲓ ⲇⲉ ⲛ̀ϫⲉ ⲡⲓⲣⲉϥⲁⲣⲉϩ ⲛ̀ⲧⲉ ⲡⲓⲙⲁ ⲛ̀ⲥⲱⲛϩ ⲟⲩⲟϩ ⲉⲧⲁϥⲛⲁⲩ ⲉ̀ⲛⲓⲣⲱⲟⲩ ⲛ̀ⲧⲉ ⲡⲓϣ̀ⲧⲉⲕⲟ ⲉⲩⲟⲩⲏⲛ ⲁϥⲑⲱⲕⲉⲙ ⲛ̀ⲧⲉϥⲥⲏϥⲓ ⲉϥⲛⲁϧⲟⲑⲃⲉϥ ⲉϥⲙⲉⲩⲓ̀ ϫⲉ ⲁⲩⲫⲱⲧ ⲛ̀ϫⲉ ⲛⲏⲉⲧⲥⲱⲛϩ *(Acts 16:27)*

So You want to Learn Coptic?

8. VERBS WITH THEIR OWN RULES

8.1. Some unusual verbs

Every language has rules, or laws guiding grammar. Whereas most verbs are law abiding, some verbs have poked their tongue out at convention and chosen their own rules of grammar. These verbs are reasonably common, so they can't be ignored. We'll just have to go along and learn them.

The first of these verbs we'll look at is:

ⲭⲱ *(to say)*

which has the following forms:

infinitive	prenominal	pronominal	qualitative
ⲭⲱ	ⲭⲉ⁻	ⲭⲟ⫽ ⲭⲟⲧ⫽	—

The infinitive

So far so normal, so how does this verb differ? The first way it differs is that the infinitive is always followed by the word ⲙⲙⲟⲥ. This word has rather unflatteringly been called a "dummy word", meaning that it always has to follow ⲭⲱ, but though it could be literally translated as 'it' is usually left untranslated.

E.g. ϯⲭⲱ ⲙⲙⲟⲥ ⲛⲱⲧⲉⲛ

"I say (it) to you"

So in the above sentence, the direct object is represented by ⲙⲙⲟⲥ, and the indirect object by ⲛⲱⲧⲉⲛ.

Pronominal form

You'll note that there are two different pronominal forms for ⲭⲱ. The first form ⲭⲟ⫽ is used to quote text. It always takes ⲥ as its pronominal suffix **(5.3.i)**, so that in doing so it literally has the meaning of 'said *it*.' Note that the pronominal form in itself doesn't tell you who is being spoken to, as the pronoun ⲥ only ever refers to what is being said, not who it's being said to.

E.g. ⲁϥϫⲟⲥ

"he said (it)"

Now, with both forms of this verb, the conjunction ϫⲉ **(6.1.ii)** always comes before whatever is being said:

So, finishing of our two examples:

†ϫⲱ ⲙ̀ⲙⲟⲥ ⲛⲱⲧⲉⲛ ϫⲉ ⲫⲁⲓ ⲡⲉ Ⲡⲭ̅ⲥ̅

"I say to you that "this is the Christ"

ⲁϥϫⲟⲥ ϫⲉ ⲫⲁⲓ ⲡⲉ Ⲡⲭ̅ⲥ̅

"He said this is the Christ"

The second form ϫⲟⲧ⸍ is always used with the suffix ⲟⲩ. It is not used to quote text, but to indirectly refer to what was said:

E.g. ⲛⲁⲓ ⲇⲉ ⲧⲏⲣⲟⲩ ⲁ Ⲓⲏⲥ ϫⲟⲧⲟⲩ ⲛ̀ⲛⲓⲙⲏϣ ϧⲉⲛ ϩⲁⲛⲡⲁⲣⲁⲃⲟⲗⲏ

(Matthew 13:34)

"and all these things Jesus said to the multitude in parables"

(Note that the ϫⲟⲧⲟⲩ here refers to the ⲛⲁⲓ which is the plural demonstrative pronoun meaning 'these' **(2.2.ii)**.)

The construct form

The construct form is just ϫⲉ on its own. As with ϫⲟⲧⲟⲩ, it's used to refer indirectly to speech rather than to quote it:

E.g. ⲁϥϫⲉ ⲕⲉⲡⲁⲣⲁⲃⲟⲗⲏ ⲛⲱⲟⲩ

"He said another parable to them" *(Luke 6:39)*

Note that the actual words of the parable weren't quoted, but that reference was only made to a parable having been said.

Past infinitive

You'll notice that as with other verbs, the infinitive was combined with the ⲁϥ to produce the past tense. There is however also a special form for ϫⲱ which is used exclusively for the past tense called the *past infinitive* which is ⲡⲉϫⲉ

Now, this infinitive only ever comes before the subject, unlike most other verbs where the subject comes before the infinitive:

ⲡⲉϫⲉ ⲒⲎⲤ ⲛⲱⲟⲩ *(Matthew 9:15)*
"Jesus said to them"

Once again, this verb has a special pronominal form for the past tense. Even though the pronoun is attached to the end of the verb, it indicates the subject, *not* the object. That is it tells you who the speaker is, rather than what the speaker said.

ⲡⲉϫⲏⲓ	I said
ⲡⲉϫⲁⲕ	you said (m)
ⲡⲉϫⲉ	you said (f)
ⲡⲉϫⲁϥ	he said
ⲡⲉϫⲁⲥ	she said
ⲡⲉϫⲁⲛ	we said
ⲡⲉϫⲱⲧⲉⲛ	you said (plural)
ⲡⲉϫⲱⲟⲩ	they said

This form also uses the indirect object (**5.7**) to indicate who was spoken to. If speech is to be quoted, our friend ϫⲉ is again used to precede the quote:

E.g. ⲡⲉϫⲁϥ ⲛⲏⲓ ϫⲉ ⲫⲁⲓ ⲡⲉ Ⲡⲭⲥ
"He said to me "this is the Christ""

`ϩⲛⲉ

The next irregular verb we'll look at is ϩⲛⲉ, which means "it is pleasing to", "to be willing" or "to be content", "agree."

This has two main uses. In the first case, it is used with another verb, often being translated as an adverb to say that the first verb was performed willingly. In these cases, ϩⲛⲉ is conjugated in the following way after the verb.

So You want to Learn Coptic?

ⲉϩⲛⲏⲓ	I willingly
ⲉϩⲛⲁⲕ	you willingly (m)
ⲉϩⲛⲉ	you willingly (f)
ⲉϩⲛⲁϥ	he willingly
ⲉϩⲛⲁⲥ	she willingly
ⲉϩⲛⲁⲛ	we willingly
ⲉϩⲛⲱⲧⲉⲛ	you willingly (pl)
ⲉϩⲛⲱⲟⲩ	they willingly

E.g. ⲁⲓⲣⲓ ⲙ̀ⲫⲁⲓ ⲉϩⲛⲏⲓ
"I did willingly"

In the second case, it is used with the relative converter ⲉⲧ (5.1.v) which comes after one of the forms from the table above, so ⲉⲧⲉϩⲛⲉⲓ means "which I wish."

E.g. ϩⲱⲃ ⲛⲓⲃⲉⲛ ⲉⲧⲉϩⲛⲱⲟⲩ
"all that they wish"

As with the other tenses we've come across, the relative converter may be combined with the article ⲡ to form the relative substantial ⲡⲉⲧ to convert the verb to a noun. So for example,

ⲡⲉⲧⲉ̀ϩⲛⲁⲕ means "that which is pleasing to you" or "your will."

ⲣⲁⲛⲉ- ⲣⲁⲛ⸗

This particular verb has the meaning "to please." It's special because it doesn't actually have an infinitive form; so it can only be used with the construct or pronominal forms.
Example:

ⲛⲏⲉⲑⲟⲩⲁⲃ ⲧⲏⲣⲟⲩ ⲉ̀ⲧⲁϥⲣⲁⲛⲁⲕ *(Commemoration of the Saints, Liturgy of St.Basil)*
"all the saints who have pleased you"

Adverbs

ⲟⲩⲉⲧ−

This verb, which means "to be distinct, different" is like ⲣⲁⲛ⸌ because it doesn't have an infinitive form. However, unlike ⲣⲁⲛ⸌ ⲟⲩⲉⲧ doesn't have a pronominal form either; in fact it only has a construct form:

E.g. ⲁⲗⲗⲁ ⲟⲩⲉⲧ ⲥⲁⲣⲝ ⲙⲉⲛ ⲛ̀ⲧⲉ ⲛⲓⲣⲱⲙⲓ ⲟⲩⲉⲧ ⲥⲁⲣⲝ ⲛ̀ⲧⲉ ⲛⲓⲧⲉⲃⲛⲱⲟⲩⲓ *(1 Corinthians 15:39)*

"but indeed the flesh of the men is different, the flesh of the beasts is different"

Vocab			
ⲁ̀ⲫⲉ	head (f)	ⲣⲉϥϯⲱⲙⲥ	Baptist (m)
ⲅⲁⲍⲟⲫⲩⲗⲁⲕⲓⲟⲛ	treasury (Gk,m)	ⲥⲱⲛⲧ ⲥⲉⲛⲧ− ⲥⲟⲛⲧ⸌	to create (v.t)
Ⲏⲣⲱⲇⲏⲥ	Herod (prop. noun)	ϩⲓⲛⲓ ϩⲉⲛ− ϩⲉⲛ⸌	to move self forward, backward
ⲓⲣⲓ ⲉⲣ− ⲁⲓ⸌ ⲟⲓ	to do, make (v.t)	ϩⲗⲟϫ	sweetness (m)
ⲙⲉⲧⲁⲛⲟⲓⲁ	repentance (Gk,f)	ϩⲱⲃ	thing (m)
ⲙ̀ⲫⲣⲏϯ	like, as (adv.)	ϭⲟⲥϫⲉⲥ	to dance (v.i)
Ⲡⲓⲗⲁⲧⲟⲥ	Pilate (prop.noun)	ϯⲱⲙⲥ	to baptize (v.t)
ⲡⲓⲟⲩⲁⲓ ⲡⲓⲟⲩⲁⲓ	each one		

Exercise 8.1

a) ⲡⲉϫⲉ Ⲡⲓⲗⲁⲧⲟⲥ ⲛⲱⲟⲩ *(Matthew 27:17)*

b) ⲁϥϫⲉ ϩⲱⲃ ⲛⲓⲃⲉⲛ ⲛⲏⲓ ⲉⲧⲁⲓⲁⲓⲧⲟⲩ *(John 4:39)*

c) ⲙ̀ⲫⲣⲏϯ ⲉⲧⲉϩⲛⲏⲓ ⲁ̀ⲛⲟⲕ ⲁⲛ ⲁⲗⲗⲁ ⲙ̀ⲫⲣⲏϯ ⲉⲧⲉϩⲛⲁⲕ ⲛ̀ⲑⲟⲕ *(Matthew 26:39)*

d) ⲁϥⲣⲁⲛⲁϥ ⲙ̀Ⲫϯ *(Hebrews 11:5)*

e) ⲡⲉϫⲉ Ⲛⲁⲑⲁⲛⲁⲏⲗ ⲛⲁϥ *(John 1:48)*

f) ⲛⲁⲕⲉϩⲓⲱⲓϣ ⲉⲕⲭⲱ ⲙ̀ⲙⲟⲥ ϫⲉ ⲁ̀ⲛⲟⲕ ⲙⲉⲛ ϯⲱⲙⲥ ⲛⲱⲧⲉⲛ ϧⲉⲛ ⲟⲩⲙⲱⲟⲩ ⲙ̀ⲙⲉⲧⲁⲛⲟⲓⲁ ⲉ̀ⲡ̀ⲭⲱ ⲉ̀ⲃⲟⲗ ⲛ̀ⲧⲉ ⲛⲓⲛⲟⲃⲓ *(Doxology for Paramoun of feast of Epiphany)*

g) ⲛⲁⲓⲥⲁϫⲓ ⲁϥϫⲟⲧⲟⲩ ϧⲉⲛ ⲡⲓⲅⲁⲍⲟⲫⲩⲗⲁⲕⲓⲟⲛ *(John 8:20)*

h) ⲁϥϫⲉ ⲧⲁⲓⲡⲁⲣⲁⲃⲟⲗⲏ ⲛⲱⲟⲩ ⲉϥϫⲱ ⲙ̀ⲙⲟⲥ *(Luke 15:3)*

i) ⲁⲕⲥⲱⲛⲧ ⲛ̀ϩⲱⲃ ⲛⲓⲃⲉⲛ ⲟⲩⲟϩ ⲡⲉⲧⲉϩⲛⲁⲕ ⲁϥϣⲱⲡⲓ ⲟⲩⲟϩ ⲁⲩⲥⲱⲛⲧ *(Revelation 4:11)*

j) ⲛ̀ⲑⲟⲥ ⲇⲉ ⲡⲉϫⲁⲥ ϫⲉ ϯⲁⲫⲉ ⲛ̀ⲓⲱⲁⲛⲛⲏⲥ ⲡⲓⲣⲉϥϯⲱⲙⲥ *(Mark 6:24)*

k) ⲟⲩⲟϩ ⲟⲩⲉⲧ ⲡ̀ϩ̀ⲗⲟϫ ⲙ̀ⲡⲓⲟⲩⲁⲓ ⲡⲓⲟⲩⲁⲓ *(hom vat ii pg.207)*

l) ⲁⲩϫⲉ ⲫⲁⲓ ⲡⲉ Ⲉⲙⲙⲁⲛⲟⲩⲏⲗ *(Doxology for Palm Sunday)*

m) ϯϫⲱ ⲙ̀ⲙⲟⲥ ⲛⲱⲧⲉⲛ ϫⲉ ϩⲉⲛ ⲑⲏⲛⲟⲩ ⲉ̀ⲃⲟⲗ ϩⲁ ⲛⲁⲓⲣⲱⲙⲓ *(Acts 5:38)*

n) ⲁⲥϭⲟⲥϫⲉⲥ ⲛ̀ϫⲉ ϯϣⲉⲣⲓ ⲛ̀ⲏⲣⲱⲇⲓⲁⲥ ϧⲉⲛ ⲑⲙⲏϯ ⲟⲩⲟϩ ⲁⲥⲣⲁⲛⲁϥ ⲛ̀ⲏⲣⲱⲇⲏⲥ *(Matthew 14:6)*

o) ⲁⲩⲓⲣⲓ ⲛⲁϥ ⲛ̀ϩⲱⲃ ⲛⲓⲃⲉⲛ ⲉⲧⲉϩⲛⲱⲟⲩ *(Matthew 17:12)*

8.2. The impersonal verbs

The term 'impersonal' doesn't sound very friendly; but no disrespect is intended to the verb it describes. It simply means that the verb isn't being performed by a person, hence the term 'impersonal'.

There are two main groups of impersonal verbs in Coptic. Those where the subject of the sentence is 'it', which is represented by the third person singular feminine form, and those which are purely impersonal, in that they do not use any form of the subject at all.

8.2.i. Subject is 'it'

| ⲁⲥϣⲱⲡⲓ | it happened |
| ⲥ̀ϣⲉ | it is appropriate, fitting |

Adverbs

ⲥⲉⲙ̅ⲡ̅ϣⲁ	it is befitting to, it is proper to

Let's take ⲁⲥϣⲱⲡⲓ as our first example. This form uses the feminine singular form of the verb, as indicated by the ⲥ so it would literally be translated as 'she happened', but because it is being used as an impersonal verb here, it is translated as 'it happened.' Now ϣⲱⲡⲓ isn't always used as impersonal verb, for example ⲁϥϣⲱⲡⲓ means 'he became,' and ⲁⲥϣⲱⲡⲓ can mean "she became", but in the use of the impersonal expression it means "it happened."

E.g. ⲁⲥϣⲱⲡⲓ ⲛ̅ϫⲉ ⲟⲩⲛⲓϣϯ ⲛ̅ϩⲟϯ ⲉ̀ϩⲣⲏⲓ ⲉϫⲉⲛ ϯⲉⲕⲕⲗⲏⲥⲓⲁ ⲧⲏⲣⲥ
(Acts 5:11)
"a great fear came (happened) down upon the whole Church"

Likewise, ⲥ̀ϣⲉ would literally mean 'she is appropriate' but as with the previous example, it is translated to mean 'it is appropriate.' It is used before another verb to tell you that that verb is "appropriate to do." Unlike ϣⲱⲡⲓ, ⲥ̀ϣⲉ is only ever used as an impersonal expression.
Also unlike ⲁⲥϣⲱⲡⲓ, ⲥ̀ϣⲉ needs to be followed by an ⲉ̀.

E.g ⲥ̀ϣⲉ ⲛⲁⲛ ⲉ̀ϯϩⲱϯ ⲙ̅ⲡⲟⲩⲣⲟ *(Luke 20:22)*
"It is appropriate for us to pay tribute to the king"

Alternatively, it may be followed by the subjunctive **(6.2)**:
E.g. ⲡⲓⲙⲁ ⲉ̀ⲧⲥ̀ϣⲉ ⲛ̅ⲧⲟⲩϯϩⲁⲡ ⲉ̀ⲣⲟⲓ *(Acts 25:10)*
"the place where it is appropriate for me to be judged"

To use the negative form, we simply use our old friend ⲁⲛ **(239).**

E.g. ⲥ̀ϣⲉ ⲛⲁⲕ ⲁⲛ ⲉ̀ϭⲓ ϯⲥ̀ϩⲓⲙⲓ ⲙ̅ⲡⲉⲕⲥⲟⲛ *(Mark 6:18)*
"it is not appropriate for you to take the wife of your brother"

As with ϣⲱⲡⲓ, ⲉⲙ̅ⲡ̅ϣⲁ is not always an impersonal verb, but it can be used as one when preceded by ⲥ̀. It likes to be followed by ⲛ̀.

So You want to Learn Coptic?

ⲥⲉⲙⲡϣⲁ ⲛ̀ⲥⲱⲧⲉⲙ ⲛ̀ⲥⲁ Ⲫϯ *(Acts 5:29)*
"it is appropriate to obey God"

8.2.ii. *No subject at all*

As mentioned above, these impersonal verbs have no subject indicated at all. Some examples are shown below.

ⲟⲩⲟⲛ	there is
ⲙ̀ⲙⲟⲛ	there is no
ϩⲱϯ	it is necessary

Ⲟⲩⲟⲛ is referred to as the *existential*, because it has the important role of telling us that something exists, and its negative form ⲙ̀ⲙⲟⲛ is referred to as the negative existential which conversely tells us if it doesn't exist. The noun following the existential is always preceded by an indefinite article, and that following the negative existential has no article at all.

E.g: ⲟⲩⲟⲛ ⲟⲩⲣⲱⲙⲓ
"there is a man"

ⲙ̀ⲙⲟⲛ ⲣⲱⲙⲓ
"there is no man"

Only the imperfect is used to make the past tense of this verb **(7.1)**, which is made by taking the presubject form ⲛⲉ and putting before the ⲟⲩⲟⲛ.

E.g. ⲛⲉ ⲟⲩⲟⲛ ⲟⲩⲣⲱⲙⲓ
"There was a man"

As with other verbs used in the imperfect, an optional ⲡⲉ can be placed at the end of the sentence to give the same meaning:

ⲛⲉ ⲟⲩⲟⲛ ⲟⲩⲣⲱⲙⲓ ⲡⲉ

In fact, this particular construction is used many times in the Bible, including John 1:1

Ϧⲉⲛ ϯⲁⲣⲭⲏ ⲛⲉ ⲡ̀ⲥⲁϫⲓ ⲡⲉ
"In the beginning was the word"

ϩⲱϯ

As was mentioned in **(6.2)**, the impersonal verb ϩⲱϯ, which means "it is necessary" is used with the subjunctive.

When a noun is the subject of the sentence, the pre subject form ⲛ̀ⲧⲉ is used.

E.g. ϩⲱϯ ⲛ̀ⲧⲉ ⲡ̀ϣⲏⲣⲓ ⲙ̀ⲫⲣⲱⲙⲓ ϭⲓ ⲛ̀ⲟⲩⲙⲏϣ ⲛ̀ϭⲓⲥⲓ *(Mark 8:31)*

"it is necessary for the son of man to receive many sufferings"

When a pronoun is being used as the subject, the conjugated form of the subjunctive is used.

E.g. ϩⲱϯ ⲛ̀ⲧⲁⲛⲁⲩ ⲉ̀ⲧⲕⲉⲣⲱⲙⲏ *(Acts 19:21)*

"it is necessary that I also see Rome"

Sometimes, ⲡⲉ is placed in between ϩⲱϯ and the subjunctive.

E.g. ϩⲱϯ ⲡⲉ ⲛ̀ⲧⲟⲩϣⲱⲡⲓ *(Mark 13:7)*

"it is necessary that they happen"

Vocab			
ⲕⲁϩⲥ	custom, habit (f)	Ⲣⲱⲙⲏ	Rome (prop.noun)
ⲑⲱⲟⲩϯ ⲑⲟⲩⲉⲧ⸗ ⲑⲟⲩⲱⲧ⸗ ⲑⲟⲩⲏⲧ	to assemble, gather, congregate (v.i)	ϣⲱⲡ ϣⲉⲡ⸗ ϣⲟⲡ⸗ ϣⲏⲡ	to receive, accept(v.t)
ⲙⲉⲣⲟⲥ	part, share (m)	ϫⲱⲣⲓ	strong, bold (adj.)

Exercise 8.2

a) ϩⲱϯ ⲡⲉ ⲛ̀ⲧⲉ ⲛⲓⲫⲏⲟⲩⲓ ϣⲟⲡϥ ⲉ̀ⲣⲱⲟⲩ *(Acts 3:21)*

b) ⲓⲥϫⲉ ⲇⲉ ⲟⲩⲟⲛ ⲟⲩⲁⲓ ϧⲉⲛ ⲑⲏⲛⲟⲩ *(James 1:5)*

c) ⲟⲩⲟϩ ⲥⲉϩⲓⲱⲓϣ ⲛⲁⲛ ⲛ̀ϩⲁⲛⲕⲉⲕⲁϩⲥ ⲛⲁⲓ ⲉ̀ⲧⲉⲥϣⲉ ⲛⲁⲛ ⲁⲛ ⲉ̀ϣⲟⲡⲟⲩ *(Acts 16:21)*

d) ⲙ̀ⲙⲟⲛ ⲟⲩⲙⲏϣ ⲛ̀ⲥⲁⲃⲉ ⲕⲁⲧⲁ ⲥⲁⲣⲝ̅ ⲙ̀ⲙⲟⲛ ⲟⲩⲙⲏϣ ⲛ̀ϫⲱⲣⲓ *(1 Corinthians 1:26)*

So You want to Learn Coptic?

e) ⲉⲧⲁϥⲉⲙⲓ ⲇⲉ ⲛ̇ϫⲉ ⲡⲁⲩⲗⲟⲥ ϫⲉ ⲟⲩⲟⲛ ⲟⲩⲙⲉⲣⲟⲥ *(Acts 23:6)*

f) ⲥ̇ϣⲉ ⲅⲁⲣ ⲛ̇ⲧⲉϥⲛⲁϩϯ *(Hebrews 11:6)*

g) ⲛⲉ ⲟⲩⲟⲛ ⲟⲩⲙⲏϣ ⲇⲉ ⲉⲩⲑⲟⲩⲏⲧ *(Acts 1:15)*

h) ⲛⲏ ⲉ̇ⲧⲉ ⲥ̇ϣⲉ ⲛ̇ⲁⲓⲧⲟⲩ ⲁⲛ *(Leviticus 4:2)*

i) ⲓⲥϫⲉ ⲟⲩⲟⲛ ⲟⲩϩⲱⲃ ⲉϥϩⲱⲟⲩ ϧⲉⲛ ⲡⲁⲓⲣⲱⲙⲓ *(Acts 25:5)*

j) ⲙ̇ⲙⲟⲛ ⲟⲩⲥ̇ϩⲓⲙⲓ ⲭⲱⲣⲓⲥ ⲣⲱⲙⲓ ⲟⲩⲇⲉ ⲣⲱⲙⲓ ⲭⲱⲣⲓⲥ ⲥ̇ϩⲓⲙⲓ ϧⲉⲛ Π̅ⲟ̅ⲥ̅ *(1 Corinthians 11:11)*

Practice text 11
Acts 9:10

ⲛⲉ ⲟⲩⲟⲛ ⲟⲩⲙⲁⲑⲏⲧⲏⲥ ⲇⲉ ϧⲉⲛ ⲇⲁⲙⲁⲥⲕⲟⲥ ⲉ̇ⲡⲉϥⲣⲁⲛ ⲡⲉ ⲁⲛⲁⲛⲓⲁⲥ. ⲡⲉϫⲉ Π̅ⲟ̅ⲥ̅ ⲇⲉ ⲛⲁϥ ϧⲉⲛ ⲟⲩϩⲟⲣⲁⲙⲁ ϫⲉ ⲁⲛⲁⲛⲓⲁⲥ ⲛ̇ⲑⲟϥ ⲇⲉ ⲡⲉϫⲁϥ ϫⲉ ϩⲏⲡⲡⲉ ⲁ̇ⲛⲟⲕ Π̅ⲟ̅ⲥ̅

Vocab

ϩⲏⲡⲡⲉ	behold (interj) (14.2.i)	ϩⲟⲣⲁⲙⲁ	dream

8.3. Not quite a verb, not quite an adjective- the adjective verbs

There are certain words in Coptic that are classified somewhere in between adjectives and verbs. Like verbs, they take a subject, and have both pronominal and construct forms, however, they are also like adjectives because they express a quality of the subject. Because they have the properties of both, they are called the adjective verbs, or *verboids*.

One such verboid is ⲛⲁⲛⲉ-, ⲛⲁⲛⲉ⸗ which means *"to be good."*

The word order used with these words is a little different from what you might expect. You see, the adjective verbs come before the noun they're describing. The other difference is that the adjective verb has a 'built in' 'is.' So in the following example:

ⲛⲁⲛⲉ ⲡⲉⲧⲉⲛϣⲟⲩϣⲟⲩ

Means your *"your boasting is good"*, not *"good your boasting."*

Adverbs

The adjective verb can also be used to precede a verb,

E.g. ⲛⲁⲛⲉ ⲟⲩⲱⲛϩ ⲉⲃⲟⲗ ⲙ̀Ⲡⲟ̅ⲥ̅ *(Psalm 91:1 92:1)*
"It is good to give thanks to the Lord"

The pronoun form uses similar subject endings as for the verbs **(5.3.i)**, as shown in the table below:

ⲛⲁⲛⲏⲓ	I am good
ⲛⲁⲛⲉⲕ	you are good (m)
ⲛⲁⲛⲉ	you are good (f)
ⲛⲁⲛⲉϥ	he is good
ⲛⲁⲛⲉⲥ	she is good
ⲛⲁⲛⲉⲛ	we are good
ⲛⲁⲛⲉⲧⲉⲛ	you are good (plural)
ⲛⲁⲛⲉⲩ	they are good
ⲛⲁⲛⲉ	pre subject form

What if you wanted to say something like "the good man"? You couldn't write ⲛⲁⲛⲉ ⲡⲓⲣⲱⲙⲓ because that would mean "the man is good." So what do you do? You use our good friend the relative pronoun **(5.1.v)**. You'll recall that the prefix ⲉⲧ /ⲉⲑ has the meaning of "which" or "who." It can be attached to the adjective-verb, so if you add it to ⲛⲁⲛⲉϥ you'll get ⲉⲑⲛⲁⲛⲉϥ. (Note the choice of ⲉⲑ being a vilminor letter **(2.1.i)**).

Then add ⲡⲓⲣⲱⲙⲓ to the front and you get: ⲡⲓⲣⲱⲙⲓ ⲉⲑⲛⲁⲛⲉϥ which literally means "the man who is good" or "the good man."

What if what you wanted to say "*a good man*"? You will recall that when there is an indefinite article (i.e. "a"), the relative converter is ⲉ— so you get:

ⲟⲩⲣⲱⲙⲓ ⲉ̀ⲛⲁⲛⲉϥ

So You want to Learn Coptic?

Some other adjective verbs are shown below:

ⲛⲁⲁ⸗	to be great
ⲛⲉⲥⲱ⸗	to be beautiful
ⲛⲁϣⲱ⸗	to be numerous
ⲱⲟⲩⲛⲓⲁⲧ⸗ ⲛⲁⲓⲁⲧ⸗	to be blessed

Vocab			
ⲙⲓⲥⲓ	birth (m)	ⲯⲁⲗⲙⲟⲥ	Psalm (Gk,m)
ⲛⲁⲏⲧ	compassionate person (m)	ⲱⲗⲓ ⲉⲗ— ⲟⲗ⸗ ⲟⲗ (q)	to take, hold (v.t)
ⲛⲟⲩⲃ	gold, money (m)	ϣϣⲏⲛ	tree (m)
ⲣⲉϥϯⲱⲙⲥ	Baptist (m)		

Exercise 8.3

a) ⲥⲙⲟⲩ ⲉⲠ̅ⲟ̅ⲥ̅ ϫⲉ ⲛⲁⲛⲉ ⲟⲩⲯⲁⲗⲙⲟⲥ (Psalm **146:1** 147:1)

b) ⲁⲙⲏⲛ ϯϫⲱ ⲙ̀ⲙⲟⲥ ⲛⲱⲧⲉⲛ ϫⲉ ⲙ̀ⲡⲉ ⲟⲩⲟⲛ ⲧⲱⲛϥ ϧⲉⲛ ⲛⲓⲙⲓⲥⲓ ⲛ̀ⲧⲉ ⲛⲓϩⲓⲟⲙⲓ ⲉⲛⲁⲁϥ ⲉⲓⲱⲁⲛⲛⲏⲥ ⲡⲓⲣⲉϥϯⲱⲙⲥ (Matthew 11:11)

c) ⲛⲁⲛⲉⲥ ⲁⲛ ⲉⲉⲗ ⲡ̀ⲱⲓⲕ ⲛ̀ⲛⲓϣⲏⲣⲓ (Mark 7:27)

d) Ⲡⲓⲛⲟⲩⲃ ⲇⲉ ⲛ̀ⲧⲉ ⲡⲓⲕⲁϩⲓ ⲉⲧⲉ ⲙ̀ⲙⲁⲩ ⲛⲁⲛⲉϥ (Genesis 2:12)

e) ⲱⲟⲩⲛⲓⲁⲧⲟⲩ ⲛ̀ⲛⲓⲛⲁⲏⲧ (Matthew 5:7)

f) ⲟⲩⲟϩ ⲁⲥⲛⲁⲩ ⲛ̀ϫⲉ ϯⲥϩⲓⲙⲓ ϫⲉ ⲛⲁⲛⲉ ⲡⲓϣϣⲏⲛ (Genesis 3:6)

g) ⲭⲉⲣⲉ ⲛⲉ Ⲙⲁⲣⲓⲁ ϯϭⲣⲟⲙⲡⲓ ⲉⲑⲛⲉⲥⲱⲥ (*response preceding the reading of the Acts, Divine Liturgy*)

9. ADVERBS

Perhaps one of the first things you'd notice when looking at the word 'adverb' is that it contains the word 'verb', so you would think that the word 'adverb' would have something to do with verbs. You may even remember back to primary school, when you learnt that adverbs describe verbs. Indeed some adverbs do in fact describe verbs, but that's not all they're limited to. In fact, they are also used to describe time, place and manner, and it is these three categories which we shall look at first:

9.1. Adverbs of time and place:

These adverbs are used to describe the time a particular event occurred, or the position of something relative to another. If you take a look at the table below, you will notice quite a few of the Coptic adverbs here start with either an ⲛ̀ or an ⲙ̀. This is because many Coptic adverbs are formed by adding either the ⲛ̀ or the ⲙ̀ (depending on the rules in **(2.4.i)**) to a noun.

For example, ⲡⲁⲓⲙⲁ means "this place"

ⲙ̀ⲡⲁⲓⲙⲁ means "of this place" or 'here.'

Most of the other Coptic adverbs in the following table are formed in a similar way.

(ⲉⲧⲉ) ⲙⲙⲁⲩ	there	ⲙ̀ⲫⲟⲟⲩ	today
ⲓⲥϫⲉⲛ	since	ⲡⲁⲗⲓⲛ (ⲟⲛ)	again, once more (Gk)
ⲙ̀ⲙⲏⲛⲓ	every day, daily	ⲛ̀ⲑⲙⲏϯ	in the midst
ⲙ̀ⲛⲁⲓ	here	ⲛ̀ⲕⲉⲥⲟⲡ	again
ⲙ̀ⲡⲁⲓⲙⲁ	of this place, here	ⲛ̀ⲣⲁⲥϯ	tomorrow
ⲙ̀ⲡⲉⲙⲑⲟ	before, in front of, facing	ⲛ̀ϯⲟⲩⲛⲟⲩ	immediately, at once
ⲙ̀ⲡⲓⲉϩⲟⲟⲩ	by day	ϧⲉⲛ ϯⲟⲩⲛⲟⲩ	immediately, at once
ⲙ̀ⲡⲓⲥⲏⲟⲩ	at that time	ⲟⲛ	also
ⲙ̀ⲡⲓⲭⲱⲣⲉϩ	in the evening	ϯⲛⲟⲩ	now, at this time

9.1.i. Telling the time

As mentioned above, adverbs are also used to describe the time, giving us the opportunity to look at the way in whch the Copts used to talk about the time.

The hour

Think back to Biblical times, and try to work out how people could tell what hour they were in. Remember, there were of course no clocks back then. During the day, they would have judged the hour by the position of the sun in the sky, which could be more accurately measured with the sundial (which incidentally was invented in Egypt). Thus the daylight hours were divided into the hours of the day, corresponding to the hours of sunlight (from 6:00am to 6:00pm), and the hours of the night. Some of these hours were allocated to the time of prayer.

The first hour corresponded to 6:00am, the third hour to 9:00am, the sixth to 12:00pm, the ninth to 3:00pm, and the twelfth to 6:00pm.

In Coptic, you would say it was the sixth hour by literally saying "the time of the hour six".

The word for hour is ⲁϫⲡ and the word for time is ⲛⲁⲩ.

So the combination is ⲫⲛⲁⲩ ⲛⲁϫⲡ ⲋ̅

Similarly, the "third hour" is ⲫⲛⲁⲩ ⲛⲁϫⲡ ⲅ̅

Now to say that something occurred in the sixth hour, you can either use the ⲙ̀/ⲛ̀ construction **(2.4.i)** or the preposition ϧⲉⲛ:

E.g. ⲱ ⲫⲏ ⲉⲧⲁϥϫⲉⲙϯⲡⲓ ⲙ̀ⲫⲙⲟⲩ ϧⲉⲛ ⲧⲥⲁⲣⲝ ⲙ̀ⲫⲛⲁⲩ ⲛⲁϫⲡ ⲯⲓϯ *(Troparion of the Ninth Hour, Liturgy of the Hours)*

"O who tasted death in the flesh in the ninth hour"

ϧⲉⲛ ⲫⲛⲁⲩ ⲛⲁϫⲡ ⲥⲟⲟⲩ *(Troparion of the sixth hour, Liturgy of the Hours)*

"in the sixth hour"

The same rules also apply for more general times of the day:

Periods of the day

When you're not sure about the exact hour, you can use the more general descriptions of the periods from the table below:

| ⲙⲉⲣⲓ | midday | ⲛ̀ⲣⲁⲥϯ | tomorrow |
| ⲙ̀ⲫⲟⲟⲩ | today | ⲛ̀ⲥⲁϥ | yesterday |

| ⲣⲟⲩϩⲓ/ ϩⲁⲛⲁⲣⲟⲩϩⲓ | evening | ϣⲱⲣⲡ | morning (m) |

E.g. ⲣⲟⲩϩⲓ ⲛⲉⲙ ϣⲱⲣⲡ ⲛⲉⲙ ⲙⲉⲣⲓ †ⲛⲁⲥⲁϫⲓ (*Psalm 54:15 55:17*)
"*evening and morning and midday I will speak*"

Placing events at these more general times also uses either the ⲙ̀/ⲛ̀ construction or ϧⲉⲛ with the adverb.
So for example:

ϧⲉⲛ ⲡⲓⲉ̀ϩⲟⲟⲩ ⲙ̀ⲙⲁϩ ⲥⲟⲟⲩ (*Troparion for 6th hour, Liturgy of the hours*)
"*in the sixth day*"

ⲙ̀ⲫⲛⲁⲩ ⲛ̀ⲣⲟⲩϩⲓ (*Zechariah 14:7*)
"*in the time of the evening*"

Time for the present

Much of the Coptic we've learnt here is based on what was found in writings by the Copts in the first Millennium. This sometimes leads to difficulties when we can't find the exact expressions for things we'd like to say now which weren't recorded in these writings. For these expressions, we often have to rely on families who have continued to speak the language, or to make an educated guess as to how the Copts would have said them. Asking the time seems to be a good example. Given that most Coptic texts are either Biblical scriptures, homilies or martyrologies, you won't find the question 'what is the time' too many times. However, modern day Coptic grammar books printed in Egypt have four different questions for asking the time. These questions below borrow in advance from constructions which we'll meet later in **(13.3)**.

ⲟⲩⲏⲣ ⲧⲉ †ⲁϫⲡ	what is the time?
†ⲁϫⲡ ⲟⲩⲏⲣ	
ⲟⲩ ⲧⲉ †ⲁϫⲡ	
†ⲁϫⲡ ⲟⲩⲏⲣ †ⲛⲟⲩ	what is the time now?

Now in giving the answer, we have to consider that the way we talk about the time now is different to the way the Copts talked about it, and that whether they spoke about minutes or seconds is a matter for debate. In any case, modern day Arabic Coptic grammar books have derived ways of talking about minutes and seconds, as well as expressions for dividing up the time which are similar to what we'd use today. This means that using the numbers from **(4)**, the adverbs above, and the vocab below, you can tell somebody the time in Coptic in a similar way to what you would say in Arabic or English:

Vocab			
ⲁϫⲡ/ ⲟⲩⲛⲟⲩ	hour (m)	ⲥⲟⲩⲥⲟⲩ	very short time, minute (m)
ⲣⲉ⁻ϥⲧⲟⲩ	quarter (m)	ⲫⲁϣⲓ/ ϫⲟⲥ	half (m)
ⲣⲓⲕⲓ ⲙⲃⲁⲗ	blink of an eye, moment, second (m)	ϣⲁⲧⲉⲛ	except (prep)

Here are some example combinations. Note that some of the expressions don't need a copula or a preposition.

ϯⲁϫⲡ ⲧⲉ ⲟⲩⲓ / ϯⲁϫⲡ ⲟⲩⲓ

"it is one o'clock"

ϯⲁϫⲡ ⲟⲩⲓ ⲛⲉⲙ ⲟⲩⲫⲁϣⲓ ⲙⲙⲉⲣⲓ

"the first hour and a half (one thirty) in the afternoon"

ϯⲁϫⲡ ϣⲟⲙⲧ ϣⲁⲧⲉⲛ ⲙⲏⲧ ⲛⲥⲟⲩⲥⲟⲩ ⲛⲧⲟⲟⲩⲓ

"the time is ten to three in the morning" (literally: the third hour except for ten minutes in the morning)

ⲥⲛⲟⲩϯ ⲛⲉⲙ ⲙⲏⲧ ⲛⲥⲟⲩⲥⲟⲩ

"10 past 2"

ⲥⲟⲟⲩ ⲟⲩϫⲟⲥ

"6:30"

The day

Realising what day it is is one of the first things that comes into your mind when waking up in the morning. Isn't it funny how this affects your mood? Without the structure of the days of the week we'd really be quite lost. The Copts also saw the value of dividing the week into days, and they also had seven days in their week.

The English days are in part named after Scandinavian gods. The Copts had a much more pragmatic approach, simply naming the days according to their place in the week.

Hence Sunday is "the first", i.e. ⲡⲓⲟⲩⲁⲓ, Monday is "the second", ⲡⲓⲥⲛⲁⲩ, and so on all the way to Saturday (ⲡⲓϣⲁϣϥ).

Adverbs

Some days also began to borrow other names from Greek. As Sunday is the Lord's day, it was also called †ⲕⲩⲣⲓⲁⲕⲏ which means "the Lordly."

Friday is also †ⲡⲁⲣⲁⲥⲕⲉⲩⲏ *"the day of preparation"*

and Saturday is ⲡⲥⲁⲃⲃⲁⲧⲟⲛ *"the Sabbath"*

You can take a look at the days in the table below:

Sunday	ⲡⲓⲟⲩⲁⲓ / †ⲕⲩⲣⲓⲁⲕⲏ
Monday	ⲡⲓⲥⲛⲁⲩ
Tuesday	ⲡⲓϣⲟⲙⲧ
Wednesday	ⲡⲓϥⲧⲟⲩ
Thursday	ⲡⲓϯⲟⲩ
Friday	ⲡⲓⲥⲟⲟⲩ / †ⲡⲁⲣⲁⲥⲕⲉⲩⲏ
Saturday	ⲡⲓϣⲁϣϥ / ⲡⲥⲁⲃⲃⲁⲧⲟⲛ

Months of the Coptic Calendar

Most Copts would be familiar with the different Coptic months which have continued to this day in the Coptic Orthodox Church. The Copts had 13 months altogether, 12 of these were 30 days long, but the 13th was only 5 days for most years and 6 days on leap years. This month is given the cute name of ⲡⲓⲕⲟⲩϫⲓ *"the little."*

The names of the months in Arabic as we know them are actually transliterated from the Sahidic dialect. The Bohairic and Sahidic names, along with their current Arabic pronunciation, as well as the time to which they correspond in the Gregorian calendar, are shown below.

Bohairic	**Sahidic**	**Current Arabic Pronunciation**	**Time of year**
ⲑⲱⲟⲩⲧ	ⲑⲟⲟⲩⲧ	Tut	Early September- Mid October
Ⲡⲁⲟⲡⲓ	Ⲡⲁⲁⲡⲉ	Babah	Mid October- Mid November
Ⲁⲑⲱⲣ	Ϩⲁⲧⲱⲣ	Hatour	Mid November- Mid December

So You want to Learn Coptic?

Ⲭⲟⲓⲁⲕ	Ⲕⲓⲁϩⲕ	Kiakh	Mid December- Early January
Ⲧⲱⲃⲓ	Ⲧⲱⲃⲉ	Tubah	Early January- Early February
Ⲙⲉϣⲓⲣ	Ⲙϣⲓⲣ	Amshir	Early February- Early March
Ⲫⲁⲙⲉⲛⲱⲑ	Ⲡⲁⲣⲙϩⲁⲧ	Baramhat	Early March- Early April
Ⲫⲁⲣⲙⲟⲩⲑⲓ	Ⲡⲁⲣⲙⲟⲩⲧⲉ	Baramudah	Early April – Early May
Ⲡⲁϣⲟⲛⲥ	Ⲡⲁϣⲟⲛⲥ	Bashans	Early May- Early June
Ⲡⲁⲱⲛⲓ	Ⲡⲁⲱⲛⲉ	Baouna	Early June- Early July
Ⲉⲡⲏⲡ	Ⲉⲡⲉⲡ	Abib	Early July- Early August
Ⲙⲉⲥⲱⲣⲏ	Ⲙⲉⲥⲱⲣⲏ	Misra	Early August- Early September
ⲡⲓⲕⲟⲩϫⲓ	Ⲉⲡⲁⲅⲟⲙⲉⲛⲁⲓ	Nasi	Early September till 10th September

Vocab			
ⲁⲃⲟⲧ	month (m)	ⲣⲟⲙⲡⲓ	year (f)
ⲁϩⲟ	treasure (m)	ⲣⲱϧ ⲣⲉⲕϩ- ⲣⲟⲕϩ⸗ ⲣⲟⲕϩ	to strike, convulse (v.t)
Ⲇⲉⲙⲟⲛ	demon (m)	ⲥⲏⲟⲩ	time (m)
Ⲇⲓⲁⲃⲟⲗⲟⲥ	devil (m)	ϫⲁϫⲓ	enemy (m)
ⲓⲛⲓ, ⲟⲛⲓ (q)	to liken, resemble (v.i)	ϣⲱⲧ	merchant, trader (m)
ⲙⲟϩ, ⲙⲉϩ	to fill, to be filled (q)	ϩⲁⲛⲁⲣⲟⲩϩⲓ / ⲣⲟⲩϩⲓ	evening (m), at the time of evening (adv.)
	to burn, to be on fire (q)	ϫⲉⲙϯⲡⲓ	to taste (v.t)

ⲣⲁⲥϯ	morrow (m)	ϫⲱⲛⲧ	anger (m)

Exercise 9.1

a) ⲡⲁⲗⲓⲛ ⲟⲛ ⲁϥⲟⲗϥ ⲛ̇ϫⲉ ⲡⲓⲇⲓⲁⲃⲟⲗⲟⲥ ⲉϫⲉⲛ ⲟⲩⲧⲱⲟⲩ   (Matthew 4:8)

b) ⲡⲁⲗⲓⲛ ⲥ̀ⲟⲛⲓ ⲛ̇ϫⲉ ϯⲙⲉⲧⲟⲩⲣⲟ ⲛ̇ⲧⲉ ⲛⲓⲫⲏⲟⲩⲓ̀ ⲛ̇ⲟⲩⲣⲱⲙⲓ ⲛ̇ϣⲱⲧ
(Matthew 13:45)

c) ⲡⲉⲛⲱⲓⲕ ⲛ̇ⲧⲉ ⲣⲁⲥϯ ⲙⲏⲓϥ ⲛⲁⲛ ⲙ̇ⲫⲟⲟⲩ   (Matthew 6:11)

d) ϣⲁϣϥ ⲛ̇ⲥⲟⲡ ⲙ̇ⲙⲏⲛⲓ   (Sunday Theotokia)

e) ⲁ ⲡ̇ϫⲱⲛⲧ ⲙ̇ⲡⲟ̅ⲥ̅ ⲙⲟϩ ⲉⲑⲃⲉ ⲛⲓⲛⲟⲃⲓ ⲉⲣⲉ ⲡⲓⲗⲁⲟⲥ ⲓⲣⲓ ⲙ̇ⲙⲱⲟⲩ
ⲙ̇ⲡⲓⲥⲏⲟⲩ ⲉ̀ⲧⲉ ⲙ̇ⲙⲁⲩ   (hom vat ii pg.224)

f) ϧⲉⲛ ϯⲟⲩⲛⲟⲩ ⲁ ⲡⲓⲇⲉⲙⲱⲛ ⲣⲱϧⲧ ⲛ̇ⲧ̇ⲥ̀ϩⲓⲙⲓ   (Acta pg.7)

g) ⲁⲥϣⲱⲡⲓ ϧⲉⲛ ϯⲙⲁϩⲗ̅ †††ⲛ̇ⲣⲟⲙⲡⲓ ϧⲉⲛ ⲡⲓⲁ̀ⲃⲟⲧ ⲙ̇ⲙⲁϩⲇ̅   (Ezekiel 1:1)

h) ⲫⲁⲓ ⲁϥⲓ̀ ϩⲁ ⲓⲏ̅ⲥ̅ ⲛ̇ⲉ̀ϫⲱⲣϩ   (John 3:2)

9.2. Adverbs of manner:

Now we finally come to the adverbs used to describe verbs. These are often formed by using the attributive construction **(2.4.i)** with either a noun or an infinitive as can be seen with the examples shown in the table below:

Infinitive/ noun		Adverb	
ⲡⲁⲓⲣⲏϯ	this way, this manner (m)	ⲙ̇ⲡⲁⲓⲣⲏϯ	in this manner, in this way
ϭⲱⲗⲉⲙ	to hasten	ⲛ̇ϭⲱⲗⲉⲙ	quickly
ϫⲱⲡ	to hide	ⲛ̇ϫⲱⲡ	secretly
ϣⲱⲣⲡ	to be early (v.t)	ⲛ̇ϣⲱⲣⲡ	early

---

††† You may need to refer to **(4.1.ii)** for a reminder of this construction

So You want to Learn Coptic?

Some other adverbs of manner however, are not derived from nouns:

ⲁⲗⲏⲑⲱⲥ	truly (Gk)	ⲙ̅ⲙⲁϣⲱ	very, greatly
ⲁⲣⲏⲟⲩ	perhaps, may be	ⲧⲟⲛⲟⲩ	very, greatly
ⲉⲛⲉϩ	ever	ϫⲉ ⲟⲩⲏⲓ	indeed
ⲕⲁⲗⲱⲥ	righteously, good, truly		

Adverbs of manner may also be formed by using the *prepositional phrase*. Judging by the name, you'd guess that these have something to do with prepositions. The preposition used is in fact ϧⲉⲛ, which comes before a noun that has an indefinite article before it. The quality of the adverbial phrase is derived from this noun.

E.g. ϧⲉⲛ ⲟⲩⲣⲁϣⲓ could be literally translated as "in a joy" but is better translated as *'joyfully'*. Other examples are:

ϧⲉⲛ ⲟⲩⲱⲛϩ ⲉⲃⲟⲗ *'openly', 'publicly'*

ϧⲉⲛ ⲟⲩⲙⲟⲩⲛ ⲉⲃⲟⲗ *'continually'*

Vocab			
ⲙⲟⲩⲛ ⲉⲃⲟⲗ	to continue, to endure (v.i)	ⲡⲁⲧⲣⲓⲁⲣⲭⲏⲥ	patriarch, father (m)
ⲟⲩⲱⲛϩ ⲉⲃⲟⲗ	to reveal, give thanks (v.i)	ϭⲓⲛϫⲟⲛⲥ	violence, oppression, iniquity (m)

Exercise 9.2

a) ⲡⲥⲏⲟⲩ ⲛ̅ⲣⲱⲙⲓ ⲛⲓⲃⲉⲛ ⲁϥⲓ ⲙ̅ⲡⲁⲙⲑⲟ ϫⲉ ⲟⲩⲏⲓ ⲁ ⲡⲕⲁϩⲓ ⲙⲟϩ ⲛ̅ϭⲓⲛϫⲟⲛⲥ ⲉⲃⲟⲗ (Genesis 6:13)

b) ⲛ̅ⲧⲟⲩⲛⲟⲩ ⲁϥϩⲓⲧϥ ⲉⲡϣⲱⲓ ⲛ̅ⲭⲱⲗⲉⲙ (S.Pachomii vita. pg.2)

c) ϯⲛⲏⲟⲩ ⲛ̅ⲭⲱⲗⲉⲙ (Revelation 3:11)

d) ⲁⲩϣⲟⲡⲧⲉⲛ ⲉⲣⲱⲟⲩ ϧⲉⲛ ⲟⲩⲣⲁϣⲓ ⲛ̅ϫⲉ ⲛⲓⲥⲛⲏⲟⲩ (Acts 21:17)

e) ⲚⲒⲢⲰⲘⲒ ⲚⲈⲚⲤⲚⲎⲞⲨ ⳽ϢⲈ ⲈⲤⲀϪⲒ ⲚⲈⲘⲰⲦⲈⲚ ϦⲈⲚ ⲞⲨⲰⲚϨ ⲈⲂⲞⲖ ⲈⲐⲂⲈ ⲠⲈⲚⲠⲀⲦⲢⲒⲀⲢⲬⲎⲤ ⲆⲀⲨⲒⲆ *(Acts 2:29)*

f) ϦⲈⲚ ⲞⲨⲘⲈⲐⲘⲎⲒ ⲄⲀⲢ ⲀⲨⲐⲰⲞⲨϮ ϦⲈⲚ ⲦⲀⲒⲠⲞⲖⲒⲤ *(Acts 4:27)*

g) ⲚⲐⲞϤ ⲆⲈ ⲠⲈϪⲀϤ ⲚⲰⲞⲨ ϪⲈ ⲔⲀⲖⲰⲤ ⲀϤⲈⲢⲠⲢⲞⲪⲎⲦⲈⲨⲒⲚ ⲈⲐⲂⲈ ⲐⲎⲚⲞⲨ ⲚϪⲈ ⲎⲤⲀⲒⲀⲤ *(Mark 7:6)*

9.3. Adverbs of situation

Adverbs of situation are used to describe the position and direction of one thing compared to something else. You may notice that this definition is uncomfortably close to that of the preposition **(5.1.iii)**. The difference however is that these adverbs also include a sense of direction as opposed to just position. In fact, they're constructed by adding two words together:

a) a preposition indicating 'direction'
b) a base word which refers to a position.

Confused? Let's look at an example.

The preposition `Ⲉ` means 'to' or 'toward'

The noun `ϦⲞⲨⲚ` means 'inward part.'

The combination `ⲈϦⲞⲨⲚ` therefore means 'inwards' with the idea of the movement of 'going inside.'

Of the prepositions we've looked at, only three are used to make up compound prepositions. These are:

Ⲉ	to, toward (with the idea of motion)
Ⲛ	in, at (without the idea of motion)
ⲤⲀ	at the side of

The table below will show how these prepositions combine with certain base nouns to give different adverbs. There are a couple of points to note here; the first is that each preposition doesn't necessarily link with each base noun. The second is that two different adverbs which are made up from the same base noun but with different prepositions often end up having the same meaning even though their forms are different.

Base noun		Adverb	Base noun	Adverb	
ⲃⲟⲗ	outside (m)	ⲉ̀ⲃⲟⲗ	out, away	ⲥⲁⲃⲟⲗ	outside
ⲡⲉⲥⲏⲧ	the bottom	ⲉ̀ⲡⲉⲥⲏⲧ	downwards	ⲥⲁⲡⲉⲥⲏⲧ ⲙ̀ⲡⲉⲥⲏⲧ	beneath
ⲡ̀ϣⲱⲓ	that which is high, above (m)	ⲉ̀ⲡ̀ϣⲱⲓ	upwards	ⲥⲁⲡ̀ϣⲱⲓ ⲙ̀ⲡ̀ϣⲱⲓ	above
ⲫⲁϩⲟⲩ	hinder part, back (m)	ⲉ̀ⲫⲁϩⲟⲩ	backwards	ⲥⲁⲫⲁϩⲟⲩ	behind, after
ϧⲟⲩⲛ	inward part (m)	ⲉ̀ϧⲟⲩⲛ	inward	ⲥⲁϧⲟⲩⲛ ⲛ̀ϧⲟⲩⲛ	inside
ϧⲣⲏⲓ	down, lower part	ⲉ̀ϧⲣⲏⲓ	downward	ⲛ̀ϧⲣⲏⲓ	below, from below
ϩⲏ	beginning (m)	ⲉ̀ⲧϩⲏ	forward, ahead		
ϩⲣⲏⲓ	upper part (m)	ⲉ̀ϩⲣⲏⲓ	upward	ⲛ̀ϩⲣⲏⲓ	up

You may remember the verb ϣⲉ ⲛ⸗ from section (**5.8**) which means "to go." This verb actually makes a special use of the adverbs of situation. To illustrate, consider how you'd go about saying "I am going to the city"?

We had already said that "I am going" is ϯϣⲉ ⲛⲏⲓ

You may remember that 'the city' is ϯⲃⲁⲕⲓ.

So now all you need is 'to,' which in Coptic is ⲉ̀. Unfortunately, Coptic isn't satisfied with only using a simple preposition for 'to', but likes to add a bit more information with an adverb before the ⲉ̀. So, it actually wants you to say "I am going *inside* to the city."

I.e. ϯϣⲉ ⲛⲏⲓ ⲉϧⲟⲩⲛ ⲉϯⲃⲁⲕⲓ

In the next example, a different adverb is used with the ⲉ̀:

ⲧⲉⲛⲛⲁϣⲉ ⲛⲁⲛ ⲉ̀ϩⲣⲏⲓ ⲉⲓ̅ⲗ̅ⲙ̅ *(Matthew 20:18)*
"we are going up to Jerusalem"

If on the other hand, someone really is just going to a place, without actually going 'inside it' or 'up to it', then one can get away without using an adverb.

E.g. Ⲏⲥⲁⲩ ⲇⲉ ϣⲉⲛⲁϥ ⲉ̀ⲧⲕⲟⲓ *(Genesis 27:5)*
"And Esau went to the field"

Vocab			
Ⲏⲥⲁⲩ	Esau (prop.noun)	ⲛⲁⲕϩⲓ	pain, birth pain (f)
ⲕⲟⲓ	field (f)	ϭⲁⲗⲁⲩϫ	feet (pl)
ⲙⲟⲕⲙⲉⲕ	to think, ponder, meditate (v.i)	ϭⲁⲗⲟϫ	foot, knee

Exercise 9.3

a) ⲁⲥⲓ̀ ⲉ̀ⲃⲟⲗ ⲥⲁⲫⲁϩⲟⲩ ⲙ̀ⲙⲟϥ *(Matthew 9:20)*

b) ⲁϥⲓ̀ ⲥⲁⲃⲟⲗ ⲛ̀ϯⲃⲁⲕⲓ *(Matthew 21:17)*

c) ⲛⲁⲩⲙⲟⲕⲙⲉⲕ ⲛ̀ϧⲣⲏⲓ ⲛ̀ϧⲏⲧⲟⲩ *(Matthew 21:25)*

d) ⲛⲁⲓ ⲇⲉ ⲧⲏⲣⲟⲩ ϩⲛ ⲙ̀ⲙⲓⲛⲁϩⲕⲓ ⲛⲉ *(Matthew 24:8)*

e) ⲥⲁⲡⲉⲥⲏⲧ ⲛ̀ⲛⲉⲕϭⲁⲗⲁⲩϫ *(Matthew 22:44)*

f) ⲧⲟⲧⲉ ⲉⲧⲁⲩϣⲉ ⲉ̀ϧⲟⲩⲛ ⲁⲩϣⲉ ⲉ̀ϩⲣⲏⲓ ⲉ̀ⲟⲩⲙⲁ ⲉϥⲥⲁⲡϣⲱⲓ ⲡⲓⲙⲁ ⲉ̀ⲛⲁⲩϣⲟⲡ ⲛ̀ϧⲏⲧϥ ⲛ̀ϫⲉ ⲡⲉⲧⲣⲟⲥ ⲛⲉⲙ ⲓⲱⲁⲛⲛⲏⲥ ⲛⲉⲙ ⲓⲁⲕⲱⲃⲟⲥ ⲛⲉⲙ Ⲁⲛⲇⲣⲉⲁⲥ ⲛⲉⲙ Ⲫⲓⲗⲓⲡⲡⲟⲥ ⲛⲉⲙ Ⲑⲱⲙⲁⲥ *(Acts 1:13)*

9.4. Making Comparisons

It's hard to listen in on a conversation between 2 kids which doesn't include some sort of comparison. Comparisons certainly don't stop when the kids grow though, they just take a different form, so that "I can run faster than you" changes to "this model offers superior handling and acceleration". Words used for making comparisons also fall under the category of adverbs, and shall be presented in this section:

9.4.i. When things are the same

The first type of comparison is where things are actually similar to each other. This is the equivalent to the English word 'like' or 'as.' There are two forms which can be used for this:

a) ⲙ̀ⲫⲣⲏϯ ⲛ̀ (ⲙ̀)

b) ϩⲱⲥ

E.g. ⲙ̀ⲫⲣⲏϯ ⲛ̀ⲟⲩⲕⲩⲑⲁⲣⲁ *(Doxology for Morning Raising of Incense)*
"like a harp"

ϩⲱⲥ is translated 'as.' It's not only used in the comparative sense, but also in the sense of describing two events occurring the same time, as in "he looked at the sky as he washed the car."

E.g. ϩⲱⲥ ⲇⲉ ⲉⲩⲙⲟϣⲓ ϩⲓ ⲡⲓⲙⲱⲓⲧ ⲁⲩⲓ ϩⲓϫⲉⲛ ⲟⲩⲙⲱⲟⲩ *(Acts 8:36)*
"and as they were walking on the path they came upon (a) water"

9.4.ii. More than

We again have a choice of two adverbs when we want to say that something is greater than another:

ⲉ̀ϩⲟⲧⲉ *"above"*

ⲛ̀ϩⲟⲩⲟ *"more"*

E.g. ⲥⲉⲙ̀ⲡϣⲁ ⲛ̀ⲥⲱⲧⲉⲙ ⲛ̀ⲥⲁ ⲫϯ ⲉ̀ϩⲟⲧⲉ ⲛⲓⲣⲱⲙⲓ *(Acts 5:29)*
"it is appropriate to obey God more than the people"

Vocab			
ⲁⲕⲧⲓⲛ	light, ray (Gk,m)	ⲙⲉⲧⲙⲉⲑⲣⲉ	witness (m)
ⲁⲛϣⲟ	thousands	ⲧⲁϩⲛⲟ ⲧⲁϩⲛⲉ⸗ ⲧⲁϩⲛⲟ/	to hinder, hamper (v.t)
ⲁⲩⲗⲏ, ⲁⲩⲗⲏⲟⲩ	courtyard, (Gk,f) courtyards (pl)	ⲭⲏⲣⲁ	widow (f)

Adverbs

ⲁϣⲁⲓ, ⲟϣ	to multiply, to be abundant (qual)	ϩⲏⲕⲓ	poor, needy person(m)
ⲕⲩⲑⲁⲣⲁ	harp (Gk,f)	ϩⲓⲁⲕⲧⲓⲛ	to "throw light", shine, illuminate
ⲗⲁⲙⲡⲣⲟⲥ	brilliant, bright (adj)	ϭⲓⲥⲓ ϭⲉⲥ— ϭⲁⲥ⳱ ϭⲟⲥⲓ	to exalt (v.t), to be exalted

Exercise 9.4

a) ⲁⲩϣⲱⲡⲓ ⲙ̄ⲙⲁⲣⲧⲩⲣⲟⲥ ⲉⲩⲟϣ ⲙ̄ⲫⲣⲏϯ ⲛ̄ⲛⲓⲥⲓⲟⲩ ⲛ̄ⲧⲉ ⲧ̄ⲫⲉ *(hom vatt ii pg66)*

b) ⲡⲉⲱⲟⲩ ⲙⲁⲣⲓⲁ ϭⲟⲥⲓ ⲉϩⲟⲧⲉ ⲧ̄ⲫⲉ *(Sunday Theotokia)*

c) ⲛⲁⲛⲉ ⲟⲩⲉϩⲟⲟⲩ ϧⲉⲛ ⲛⲉⲕⲁⲩⲗⲏⲟⲩ ⲉϩⲟⲧⲉ ϩⲁⲛⲁⲛϣⲟ *(Psalm 83:11 84:10)*

d) ⲧⲉϩⲓⲁⲕⲧⲓⲛ ⲉⲃⲟⲗ ⲉϩⲟⲧⲉ ⲫⲣⲏ ⲧⲉⲟⲓ ⲛ̄ⲗⲁⲙⲡⲣⲟⲥ ⲉϩⲟⲧⲉ ⲛⲓⲭⲉⲣⲟⲩⲃⲓⲙ *(Sunday Theotokia, Midnight Praises)*

e) ϩⲓⲛⲁ ⲇⲉ ⲛ̄ⲧⲁϣⲧⲉⲙⲧⲁϩⲛⲟ ⲙ̄ⲙⲟⲕ ⲛ̄ϩⲟⲩⲟ *(Acts 24:4)*

f) ⲓⲥϫⲉ ⲧⲉⲛϭⲓ ⲛ̄ϯⲙⲉⲧⲙⲉⲑⲣⲉ ⲛ̄ⲧⲉ ⲛⲓⲣⲱⲙⲓ ϯⲙⲉⲧⲙⲉⲑⲣⲉ ⲛ̄ⲧⲉ ⲫϯ ⲟⲩⲛⲓϣϯ ⲧⲉ ⲛ̄ϩⲟⲩⲟ *(1 John 5:9)*

g) ⲟⲩⲟϩ ⲡⲉϫⲁϥ ϫⲉ ⲁⲗⲏⲑⲱⲥ ϯϫⲱ ⲙ̄ⲙⲟⲥ ⲛⲱⲧⲉⲛ ϫⲉ ⲧⲁⲓⲭⲏⲣⲁ ⲛ̄ϩⲏⲕⲓ ⲁⲥϩⲓⲟⲩⲓ ⲉϩⲟⲧⲉ ⲛⲁⲓ ⲧⲏⲣⲟⲩ *(Luke 21:3)*

So You want to Learn Coptic?

10. MORE TENSES

We have already met the most commonly used present, past and future tenses, but that was only the tip of the iceberg; in this chapter we'll look at some of the other variations of these tenses, and the situations where they're used.

10.1. In the habit- the habitual tense

The habitual tense is another type of present tense. To understand the difference between this tense and the first present **(5.1)**, consider the difference between saying "he is walking" and "he walks." Both sentences are in the present tense but they're not quite the same. "He is walking" implies that 'He' is walking at this very moment, but "he walks" just says that 'he' usually, or is in the habit of walking, he may not be walking right now but you know that from time to time he walks. As you've probably come to expect by now, Coptic also has a habitual tense which is conjugated by adding the appropriate prefix from the table below to the verb:

ϢⲀⲒ–	1st person (s)
ϢⲀⲔ–	2nd person (m)
ϢⲀⲢⲈ–	2nd person (f)
ϢⲀϤ–	3rd person (m)
ϢⲀⲤ–	3rd person (f)
ϢⲀⲚ–	1st person (pl)
ϢⲀⲢⲈⲦⲈⲚ–	2nd person (pl)
ϢⲀⲨ–	3rd person (pl)
ϢⲀⲢⲈ	Pre subject form

Two of these forms are nicely illustrated in this example:

ϢⲀϤⲪⲰⲦ ⲞⲨⲞϨ ϢⲀϤⲬⲀ ⲚⲒⲈⲤⲰⲞⲨ ⲞⲨⲞϨ ϢⲀⲢⲈ ⲠⲒⲞⲨⲰⲚϢ

ϨⲞⲖⲘⲞⲨ ⲞⲨⲞϨ ϢⲀϤⲬⲞⲢⲞⲨ ⲈⲂⲞⲖ *(John 10:12)*

"He flees and he leaves the sheep and the wolf steals them and he scatters them"

So You want to Learn Coptic?

Vocab			
ⲁⲗⲟⲩ	Youth, child (m.f)	ⲟⲩⲱⲛϣ	wolf (m)
ⲁⲗⲱⲟⲩⲓ	children (pl)	ⲥⲙⲏ	voice (f)
ⲁⲥⲕⲟⲥ	wineskin, leather bag (m)	ⲧⲁⲕⲟ ⲧⲁⲕⲉ⸗ ⲧⲁⲕⲟ⸍ ⲧⲁⲕⲏⲟⲩⲧ	to destroy, lose (v.t)
ⲉⲥⲱⲟⲩ	sheep (m)	ϣⲱⲙ	summer (m)
ⲏⲣⲡ	wine (m)	ϩⲓⲟⲩⲓ ϩⲓ⸗ ϩⲓⲧ⸍ ϩⲓⲟⲩⲓ	to strike, cast, lay (v.t)
ⲑⲉϣⲉ	neighbour, borderer (mf)	ϩⲱⲗⲉⲙ ϩⲉⲗⲉⲙ⸗ ϩⲟⲗⲙ⸍	to seize, rob (v.t)
ⲑⲉϣⲉⲩ	neighbours (pl)	ϫⲉⲥⲕⲓϯ	drachma (f) (currency unit)
ⲓⲛⲓ ⲉⲛ⸗ ⲉⲛ⸍	to bring (v.t)	ϫⲱⲣ ϫⲉⲣ⸗ ϫⲟⲣ⸍ ϫⲏⲣ	
ⲙⲟⲩⲣ ⲙⲉⲣ⸗ ⲙⲟⲣ⸍ ⲙⲏⲣ	to bind (v.t)	ⲉⲃⲟⲗ	to scatter, disperse (v.t)

Exercise 10.1

a) ϣⲁⲩϩⲓ ⲏⲣⲡ ⲙ̀ⲃⲉⲣⲓ ⲉ̀ⲁⲥⲕⲟⲥ ⲙ̀ⲃⲉⲣⲓ *(Matthew 9:17)*

b) ⲛⲓⲥⲁϫⲓ ⲛ̀ⲧⲉ Ⲫϯ ϣⲁϥⲥⲱⲧⲉⲙ ⲉ̀ⲣⲱⲟⲩ *(John 8:47)*

c) ⲉⲕⲟⲓ ⲛ̀ⲁⲗⲟⲩ ϣⲁⲕⲙⲟⲣⲕ ⲙ̀ⲙⲁⲩⲁⲧⲕ *(John 21:18)*

d) ϣⲁⲣⲉⲧⲉⲛⲉ̀ⲙⲓ ϫⲉ ϥ̀ϧⲉⲛⲧ ⲛ̀ϫⲉ ⲡⲓϣⲱⲙ *(Matthew 24:32)*

e) ϣⲁⲥⲙⲟⲩϯ ⲉ̀ⲛⲉⲥϣ̀ⲫⲉⲣⲓ ⲛⲉⲙ ⲛⲉⲥⲑⲉϣⲉⲩ ⲉⲥϫⲱ ⲙ̀ⲙⲟⲥ ϫⲉ ⲣⲁϣⲓ ⲛⲉⲙⲏⲓ ϫⲉ ⲁⲓϫⲓⲙⲓ ⲛ̀ⲧⲁϫⲉⲥⲕⲓϯ ⲉ̀ⲧⲁⲥⲧⲁⲕⲟ *(Luke 15:9)*

f) ϣⲁⲣⲉ ⲛⲓⲉⲥⲱⲟⲩ ⲥⲱⲧⲉⲙ ⲉ̀ⲧⲉϥϲ̀ⲙⲏ ⲟⲩⲟϩ ϣⲁϥⲙⲟⲩϯ ⲉ̀ⲛⲉϥⲉ̀ⲥⲱⲟⲩ ⲕⲁⲧⲁ ⲛⲟⲩⲣⲁⲛ ⲟⲩⲟϩ ϣⲁϥⲉ̀ⲛⲟⲩ ⲉ̀ⲃⲟⲗ *(John 10:3)*

More tenses

10.1.i. *Negative habitual*

As with the other tenses, the habitual also has a negative counterpart, which is called the negative habitual. It's used when you want to say that something is not usually done, or not in the habit of being done. As with the affirmative habitual, the negative habitual form also attaches to the infinitive:

1st person (s)	ⲙ̀ⲡⲁⲓ–
2nd person (m)	ⲙ̀ⲡⲁⲕ–
2nd person (f)	ⲙ̀ⲡⲁⲣⲉ–
3rd person (m)	ⲙ̀ⲡⲁϥ–
3rd person (f)	ⲙ̀ⲡⲁⲥ–
1st person (pl)	ⲙ̀ⲡⲁⲛ–
2nd person (pl)	ⲙ̀ⲡⲁⲣⲉⲧⲉⲛ–
3rd person (pl)	ⲙ̀ⲡⲁⲩ–
Pre subject form	ⲙ̀ⲡⲁⲣⲉ

So using our friend ⲙⲟϣⲓ again, the *"man does not walk"* would be ⲙ̀ⲡⲁⲣⲉ ⲡⲓⲣⲱⲙⲓ ⲙⲟϣⲓ, and *"we do not walk"* would be ⲙ̀ⲡⲁⲛⲙⲟϣⲓ

Vocab			
ⲉⲣϩⲱⲃ	to work, labour (v.i)	ⲣⲉϥϭⲓⲟⲩⲓ	thief (m)
ⲙⲁⲛⲙ̀ⲧⲟⲛ	place of rest (m)	ϭⲓⲱⲙⲥ	to immerse, baptise (v.i)
ⲙⲉⲑⲙⲏⲓ	righteousness truth (f)	ϣⲱⲧ ϣⲉⲧ– ϣⲁⲧ⸗ ϣⲏⲧ	to cut, slay, slaughter (v.t)
ⲣⲉϥⲉⲣⲛⲟⲃⲓ	sinner (m)		

Exercise 10.2

a) ⲉϥⲕⲱϯ ⲛ̀ⲥⲁ ⲙⲁⲛⲙ̀ⲧⲟⲛ ⲟⲩⲟϩ ⲙ̀ⲡⲁϥϫⲓⲙⲓ (Matthew 12:43)

b) ⲧⲉⲛⲉ̀ⲙⲓ ϫⲉ ⲙ̀ⲡⲁⲣⲉ Ⲫϯ ⲥⲱⲧⲉⲙ ⲉ̀ϩⲁⲛⲣⲉϥⲉⲣⲛⲟⲃⲓ *(John 9:31)*

c) ⲡⲓⲣⲉϥϭⲓⲟⲩⲓ ⲇⲉ ⲛ̀ⲑⲟϥ ⲙ̀ⲡⲁϥⲓ̀ ⲉⲃⲏⲗ ⲁⲣⲏⲟⲩ ⲛ̀ⲧⲉϥϭⲓⲟⲩⲓ̀ ⲟⲩⲟϩ ⲛ̀ⲧⲉϥϣⲱⲧ ⲟⲩⲟϩ ⲛ̀ⲧⲉϥⲧⲁⲕⲟ *(John 10:10)*

d) ⲙ̀ⲡⲁⲩϩⲓ ⲏⲣⲡ ⲙ̀ⲃⲉⲣⲓ ⲉ̀ⲁⲥⲕⲟⲥ ⲛ̀ⲁⲡⲁⲥ *(Matthew 9:17)*

e) ⲡ̀ϫⲱⲛⲧ ⲅⲁⲣ ⲙ̀ⲫ̀ⲣⲱⲙⲓ ⲙ̀ⲡⲁϥⲉⲣϩⲱⲃ ⲉ̀ϯⲙⲉⲑⲙⲏⲓ ⲛ̀ⲧⲉ Ⲫϯ *(James 1:20)*

Relative conversion of habitual

We first met the relative converter in **(5.1.v)**, which as we saw can be translated as 'which', 'who' or 'when.' The circumstantial can also be used with the relative converter, and conveniently this is done very easily by simply attaching ⲉ̀ before the habitual form. Remember that the resumptive morph still has to come somewhere after the verb. **(p106)**

E.g. ⲡⲓⲙⲁ ⲉ̀ϣⲁϥϣⲉ ⲛⲁϥ ⲉ̀ϧⲟⲩⲛ ⲉ̀ⲣⲟϥ *(Mark 6:56)*

"the place which he goes inside"

Vocab			
ⲃⲁⲉⲙⲡⲓ	goat (f)	ⲙⲉⲓ ⲙⲉⲛⲣⲉ- ⲙⲉⲛⲣⲓⲧ⸗ ⲙⲁⲓ (p.c^{‡‡‡})	to love (v.t)
ⲥⲁⲓⲏ	beautiful person, thing (f)	ⲙ̀ⲫ̀ⲣⲏϯ	like, as (adv)
ⲥⲁϩⲟⲩⲓ ⲥ̀ϩⲟⲩⲉⲣ- ⲥ̀ϩⲟⲩⲱⲣ⸗ ⲥ̀ϩⲟⲩⲟⲣⲧ	to rebuke, curse (v.t)	ⲡⲩⲗⲏ	gate (Gk,f)

---

‡‡‡ p.c has nothing to do with political correctness, but rather stands for participium coniunctum. This scary sounding Latin phrase simply refers to certain nouns which are formed by adding '-ing' to the infinitive. So the p.c of 'to love' is 'loving'. Bear in mind that there are very few verbs which have a p.c form.

More tenses

ⲟⲩⲱⲙ ⲟⲩⲉⲙ– ⲟⲩⲟⲙ⳱	to eat (v.t)	ⲧⲁⲡⲁⲛⲏ	food (Gk,pl)
ⲫⲱⲣⲝ ⲫⲉⲣⲝ– ⲫⲟⲣⲝ⳱ ⲫⲟⲣⲝ	to divide, separate (v.t)	ⲫⲁⲛⲓϫⲱⲓⲧ	"of the olives" (prop. noun)
ⲙⲁⲛⲉⲥⲱⲟⲩ	shepherd (m)		

Exercise 10.3

a) ⲡⲏⲣⲡ ⲛⲉⲙ ⲡⲓⲧⲁⲡⲁⲛⲏ ⲉϣⲁⲣⲉ ⲡⲟⲩⲣⲟ ⲟⲩⲱⲙ ⲉ̇ⲃⲟⲗ ⲛ̇ϧⲏⲧⲟⲩ
(hom vatt ii pg.74)

b) ϯⲡⲩⲗⲏ ⲛⲧⲉ ⲡⲓⲉⲣⲫⲉⲓ ⲑⲏ ⲉ̇ϣⲁⲩⲙⲟⲩϯ ⲉⲣⲟⲥ ϫⲉ ϯⲥⲁⲓⲛ *(Acts 3:2)*

c) ⲡⲓⲧⲱⲟⲩ ⲉ̇ϣⲁⲩⲙⲟⲩϯ ⲉⲣⲟϥ ϫⲉ ⲫⲁⲛⲓϫⲱⲓⲧ *(Acts 1:12)*

d) ⲛⲏ ⲉ̇ϣⲁⲓⲙⲉⲛⲣⲓⲧⲟⲩ ϣⲁⲓⲥⲁϩⲱⲟⲩ ϣⲁⲓϯⲥ̇ⲃⲱ ⲛⲱⲟⲩ *(Revelation 3:19)*

e) ⲙ̇ⲫⲣⲏϯ ⲙ̇ⲡⲓⲙⲁⲛⲉⲥⲱⲟⲩ ⲉ̇ϣⲁϥⲫⲱⲣⲝ ⲛ̇ⲛⲓⲉⲥⲱⲟⲩ ⲉ̇ⲃⲟⲗ ϧⲉⲛ ⲛⲓⲃⲁⲉⲙⲡⲓ *(Matthew 25:32)*

10.2. Back to the future- the emphatic future tense

We already met the first future tense in **(5.9)**, so why would we want another future tense? The future tense we'll deal with in this section is actually quite different from the first future, in that it not only says that something *will* happen, but it adds the meaning that it will *definitely* happen. This tense is used for emphasis (hence the name), and is also used for giving commands, e.g "you *will* wash the car." As with all the other tenses we've met, this tense is made up by adding the relevant prefix to the infinitive, as you can see in the table below:

ⲉⲓⲉ–	I *will*
ⲉⲕⲉ–	You *will* (m)
ⲉⲣⲉ–	You *will* (f)
ⲉϥⲉ–	He *will*
ⲉⲥⲉ–	She *will*

So You want to Learn Coptic?

ⲉⲛⲉ—	We *will*
ⲉⲣⲉⲧⲉⲛⲉ̀—	You *will* (plural)
ⲉⲩⲉ—	They *will*
ⲉⲣⲉ	pre subject form

To highlight the use of the emphatic future, let's look at what Archangel Gabriel said to the Virgin Saint .Mary when talking to her about the Lord to whom she would give birth:

ⲫⲁⲓ ⲉϥⲉⲉⲣⲟⲩⲛⲓϣϯ ⲟⲩⲟϩ ⲉⲩⲉⲙⲟⲩϯ ⲉⲣⲟϥ ϫⲉ ⲡ̀ϣⲏⲣⲓ ⲙ̀ⲡⲉⲧϭⲟⲥⲓ ⲟⲩⲟϩ ⲉϥⲉϯ ⲛⲁϥ ⲛ̀ϫⲉ Ⲡ̅ⲟ̅ⲥ̅ Ⲫ̀ϯ ⲙ̀ⲡ̀ⲑ̀ⲣⲟⲛⲟⲥ ⲛ̀Ⲇⲁⲩⲓⲇ ⲡⲉϥⲓⲱⲧ
(Luke 1:32)
"He (this) will be great and He will be called 'the Son of the Highest' and the Lord God will give Him the throne of David His father."

Perhaps the most familiar example of the emphatic future is used to conclude the Divine Liturgy.

ⲁⲙⲏⲛ ⲉⲥⲉϣⲱⲡⲓ

"Amen it shall be"

As with the past perfect, the third person plural may also be used to imply a passive tense **(p103)**.

E.g. ⲡⲁⲏⲓ ⲉⲩⲉⲙⲟⲩϯ ⲉⲣⲟϥ ϫⲉ ⲟⲩⲏⲓ ⲙ̀ⲡⲣⲟⲥⲉⲩⲭⲏ *(Matthew 21:13)*
"my house will be called a house of prayer"

As the name implies, the pre subject form ⲉⲣⲉ comes before the subject. With the other tenses which we've seen, we've noticed that the infinitive doesn't have any prefixes added to it when the pre subject form is being used. However, with the emphatic future, the verb is sometimes conjugated even when the pre subject form is being used.

E.g. ⲟⲩⲟϩ ⲉⲣⲉ ⲡⲟⲩⲥⲱⲙⲁ ⲉϥⲉϣⲱⲡⲓ ϩⲓ ⲛⲓϣ̀ⲑⲉϩ ⲛ̀ⲧⲉ ϯⲛⲓϣϯ

ⲙ̀ⲃⲁⲕⲓ *(Revelation 11:8)*
"and their body will be on the streets of the great city"

Vocab

ⲑⲉⲃⲓⲟ ⲑⲉⲃⲓⲉ- ⲑⲉⲃⲓⲟ⸍ ⲑⲉⲃⲓⲏⲟⲩⲧ	to be humble, to humiliate (v.t)	ⲥⲁⲣⲏⲥ	southern side, south (m)
ⲓⲣⲓ ⲉⲣ- ⲁⲓ⸍ ⲟⲓ	to do, make (v.t)	ⲥⲓⲱⲛ	Zion (prop. noun)
ⲓⲱϯ	dew (f)	ⲥⲟⲗⲥⲉⲗ	adornment (m)
ⲕⲣⲓⲥⲓⲥ	judgement (f)	ϩⲓⲟⲩⲓ ϩⲓ- ϩⲓⲧ⸍ ϩⲱⲟⲩⲓ	to cast, strike, throw (v.t)
ϣⲑⲉϩ	street (m)	ⲉ̀ϧⲣⲏⲓ	to throw down
ⲛⲟⲙⲟⲥ	law (m)	ϩ̀ⲣⲱ	furnace, oven (f)
ⲡⲣⲟⲥⲉⲩⲭⲏ	prayer (f)		

Exercise 10.4

a) ⲟⲩⲟϩ ⲫⲏⲉⲧⲉ ⲛ̀ϥⲛⲁϩⲓⲧϥ ⲉ̀ϧⲣⲏⲓ ⲁⲛ ⲛ̀ⲧⲉϥⲟⲩⲱϣⲧ ϧⲉⲛ ϯⲟⲩⲛⲟⲩ ⲉⲧⲉⲙⲙⲁⲩ ⲉⲩⲉ̀ϩⲓⲧϥ ⲉ̀ϯϩ̀ⲣⲱ ⲛ̀ⲭ̀ⲣⲱⲙ (Daniel 3:6)

b) ⲉ̀ⲃⲟⲗϧⲉⲛ ⲛⲉⲕϫⲓϫ ⲡ̀ⲟⲩⲣⲟ ⲉϥⲉ̀ⲛⲁϩⲙⲉⲛ (Daniel 3:17)

c) ⲡⲓⲙⲁ ⲅⲁⲣ ⲉⲧⲉ ⲡⲉⲕⲁϩⲟ ⲙ̀ⲙⲟϥ ⲉϥⲉ̀ϣⲱⲡⲓ ⲙ̀ⲙⲁⲩ ⲛ̀ϫⲉ ⲡⲉⲕⲕⲉϩⲏⲧ (Matthew 6:21)

d) ⲉϥⲉ̀ⲉⲣⲙⲉⲗⲉⲧⲁⲛ ϧⲉⲛ ⲡⲉϥⲛⲟⲙⲟⲥ ⲙ̀ⲡⲓⲉ̀ϩⲟⲟⲩ ⲛⲉⲙ ⲡⲓⲉ̀ϫⲱⲣϩ (Psalm 1:2 1:2)

e) ⲟⲩⲟϩ ⲉⲣⲉ ⲫⲛⲟⲩϯ ϯⲛⲁⲕ ⲉ̀ⲃⲟⲗϧⲉⲛ ϯⲓⲱϯ ⲛ̀ⲧⲉ ϯⲫⲉ (Genesis 27:28)

f) ⲉⲣⲉ ⲫϯ ⲓⲛⲓ ⲛ̀ⲧⲉϥϫⲓϫ ⲉ̀ϫⲉⲛ ⲡⲓⲥⲟⲗⲥⲉⲗ ⲧⲏⲣϥ ⲛ̀ⲧⲉ ϯⲫⲉ ⲛⲉⲙ ⲉ̀ϫⲉⲛ ⲛⲓⲟⲩⲣⲱⲟⲩ ⲛ̀ⲧⲉ ⲡ̀ⲕⲁϩⲓ (Isaiah 24:21)

g) ⲉⲣⲉ ⲫϯ ⲑⲉⲃⲓⲟ ⲛ̀ⲛⲓⲁⲣⲭⲱⲛ ⲛ̀ⲧⲉ ⲛⲉⲛϣⲏⲣⲓ ⲛ̀ⲥⲓⲱⲛ (Isaiah 3:17)

So You want to Learn Coptic?

h) ⲁⲣⲉⲧⲉⲛⲥⲱⲧⲉⲙ ϫⲉ ⲁⲩϫⲟⲥ ϫⲉ ⲉⲕⲉⲙⲉⲛⲣⲉ ⲡⲉⲕϣⲫⲏⲣ ⲟⲩⲟϩ ⲉⲕⲉⲙⲉⲥⲧⲉ ⲡⲉⲕϫⲁϫⲓ *(Matthew 5:43)*

i) ⲟⲩⲟϩ ⲙⲉⲛⲉⲛⲥⲁ ⲅ̄ ⲛ̇ⲉϩⲟⲟⲩ ⲉϥⲉⲧⲱⲛϥ *(Matthew 20:19)*

j) ϯⲟⲩⲣⲱ ⲛ̇ⲧⲉ ⲥⲁⲣⲏⲥ ⲉⲥⲉⲧⲱⲛⲥ ϧⲉⲛ ϯⲕⲣⲓⲥⲓⲥ ⲛⲉⲙ ⲡⲁⲓϫⲱⲟⲩ ⲟⲩⲟϩ ⲉⲥⲉϯϩⲁⲡ ⲉⲣⲟϥ *(Matthew 12:42)*

Confusion Corner

The many meanings of ⲉⲣⲉ

We've come across the little word ⲉⲣⲉ a number of times now, so this is a good opportunity to summarise its different uses. Remember that ⲉⲣⲉ comes before a noun in all these cases.

1) Used as a relative converter **(5.1.v)**, where it means 'which, who or when.'
2) Used as the pre subject form of the circumstantial conversion **(7.2)** where it can often be translated as 'while' or 'as.' Remember that when the circumstantial is used with the future tense, it takes the meaning of 'about to.' **(7.2.ii)**.
3) As the pre subject form of the emphatic future **(10.2)**.

Practice text 12
*Psalm **19:1-7** 20:1-6*

Ⲉϥⲉⲥⲱⲧⲉⲙ ⲉⲣⲟⲕ ⲛ̀ϫⲉ Ⲡ̀ϭⲟⲓⲥ ϧⲉⲛ ⲡⲓⲉ̀ϩⲟⲟⲩ ⲛ̀ⲧⲉ ⲡⲉⲕϩⲟϫϩⲉϫ.

Ⲉϥⲉϯ ⲉ̀ϩⲣⲏⲓ ⲉϫⲱⲕ ⲛ̀ϫⲉ ⲫ̀ⲣⲁⲛ ⲙ̀Ⲫⲛⲟⲩϯ ⲛ̀Ⲓⲁⲕⲱⲃ.

Ⲉϥⲉⲟⲩⲱⲣⲡ ⲛⲁⲕ ⲛ̀ⲟⲩⲃⲟⲏⲑⲓⲁ ⲉ̀ⲃⲟⲗ ϧⲉⲛ ⲡⲉⲑⲟⲩⲁⲃ.

Ⲉϥⲉϣⲟⲡⲕ ⲉⲣⲟϥ ⲉ̀ⲃⲟⲗ ϧⲉⲛ Ⲥⲓⲱⲛ ⲉϥⲉⲉⲣⲫ̀ⲙⲉⲩⲓ ⲛ̀ⲛⲉⲕϣⲟⲩϣⲱⲟⲩϣⲓ ⲧⲏⲣⲟⲩ ⲛⲉⲕϭⲗⲓⲗ ⲥⲉⲕⲉⲛⲓⲱⲟⲩⲧ ⲛⲁϥ.

Ⲉϥⲉϯ ⲛⲁⲕ ⲛ̀ϫⲉ Ⲡ̀ϭⲟⲓⲥ ⲕⲁⲧⲁ ⲡⲉⲕϩⲏⲧ ⲟⲩⲟϩ ⲡⲉⲕⲥⲟϭⲛⲓ ⲧⲏⲣϥ ⲉϥⲉϫⲟⲕϥ ⲉ̀ⲃⲟⲗ.

Ⲉⲛⲉⲟⲩⲱⲛϩ ⲛⲁⲕ ⲉ̀ⲃⲟⲗ Ⲡ̀ϭⲟⲓⲥ ϧⲉⲛ ⲡⲉⲕⲛⲟϩⲉⲙ ⲟⲩⲟϩ ϧⲉⲛ ⲫ̀ⲣⲁⲛ ⲙ̀Ⲡⲉⲛⲛⲟⲩϯ ⲉⲛⲉⲁⲓⲁⲓ.

Ⲉⲣⲉ Ⲡ̀ϭⲟⲓⲥ ϫⲉⲕ ⲛⲉⲕⲉⲧⲏⲙⲁ ⲧⲏⲣⲟⲩ ⲉ̀ⲃⲟⲗ.

Vocab			
ⲃⲟⲏⲑⲓⲁ	help, aid, cure (f)	ⲥⲟϭⲛⲓ	counsel (m)
ⲉⲧⲏⲙⲁ	request, demand (m)	ϣⲟⲩϣⲱⲟⲩϣⲓ	sacrifice (m)
ⲉ̀ϩⲟⲟⲩ	day (m)	ϩⲟϫϩⲉϫ	trouble, tribulation (m)
ⲕⲉⲛⲓ, ⲕⲉⲛⲓⲱⲟⲩⲧ	to make fat, to be fattened (q)	ϫⲱⲕ ϫⲉⲕ– ϫⲟⲕ⸗ ϫⲏⲕ	
ⲙⲉⲩⲓ	thought, remembrance (m)	ⲉ̀ⲃⲟⲗ	to complete, perfect (v.t)
ⲛⲟϩⲉⲙ	to save (v.t)	ϭⲗⲓⲗ	burnt offering (m)
ⲟⲩⲓⲛⲁⲙ	right hand (f)	ϯⲉ̀ϩⲣⲏⲓ ⲉϫⲉⲛ	to put upon (v.t)
ⲡⲉⲑⲟⲩⲁⲃ	the Holy, Sanctuary (m)		

So You want to Learn Coptic?

10.2.i.   *Negative emphatic future*

The emphatic also has a negative form, used to insist that something will *not* happen. This tense is called the negative emphatic future, and it's conjugated as follows:

ⲛ̀ⲛⲁ-	I *will* not
ⲛ̀ⲛⲉⲕ-	You *will* not (m)
ⲛ̀ⲛⲉ-	You *will* not (f)
ⲛ̀ⲛⲉϥ-	He *will* not
ⲛ̀ⲛⲉⲥ-	She *will* not
ⲛ̀ⲛⲉⲛ-	We *will* not
ⲛ̀ⲛⲉⲧⲉⲛ-	You *will* not (plural)
ⲛ̀ⲛⲟⲩ-	They *will* not
ⲛ̀ⲛⲉ	pre subject form

E.g. ⲁϥⲭⲱ ⲛ̀ⲟⲩϩⲱⲛ ⲟⲩⲟϩ ⲛ̀ⲛⲉϥⲥⲓⲛⲓ   *(Psalm 148:6 148:6)*

"He set a command, it shall not pass"

ⲁⲙⲟⲛⲓ	to seize, hold (v.t)	ⲡⲉⲧϩⲱⲟⲩ	that which is evil (m)
ⲁⲩⲭⲁⲗ	ship anchor (m)	ⲥⲓⲛⲓ	to pass by, pass away (v.i)
ⲉⲧⲓ	after, during, and (Gk.conj.)	ϣⲟⲃⲓ	hypocrite (m)
ⲑⲏⲟⲩ	wind, breath (m)	ϧⲁⲧϩⲏ	before, in front of (prep)
ⲛⲟϩ	rope, cord (m)	ϩⲱⲛ	command (m)

Exercise 10.5

a)   ϣⲁⲣⲁⲙⲟⲛⲓ ⲛ̀ⲛⲓⲛⲟϩ ⲛⲉⲙ ⲛⲓⲁⲩⲭⲁⲗ ⲉ̀ⲣⲉⲣϩⲟϯ ϫⲉ ⲛ̀ⲛⲉ ⲛⲓⲑⲏⲟⲩ

ⲓ̀ ⲉ̀ϫⲱⲟⲩ   *(hom vat ii pg.206)*

b) ⲙ̄ⲛⲁⲉⲣϩⲟϯ ϧⲁⲧϩⲏ ⲛ̄ϩⲁⲛⲡⲉⲧϩⲱⲟⲩ ϫⲉ ⲛ̄ⲑⲟⲕ ⲕⲭⲏ ⲛⲉⲙⲏⲓ
(Psalm **22**:4 23:4)

c) ⲛ̄ⲛⲉ ⲧⲁⲓⲅⲉⲛⲉⲁ ⲥⲓⲛⲓ ϣⲁⲧⲉ ⲛⲁⲓ ⲧⲏⲣⲟⲩ ϣⲱⲡⲓ (*Luke 21:32*)

d) ⲧⲫⲉ ⲛⲉⲙ ⲡⲕⲁϩⲓ ⲥⲉⲛⲁⲥⲓⲛⲓ ⲛⲁⲥⲁϫⲓ ⲇⲉ ⲛ̄ⲛⲟⲩⲥⲓⲛⲓ (*Luke 21:33*)

e) ⲛ̄ⲛⲉ ⲟⲩⲧⲁϩ ⲓ ⲉⲃⲟⲗ ⲛ̄ϧⲏϯ ϣⲁ ⲉⲛⲉϩ (*Matthew 21:19*)

f) ⲉⲧⲓ ⲕⲉ ⲍ̄ ⲛⲉϩⲟⲟⲩ ⲡⲉ ⲛ̄ⲛⲉⲕⲙⲁⲩ ⲉⲡⲓⲕⲁϩⲓ (*hom vat pg.225*)

g) ⲛ̄ⲛⲉⲧⲉⲛⲉⲣ ⲙ̄ⲫⲣⲏϯ ⲛ̄ⲛⲓϣⲟⲃⲓ (*Matthew 6:16*)

10.3. The imperfect future

No one really expects the future to be perfect, and things often just don't work out the way you expect. The imperfect future tense describes situations where the expected future hasn't quite occurred. To elaborate further, there are two different situations where it is used:

1. Where something was about to happen

2. Where something would have happened but for something else happening before it e.g. "If I had studied I would have passed":

10.3.i. 1) Was about to...

For the construction of the first type of imperfect future, the imperfect tense (**7.1**) is combined with the first future (**5.9**) to give the meaning of 'about to' as in the table below:

ⲛⲁⲓⲛⲁ−...(ⲡⲉ)	I was about to
ⲛⲁⲕⲛⲁ−...(ⲡⲉ)	You were about to (m)
ⲛⲁⲣⲉⲛⲁ−...(ⲡⲉ)	You were about to (f)
ⲛⲁϥⲛⲁ−...(ⲡⲉ)	He was about to
ⲛⲁⲥⲛⲁ−...(ⲡⲉ)	She was about to
ⲛⲁⲛⲛⲁ−...(ⲡⲉ)	We were about to
ⲛⲁⲣⲉⲧⲉⲛⲛⲁ−...(ⲡⲉ)	You were about to (pl)

So You want to Learn Coptic?

ⲛⲁⲩⲛⲁ–...(ⲡⲉ)	They were about to
ⲛⲁⲣⲉ...ⲛⲁ...(ⲡⲉ)	Pre subject form

E.g. ⲑⲁⲓ ⲛⲁⲥⲛⲁⲙⲟⲩ ⲡⲉ *(Luke 8:42)*
"*she was about to die*"

In this example, the ⲛⲁⲥ is the imperfect for the third person singular (meaning "she was") which is then combined with the future converter ⲛⲁ(5.9). The construction is completed with the ⲡⲉ at the end which you may recall was an optional extra with the past imperfect.

ⲛⲁⲩⲛⲁⲫⲱϧ ⲇⲉ ⲡⲉ ⲛ̀ϫⲉ ⲛⲓϣⲛⲏⲟⲩ *(Luke 5:6)*
"*and the nets were about to break*"

2) It would have…

The second type of future imperfect is used to describe two hypothetical events, with the second event being conditional on the first having occurred. Let's walk through an example to make things clearer:

Ⲡⲁⲟ̅ⲥ̅ ⲉ̀ⲛⲁⲕⲭⲏ ⲙ̀ⲡⲁⲓⲙⲁ ⲛⲁⲣⲉ ⲡⲁⲥⲟⲛ ⲛⲁⲙⲟⲩ ⲁⲛ ⲡⲉ *(John 11:32)*
"*My Lord, if you had been here my brother would not have died*"

There are two hypothetical events which occur here.
The first is a hypothetical event which could have occurred in the past; "if you had been here".
The second is the hypothetical event which would have occurred later on had the first event occurred ("my brother would not have died.")

For the first event, the imperfect is combined with the ⲉ̀ of the circumstantial (7.1) so we get: Ⲡⲁⲟ̅ⲥ̅ ⲉ̀ⲛⲁⲕⲭⲏ.

The imperfect for you (m) is ⲛⲁⲕ, which is combined with the ⲉ̀, for the combination ⲉ̀ⲛⲁⲕ to mean "if you were."

For the second hypothetical, the imperfect is combined with the future converter, using the same construction which was used for the first type of future

More tenses

imperfect. So ⲛⲁⲣⲉ (the presubject form of the imperfect) comes before ⲡⲁⲥⲟⲛ which is the subject, and the ⲛⲁ comes before the verb ⲙⲟⲩ (to die).

Note the optional ⲡⲉ which has been used at the end of the sentence.

It is also useful to remember that the ⲉⲛⲁⲣⲉ of the future imperfect which is constructed by adding the imperfect presubject form ⲛⲁⲣⲉ to the circumstantial ⲉ is sometimes shortened to just ⲉⲛⲉ.

Vocab			
ⲉⲣⲇⲓⲁⲕⲣⲓⲛⲓⲛ	to examine (v.t)	ϣⲛⲉ	net
ⲉⲣⲟⲩⲱ	to reply, to answer (v.i)	ϣⲛⲏⲟⲩ	nets (pl)
ⲟⲩⲱϣ ⲟⲩⲁϣ⁻ ⲟⲩⲉϣ⁻ ⲟⲩⲁϣ⁄	to desire, want (v.t)	ϫⲱⲕ ϫⲉⲕ⁻ ϫⲟⲕ⁄ ϫⲏⲕ	
ⲥⲁⲙⲡⲉⲧϩⲱⲟⲩ	evil person (m)	ⲉⲃⲟⲗ	to complete, accomplish, fulfil (v.t)

Exercise 10.6:

a) ⲟⲩⲟϩ ⲧⲉⲧⲉⲛϫⲱ ⲙⲙⲟⲥ ϫⲉ ⲉⲛⲁⲛϫⲏ ϧⲉⲛ ⲛⲓⲉϩⲟⲟⲩ ⲛⲧⲉ ⲛⲉⲛⲓⲟϯ ⲛⲁⲛⲛⲁϣⲱⲡⲓ ⲉⲛⲟⲓ ⲛϣⲫⲏⲣ ⲉⲣⲱⲟⲩ ⲁⲛ ⲡⲉ ϧⲉⲛ ⲡⲓⲥⲛⲟϥ ⲛⲧⲉ ⲛⲓⲡⲣⲟⲫⲏⲧⲏⲥ *(Matthew 23:30)*

b) ϫⲉ ⲉⲛⲉ ⲁⲕⲟⲩⲱϣ ϣⲟⲩϣⲱⲟⲩϣⲓ ⲛⲁⲓⲙⲁϯ ⲟⲛ ⲡⲉ *(Psalm 50:18 51:16)*

c) ⲫⲏ ⲉⲛⲁϥⲛⲁϫⲟⲕϥ ⲉⲃⲟⲗ ϧⲉⲛ Ⲓⲗ̅ⲏ̅ⲙ̅ *(Luke 9:31)*

d) ⲉⲛⲁⲛⲉⲣⲇⲓⲁⲕⲣⲓⲛⲓⲛ ⲅⲁⲣ ⲙⲙⲟⲛ ⲛⲁⲩⲛⲁϯϩⲁⲡ ⲉⲣⲟⲛ ⲁⲛ ⲡⲉ *(1 Corinthians 11:31)*

e) ⲁⲩⲉⲣⲟⲩⲱ ⲡⲉϫⲱⲟⲩ ⲛⲁϥ ⲉⲛⲉ ⲫⲁⲓ ⲟⲩⲥⲁⲙⲡⲉⲧϩⲱⲟⲩ ⲁⲛ ⲡⲉ ⲛⲁⲛⲛⲁⲧⲏⲓϥ ⲛⲁⲕ ⲁⲛ ⲡⲉ *(John 18:30)*

So You want to Learn Coptic?

10.4. Giving orders- the imperative

The word 'imperative' is related to the word 'empire,' which is related to the word 'emperor.' Now I'm not exactly sure of all the things that emperors did, but I know that one thing they did for sure was to give orders. This role of giving orders is so important that a whole tense is devoted to it, called the *imperative* tense.

In English, verbs in the imperative look just the same as verbs which aren't. For example, the 'stand' in the order 'stand over there' is just the same as the 'stand' in the statement "I stand all day long."

Now although many verbs in Coptic look identical in their imperative and non imperative forms, many other verbs take on a special imperative form. Of those that don't change, some only use their infinitive form for their imperative, whereas others use only their construct or their pronominal form.

Some of the verbs which don't change for their imperative form are shown in the table below:

Non imperative form	Imperative	Imperative translation
ⲙⲟϣⲓ	ⲙⲟϣⲓ	walk!
ϩⲱⲥ	ϩⲱⲥ	sing, praise!
ⲥⲱⲧⲉⲙ	ⲥⲱⲧⲉⲙ	listen, obey!
ⲧⲱⲟⲩⲛ	ⲧⲱⲛ⸗ (pronominal form)	arise!
ⲙⲉⲓ	ⲙⲉⲛⲣⲉ– (construct form)	love!
ⲛⲟϩⲉⲙ	ⲛⲁϩⲙ⸗ (pronominal form)	save!

Whereas the non imperative form takes the subject prefix before the verb, as in ⲭⲙⲟϣⲓ- *"you are walking"*, the imperative doesn't take any prefix, so to give the command 'walk' you just say ⲙⲟϣⲓ.

Other examples:

ⲛⲁϩⲙⲉⲛ ⲉⲃⲟⲗϩⲁ ⲡⲓⲡⲉⲧϩⲱⲟⲩ *(Prayer of thanksgiving)*
"save us from the evil"

ⲧⲉⲛ ⲑⲏⲛⲟⲩ ⲉ ⲉⲡϣⲱⲓ ⲛⲓϣⲏⲣⲓ ⲛⲧⲉ ⲡⲓⲟⲩⲱⲓⲛⲓ (ϫⲉⲛ ⲑⲏⲛⲟⲩ *introductory hymn to Midnight praises)*
"rise up children of the light"

ⲟⲩⲛⲟϥ ⲙⲙⲟ Ⲙⲁⲣⲓⲁ *(Aspasmoc Adam)*
"rejoice O Mary"[§§§]

As mentioned above, there are other verbs which do change their form in the imperative. These verbs take on one of two special imperative forms which make an adjustment to the original verb.

10.4.i. Verbs which take an ⲁ-

Most of these verbs change to the imperative by simply adding an ⲁ- before the infinitive. Examples:

Non imperative form	Imperative form	Imperative translation
ⲛⲁⲩ	ⲁⲛⲁⲩ	see!
ⲟⲩⲱⲙ	ⲁⲟⲩⲱⲙ	eat!
ⲟⲩⲱⲛ	ⲁⲟⲩⲱⲛ	open!

Some verbs which take the ⲁ- change their form completely, and have a different imperative form for each of the infinitive, pronominal and construct forms.

Non imperative form	Imperative form	Imperative translation
ⲓⲛⲓ ⲉⲛ- ⲉⲛ⸗	ⲁⲛⲓⲟⲩⲓ ⲁⲛⲓ- ⲁⲛⲓⲧ⸗	bring!
ⲓⲣⲓ ⲉⲣ- ⲁⲓ⸗	ⲁⲣⲓⲟⲩⲓ ⲁⲣⲓ- ⲁⲣⲓⲧ⸗	make!, do!
ⲱⲗⲓ ⲉⲗ- ⲟⲗ⸗	ⲁⲗⲓⲟⲩⲓ ⲁⲗⲓ- ⲁⲗⲓⲧ⸗	lift up!, hold!, take!, remove!
ϫⲱ ϫⲉ- ϫⲟ⸗	ⲁϫⲱ ⲁϫⲉ- ⲁϫⲟ⸗	say!

E.g. ⲁϫⲟⲥ ⲛ̀ⲧϣⲉⲣⲓ ⲛ̀ⲥⲓⲱⲛ *(Matthew 21:5)*

[§§§] Remember that ⲟⲩⲛⲟϥ ⲙⲙⲟ⸗ is a reflexive verb **(5.8)**, this explains the ⲙⲙⲟ in the imperative.

So You want to Learn Coptic?

"say to the daughter of Zion"

Did you notice that the imperative form of ⲉⲣ is ⲁⲣⲓ? Recall from the section on compound verbs in (5.6) that many verbs were formed by adding the construct form of ⲓⲣⲓ (ⲉⲣ⁻) to quite a large number of nouns. These same nouns also attach to the construct form of the imperative ⲁⲣⲓⲟⲩⲓ (ⲁⲣⲓ⁻) to form the imperative of those verbs, as with the examples in the table below:

Infinitive	imperative translation	Imperative	imperative translation
ⲉⲣⲃⲟⲏⲑⲓⲛ	to help, support	ⲁⲣⲓⲃⲟⲏⲑⲓⲛ	help! support!
ⲉⲣⲥⲟⲃⲧ	to make a wall around, protect	ⲁⲣⲓⲥⲟⲃⲧ	make a wall around!, protect!
ⲉⲣⲡⲣⲉⲥⲃⲉⲩⲓⲛ	to intercede	ⲁⲣⲓⲡⲣⲉⲥⲃⲉⲩⲓⲛ	intercede!
ⲉⲣⲫⲙⲉⲩⲓ	to remember	ⲁⲣⲓⲫⲙⲉⲩⲓ	remember!
ⲉⲣϩⲙⲟⲧ	to grant, bestow	ⲁⲣⲓϩⲙⲟⲧ	grant that!

10.4.ii. Verbs which take ⲙⲁ-.

The imperative of these verbs simply adds ⲙⲁ- to the infinitive form. This group includes all those compound verbs which are linked with the verb ϯ.

Infinitive		Imperative	
ⲧⲁⲗϭⲟ	to heal	ⲙⲁⲧⲁⲗϭⲟ	heal!
ⲧⲁϫⲣⲟ	to strengthen	ⲙⲁⲧⲁϫⲣⲟ	strengthen!
ⲧⲟⲩⲃⲟ	to purify	ⲙⲁⲧⲟⲩⲃⲟ	purify!
ϣⲉ ⲛ/	to go	ⲙⲁϣⲉ ⲛ/	go!
ϯⲱⲟⲩ	glorify	ⲙⲁⲱⲟⲩ	glorify!
ϯϩⲟ	to ask	ⲙⲁϯϩⲟ	ask!

More tenses

As mentioned above, this form replaces all those verbs which are linked with ϯ.

This includes the verb ϯ (to give) itself.

| ϯ ϯ- ⲧⲏⲓ⸗ | ⲙⲟⲓ ⲙⲁ- ⲙⲏⲓ⸗ | give! |

E.g. ⲙⲟⲓ ⲛⲏⲓ ⲛ̀ⲧⲁⲥⲱ *(John 4:7)*
"give me so that I drink"

Some exceptions

Two verbs in particular don't look anything like their non imperative form. Unlike the other imperative forms we've met, these verbs take different forms according to gender and number.

Infinitive	masculine singular	feminine singular	plural
ⲓ̀	ⲁⲙⲟⲩ	ⲁⲙⲏ	ⲁⲙⲱⲓⲛⲓ
ϭⲓ	ⲙⲟ	ⲙⲉ	ⲙⲱⲓⲛⲓ

Vocab			
ⲉⲛⲕⲟⲧ	to sleep, lay down, pass away (v.i)	ⲭⲱ ⲉ̀ⲃⲟⲗ	to forgive (v.t)
ⲓϣⲓ ⲉϣ- ⲁϣ⸗ ⲁϣⲓ	to hang up, crucify (v.t)	ϣⲱⲛⲓ	to be sick (v.i)
ⲙⲁⲛⲙⲟϣⲓ	place of walking (crossing) (m)	ϩⲁⲓ	husband (m)
ⲙ̀ⲙⲁⲩ	there (adv)	ϩⲩⲙⲛⲟⲥ	hymn (m)
ⲙ̀ⲛⲁⲓ	here (adv)	ϫⲟⲩϣⲧ	to look, see (v.i)
ⲙ̀ⲧⲟⲛ	to rest, repose (v.i)	ϭⲓⲥⲓ	the height, highest (m)
ⲧⲁⲗϭⲟ ⲧⲁⲗϭⲉ- ⲧⲁⲗϭⲟ⸗	to heal, to make to cease (v.i)		

So You want to Learn Coptic?

Exercise 10.7

a) ⲁⲣⲓϩⲟϯ ϧⲁⲧϩⲏ ⲙ̀ⲫϯ ⲟⲩⲟϩ ⲙⲁⲱⲟⲩ ⲛⲁϥ ϫⲉ ⲁⲥⲓ ⲛ̀ϫⲉ ϯⲟⲩⲛⲟⲩ ⲛ̀ⲧⲉ ⲡⲉϥϩⲁⲡ *(Revelation 14:7)*

b) ⲙⲁⲡⲓⲁⲗⲟⲩ ϣⲉⲛⲟⲩϯ ⲛⲏⲓ ⲛ̀ⲧⲉϥϫⲟⲩϣⲧ ⲉ̀ⲛⲓⲉⲥⲱⲟⲩ ⲛⲉⲙⲏⲓ *(SinArch page 8)*

c) ⲙⲁⲧⲁⲗϭⲟ ⲙ̀ⲡⲉⲕⲗⲁⲥ ⲉ̀ⲃⲟⲗϩⲁ ⲡⲓⲡⲉⲧϩⲱⲟⲩ *(Psalm **33:14** 34:13)*

d) ⲙⲁϣⲉⲛⲱⲧⲉⲛ ⲇⲉ ⲉ̀ⲃⲟⲗ ⲉ̀ⲛⲓⲙⲁⲛⲙⲟϣⲓ ⲛ̀ⲧⲉ ⲛⲓⲙⲱⲓⲧ *(Matthew 22:9)*

e) ⲡⲉϫⲉ Ⲓⲏⲥ ⲛⲁⲥ ϫⲉ ⲙⲁϣⲉ ⲛⲉ ⲙⲟⲩϯ ⲉ̀ⲡⲉϩⲁⲓ ⲟⲩⲟϩ ⲁⲙⲏ ⲉ̀ⲙ̀ⲛⲁⲓ *(John 4:16)*

f) ⲁⲛⲁⲩ ⲟⲩⲛ ⲙⲏⲡⲱⲥ ⲛ̀ⲧⲉϥⲓ̀ ⲉϫⲉⲛ ⲑⲏⲛⲟⲩ ⲛ̀ϫⲉ ⲫⲏ ⲉ̀ⲧⲁⲩϫⲟϥ ϧⲉⲛ ⲛⲓⲡ̀ⲣⲟⲫⲏⲧⲏⲥ *(Acts 13:40)*

g) ⲙⲁⲑⲁⲙⲓⲟ ⲛⲁⲛ ⲛ̀ϩⲁⲛⲛⲟⲩϯ *(Acts 7:40)*

h) ⲡⲉϫⲉ ⲡⲓⲗⲁⲧⲟⲥ ⲛⲱⲟⲩ ϫⲉ ⲙⲱⲓⲛⲓ ⲉⲣⲟϥ ⲛ̀ⲑⲱⲧⲉⲛ ⲁϣϥ *(John 19:6)*

i) Ⲡⲓⲁⲅⲅⲉⲗⲟⲥ ⲛ̀ⲧⲉ ⲡⲁⲓⲉ̀ϩⲟⲟⲩ ⲉⲧϭⲟⲥⲓ ⲉ̀ⲡ̀ϭⲓⲥⲓ ⲛⲉⲙ ⲡⲁⲓϩⲩⲙⲛⲟⲥ ⲁⲣⲓⲡⲉⲛⲙⲉⲩⲓ̀ ϧⲁⲧϩⲏ ⲙ̀Ⲡ̄ⲟ̄ⲥ̄ ⲛ̀ⲧⲉϥⲭⲁ ⲛⲉⲛⲛⲟⲃⲓ ⲛⲁⲛ ⲉ̀ⲃⲟⲗ. Ⲛ̀ⲏⲉⲧϣⲱⲛⲓ ⲙⲁⲧⲁⲗϭⲱⲟⲩ ⲛⲏⲉ̀ⲧⲁⲩⲉⲛⲕⲟⲧ Ⲡ̄ⲟ̄ⲥ̄ ⲙⲁⲙ̀ⲧⲟⲛ ⲛⲱⲟⲩ ⲛⲉⲛⲥ̀ⲛⲏⲟⲩ ⲉⲧⲭⲏ ϧⲉⲛ ϩⲟϫϩⲉϫ ⲛⲓⲃⲉⲛ Ⲡⲁ̄ⲟ̄ⲥ̄ ⲁ̀ⲣⲓⲃⲟⲓ̀ⲑⲓⲛ ⲉ̀ⲣⲟⲛ ⲛⲉⲙⲱⲟⲩ *(Conclusion to Batoc Theotokia)*

More tenses

Practice text 13
Psalm **34:1-3** *35:1-3*

David's supplications to the Lord in the times of his greatest distress would often take the form of the imperative, as this reading text shows.

Ⲙⲁϩⲁⲡ Ⲡ϶ⲟⲓⲥ ⲛ̀ⲛⲉⲧϭⲓ ⲙ̀ⲙⲟⲓ ⲛ̀ϫⲟⲛⲥ ⲟⲩⲟϩ ⲃⲱⲧⲥ ⲛ̀ⲛⲉⲧⲃⲱⲧⲥ ⲉ̀ⲣⲟⲓ. Ϭ'ⲓ ⲛ̀ⲟⲩϩⲟⲡⲗⲟⲛ ⲛⲉⲙ ⲟⲩϣⲉⲃϣⲓ ⲧⲱⲛⲕ ⲁ̀ⲣⲓⲃⲟⲏⲑⲓⲛ ⲉ̀ⲣⲟⲓ. ⲑⲱⲕⲉⲙ ⲛ̀ⲧⲉⲕⲥⲏϥⲓ ⲟⲩⲟϩ ⲙⲁϣⲑⲁⲙ ⲉ̀ϩⲣⲉⲛ ⲛⲏⲉⲧϭⲟϫⲓ ⲛ̀ⲥⲱⲓ ⲁ̀ϫⲟⲥ ⲛ̀ⲧⲁⲯⲩⲭⲏ ϫⲉ ⲁ̀ⲛⲟⲕ ⲡⲉ ⲡⲉⲟⲩϫⲁⲓ.

ⲃⲟⲏⲑⲓⲛ	to help, support (v.t)	ϣⲑⲁⲙ	to shut (v.t)
ⲃⲱⲧⲥ	to fight (v.t)	ϩⲟⲡⲗⲟⲛ	weapon (m)
ⲉ̀ϩⲣⲉⲛ	in front of (**Appendix 3**)	ϭⲓⲛϫⲟⲛⲥ	to use violence, do evil (v.t)
ⲑⲱⲕⲉⲙ	to draw out (knife or sword) v.t	ϭⲟϫⲓ ⲛ̀ⲥⲱ⸗	to persecute
ⲟⲩϫⲁⲓ	salvation (m)	ϯϩⲁⲡ	to judge (v.t)
ϣⲉⲃϣⲓ	shield (f)		

10.4.iii. The negative imperative

As surely as the emperors gave orders for things to be done, they also gave orders for things *not* to be done, hence we also have the negative imperative form. This form is actually much easier to remember than that for the affirmative imperative, as the only change is adding **ⲙ̀ⲡⲉⲣ⁻** before the infinitive for *any* verb you wish to convert, so there are no ⲁ⁻'s and no ⲙⲁ⁻'s to worry about.

E.g. *"Do not give"* is **ⲙ̀ⲡⲉⲣϯ**

ⲁ̀ⲛⲟⲕ ⲡⲉ ⲙ̀ⲡⲉⲣϩⲟϯ *(Mark 6:50)*

"It is I, do not fear"

So You want to Learn Coptic?

Vocab			
ⲉⲣⲛⲱⲓⲕ	to fornicate, commit adultery (v.i)	ϧⲱⲧⲉⲃ	to kill, murder (v.t)
ⲙⲉⲛⲣⲏⲧ	beloved (m)	ϩⲟⲣⲁⲙⲁ	vision, appearance (m, Gk)
ⲙⲉⲛⲣⲁϯ	beloved (pl)	ϥⲓⲣⲱⲟⲩϣ	to worry, take care of (v.i)
ⲛⲟⲩϫ	false, untrue (adj)	ϭⲓⲟⲩⲓ	to steal (v.t)
ⲧⲁⲥⲑⲟ	to return, bring back (v.t)	ϭⲟϫⲓ	to run, pursue (v.i)
ⲭⲁⲣⲱ⸗	to be silent (v.i)		

Exercise 10.8

a) ⲛⲁⲙⲉⲛⲣⲁϯ ⲙ̀ⲡⲉⲣⲛⲁϩϯ ⲉ̀ⲡ̅ⲛ̅ⲁ̅ ⲛⲓⲃⲉⲛ *(1 John 4:1)*

b) ⲙⲁϣⲉ ⲛⲉ ⲓⲥϫⲉⲛ ϯⲛⲟⲩ ⲙ̀ⲡⲉⲣⲧⲁⲥⲑⲟ ⲉ̀ⲉⲣⲛⲟⲃⲓ *(John 8:11)*

c) ⲙ̀ⲡⲉⲣⲣⲁϣⲓ ϧⲉⲛ ⲫⲁⲓ *(Luk 10:20)*

d) ⲙ̀ⲡⲉⲣϥⲓⲣⲱⲟⲩϣ ϧⲁ ⲡⲓⲣⲁⲥϯ *(Matthew 6:34)*

e) ⲙ̀ⲡⲉⲣϣⲉ ⲛⲱⲧⲉⲛ ⲟⲩⲇⲉ ⲙ̀ⲡⲉⲣϭⲟϫⲓ *(Luke 17:23)*

f) ⲙ̀ⲡⲉⲣϯϩⲁⲡ ϩⲓⲛⲁ ⲛ̀ⲧⲟⲩϣⲧⲉⲙϯϩⲁⲡ ⲉⲣⲱⲧⲉⲛ *(Matthew 7:1)*

g) ⲡⲉϫⲉ Ⲡ̅ⲟ̅ⲥ̅ ⲇⲉ ⲙ̀ⲡⲁⲩⲗⲟⲥ ⲉⲃⲟⲗ ϩⲓⲧⲉⲛ ⲟⲩϩⲟⲣⲁⲙⲁ ϧⲉⲛ ⲡⲓⲉ̀ϫⲱⲣϩ ϫⲉ ⲙ̀ⲡⲉⲣⲉⲣϩⲟϯ ⲁⲗⲗⲁ ⲥⲁϫⲓ ⲟⲩⲟϩ ⲙ̀ⲡⲉⲣⲭⲁⲣⲱⲕ *(Acts 18:9)*

h) ⲙ̀ⲡⲉⲣⲙⲉⲛⲣⲉ ⲡⲓⲕⲟⲥⲙⲟⲥ ⲟⲩⲇⲉ ⲛⲏ ⲉⲧϣⲟⲡ ϧⲉⲛ ⲡⲓⲕⲟⲥⲙⲟⲥ *(1 John 2:15)*

i) ⲛⲓⲉⲛⲧⲟⲗⲏ ⲕ̀ⲥⲱⲟⲩⲛ ⲙ̀ⲙⲱⲟⲩ ⲙ̀ⲡⲉⲣϧⲱⲧⲉⲃ ⲙ̀ⲡⲉⲣⲉⲣⲛⲱⲓⲕ ⲙ̀ⲡⲉⲣϭⲓⲟⲩⲓ ⲙ̀ⲡⲉⲣⲉⲣⲙⲉⲑⲣⲉ ⲛ̀ⲛⲟⲩϫ *(Mark 10:19)*

Practice text 14
Psalm 6:2-4 6:1-3

As we shall see in the following passage, David also made used of the negative imperative in his prayers and petitions to the Lord.

Ⲡ̅ⲟ̅ⲥ̅ ⲙ̀ⲡⲉⲣⲥⲟϩⲓ ⲙ̀ⲙⲟⲓ ϧⲉⲛ ⲡⲉⲕϫⲱⲛⲧ ⲟⲩⲇⲉ ⲛ̀ϩ̀ⲣⲏⲓ ϧⲉⲛ ⲡⲉⲕⲙ̀ⲃⲟⲛ. ⲙ̀ⲡⲉⲣϯ ⲥ̀ⲃⲱ ⲛⲏⲓ. ⲛⲁⲓ ⲛⲏⲓ Ⲡ̅ⲟ̅ⲥ̅ ϫⲉ ⲁ̀ⲛⲟⲕ ⲟⲩⲁⲥⲑⲉⲛⲏⲥ. ⲙⲁⲧⲁⲗϭⲟⲓ Ⲡ̅ⲟ̅ⲥ̅ ϫⲉ ⲛⲁⲕⲁⲥ ⲁⲩϣ̀ⲑⲟⲣⲧⲉⲣ ⲟⲩⲟϩ ⲁ̀ⲧⲁⲯⲩⲭⲏ ϣ̀ⲑⲟⲣⲧⲉⲣ ⲉ̀ⲙⲁϣⲱ

Vocab			
ⲁⲥⲑⲉⲛⲏⲥ	weak, feeble, (Gk,m)	ϣ̀ⲑⲟⲣⲧⲉⲣ	to be disturbed, troubled
ⲙ̀ⲃⲟⲛ	wrath (m)	ϫⲱⲛⲧ	anger (m)
ⲥⲟϩⲓ	to reprove, correct, admonish (v.t)	ϯⲥ̀ⲃⲱ	to teach, reprove

10.4.iv. A Milder imperative- The 'Optative'

There is a milder, more gentle way of giving instructions. This way is more of an encouragement rather than an order. Think of it as the difference between saying 'let us go to the beach' or 'let us pray', as opposed to 'go the beach!' or 'pray!.'

This form is called the *Optative*. It's unique amongst the tenses because it doesn't actually have a second person form. It is formed around the stem ⲙⲁⲣ⫽ and is conjugated as in the following table:

ⲙⲁⲣⲉ	pre subject form
ⲙⲁⲣⲓ⫽	may I
ⲙⲁⲣⲉϥ⫽	may he
ⲙⲁⲣⲉⲥ⫽	may she
ⲙⲁⲣⲟⲩ⫽	may they
ⲙⲁⲣⲉⲛ⫽	may we

So You want to Learn Coptic?

The optative can then be attached to either the infinitive or the pronominal form of the verb. E.g:

ϩⲱⲥ *"to praise"*

ⲙⲁⲣⲉⲛϩⲱⲥ *"let us praise"*

Vocab			
ⲛⲟϩⲉⲙ ⲛⲁϩⲉⲙ– ⲛⲁϩⲙ⸗ ⲛⲟϩⲉⲙ	to save, deliver (v.t)	ⲧⲟⲩⲃⲟ	to be, become pure, to purify (v.t)
ⲟⲩⲱϣ ⲟⲩⲉϣ– ⲟⲩⲁϣ⸗	to desire, to love (v.t)	ϩⲱⲥ	to praise (v.t)
ⲥⲱⲧⲉⲙ ⲥⲟⲑⲙ⸗	to hear, listen (v.t)	ⲭⲱⲣ ⲉⲃⲟⲗ	to disperse, scatter (v.t)

Exercise 10.9

a) ⲙⲁⲣⲉⲛϩⲱⲥ ⲉⲠ̅ⲟ̅ⲥ̅ *(Exodus 15:21)*

b) ⲙⲁⲣⲉϥⲧⲟⲩⲃⲟ ⲛ̇ϫⲉ ⲡⲉⲕⲣⲁⲛ *(Matthew 6:9)*

c) ⲙⲁⲣⲉⲥⲓ̇ ⲛ̇ϫⲉ ⲧⲉⲕⲙⲉⲧⲟⲩⲣⲟ *(Matthew 6:10)*

d) ⲙⲁⲣⲓ ⲥⲱⲧⲉⲙ ⲉ̇ⲡⲉⲕⲛⲁⲓ *(Psalm **142:8** 143:8)*

e) ⲙⲁⲣⲟⲩⲭⲱⲣ ⲉ̇ⲃⲟⲗ ⲛ̇ϫⲉ ⲛⲉⲕϫⲁϫⲓ ⲧⲏⲣⲟⲩ *(Numbers 10:35)*

f) ⲙⲁⲣⲉϥⲛⲁϩⲙⲉϥ ϯⲛⲟⲩ ⲓⲥϫⲉ ϥ̇ⲟⲩⲁϣϥ *(Matthew 27:43)*

g) ⲛⲑⲱⲧⲉⲛ ϩⲱⲧⲉⲛ ⲫⲏ ⲉⲧⲁⲣⲉⲧⲉⲛⲥⲟⲑⲙⲉϥ ⲓⲥϫⲉⲛ ϩⲏ ⲙⲁⲣⲉϥϣⲱⲡⲓ ϧⲉⲛ ⲑⲏⲛⲟⲩ[****] *(1 John 2:24)*

[****] Confused about the ϧⲉⲛ ⲑⲏⲛⲟⲩ? Refer to (**5.5**) for a reminder

10.5. When or if- The conditional

Sometimes, things we want have to wait till other things get done. For example, in the sentence *"I will buy a car, when I get lots of money"*, buying the car depends on getting money first. The key word here is 'when', which implies that a certain event has to take place before the next event can occur. In other words, the second event is *conditional* on the first event taking place first, hence the name of the condtional tense. The conditional is whole tense which carries the meaning of 'when' or 'if'. Superficially, this tense actually looks like the past perfect tense **(5.2)**, except that it has a ϣⲁⲛ stuck in between the pronoun and the verb as well:

ⲁⲓϣⲁⲛ⁻	when I, if I
ⲁⲕϣⲁⲛ⁻	when you, if you (m)
ⲁⲣⲉϣⲁⲛ⁻	when you, if you (f)
ⲁϥϣⲁⲛ⁻	when he, if he
ⲁⲥϣⲁⲛ⁻	when she, if she
ⲁⲛϣⲁⲛ⁻	when we
ⲁⲣⲉⲧⲉⲛϣⲁⲛ⁻	when you (plural)
ⲁⲩϣⲁⲛ⁻	when they
ⲁⲣⲉϣⲁⲛ⁻	pre subject form

In Coptic, this tense is used for both 'when' and 'if', which clearly don't always mean the same thing, so it's up to you to look at the context to decide which meaning is the most appropriate.

E.g. ⲁⲣⲓ ⲡⲁ ⲙⲉⲩⲓ Ⲡⲁ ⲟ̅ⲥ̅ ⲁⲕϣⲁⲛⲓ ϧⲉⲛ ⲧⲉⲕⲙⲉⲧⲟⲩⲣⲟ *(Hymn for service of Great Friday)*
"remember me my Lord when you come into your kingdom"

ⲕⲁⲛ is a special word which is often used with the conditional which gives the meaning of 'even if.'

E.g. ⲕⲁⲛ ⲁⲓϣⲁⲛϭⲓ ⲛⲉⲙ ⲛⲉϥϩ̀ⲃⲱⲥ ϯⲛⲁⲛⲟϩⲉⲙ *(Mark 5:28)*
"If I even touch his garments I shall be saved"

The word ⲉϣⲱⲡ which also means 'if or when' is often used with the conditional. In these cases, it's left untranslated as the rest of the conditional construction is enough to give the meaning of the conditional to the clause. On the other hand, ⲉϣⲱⲡ can also be used without the rest of the conditional construction, in which case it is translated;

E.g. ⲉϣⲱⲡ ⲇⲉ ⲁϥϣⲁⲛⲓ ⲛ̀ϫⲉ ⲡ̀ϣⲏⲣⲓ ⲙ̀ⲫⲣⲱⲙⲓ ϧⲉⲛ ⲡⲉϥⲱⲟⲩ ⲛⲉⲙ ⲛⲉϥⲁⲅⲅⲉⲗⲟⲥ ⲧⲏⲣⲟⲩ ⲛⲉⲙⲁϥ ⲧⲟⲧⲉ ⲉϥⲉϩⲉⲙⲥⲓ ϩⲓϫⲉⲛ ⲡ̀ⲑ̀ⲣⲟⲛⲟⲥ ⲛ̀ⲧⲉ ⲡⲉϥⲱⲟⲩ *(Matthew 25:31)*

"and when the son of man comes in his glory and all his angels with Him then he will sit on the throne of His Glory"

ⲉ̀ϣⲱⲡ ⲧⲉⲧⲉⲛⲙⲉⲓ ⲙ̀ⲙⲟⲓ ⲧⲉⲧⲉⲛⲛⲁⲁⲣⲉϩ ⲉ̀ⲛⲁⲉ̀ⲛⲧⲟⲗⲏ *(John 14:15)*

"if you love me you will keep my commandments"

Vocab			
ⲁⲣⲉϩ	to guard, to keep, to study (v.t)	ⲡⲁⲧϣⲉⲗⲉⲧ	bridegroom (m)
ⲉⲣⲛⲏⲥⲧⲉⲩⲓⲛ	to fast (v.i)	ⲥⲉⲃⲓ	circumcision (m)
ⲉⲣⲥ̀ⲕⲁⲛⲇⲁⲗⲓⲍⲉⲥⲑⲉ	to stumble (v.i)	ⲧⲟⲩⲛⲟⲥ ⲧⲟⲩⲛⲟⲥ- ⲧⲟⲩⲛⲉⲥ- ⲧⲟⲩⲛⲟⲥ⸗	to raise, arouse (v.t)
ⲑ̀ⲣⲟⲛⲟⲥ	throne (m)	ϩⲏⲟⲩ	profit, gain (m)
ⲙⲉⲧⲟⲩⲣⲟ	kingdom (f)	ϭⲓ ⲛⲉⲙ⸗	to touch (v.t)
ⲛⲟⲙⲟⲥ	law (m)		

Exercise 10.10

a) ⲡⲉⲧⲣⲟⲥ ⲇⲉ ⲡⲉϫⲁϥ ⲛⲁϥ ϫⲉ ⲕⲁⲛ ⲁⲩϣⲁⲛⲉⲣⲥ̀ⲕⲁⲛⲇⲁⲗⲓⲍⲉⲥⲑⲉ ⲧⲏⲣⲟⲩ ⲁⲗⲗⲁ ⲁ̀ⲛⲟⲕ ⲁⲛ *(Mark 14:29)*

More tenses

b) ⲥⲉⲛⲏⲟⲩ ⲇⲉ ⲛ̀ϫⲉ ϩⲁⲛⲉ̀ϩⲟⲟⲩ ⲉ̀ϣⲱⲡ ⲁⲩϣⲁⲛⲱⲗⲓ ⲙ̀ⲡⲓⲡⲁⲧϣⲉⲗⲉⲧ ⲉ̀ⲃⲟⲗ ϩⲁⲣⲱⲟⲩ ⲧⲟⲧⲉ ⲉⲩⲉⲉⲣⲛⲏⲥⲧⲉⲩⲓⲛ *(Matthew 9:15)*

c) ⲁⲩϣⲁⲛⲥⲱⲧⲉⲙ ϣⲁⲩϣⲉⲡ ⲡⲓⲥⲁϫⲓ ⲉⲣⲱⲟⲩ ϧⲉⲛ ⲟⲩⲣⲁϣⲓ *(Luke 8:13)*

d) ⲉⲣⲉⲧⲉⲛⲉ̀ϭⲓ ⲛ̀ⲟⲩϫⲟⲙ ⲉ̀ϣⲱⲡ ⲁⲣⲉϣⲁⲛ ⲡⲓⲡ͞ⲛ͞ⲁ ⲉⲑⲟⲩⲁⲃ ⲓ̀ ⲉ̀ϩⲣⲏⲓ ⲉϫⲉⲛ ⲑⲏⲛⲟⲩ *(Acts 1:8)*

e) ⲁⲓϣⲁⲛϭⲓ ⲇⲉ ⲛ̀ⲟⲩⲥⲛⲟⲩ †ⲛⲁⲟⲩⲱⲣⲡ ⲛ̀ⲥⲱⲕ *(Acts 24:25)*

f) ⲟⲩⲟⲛ ϩⲛⲟⲩ ⲅⲁⲣ ⲙ̀ⲡⲓⲥⲉⲃⲓ ⲉ̀ϣⲱⲡ ⲁⲕϣⲁⲛⲓⲣⲓ ⲙ̀ⲡⲓⲛⲟⲙⲟⲥ *(Romans 2:25)*

g) ⲉϥⲉⲧⲟⲩⲛⲟⲥϥ ⲛ̀ϫⲉ Ⲡ͞ⲟ͞ⲥ ⲕⲁⲛ ⲉ̀ϣⲱⲡ ⲁϥⲓⲣⲓ ⲛ̀ϩⲁⲛⲛⲟⲃⲓ ⲉⲩⲉⲭⲁⲩ ⲛⲁϥ ⲉ̀ⲃⲟⲗ *(James 5:15)*

10.5.i.   Negative of the conditional

If there is a chance that something will happen, there is also a chance that it will not happen, hence the reason for the negative conditional tense, used to express the meaning of 'if not.' The construction for the negative conditional will actually be a little familiar (at least it should be familiar, depending on your memory); as back in **(6.2.ii)** we saw that the negative of the subjunctive is formed by placing an **ϣⲧⲉⲙ** between the subjunctive and the verb. **ϣⲧⲉⲙ** is also used when forming the negative of the conditional. Here the **ϣⲧⲉⲙ** is swapped for the **ϣⲁⲛ** of the affirmative conditional as in the table below:

ⲁⲓϣⲧⲉⲙ-	if I do not
ⲁⲕϣⲧⲉⲙ-	if you do not (m)
ⲁⲣⲉϣⲧⲉⲙ-	if you do not (f)
ⲁϥϣⲧⲉⲙ-	if he does not
ⲁⲥϣⲧⲉⲙ-	if she does not
ⲁⲛϣⲧⲉⲙ-	if we do not

So You want to Learn Coptic?

ⲁⲣⲉⲧⲉⲛϣⲧⲉⲙ-	if you do not (plural)
ⲁⲩϣⲧⲉⲙ-	if they do not
ⲁⲣⲉϣⲧⲉⲙ-	pre subject form

E.g. ϯⲛⲟⲩ ⲇⲉ ⲁⲣⲉⲧⲉⲛϣⲧⲉⲙ ⲟⲩⲱϣⲧ ⲙ̅ⲙⲟⲥ ⲥⲉⲛⲁϩⲓ ⲑⲏⲛⲟⲩ ⲉ̀ϩⲣⲏⲓ ⲉ̀ϯϩⲣⲱ ⲙ̀ⲭⲣⲱⲙ *(hom vatt ii pg.81)*

"and now if you do not worship it you will be thrown down into the furnace of fire"

Vocab			
ⲁⲛⲟⲙⲟⲥ	lawless (adj Gk)	ⲉⲣⲙⲉⲧⲁⲛⲟⲓⲛ	to repent (Gk, v.i)
Ⲃⲁⲥⲓⲗⲓⲧⲏⲥ	Basil (prop.noun)	ⲓⲱⲓ ⲓⲁ̄— ⲓⲁ⸗	to wash (v.t)
Ⲇⲓⲟⲕⲗⲏⲧⲓⲁⲛⲟⲥ	Diocletian (prop noun)	ⲫⲱⲛ ⲉ̀ⲃⲟⲗ	to flow, pour out (v.i)
ⲉⲣⲕⲁⲧⲁⲅⲓⲛⲱⲥⲕⲓⲛ	to condemn (Gk)	ϭⲗⲟϫ	bed (m)

Exercise 10.11

a) ⲛⲁⲙⲉⲛⲣⲁϯ ⲉϣⲱⲡ ⲁⲣⲉϣⲧⲉⲙ ⲡⲉⲛϩⲏⲧ ⲉⲣⲕⲁⲧⲁⲅⲓⲛⲱⲥⲕⲓⲛ ⲙ̀ⲙⲟⲛ *(1 John 3:21)*

b) ⲉϣⲱⲡ ⲅⲁⲣ ⲁⲣⲉⲧⲉⲛ ϣⲧⲉⲙⲛⲁϩϯ ϫⲉ ⲁⲛⲟⲕ ⲡⲉ ⲧⲉⲧⲉⲛⲛⲁⲙⲟⲩ ⲛ̀ϩⲣⲏⲓ ϧⲉⲛ ⲛⲉⲧⲉⲛⲛⲟⲃⲓ *(John 8:24)*

c) ϯϫⲱ ⲙ̀ⲙⲟⲥ ⲛⲱⲧⲉⲛ ϫⲉ ⲁⲣⲉⲧⲉⲛϣⲧⲉⲙⲟⲩⲱⲙ ⲛ̀ⲧⲥⲁⲣⲝ ⲙ̀ⲡϣⲏⲣⲓ ⲙ̀ⲫⲣⲱⲙⲓ *(John 6:53)*

d) ⲛⲓⲫⲁⲣⲓⲥⲉⲟⲥ ⲅⲁⲣ ⲛⲉⲙ ⲛⲓⲓⲟⲩⲇⲁⲓ ⲧⲏⲣⲟⲩ ⲙ̀ⲡⲁⲩⲟⲩⲱⲙ ⲁⲩϣⲧⲉⲙⲓⲁⲧⲟⲧⲟⲩ ⲛ̀ⲟⲩⲙⲏϣ ⲛ̀ⲥⲟⲡ *(Mark 7:3)*

e) ϯⲛⲁϩⲓⲥ ⲉ̀ⲡϭⲗⲟϫ ⲛⲉⲙ ⲛⲏ ⲉⲧⲁⲩⲉⲣⲛⲱⲓⲕ ⲛⲉⲙⲁⲥ ⲉ̀ⲟⲩⲛⲓϣϯ ⲛ̀ϩⲟϫϩⲉϫ ⲉϣⲱⲡ ⲁⲥϣⲧⲉⲙⲉⲣⲙⲉⲧⲁⲛⲟⲓⲛ *(Revelation 2:22) f)* ⲡⲉϫⲁϥ ⲙ̀ⲡⲟⲩⲣⲟ ⲛ̀ⲁⲛⲟⲙⲟⲥ Ⲇⲓⲟⲕⲗⲧⲓⲁⲛⲟⲥ ϫⲉ ϥⲟⲛϩ ⲛ̀ϫⲉ Ⲡⲁ⳪ Ⲓⲏ̅ⲥ̅ Ⲡⲭ̅ⲥ̅ ⲁⲕϣ̀ⲧⲉⲙⲉⲛϩⲁⲓ ϩⲁⲣⲟⲓ ϩⲱ ⲛ̀ⲧⲉⲕⲟⲩⲟⲣⲡⲧ ⲉ̀ϩⲣⲏⲓ ⲉ̀ϫⲏⲙⲓ ⲛ̀ⲧⲟⲩⲫⲱⲛ ⲡⲁⲥ̀ⲛⲟϥ ⲉ̀ⲃⲟⲗ ϧⲉⲛ ⲡⲓⲙⲁ ⲉ̀ⲧⲉ ⲙ̀ⲙⲁⲩ ⲙ̀ⲫⲣⲏϯ ⲙ̀ⲡⲁⲓⲱⲧ Ⲃⲁⲥⲓⲗⲓⲧⲏⲥ ⲛⲉⲙ ⲛⲁⲥ̀ⲛⲏⲟⲩ ⲧⲏⲣⲟⲩ ϯⲛⲁⲱⲗⲓ ⲛ̀ⲧⲉⲕⲁⲫⲉ *(AmHyv pg29)*

> ### Practice text 15
> *Matthew 18:15-17*
>
> Ⲉϣⲱⲡ ⲇⲉ ⲁⲣⲉϣⲁⲛ ⲡⲉⲕⲥⲟⲛ ⲉⲣⲛⲟⲃⲓ ⲉ̀ⲣⲟⲕ ⲙⲁϣⲉ ⲛⲁⲕ ⲟⲩⲟϩ ⲥⲁϩⲱϥ ⲟⲩⲧⲱⲕ ⲛⲉⲙⲁϥ ⲙ̀ⲙⲁⲩⲁⲧⲕ ⲉϣⲱⲡ ⲁϥϣⲁⲛⲥⲱⲧⲉⲙ ⲛ̀ⲥⲱⲕ ⲉⲕⲉ̀ϫⲉⲙϩⲏⲟⲩ ⲙ̀ⲡⲉⲕⲥⲟⲛ. ⲉϣⲱⲡ ⲇⲉ ⲁϥϣ̀ⲧⲉⲙⲥⲱⲧⲉⲙ ⲛ̀ⲥⲱⲕ ϭⲓ ⲛ̀ⲕⲉⲟⲩⲁⲓ ⲓⲉ ⲕⲉⲃ̅ ⲛⲉⲙⲁⲕ ϩⲓⲛⲁ ⲉ̀ⲃⲟⲗ ϧⲉⲛ ⲣⲱϥ ⲙ̀ⲙⲉⲑⲣⲉ ⲃ̅ ⲓⲉ ⲅ̅ ⲛ̀ⲧⲉ ⲥⲁϫⲓ ⲛⲓⲃⲉⲛ ⲟϩⲓ ⲉ̀ⲣⲁⲧⲟⲩ. ⲉϣⲱⲡ ⲇⲉ ⲁϥϣ̀ⲧⲉⲙⲥⲱⲧⲉⲙ ⲛ̀ⲥⲱⲟⲩ ⲁϫⲟⲥ ⲛ̀ϯⲉⲕⲕⲗⲏⲥⲓⲁ. ⲉϣⲱⲡ ⲇⲉ ⲁϥϣ̀ⲧⲉⲙⲥⲱⲧⲉⲙ ⲛ̀ⲥⲁ ϯⲉⲕⲕⲗⲏⲥⲓⲁ ⲉϥⲉ̀ϣⲱⲡⲓ ⲛ̀ⲧⲟⲧⲕ ⲙ̀ⲫⲣⲏϯ ⲛ̀ⲟⲩⲉⲑⲛⲓⲕⲟⲥ ⲛⲉⲙ ⲟⲩⲧⲉⲗⲱⲛⲏⲥ
>
> | Vocab | | | |
> |---|---|---|---|
> | ⲉⲑⲛⲓⲕⲟⲥ | foreigner, Gentile, heathen (Gk,m) | ⲣⲱϥ | (his) mouth **15.4** |
> | ⲛ̀ⲧⲟⲧⲕ | to you **(Appendix 3)** | ⲥⲟϩⲓ ⲥⲁϩⲱ⳱ | to blame, rebuke, correct, admonish (v.t) |
> | ⲟⲩⲧⲉ ⲟⲩⲧⲱ⳱ | between, among | ⲧⲉⲗⲱⲛⲏⲥ | tax collector (Gk, m) |
> | ⲟϩⲓ ⲉⲣⲁⲧ⳱ | to stand (vi, reflex) | ϫⲉⲙϩⲏⲟⲩ | to profit, gain |

So You want to Learn Coptic?

11. MORE ON THE INFINITIVE

Up till now, we've focussed mainly on the different forms and tenses derived from the infinitive. In this chapter though, we'll concentrate more on the grammatical structures which involve the infinitive itself as a unit.

11.1. Making things happen- the causative

The infinitive has another special form which we'll get acquainted with here. The prefix (ⲉ̀)ⲑⲣⲉ⳱ is added before the infinitive to give the meaning of 'causing it to happen' or 'in order to', hence the construction is called the 'causative infinitive.' The infinitive form which does not take the causative (that is the one we have dealt with all along) is known as the 'simple infinitive'. Let's take an example of making a causative infinitive by applying the construction to the simple infinitive ϩⲱⲥ *'to praise.'*

The prefix (ⲉ̀)ⲑ̀ⲣ(ⲉ)⳱ first adds a letter to the stem depending on the person and number of the subject. The new combination is then placed before the infinitive, as in the examples below:

(ⲉ)ⲑⲣⲓϩⲱⲥ	so that I praise
(ⲉ)ⲑⲣⲉⲕϩⲱⲥ	so that you praise (m)
(ⲉ)ⲑⲣⲉϩⲱⲥ	so that you praise (f)
(ⲉ)ⲑⲣⲉϥϩⲱⲥ	so that he praise
(ⲉ)ⲑⲣⲉⲥϩⲱⲥ	so that she praise
(ⲉ)ⲑⲣⲉⲛϩⲱⲥ	so that we praise
(ⲉ̀)ⲑⲣⲉⲧⲉⲛϩⲱⲥ (ⲉ)ⲑⲣⲉⲧⲉⲧⲉⲛϩⲱⲥ	so that you praise (plural)
(ⲉ)ⲑⲣⲟⲩϩⲱⲥ	so that they praise

So You want to Learn Coptic?

E.g. ⲙⲁϩⲑⲏⲧⲉⲛ ⲇⲉ ⲉ̀ⲡⲉⲧⲉⲛⲧⲁⲓⲟ ⲙ̀ⲡⲉⲣⲁⲓϥ ⲙ̀ⲡⲉⲙⲑⲟ ⲛ̀ⲛⲓⲣⲱⲙⲓ

ⲉⲑⲣⲟⲩⲛⲁⲩ ⲉⲣⲱⲧⲉⲛ *(Matthew 6:1)*

"And Give heed to your gift, do not make it before men that they see you"

ⲑ̀ⲣⲉ⫽ can also be used as a verb in its own right with the meaning of 'to cause.' The construction then takes the following form:

ⲑ̀ⲣⲉ⫽ + optional object marker + object + infinitive

Note that the infinitive stands at the end of the construction without having any letters attached to it, that is the 'to' in 'cause to' is inferred in the translation but doesn't actually have an equivalent in the Coptic.

E.g. ⲁϥⲑ̀ⲣⲉ ⲡⲱⲛϧ ⲉⲣⲟⲩⲱⲓⲛⲓ ⲉ̀ⲣⲟⲛ   *(Second verse Doxology of the Resurrection)*

"He caused the life to shine on us"

Vocab			
ⲥⲁⲙ̀ⲡⲉⲑⲛⲁⲛⲉⲩ	beneficient, good	ⲥⲁⲙ̀ⲡⲉⲧϩⲱⲟⲩ	evil doer, sinner

Exercise 11.1

a) ⲥⲉⲑ̀ⲣⲟⲩ ⲛ̀ⲑ̀ⲃⲁⲕⲓ ⲙ̀Ⲫϯ ⲟⲩⲛⲟϥ   *(Psalm 45:4 46:4)*

b) ϫⲉ ⲉϥⲑ̀ⲣⲟ ⲙ̀ⲡⲉϥⲣⲏ ϣⲁⲓ ⲉϫⲉⲛ ⲛⲓⲥⲁⲙ̀ⲡⲉⲧϩⲱⲟⲩ ⲛⲉⲙ ⲛⲓⲥⲁⲙ̀ⲡⲉⲑⲛⲁⲛⲉⲩ   *(Matthew 5:45)*

c) ⲉⲓⲉ̀ⲑ̀ⲣⲉ ⲡⲉⲕⲣⲁⲛ ⲉⲣⲛⲓϣϯ   *(Genesis 12:2)*

d) ⲁⲩⲑ̀ⲣⲉϥϩⲉⲙⲥⲓ ⲥⲁⲡ̀ϣⲱⲓ ⲙ̀ⲙⲱⲟⲩ   *(Matthew 21:7)*

e) ϯⲛⲁⲑ̀ⲣⲉ ⲛⲉⲧⲉⲛⲥⲱⲙⲁ ⲉⲣⲟⲩⲱⲓⲛⲓ ⲙ̀Ⲫ̀ⲣⲏϯ ⲙ̀Ⲫ̀ⲣⲏ   *(hom vatt ii pg.87)*

More on the infinitive

Practice text 16
Panéric des trois enfants de Babylone, Homélies Coptes de Vaticaine pg.87

ϯⲛⲁϭⲟ̅ⲛⲧ ⲛⲉⲧⲉⲛⲣⲁⲛ ϧⲉⲛ ϯⲉⲕⲕ̅ⲗⲏⲥⲓⲁ ⲛ̅ⲛⲓϣⲟⲣⲡ ⲙ̅ⲙⲓⲥⲓ ϯⲛⲁⲑⲣⲟⲩϩⲓⲱⲓϣ ⲙ̅ⲙⲟϥ ϧⲉⲛ ⲡⲓⲕⲟⲥⲙⲟⲥ ⲧⲏⲣϥ. ⲉϣⲱⲡ ⲁⲓϣⲁⲛⲓ ϧⲉⲛ ⲧⲁⲡⲁⲣⲟⲩⲥⲓⲁ ϯⲛⲁⲑⲣⲉ ⲛⲉⲧⲉⲛⲥⲱⲙⲁ ⲉⲣⲟⲩⲱⲓⲛⲓ ⲙ̅ⲫⲣⲏϯ ⲙ̅ⲫⲣⲏ ⲟⲩⲟϩ ⲉⲑⲣⲉ ⲧⲉⲧⲉⲛϣⲱⲡⲓ ⲉⲣⲉⲧⲉⲛⲟⲓ ⲙ̅ⲩ̇ϣⲏⲣⲓ ⲙ̅ⲡⲉⲙⲑⲟ ⲛ̅ⲛⲓⲉⲑⲛⲟⲥ ⲧⲏⲣⲟⲩ

Vocab			
ⲟⲩⲧⲉ ⲟⲩⲧⲱ⸗	between, among (prep.)	ⲣⲱϥ	(his) mouth **(15.4)**
ⲟϩⲓ ⲉⲣⲁⲧ⸗	to stand (vi,reflex)	ⲥϧⲁⲓ ⲥϧⲏⲧ⁻ ⲥϧⲏⲧ⸗ ⲥϧⲏⲟⲩⲧ (q)	to write (v.t)
ⲡⲁⲣⲟⲩⲥⲓⲁ	appearance (Gk,f)		

11.1.i. Negative of the causative

The negative of the causative is really very much like the negative imperative because it also carries the meaning of ordering something to not be done. It is formed by placing ⲙ̅ⲡⲉⲛ which is the equivalent of the ⲙ̅ⲡⲉⲣ of the negative imperative **(10.4.iii)** before ⲑⲣⲉ.

E.g. ⲙ̅ⲡⲉⲛⲑⲣⲉ ⲡⲉⲧⲉⲛϩⲏⲧ ϣⲑⲟⲣⲧⲉⲣ ⲛⲁϩϯ ⲉⲫϯ ⲟⲩⲟϩ ⲛⲁϩϯ ⲉⲣⲟⲓ ϩⲱ *(John 14:1)*

"Do not cause your heart to be disturbed believe in God and believe in me also"

Vocab

ⲕⲁⲕⲓⲁ	evil, malice (Gk,f)	ϣⲱⲡ	to buy, accept (v.t)
ⲫⲟⲩⲁⲓ ⲫⲟⲩⲁⲓ	each one	ϩⲗⲓ	thing, person, nothing, anyone
ⲭⲱⲣⲁ	district, country (Gk,f)	ϫⲉⲙⲛⲟⲩϯ	to find comfort (v.i)

Exercise 11.2

a) Ⲡ̅ⲟ̅ⲥ̅ ⲙ̅ⲡⲉⲛⲑⲣⲉⲛⲧⲁⲕⲟ ⲉⲑⲃⲉ ϯⲯⲩⲭⲏ ⲛ̀ⲧⲉ ⲡⲁⲓⲣⲱⲙⲓ *(Jonah 1:14)*

b) Ⲁϥⲓ ⲛ̀ϫⲉ ⲡⲓⲥⲛⲟⲩ ⲟⲩⲟϩ ϩⲏⲡⲡⲉ ⲓⲥ ⲡⲓⲉ̀ϩⲟⲟⲩ ⲁϥϧⲱⲛⲧ ⲉ̀ϧⲟⲩⲛ ⲙ̀ⲡⲉⲛⲑⲣⲉ ⲫⲏⲉⲧϣⲱⲡ ⲣⲁϣⲓ *(Ezekiel 7:12)*

c) Ⲟⲩⲟϩ ⲫⲟⲩⲁⲓ ⲫⲟⲩⲁⲓ ⲙ̀ⲙⲱⲧⲉⲛ ⲙ̀ⲡⲉⲛⲑⲣⲉϥⲙⲉⲩⲓ ⲉ̀ⲟⲩⲕⲁⲕⲓⲁ̀ ϧⲉⲛ ⲡⲉⲧⲉⲛϩⲏⲧ *(Zechariah 8:17)*

d) Ϧⲉⲛ ⲡⲓⲥⲛⲟⲩ ⲇⲉ ⲉⲧⲉⲙ̀ⲙⲁⲩ ⲉϥⲉ̀ϫⲟⲥ ⲛ̀ϫⲉ Ⲡ̅ⲟ̅ⲥ̅ ⲛ̀Ⲓⲗ̅ⲏ̅ⲙ̅ ϫⲉ ϫⲉⲙⲛⲟⲩϯ Ⲥⲓⲱⲛ ⲙ̀ⲡⲉⲛⲑⲣⲟⲩⲃⲱⲗ ⲉ̀ⲃⲟⲗ ⲛ̀ϫⲉ ⲛⲉⲭⲓϫ *(Zephaniah 3:16)*

e) ⲟⲩⲟϩ ⲛⲏ ⲉⲧϧⲉⲛ ⲛⲓⲭⲱⲣⲁ ⲙ̀ⲡⲉⲛⲑⲣⲟⲩϣⲉ ⲉ̀ϧⲟⲩⲛ ⲉ̀ⲣⲟⲥ *(Luke 21:21)*

f) ⲙ̀ⲡⲉⲛⲑⲣⲉ ⲛ̀ϩⲏⲧ ⲙ̀ⲡⲟⲩⲣⲟ ϣⲑⲟⲣⲧⲉⲣ *(hom vatt ii pg. 95)*

11.2. Verbal substantive- making nouns from verbs

Throughout the course of this book, you may have noticed that some infinitives are identical to their corresponding nouns,
E.g.

ⲣⲁϣⲓ *"to rejoice"* (v.i)

ⲣⲁϣⲓ *"joy"* (m)

Sometimes, the prefix **ϫⲓⲛ⁄** is used before the verb to convert it to a noun which represents the 'way,' or the 'manner' in which the verb is done.
E.g.

ⲁⲣⲉϩ *'to guard, keep, study'* (v.t)

ϫⲓⲛⲁⲣⲉϩ *'act of guarding'* (m)

More on the infinitive

ⲑⲁⲙⲓⲟ *'to create' (v.t)*

ϫⲓⲛⲑⲁⲙⲓⲟ *'the act of creating' (m)*

There are also verbs where the infinitive may be converted to a noun with or without the ϫⲓⲛ. The two nouns formed in this way carry somewhat different meanings:
E.g.

ⲱⲛϩ *'to live'*

ⲱⲛϩ *'life'* (m)

ϫⲓⲛⲱⲛϩ *'way, manner of life'*

The form resulting from the conversion of the verb to the noun is called the *verbal substantive* as the substantive is understood grammatically to refer to "acting to or like a noun." The verbal substantive may be expanded to form an *adverbial phrase*. Here the verbal substantive is converted to form a phrase which adds meaning to another clause in the sentence.

The first step to making the conversion to the adverbial phrase is to add one of the four constructions in the table below to the infinitive. We'll use the infinitive ⲃⲱⲗ as an example to demonstrate what the four different end product look like in the table below:

	A	B
1	ⲡϫⲓⲛⲧⲉ ⲃⲱⲗ	ⲡϫⲓⲛⲧ⸗ⲃⲱⲗ
2	ⲡϫⲓⲛⲑⲣⲉ ⲃⲱⲗ	ⲡϫⲓⲛⲑⲣⲉ⸗ ⲃⲱⲗ

If you look at row 2, you'll notice that the substantives in that row have a ⲑⲣⲉ, so you would think that those forms would somehow be related to the causative (**11.1**) in their meaning. Unfortunately, this is one those circumstances where logic takes a back seat, because there is actually *no* difference in meaning between the forms in rows 1 and 2.

Now the forms in column A come before a noun, whereas those in B come before a pronoun. In other words, column A has the construct form (**5.3.ii**), and B has the pronominal form (**5.3.i**).

The endings used to give the subject for the form in cell B2 are the same as those which were used with ⲑⲣⲉ⳱ in **(11.1)**. The endings which follow the ⲡϫⲓⲛⲧ⳱ in B1 are given below:

	singular	plural
first person	ⲡϫⲓⲛⲧⲁ	ⲡϫⲓⲛⲧⲉⲛ
second person (m)	ⲡϫⲓⲛⲧⲉⲕ	ⲡϫⲓⲛⲧⲉⲧⲉⲛ
second person (f)	ⲡϫⲓⲛⲧⲉ	
third person (m)	ⲡϫⲓⲛⲧⲉϥ	ⲡϫⲓⲛⲧⲟⲩ
third person (f)	ⲡϫⲓⲛⲧⲉⲥ	
prenominal form	ⲡϫⲓⲛⲧⲉ	

The next step to forming the adverbial phrase is to add either the preposition ⲉ̀ or ϧⲉⲛ to any of the four constructions above. Adding ⲉ̀ gives the meaning of "in order to", and adding ϧⲉⲛ gives the meaning of 'when.'

Something very important to note here (which will save you a lot confusion) is that when the verbal substantive is used in the adverbial phrase, it no longer carries the same meaning as when it was just a verbal substantive. This point is illustrated in the example below:

E.g. ⲥⲱⲧⲉⲙ Ⲫϯ ⲉ̀ ⲧⲁⲡⲣⲟⲥⲉⲩⲭⲏ ϧⲉⲛ ⲡϫⲓⲛⲧⲁⲧⲱⲃϩ *(Psalm 63:2 63:1)*
"hear O God my prayer when I pray"

ⲡϫⲓⲛⲧⲁⲧⲱⲃϩ on its own would mean *"manner of my prayer"*, but when it has the ϧⲉⲛ before it, it no longer means *"manner of my prayer"*, but in combination with ϧⲉⲛ means 'when I pray' (note that we've used the first person singular form with verbal substantive in this case.)

In the next example, the preposition used before the verbal substantive is ⲉ̀, which means 'in order to.'

E.g. ⲉⲑⲃⲉ ⲫⲁⲓ ⲁⲓ̀ ⲉ̀ⲡⲓⲕⲟⲥⲙⲟⲥ ⲉ̀ⲡϫⲓⲛⲧⲁⲉⲣⲙⲉⲑⲣⲉ ⲛ̀ϯⲙⲉⲑⲙⲏⲓ *(John 18:37)*
"for the sake of this I came to the world, to witness to the truth"

More on the infinitive

Vocab			
ⲉⲣⲡⲓⲣⲁⲍⲓⲛ	to tempt (v.t)	ⲱⲗⲓ ⲉⲗ- ⲟⲗ⳰ ⲟⲗ,ⲏⲗ	to hold, take (v.t)
ⲉⲭⲙⲁⲗⲱⲥⲓⲁ	captivity (Gk, f)	ϭⲓⲙⲱⲓⲧ ϧⲁ	to lead (v.i)
Ⲫⲓⲗⲓⲥⲧⲓⲛ	Philistine (prop.noun)		

Exercise 11.3

a) ϧⲉⲛ ⲡ̀ⲭⲓⲛⲑⲣⲉϥⲥⲱⲧⲉⲙ ⲛ̀ϫⲉ ⲡⲟⲩⲣⲟ ⲉⲡ̀ϩⲣⲱⲟⲩ ⲛ̀ⲛⲓⲙⲏϣ ⲁϥⲉⲣϣ̀ⲫⲏⲣⲓ *(hom vatt ii pg.83)*

b) ϧⲉⲛ ⲡ̀ⲭⲓⲛ ⲑ̀ⲣⲉ Ⲡ̅ⲟ̅ⲥ̅ ⲧⲁⲥⲑⲟ ⲛ̀ϯⲉⲭⲙⲁⲗⲱⲥⲓⲁ ⲛ̀ⲧⲉ Ⲥⲓⲱⲛ ⲁⲛϣⲱⲡⲓ ⲙ̀ⲫ̀ⲣⲏϯ ⲛ̀ϩⲁⲛⲟⲩⲟⲛ ⲉⲁⲩϯⲛⲟⲙϯ ⲛⲱⲟⲩ *(Psalm 125:1 126:1)*

c) ⲛⲁϥϫⲱ ⲇⲉ ⲛ̀ⲟⲩⲡⲁⲣⲁⲃⲟⲗⲏ ⲛⲱⲟⲩ ⲉⲡ̀ⲭⲓⲛⲧⲟⲩ ⲉⲣⲡⲣⲟⲥⲉⲩⲭⲉⲥⲑⲉ ⲛ̀ⲥⲏⲟⲩ ⲛⲓⲃⲉⲛ *(Luke 18:1)*

d) ϧⲉⲛ ⲡ̀ⲭⲓⲛϫⲟⲥ ϫⲉ ⲙ̀ⲫⲟⲟⲩ ⲉϣⲱⲡ ⲁⲣⲉⲧⲉⲛϣⲁⲛⲥⲱⲧⲉⲙ ⲉ̀ⲧⲉϥⲥ̀ⲙⲏ *(Hebrews 3:15)*

e) ϧⲉⲛ ⲡ̀ⲭⲓⲛ ⲑ̀ⲣⲉ Ⲫⲁⲣⲁⲱ̀ ⲭⲱ ⲙ̀ⲡⲓⲗⲁⲟⲥ ⲉ̀ⲃⲟⲗ ⲙ̀ⲡⲉϥϭⲓⲙⲱⲓⲧ ϧⲁϫⲱⲟⲩ ⲛ̀ϫⲉ Ⲫϯ ⲉ̀ⲫ̀ⲙⲱⲓⲧ ⲙ̀Ⲫⲩⲗⲓⲥⲧⲓⲛ *(Exodus 13:17)*

f) ⲁ ⲡⲓⲡ̅ⲛ̅ⲁ̅ ⲟⲗϥ ⲉⲡ̀ϣⲁϥⲉ ⲉⲡ̀ⲭⲓⲛⲧⲉ ⲡⲓⲇⲓⲁ̀ⲃⲟⲗⲟⲥ ⲉⲣⲡⲓⲣⲁⲍⲓⲛ ⲙ̀ⲙⲟϥ *(Matthew 4:1)*

11.3. Being able- the potential infinitive

Having the potential to do something means that you are able to do it, and it is this meaning that the potential infinitive carries, i.e. of "being able." This form of the infinitive is constructed by taking an ϣ̀ before the infinitive.

E.g. ϣ̀ⲥⲁϫⲓ *"to be able to speak"*

So You want to Learn Coptic?

The ϣ̄ is often combined with the noun ϫoⲙ 'power' to make ϣϫoⲙ. The combination ϣϫoⲙ is then combined with the impersonal verb oⲩoⲛ "*there is*" **(8.2.ii)**. So oⲩoⲛ ϣϫoⲙ means "there is power." The original English meaning for 'power' is actually 'ability.' So to say "there is power" actually means "there is ability", or "it is possible." To this we finally add the object marker ⲙ̄ (ⲛ̄) **(5.1.iv)**.

E.g. oⲩoⲛ ϣϫoⲙ ⲙ̄ⲡⲉⲧⲣoⲥ
"It is possible for Peter"

Naturally, the pronoun form for ⲙ̄ (ⲛ̄) which we saw in **(8.2.ii)** can also be used. So oⲩoⲛϣϫoⲙ ⲙ̄ⲙoⲓ means "there is power to me" or "I am able."

When we need to know exactly what one is able to do, we connect the preposition ⲉ̀ with the relevant verb, so for example:

oⲩoⲛ ϣϫoⲙ ⲙ̄ⲙoⲓ ⲉ̀ⲱϣ means *"I am able to read."*

An alternative construction which can be used is made by sneaking in a ϫⲉⲙ between ϣ̄ and ϫoⲙ. ϫⲉⲙ is the construct form (**5.3.ii**), of ϫⲓⲙⲓ which means "to find", so the construction literally means *"it is possible to find power."*

The dependent personal pronoun (**5.1.i**) is then attached before the new construction.

E.g. ϥϣϫⲉⲙϫoⲙ.
"He is able to find power" or *"He is able."*

This time the ⲛ̄/ⲙ̄ construction is then used on the verb that follows:

ϥϣϫⲉⲙϫoⲙ ⲛ̄ⲥⲁϫⲓ
"He is able to speak"

Vocab	
ⲃⲱⲗ ⲃⲉⲗ— ⲃoⲗ⸗ ⲃⲏⲗ (ⲉ̀ⲃoⲗ)	to loosen, undo, collapse (v.t)
ⲧoⲩⲃo ⲧoⲩⲃⲉ— ⲧoⲩⲃo⸗ ⲧoⲩⲃⲏoⲩⲧ	to clean, purify (v.t)
ϯⲗoⲅoⲥ	give account (v.i)

More on the infinitive

Exercise 11.4

a) ⲚⲀⲒ ⲈⲦⲈ ⲞⲨⲞⲚ ϢϪⲞⲘ ⲘⲘⲰⲞⲨ ⲈϮⲤⲂⲰ ⲚⲀⲔ ⲈⲠⲒⲞⲨϪⲀⲒ ⲈⲂⲞⲖ ϨⲒⲦⲈⲚ ⲠⲒⲚⲀϨϮ ⲈⲦϦⲈⲚ ⲠⲬⲤ ⲒⲎⲤ *(2 Timothy 3:15)*

b) ⲠⲀⲞⲤ ⲀⲔϢⲀⲚⲞⲨⲰϢ ⲞⲨⲞⲚ ϢϪⲞⲘ ⲘⲘⲞⲔ ⲈⲦⲞⲨⲂⲞⲒ *(Matthew 8:2)*

c) Ⲁ ⲪⲀⲒ ϪⲞⲤ ϪⲈ ⲞⲨⲞⲚ ϢϪⲞⲘ ⲘⲘⲞⲒ ⲈⲂⲈⲖ ⲠⲒⲈⲢⲪⲈⲒ ⲚⲦⲈ ⲪϮ ⲈⲂⲞⲖ *(Matthew 26:61)*

d) ⲈⲐⲂⲈ ⲪⲀⲒ Ⲁ ⁺⁺⁺⁺ϢϪⲈⲘϪⲞⲘ ⲚⲈⲢϨⲀⲖ ⲘⲘⲞⲤ ⲔⲀⲦⲀ ⲪⲞⲨⲰϢ ⲘⲠⲈⲤϨⲎⲦ *(hom vat ii pg.114)*

e) ⲐⲀⲒ ⲈⲦⲈ ⲞⲨⲞⲚ ϢϪⲞⲘ ⲘⲘⲞⲚ ⲈϮⲖⲞⲄⲞⲤ ⲈⲐⲂⲎⲦⲤ ϦⲀ ⲠⲒϢⲐⲞⲢⲦⲈⲢ *(Acts 19:40)*

11.3.i. *Not being able- the negative potential*

Unfortunately, we can't always be positive that we can do everything we want, and we have to admit that there are some things which just can't be done. Without being too negative, the Copts had devised is a special tense for expressing that things are impossible.

The construction used for this tense is similar to that for the potential infinitive. You'll recall that in the section on impersonal verbs **(8.2.ii)**, ⲞⲨⲞⲚ meant 'there is', whereas ⲘⲘⲞⲚ meant 'there isn't.' Likewise, as ⲞⲨⲞⲚ was used for the affirmative potential infinitive, so ⲘⲘⲞⲚ is used for the negative potential.

Now ⲘⲘⲞⲚ is attached before the ϢϪⲞⲘ, with the combination being used in the same way that ⲞⲨⲞⲚ ϢϪⲞⲘ was used in the section above.

E.g. ⲘⲘⲞⲚϢϪⲞⲘ ⲘⲔⲈⲚⲞⲨϮ ⲈⲚⲞϨⲈⲘ ⲘⲠⲀⲒⲢⲎϮ *(Daniel 3:29)*
"it is not possible for another god to save in this way"

⁺⁺⁺⁺ notice that the pre subject form of the past perfect **(5.2)** can be used to convert the construction to the past tense

So You want to Learn Coptic?

Sometimes you'll want to talk about something that could not have been done in the past. In these cases, the negative form of the past perfect **(5.2.i)** is combined with the ϣϫⲟⲙ without any need for the ⲙⲙⲟⲛ.

E.g. ⲙⲡⲟⲩ ϣϫⲟⲙ ⲛ̇ⲁⲙⲟⲛⲓ ⲙ̇ⲙⲟϥ *(Third verse Doxology of Resurrection)*
"They could not hold him"

Vocab			
ⲁⲙⲟⲛⲓ	to hold, seize, detain (v.t)	ⲥⲱ	to drink (v.t)
ⲉⲩⲥⲉⲃⲓⲟⲥ	Eusebius (prop.noun)	ϫⲱⲗ ⲉ̇ⲃⲟⲗ	to deny (v.i)
ⲡⲟⲗⲉⲙⲟⲥ	battle (Gk,m)		

Exercise 11.5

a) ⲙ̇ⲙⲟⲛ ϣϫⲟⲙ ⲙ̇ⲙⲟϥ ⲉ̇ⲛⲁⲩ *(John 3:3)*

b) ⲙ̇ⲙⲟⲛ ϣϫⲟⲙ ⲙ̇ⲙⲟϥ ⲉ̇ⲛⲁϩⲙⲉϥ *(Matthew 27:42)*

c) ⲙ̇ⲙⲟⲛ ϣϫⲟⲙ ⲅⲁⲣ ⲛ̇ϩⲗⲓ ⲉ̇ⲉⲣ ⲛⲁⲓⲙⲏⲓⲛⲓ ⲉⲧⲉⲕⲓⲣⲓ ⲙ̇ⲙⲱⲟⲩ ⲁⲣⲉϣⲧⲉⲙ⁂ Ⲫϯ ϣⲱⲡⲓ ⲛⲉⲙⲁϥ *(John 3:2)*

d) ⲥⲉⲥⲱⲟⲩⲛ ⲛ̇ϫⲉ ⲛⲏ ⲧⲏⲣⲟⲩ ⲉⲧϣⲟⲡ ϧⲉⲛ ⲓ̅ⲗ̅ⲏ̅ⲙ̅ ⲙ̇ⲙⲟⲛ ϣϫⲟⲙ ⲙ̇ⲙⲟⲛ ⲉ̇ϫⲱⲗ ⲉ̇ⲃⲟⲗ *(Acts 4:16)*

e) ⲙ̇ⲙⲟⲛ ϣϫⲟⲙ ⲙ̇ⲙⲱⲧⲉⲛ ⲉ̇ⲥⲱ ⲉⲃⲟⲗ ϧⲉⲛ ⲡⲓⲁⲫⲟⲧ ⲛ̇ⲧⲉ Ⲡ̅ⲟ̅ⲥ̅ ⲛⲉⲙ ⲡⲓⲁⲫⲟⲧ ⲛ̇ⲧⲉ ⲛⲓⲇⲉⲙⲱⲛ *(1 Corinthians 10:21)*

f) ⲙ̇ⲙⲟⲛ ϣϫⲟⲙ ⲙ̇ⲙⲟⲓ ⲉ̇ⲉⲣⲫⲁⲓ ϣⲁⲧⲉϥⲓ̇ ⲛ̇ϫⲉ ⲉⲩⲥⲉⲃⲓⲟⲥ ⲡⲁϣⲏⲣⲓ ⲉ̇ⲃⲟⲗϧⲉⲛ ⲡⲓⲡⲟⲗⲉⲙⲟⲥ *(AmHyv p2)*

⁂ You may need to refer to **(10.5.i)** to remind yourself of this construction

11.4. Not yet

If you've been wading your way through this book, and found the going a bit tough, you may be starting to ask "am I near the end yet?" To this the reply must be 'not yet'. In fact, there's a special construction in Coptic completely devoted to giving the meaning of 'not yet.' It is formed with either ⲙⲡⲁⲧ⳱ as the pronoun form, or ⲙⲡⲁⲧⲉ- as the construct form. An example of its usage is shown below using the verb ⲛⲁⲩ *'to see.'*

ⲙⲡⲁϯⲛⲁⲩ	I have not yet seen
ⲙⲡⲁⲧⲉⲕⲛⲁⲩ	You have not yet seen (m)
ⲙⲡⲁⲧⲉⲛⲁⲩ	You have not yet seen (f)
ⲙⲡⲁⲧⲉϥⲛⲁⲩ	He has not yet seen
ⲙⲡⲁⲧⲉⲥⲛⲁⲩ	She has not yet seen
ⲙⲡⲁⲧⲉⲛⲛⲁⲩ	We have not yet seen
ⲙⲡⲁⲧⲉⲧⲉⲛⲛⲁⲩ	You have not yet seen (pl)
ⲙⲡⲁⲧⲟⲩⲛⲁⲩ	They have not yet seen
ⲙⲡⲁⲧⲉ	Pre subject form

Now when you say "he has not seen", you're really talking in the present tense. However, if you were to look further back in time, you would want to say something '*had* not been done' as opposed to 'it has not been done'. For this case, you would need to borrow the ⲛⲉ from the plu perfect **(7.1.i)** to give the meaning of 'had', where it happily sits in front of the ⲙⲡⲁⲧ⳱ construction.

E.g. ⲛⲉ ⲙⲡⲁⲧⲉⲥⲓ ⲛϫⲉ ⲧⲉϥⲟⲩⲛⲟⲩ *(John 8:20)*
"his hour had not yet come"

As with the past imperfect **(7.1)**, you take an optional ⲡⲉ to put after the not yet construction.

E.g. ⲛⲉ ⲙⲡⲁⲧⲉϥⲓ ⲅⲁⲣ ⲡⲉ ⲛϫⲉ I̅H̅C̅ ⲉϩⲣⲏⲓ ⲉⲛϯⲙⲓ *(John 11:30)*
"for Jesus had not yet come up to the village"

So You want to Learn Coptic?

The ⲙⲡⲁⲧ⸗ construction is also commonly used to give the meaning of 'before.' The construction is identical to that used to give the 'has not', so you really need to look at the context to determine which meaning is intended.

ⲙⲡⲁⲧⲉ ⲫⲣⲏ ϩⲱⲧⲡ *(SinArch pg.8)*
"before the sun sets"

Vocab			
ⲉⲛⲭⲁⲓ	thing, possession (m)	ϫⲱⲕ ϫⲉⲕ– ϫⲟⲕ⸗ ϫⲏⲕ (ⲉⲃⲟⲗ)	to complete, fulfill (v.t)
ⲉⲣⲭⲣⲓⲁ	to need (v.i)	ϫⲱⲕ	completion, end (m)
ⲧⲱⲃϩ ⲧⲟⲃϩ⸗	to entreat, to ask (v.t)		

Exercise 11.6

a) ϥⲥⲱⲟⲩⲛ ⲅⲁⲣ ⲛϫⲉ ⲡⲉⲧⲉⲛⲓⲱⲧ ⲛⲛⲏ ⲉⲧⲉⲧⲉⲛⲉⲣⲭⲣⲓⲁ ⲙⲙⲱⲟⲩ ⲙⲡⲁⲧⲉⲧⲉⲛⲧⲟⲃϩϥ ⲉⲑⲃⲏⲧⲟⲩ   *(Matthew 6:8)*

b) ⲟⲩⲟϩ ⲁⲥϣⲱⲡⲓ ⲙⲡⲁϯϫⲉⲕ ⲛⲁⲓⲥⲁϫⲓ ⲉⲃⲟⲗ   *(Genesis 24:45)*

c) ⲁⲗⲗⲁ ⲙⲡⲁⲧⲉϥⲓ ⲛϫⲉ ⲡⲓϫⲱⲕ   *(Mark 13:7)*

d) ϫⲉ ⲙⲡⲁⲧⲉ ⲡⲁⲥⲛⲟⲩ ⲁⲛⲟⲕ ϫⲱⲕ ⲉⲃⲟⲗ   *(John 7:8)*

e) ⲛⲉ ⲙⲡⲁⲧⲉϥⲓ ⲅⲁⲣ ⲉϫⲉⲛ ⲟⲩⲟⲛ ⲙⲙⲱⲟⲩ   *(Acts 8:16)*

f) ϯⲛⲟⲩ ⲇⲉ ⲙⲡⲁⲧⲉⲛⲛⲁⲩ ⲉⲉⲛⲭⲁⲓ ⲛⲓⲃⲉⲛ   *(Hebrews 2:8)*

11.5.   When one verb leads to another

Sometimes there'll be two verbs in the sentence where the first verb is directly related to the other, as in this example:
"You know how to interpret"
Here the first verb is 'know' and the second is 'interpret.'
As you can see, the second is directly related to the first. The conjunctions we looked at in (**6.1**) wouldn't be useful to link them. In these cases, Coptic uses the preposition ⲛ

More on the infinitive

or **ⲉ** to link the verbs. As to which is used in a particular guide, there are two rough guides:

The first is that verbs which express a wish, allowing, ordering, promising, swearing, intending, and being able take **ⲉ** whereas verbs of willing, desiring, beginning, anticipating, understanding, loving, fearing take **ⲛ̀**.

E.g. **ⲛⲑⲱⲟⲩ ⲇⲉ ⲛⲁⲩⲟⲩⲱϣ ⲉⲓⲛⲓ ⲛ̀ⲛⲟⲩϫⲓϫ ⲉ̀ϩⲣⲏⲓ ⲉ̀ϫⲱϥ ⲉ̀ϧⲟⲑⲃⲉϥ** *(Acts 9:29)*
"but they desired to bring their hands down upon him to kill Him"

ⲟⲩⲟϩ ⲁϥⲉⲣϩⲏⲧⲥ ⲛ̀ϯⲥⲃⲱ ⲛⲱⲟⲩ *(Mark 8:31)*
"and he began to teach them"

The second guide is that if the second verb immediately comes after the first, it takes **ⲛ̀**, but if another word comes in between, then the second verb takes **ⲉ̀**.

We've actually already seen a bit of this with some of the verbs we've come across; the verb which immediately followed the potential infinitive **ϣϫⲉⲙ ϫⲟⲙ** took an **ⲛ̀** before it, but took **ⲉ̀** if the direct object pronoun **ⲙⲙⲟ⸗** came in between **(11.3)**. We also saw this with the impersonal verb **ⲥϣⲉ** *"it is befitting"*, here **ⲥϣⲉ** took **ⲛ̀** if the next verb immediately followed it, and again **ⲉ̀** if another word came in between **(8.2.i)**.

Vocab			
ⲉⲣⲇⲟⲕⲓⲙⲁⲍⲓⲛ	to test, try, examine (v.t)	ⲥⲙⲟⲧⲉⲛ	to be easy (v.i)
ⲁⲙⲟⲛⲓ (ⲙ̀)	to overcome, seize (v.t)	ⲉⲣϩⲁⲗ	to deceive (v.t)

Exercise 11.7

a) **ⲧⲉⲧⲉⲛⲥⲱⲟⲩⲛ ⲛ̀ⲉⲣⲇⲟⲕⲓⲙⲁⲍⲓⲛ** *(Luke 12:56)*

b) **ⲁϥϩⲉⲙⲥⲓ ⲉ̀ϯⲥⲃⲱ ⲛⲱⲟⲩ** *(John 8:2)*

c) **ϯⲉⲣϩⲉⲗⲡⲓⲥ ⲅⲁⲣ ⲉ̀ⲛⲁⲩ ⲉ̀ⲣⲱⲧⲉⲛ** *(2 John 1:12)*

d) **ⲁⲣⲓⲧⲉⲛ ⲛ̀ⲉⲙⲡ̀ϣⲁ ⲛ̀ϫⲟⲥ** *(introduction to Lord's prayer)*

So You want to Learn Coptic?

e) ⲥⲙⲟⲧⲉⲛ ⲛ̀ⲉⲣϩⲁⲗ ⲙ̀ⲙⲟⲥ *(hom vat 214)*

12. ANYONE FOR SECONDS? - THE SECOND TENSE

Perhaps the most difficult concept to grasp in Coptic is what is called the 'second tense.'

We've already looked at the 'first present tense' (**5.1**), the 'first perfect tense' (**5.2**). and the 'first future tense' (**5.9**), so why do we need a second tense then? The second tense has two key roles. The first is easy enough to understand, which is it's use in questions. The second which shall be discussed is a role that is unique to Coptic, and hence is difficult to find the equivalent of in English. But basically, it takes the emphasis in a sentence away from the verb and moves it to another part of the sentence. Let me explain further:

In an English sentence, the emphasis can be controlled by the order of the words in the sentence. For example, compare the following sentences:
"I came for this"
and
"For this I came"

Both of these sentences have similar meanings, but by changing the word order for the second sentence the emphasis shifts from the verb 'came' to 'for this.'

In Coptic sentences, the emphasis can also be switched from the verb. However, unlike English, the word order does not change. Instead, a special tense of the verb is used, which is called the second tense. There is a second tense for the present, future and past tenses.

12.1. Second present

Now, to make things a bit more confusing, the second *present* tense looks almost exactly like the first *perfect* tense! So the prefixes to the verb are as follows:

1ˢᵗ person singular	ⲁⲓ—
2ⁿᵈ person singular masculine	ⲁⲕ—
2ⁿᵈ person singular feminine	ⲁⲣⲉ—
3ʳᵈ person singular masculine	ⲁϥ—
3ʳᵈ person singular feminine	ⲁⲥ—
1ˢᵗ person plural	ⲁⲛ—
2ⁿᵈ person plural	ⲁⲣⲉⲧⲉⲛ—

So You want to Learn Coptic?

3rd person plural	ⲁⲩ–
pre subject form	ⲁⲣⲉ

You will recall that we said that the second present looks *almost* exactly like the past *perfect*. In what way does it differ?

Remember the presubject form of the past perfect? That's where the ⲁ is split from the infinitive and goes in front of the subject, as in the following example:

ⲁ ⲡⲓⲣⲱⲙⲓ ⲙⲟϣⲓ

"The man walked"

The presubject form for the second present however is ⲁⲣⲉ.

As mentioned above, when verbs are written with the second tense, the emphasis of the sentence is diverted from the verb of the sentence to another part of the sentence.

Consider this example:

ⲧⲉⲧⲉⲛϫⲱ ⲙⲙⲟⲥ ϫⲉ ⲁⲣⲉ ⲡⲓⲙⲁⲛⲟⲩⲱϣⲧ ϧⲉⲛ ⲓⲗⲏⲙ ⲡⲓⲙⲁ ⲉⲧⲉ ⲥϣⲉ ⲛⲟⲩⲱϣⲧ ⲙⲙⲟϥ *(John 4:20)*

"You say the place in Jerusalem is the place which is appropriate to worship in"

It is clear here that the emphasis in the sentence is not on the verb 'worship', but on the phrase "Jerusalem is the place", hence the second tense is used to shift emphasis away from the verb to this phrase. Unfortunately, the second tense doesn't tell you which part of the sentence the emphasis has switched to, only that it has switched away from the verb.

Now in the example above, it was clear that this example used the second tense because the pre subject form of the second tense was used.

So how do you tell them apart for the forms where the presubject form isn't used? Well, here you have to look carefully at the context of the sentence and see which one makes the most sense. Let's take an example:

ϧⲉⲛ ⲡⲁⲣⲭⲱⲛ ⲛⲧⲉ ⲛⲓⲇⲉⲙⲱⲛ ⲁϥϩⲓⲟⲩⲓ ⲛⲛⲓⲇⲉⲙⲱⲛ ⲉⲃⲟⲗ *(Matthew 9:34)*

The verb in this sentence is ϩⲓⲟⲩⲓ - *"to cast."* Now we notice the ⲁϥ in front, which means that the verb could either be in the first past perfect tense or the second present tense. If the verb was in the first past perfect tense, it would mean "he cast out."

However, since there is no reason to think that Christ no longer casts out demons, it doesn't really make sense to translate it in the past tense.

The likely tense therefore is the second present tense. In this case the emphasis is switching from the verb to another part of the sentence. As we said, the second tense does not actually tell us exactly which part of the sentence the emphasis is transferred to; just that it is away from the verb. In this case, it is quite probable that the emphasis is intended to be on the "through the chief of demons."

Hence to reflect this emphasis of the sentence, an appropriate translation would be:

"It is *through the chief of Demons* that He casts out demons"

Another example is:

Ⲁϥϯⲛⲁⲛ ⲙ̀ⲡⲉϥⲥⲱⲙⲁ ⲛⲉⲙ ⲡⲉϥⲥ̀ⲛⲟϥ ⲉⲧⲧⲁⲓⲏⲟⲩⲧ ⲟⲩⲟϩ ⲁⲛⲱⲛϧ ϣⲁ ⲉ̀ⲛⲉϩ *(ⲡⲓⲱⲓⲕ ⲛ̀ⲧⲉ ⲡ̀ⲱⲛϧ,* Hymn during Holy Communion)

Let's focus our attention on **ⲁⲛⲱⲛϧ.** Once again, the tense of this verb is either the first past perfect or the second present. Here it doesn't really make sense to say "we *lived* forever", so the second present tense applies here, and the translation is therefore "we live *forever*" with the emphasis on 'forever'. So, the final translation is:

"He gave us His body and His honoured blood and we live forever"

12.2. The second future tense

There is also a second future tense, which has the same purpose of expressing a different part of the sentence than the verb. Fortunately, the second future is quite easy to recognise because it is unique in its form in that it looks like a combined past tense with the future.

1ˢᵗ person singular	ⲁⲓⲛⲁ⁻
2ⁿᵈ person singular masculine	ⲁⲭⲛⲁ⁻
2ⁿᵈ person singular feminine	ⲁⲣⲉⲛⲁ⁻
3ʳᵈ person singular masculine	ⲁϥⲛⲁ⁻
3ʳᵈ person singular feminine	ⲁⲥⲛⲁ⁻
1ˢᵗ person plural	ⲁⲛⲛⲁ⁻
2ⁿᵈ person plural	ⲁⲣⲉⲧⲉⲛⲛⲁ⁻

So You want to Learn Coptic?

3rd person plural	ⲁⲩⲛⲁ–
pre subject form	ⲁⲣⲉ

E.g. ⲡⲓⲑⲙⲏⲓ ⲁϥⲛⲁⲱⲛϧ ⲉⲃⲟⲗ ϧⲉⲛ ⲫⲛⲁϩϯ *(Galatians 3:11)*
"the righteous will live **through faith**"

Vocab			
ⲁⲅⲁⲑⲟⲥ	good, righteous one (Gk, m)	ⲡⲁⲥⲭⲁ	Passover (Gk,m)
ⲕⲁⲧⲁⲃⲟⲗⲏ	foundation, establishment (Gk,f)	ⲣⲱⲓ	my mouth (poss.noun) **(15.4)**
ⲙⲉⲧϫⲱⲃ	weakness (f)	ϣⲟⲩϣⲟⲩ	to boast, be proud (v.t)
ⲛ̀ⲕⲟⲧ	to rest (v.i)	ϧⲁⲧⲟⲧⲕ	at, beside, under (comp. prep) **(Appendix 3)**
ⲛ̀ⲧⲟⲧⲕ	to you (comp. prep) **(Appendix 3)**	ϩⲱⲡ ϩⲉⲡ– ϩⲟⲡ⸗ ϩⲏⲡ	to hide (v.t)
ⲟⲩⲱⲛ	to open (v.t)		

Exercise 12.1

a) ⲓⲥϫⲉ ⲥⲉⲙ̀ⲡϣⲁ ⲛ̀ⲧⲁϣⲟⲩϣⲟⲩ ⲙ̀ⲙⲟⲓ ⲁⲓⲛⲁϣⲟⲩϣⲟⲩ ⲙ̀ⲙⲟⲓ ϧⲉⲛ ⲛⲁⲙⲉⲧϫⲱⲃ *(2 Corinthians 11:30)*

b) Ⲇⲓⲉⲣⲉⲧⲓⲛ ⲛ̀ⲧⲟⲧⲕ ⲱ̀ ⲡⲓⲁⲅⲁⲑⲟⲥ ⲁⲣⲓⲟⲩⲛⲁⲓ ⲛⲉⲙⲏⲓ ⲕⲁⲧⲁ ⲡⲉⲕⲛⲓϣϯ ⲛ̀ⲛⲁⲓ *(9th hour commentary of Monday Morning of the Holy Pascha)*

c) ϧⲉⲛ ⲡⲓϣⲓ ⲉ̀ⲧⲉⲧⲉⲛⲛⲁϣⲓ ⲙ̀ⲙⲟϥ ⲁⲩⲛⲁϣⲓ ⲛⲱⲧⲉⲛ ⲙ̀ⲙⲟϥ *(Matthew 7:2)*

d) ⲁⲓⲛⲁⲟⲩⲱⲛ ⲛ̀ⲣⲱⲓ ϧⲉⲛ ϩⲁⲛⲡⲁⲣⲁⲃⲟⲗⲏ ⲟⲩⲟϩ ⲛ̀ⲧⲁⲥⲁϫⲓ ⲛ̀ⲛⲏ ⲉⲧϩⲏⲡ ⲓⲥϫⲉⲛ ⲧ̀ⲕⲁⲧⲁⲃⲟⲗⲏ ⲙ̀ⲡⲓⲕⲟⲥⲙⲟⲥ *(Matthew 13:35)*

e) ⲁϫⲟⲥ ⲛⲁϥ ϫⲉ ⲡⲉϫⲉ ⲡⲓⲣⲉϥϯⲥⲃⲱ ϫⲉ ⲁ ⲡⲁⲥⲏⲟⲩ ⲁϥϧⲱⲛⲧ ⲁⲓⲛⲁⲓⲣⲓ ⲙ̀ⲡⲁⲡⲁⲥⲭⲁ ϧⲁⲧⲟⲧⲕ ⲛⲉⲙ ⲛⲁⲙⲁⲑⲏⲧⲏⲥ *(Matthew 26:18)*

f) ⲙ̀ⲡⲉⲥⲙⲟⲩ ⲛ̀ϫⲉ ϯⲁⲗⲟⲩ ⲁⲗⲗⲁ ⲁⲥⲛ̀ⲕⲟⲧ *(Mark 5:39)*

12.3. The second past tense

As with the present and future tenses, there is also a second past tense. Once again, this tense looks identical to another more common tense, which in this case is the past tense converted by the relative pronoun **(5.4)**

1ˢᵗ person singular	ⲉⲧⲁⲓ⁻
2ⁿᵈ person singular masculine	ⲉⲧⲁⲕ⁻
2ⁿᵈ person singular feminine	ⲉⲧⲁⲣⲉ⁻
3ʳᵈ person singular masculine	ⲉⲧⲁϥ⁻
3ʳᵈ person singular feminine	ⲉⲧⲁⲥ⁻
1ˢᵗ person plural	ⲉⲧⲁⲛ⁻
2ⁿᵈ person plural	ⲉⲧⲁⲣⲉⲧⲉⲛ⁻
3ʳᵈ person plural	ⲉⲧⲁⲩ⁻
pre subject form	ⲉⲧⲁ

So as with the second present, a careful study of the context is required to determine which of the tenses is intended. It's actually easier in many regards to pick out the second past tense than it is for the second present, because the alternative translation which you'd get if you used the past relative usually doesn't make any sense at all, not just contextually but also grammatically.

E.g. ⲧⲉⲛⲉⲙⲓ ϫⲉ ⲉⲧⲁⲕⲓ ⲉⲃⲟⲗ ϩⲓⲧⲉⲛ Ⲫϯ *(John 3:2)*

If you were to translate the ⲉⲧⲁⲕⲓ as if it were in the past relative, the translation would be "we know that which you came from God." The 'which' from the relative would be clearly out of place. Hence this is your clue that this word isn't in the

So You want to Learn Coptic?

past relative tense and the second past tense translation would be more appropriate, hence the correct translation would be:

"We know that you came *from God*"

Vocab			
ⲧⲁⲕⲟ ⲧⲁⲕⲉ– ⲧⲁⲕⲟ⸗ ⲧⲁⲕⲏⲟⲩⲧ	to destroy (v.t)	ϩⲓⲧⲟⲧⲕ	through you (comp. prep) **(Appendix 3)**
ⲧⲁⲫⲙⲏⲓ	truth (m)	ϩⲩⲕⲱⲛ	image, icon, likeness (f)
ⲧⲁⲫⲙⲏⲓ	truly (adv)		

Exercise 12.2

a) ⲁϥⲉⲣⲟⲩⲱ ⲛ̇ϫⲉ Ⲓⲏⲥ ⲟⲩⲟϩ ⲡⲉϫⲁϥ ϫⲉ ⲉⲧⲁⲥϣⲱⲡⲓ ⲁⲛ ⲉⲑⲃⲏⲧ ⲛ̇ϫⲉ ⲧⲁⲓⲥⲙⲏ ⲁⲗⲗⲁ ⲉⲑⲃⲉ ⲑⲏⲛⲟⲩ *(John 12:30)*

b) ⲁⲩⲉⲙⲓ ⲧⲁⲫⲙⲏⲓ ϫⲉ ⲉⲧⲁⲓⲓ ⲉ̇ⲃⲟⲗ ϩⲓⲧⲟⲧⲕ *(John 17:8)*

c) ϫⲉ ⲉⲧⲁⲓⲑⲁⲙⲓⲟ ⲙ̇ⲡⲓⲣⲱⲙⲓ ϧⲉⲛ ⲟⲩϩⲩⲕⲱⲛ ⲛ̇ⲧⲉ Ⲫϯ *(Genesis 9:6)*

d) ⲉⲧⲁⲕⲓ̇ ⲉ̇ⲙⲛⲁⲓ ⲉ̇ⲧⲁⲕⲟⲛ ⲙ̇ⲡⲁⲧⲉ ⲡⲉⲛⲥⲏⲟⲩ ϣⲱⲡⲓ *(Matthew 8:29)*

e) ⲁⲛⲟⲕ ⲉⲧⲁⲓⲓ̇ ϩⲓⲛⲁ ⲛ̇ⲧⲉ ⲟⲩⲱⲛϧ ϣⲱⲡⲓ ⲛⲱⲟⲩ *(John 10:10)*

13. ASKING QUESTIONS- THE INTERROGATIVE

Have you ever heard of an interrogation? An interrogation implies asking questions in an aggressive manner, often with the goal of acquiring a particular answer. The word 'interrogative' may therefore have an intimidating feel about it, but this is unfair, because the 'interrogative' represents something much more innocent. It simply refers to the part of speech which involves asking questions. Asking questions is fundamental to communication and to language in general, and Coptic is no exception. There are three basic constructions for the interrogative which will be discussed in this chapter.

13.1. Change of intonation

Intonation is the change in pitch one makes when speaking. Very often, a sentence written on paper could be read as either a statement or a question depending on the intonation. In English, a question mark will tell you the difference, but Coptic doesn't use question marks. Whereas other types of sentences in Coptic have ways of indicating that the sentence is a question, the sentences in this category don't have internal clues, and you have to rely on the context to determine that a question is really being asked.

E.g. ⲡⲓⲗⲁⲧⲟⲥ ⲇⲉ ⲁϥϣⲉⲛϥ ⲉϥϫⲱ ⲙ̅ⲙⲟⲥ ϫⲉ ⲛ̅ⲑⲟⲕ ⲡⲉ ⲡ̅ⲟⲩⲣⲟ ⲛ̅ⲧⲉ ⲛⲓⲓⲟⲩⲇⲁⲓ *(Luke 23:3)*

"and Pilate asked him saying 'are you the king of the Jews'?"

If we were to read ⲛ̅ⲑⲟⲕ ⲡⲉ ⲡ̅ⲟⲩⲣⲟ ⲛ̅ⲧⲉ ⲛⲓⲓⲟⲩⲇⲁⲓ on its own, we would translate it as *"you are the king of the Jews."* However, because it is preceded by ⲁϥϣⲉⲛϥ *"he asked"*, we have the clue we need to realise that the phrase is actually a question and is translated as such.

13.2. Using the interrogative particle

As indicated above, some sentences have built in clues to let you know that there is a question. We'll look at two of these particles ⲁⲛ and ⲙⲏ.

ⲁⲛ comes at the beginning of a sentence and turns it into a question. It could be roughly translated as the 'is' in 'is it?'. (It is not to be confused with the ⲁⲛ of negation which we first met in **(5.1.i)**.)

So You want to Learn Coptic?

E.g. ⲁⲛ ⲫⲁⲓ ⲡⲉ ⲡⲉⲧⲉⲛϣⲏⲣⲓ ⲫⲏ ⲉⲧⲉⲧⲉⲛϫⲱ ⲙ̀ⲙⲟⲥ ϫⲉ ⲁⲛⲙⲁⲥϥ ⲉϥⲟⲓ ⲙ̀ⲃⲉⲗⲗⲉ *(John 9:19)*

"is this your son, this who you say that 'we gave birth to him blind'?"

ⲙⲏ also starts the sentence to turn it into a question and is left untranslated. It often has a somewhat rhetorical sense, in that the speaker isn't really waiting for an answer.

E.g. ⲙⲏ ⲟⲩⲟⲛϣ̀ϫⲟⲙ ⲛ̀ⲟⲩⲃⲱⲕ ⲉ̀ϣⲱϣ ⲙ̀ⲡⲉϥⲟ̅ⲥ̅ *(AmHyv p31)*

"is it possible for a servant to despise his lord?"

The question will often be in one of the negative tenses, so that it takes the form of a negative statement, but the answer to the question is expected to be 'yes', and it doesn't really need to be answered E.g. "is not the sky blue?"

E.g. ⲙⲏ ⲁⲛⲟⲕ ⲟⲩⲣⲉⲙϩⲉ ⲁⲛ ⲙⲏ ⲁⲛⲟⲕ ⲟⲩⲁⲡⲟⲥⲧⲟⲗⲟⲥ ⲁⲛ ⲙⲏ ⲓ̅ⲏ̅ⲥ̅ ⲡ̅ⲭ̅ⲥ̅ ⲡⲉⲛϭⲟⲓⲥ ⲙ̀ⲡⲓⲛⲁⲩ ⲉ̀ⲣⲟϥ ⲙⲏ ⲛ̀ⲑⲱⲧⲉⲛ ⲁⲛ ⲡⲉ ⲡⲁϩⲱⲃ ϧⲉⲛ Ⲡ̅ⲟ̅ⲥ̅ *(1 Corinthians 9:1)*

"am I not a free person? Am I not an Apostle? Jesus Christ our Lord, did I not see Him? Are you not my work in the Lord"

Vocab			
ⲉⲣⲟⲩⲱ	to answer, reply (v.i)	ⲥⲱⲣϩ ⲥⲁⲣϩ-	to sweep (v.t)
ⲕⲟⲩⲣ	slap, blow (m)	ϣⲓⲛⲓ ϣⲉⲛ- ϣⲉⲛ⸗	to seek, ask (v.t)
ⲣⲉⲙϩⲉ	free person (m)	ϧⲏⲃⲥ	lamp (m)
ⲣⲏϯ	manner, condition (m)	ϫⲱⲓⲗⲓ, ϫⲁⲗⲏⲟⲩⲧ	to dwell, visit, to be dwelling, visiting (q)
ⲥⲱ ⲥⲉ- ⲥⲟ⸗ ⲥⲁⲩ (p.c)	to drink (v.t)	ϭⲉⲣⲟ ϭⲉⲣⲉ- ϭⲉⲣⲟ⸗ ϭⲉⲣⲏⲟⲩⲧ	to light up, burn, kindle (v.t)

Exercise 13.1

a) ⲟⲩⲟⲛ ϣϫⲟⲙ ⲙ̅ⲙⲱⲧⲉⲛ ⲉⲥⲉ ⲡⲓⲁⲫⲟⲧ ⲉϯⲛⲁⲥⲟϥ. ⲡⲉϫⲱⲟⲩ ⲛⲁϥ ϫⲉ ⲟⲩⲟⲛ ϣϫⲟⲙ ⲙ̅ⲙⲟⲛ *(Matthew 20:22)*

b) ⲙⲏ ⲙ̅ⲡⲁϥⲭⲁ ⲡⲓϥ̅ⲑ̅ ⲛ̅ⲥⲱϥ *(Luke 15:4)*

c) ⲁϥϯ ⲛ̅ⲟⲩⲕⲟⲩⲣ ⲙ̅ⲓⲏ̅ⲥ̅ ⲉϥϫⲱ ⲙ̅ⲙⲟⲥ ϫⲉ ⲁⲛ ⲫⲁⲓ ⲡⲉ ⲙ̅ⲫⲣⲏϯ ⲛ̅ⲉⲣⲟⲩⲱ ⲙ̅ⲡⲓⲁⲣⲭⲓⲉⲣⲉⲩⲥ *(John 18:22)*

d) ⲉⲧⲁⲩⲙⲟⲩϯ ⲛⲁⲩϣⲓⲛⲓ ⲡⲉ ϫⲉ ⲁⲛ ⲥⲓⲙⲱⲛ ⲫⲏ ⲉⲧⲟⲩⲙⲟⲩϯ ⲉⲣⲟϥ ϫⲉ ⲡⲉⲧⲣⲟⲥ ϥ̅ϫⲁⲗⲏⲟⲩⲧ ⲉⲡⲁⲓⲙⲁ *(Acts 10:18)*

e) ⲙⲏ ⲙ̅ⲡⲁⲥϭⲉⲣⲉ ⲟⲩϩⲏⲃⲥ ⲟⲩⲟϩ ⲛ̅ⲧⲉⲥⲥⲁⲣϩ ⲡⲓⲏⲓ *(Luke 15:8)*

f) ⲁⲛ ⲥ̅ϣⲉ ⲛⲏⲓ ⲛ̅ⲧⲁϫⲉ ϩⲗⲓ ⲛⲁⲕ *(Acts 21:37)*

g) ⲙⲏ ⲧⲁϫⲓϫ ⲁⲛ ⲁⲥⲑⲁⲙⲓⲉ ⲛⲁⲓ ⲧⲏⲣⲟⲩ *(Acts 7:50)*

13.3. Using the interrogative pronouns

The "Interrogative *pronouns*" are the standard words used for questions. They can almost be thought of as the "who, where, and why's" of Coptic. One of the important things to look out for is their position in the sentence relative to the verb; since as a general rule (which is not without exceptions), the verb is used in the second tense when the interrogative pronoun comes after the verb, but not when it comes before it.

The following pronouns stand at the beginning of the sentence:

ⲁϣ	what
ⲁϩⲟ⳥	why?
ⲉⲑⲃⲉ ⲟⲩ	why?
ⲛⲓⲙ	who ?
ⲟⲩ	what?
ⲟⲩⲏⲣ	how many?

So You want to Learn Coptic?

ⲡⲱⲥ	how is it?
ϣⲁ ⲑ̀ⲛⲁⲩ	until when?

E.g. ϯⲥ̀ϩⲓⲙⲓ ⲉⲑⲃⲉ ⲟⲩ ⲧⲉⲣⲓⲙⲓ *(John 20:15)*
"*woman, why are you crying?*"

As we said, the verb ⲣⲓⲙⲓ is not converted to the second tense because it came after the interrogative article, which in this case is ⲉⲑⲃⲉ ⲟⲩ.

If you scan down the table, you'll notice that ⲁϩⲟ⸗ differs from the other interrogative pronouns because it has to take a suffix to indicate the subject

E.g. ⲁϧⲱⲧⲉⲛ ⲧⲉⲧⲉⲛⲟϩⲓ ⲉⲣⲁⲧⲉⲛ ⲑⲏⲛⲟⲩ ⲉⲣⲉⲧⲉⲛⲥⲟⲙⲥ ⲉ̀ⲡ̀ϣⲱⲓ ⲉ̀ⲧ̀ⲫⲉ *(Acts 1:11)*
"*why do you stand up looking up to Heaven?*"

With the exception of ⲁϩⲟ⸗, these pronouns may also be linked with a noun with the attributive (ⲛ̀/ⲙ̀) construction **(2.4.i)**. In this, sense, they could be thought of as being adjectives.

E.g. ⲁϣ ⲛ̀ⲏⲓ ⲫⲏ ⲉⲧⲉⲧⲉⲛⲛⲁⲕⲟⲧϥ ⲛⲏⲓ *(Acts 7:49)*
"*what is the house which you will build me?*"

Vocab			
ⲕⲱⲧ ⲕⲉⲧ⁻ ⲕⲟⲧ⸗	to build (v.t)	ⲛ̀ⲧⲟⲧ	through me (comp prep) **(Appendix 3)**
ⲛⲉϫⲓ	womb (f)	ⲥⲟⲙⲥ	to behold, look, consider (v.i)
ⲛⲏⲃ	master, Lord (m)		

Exercise 13:2

a) ⲡⲱⲥ ⲛ̀ⲑⲟⲕ ⲟⲩⲓⲟⲩⲇⲁⲓ ⲕ̀ⲉⲣⲉⲧⲓⲛ ⲛ̀ⲧⲟⲧ ⲉ̀ⲥⲱ *(John 4:9)*

b) ⲛ̀ⲑⲟϥ ⲇⲉ ⲡⲉϫⲁϥ ϫⲉ ⲡⲱⲥ ⲟⲩⲟⲛ ϣ̀ϫⲟⲙ ⲙ̀ⲙⲟⲓ ⲉ̀ⲉⲙⲓ ⲁⲣⲉϣⲧⲉⲛ ⲟⲩⲁⲓ ϭⲓⲙⲱⲓⲧ ⲛⲏⲓ *(Acts 8:31)*

c) ⲟⲩⲏⲣ ⲛ̀ⲣⲟⲙⲡⲓ ϯⲟⲓ ⲙ̀ⲃⲱⲕ ⲛⲁⲕ *(Luke 15:29)*

d) ⲟⲩⲟϩ ⲁⲩⲱϣ ⲉⲃⲟⲗ ϧⲉⲛ ⲟⲩⲛⲓϣϯ ⲛ̀ⲥⲙⲏ ⲉⲩϫⲱ ⲙ̀ⲙⲟⲥ ϫⲉ ϣⲁ ⲑ̀ⲛⲁⲩ ϫⲉ ⲡⲉⲛⲛⲏⲃ ⲫⲏ ⲉⲑⲟⲩⲁⲃ ⲡⲓⲑ̀ⲙⲏⲓ ⲕ̀ϯϩⲁⲡ ⲁⲛ *(Revelation 6:10)*

e) ⲁϣ ⲡⲉ ⲫⲙⲁ ⲛ̀ⲧⲉ ⲡⲁⲙⲁ ⲛ̀ⲉⲙⲧⲟⲛ *(Acts 7:49)*

f) ⲛⲓⲙ ⲡⲉ ⲫ̀ⲣⲱⲙⲓ ϫⲉ ⲁⲕⲉⲣⲡⲉϥⲙⲉⲩⲓ *(Hebrews 2:6)*

g) ϯⲥ̀ϩⲓⲙⲓ ⲁϧⲟ ⲧⲉⲣⲓⲙⲓ *(John 20:13)*

h) ⲁϧⲟⲓ ⲅⲁⲣ ⲙ̀ⲡⲓⲙⲟⲩ ϧⲉⲛ ⲑ̀ⲛⲉϫⲓ *(Job 3:11)*

i) ⲡⲱⲥ ⲧⲉⲧⲉⲛⲕⲁϯ ⲁⲛ *(Mark 8:21)*

j) ⲟⲩ ⲡⲉⲧϣⲟⲡ ⲡⲁϣⲏⲣⲓ *(Genesis 22:7)*

So much for the interrogative pronouns that come before the verb, now we'll look at those that come after the verb.

ⲉⲃⲟⲗ ⲑⲱⲛ	from where
ⲉ̀ⲑⲱⲛ	whither (to where)
ⲑ̀ⲛⲁⲩ	when
ⲑⲱⲛ	where
ⲛ̀ⲑ̀ⲛⲁⲩ	when

Now here is where the second tense **(12)** comes into play; you see when these interrogative articles are used for a question, the second tense is used instead of the first. This means you have to be careful, because it might look like the verb is in the past tense whereas in fact it is in the present tense.

E.g. ⲫ̀ⲣⲉϥϯⲥ̀ⲃⲱ ⲁⲕϣⲟⲡ ⲑⲱⲛ *(John 1:38)*

Here the interrogative article is **ⲑⲱⲛ**, which comes after the verb **ϣⲟⲡ**. Hence **ϣⲟⲡ** is rendered in the second present tense, so the translation is *"teacher, where do You dwell?"* as opposed to *"teacher, where did You dwell?"*

The same also applies with the future tense when the interrogative article follows the verb, that is the verb takes the *second* future tense:

So You want to Learn Coptic?

E.g. ⲁⲩⲛⲁⲙⲉⲥ ⲠⲬⲤ ⲐⲰⲚ *(Matthew 2:4)*
"Where will the Christ be born?"

Again, as with the present tense, the second *past* tense is used if a question is asked in the past.

E.g. ⲣⲁⲃⲃⲓ ⲉ̀ⲧⲁⲕⲓ̀ ⲉⲙⲛⲁⲓ ⲚⲐⲚⲀⲨ *(John 6:25)*
"Rabbi, when did you come here"

ⲉ̀ⲧⲁⲕⲓ̀ ⲉ̀ ⲡⲁⲓⲙⲁ ⲚⲤⲀ ⲞⲨ ⲚϨⲰⲂ
"For what thing did you come to this place?"

Now, we had said above that the interrogative pronouns ⲀϢ, ⲞⲨ and ⲚⲒⲘ precede the verb, and this is in fact true, however they can also come after the verb, in this case they are used more as object nouns rather than as pronouns. When they are used in this way, the verb is also rendered in the second tense.

E.g ⲁⲣⲉⲕⲰϯ ⲚⲤⲀ ⲚⲒⲘ *(John 20:15)*
"Who are you looking for?"

ⲐⲰⲚ may also be used in a phrase where there is no other verb to ask a question. Here ⲐⲰⲚ is itself conjugated as a verb in the second tense.

E.g ⲁϥⲐⲰⲚ ⲠⲈⲔⲒⲰⲦ *(John 8:19)*
"where is your father"

ⲐⲰⲚ can still be used to mean 'where' without necessarily being in a question

E.g. ⲠⲈϪⲈ ⲐⲰⲘⲀⲤ ⲚⲀϤ ϪⲈ Ⲡ⳪ ⲦⲈⲚⲈⲘⲒ ⲀⲚ ϪⲈ ⲀⲔⲚⲀϢⲈ ⲚⲀⲔ ⲈⲐⲰⲚ *(John 14:5)*
"Thomas said to him 'Lord, we do not know where you will go"

Vocab			
ⲎⲠⲒ	number (f)	Ⲣⲁⲃⲃⲓ	Rabbi (prop. noun)
ⲘⲀⲚϢⲀϤⲈ	wilderness, desert (m)	ⲤⲀⲦⲀⲚⲀⲤ	Satan (prop. noun)
Ⲙ̀ⲔⲀϨ	pain, suffering (m)	ϬⲒⲤⲒ	weariness, suffering (m)
ⲠⲞⲖⲈⲘⲞⲤ	battle, war, fight (Gk, m)	ϨⲰⲦⲠ	to set, sink (v.i)

Exercise 13.3

a) ⲉⲧⲁϥⲛⲁⲩ ⲉⲣⲱⲟⲩ ⲉⲩⲙⲟϣⲓ ⲛ̀ⲥⲱϥ ⲡⲉϫⲁϥ ⲛⲱⲟⲩ ϫⲉ ⲁⲣⲉⲧⲉⲛⲕⲱϯ ⲛ̀ⲥⲁ ⲟⲩ *(John 1:38)*

b) ⲉⲧⲁⲧⲓ̀ ⲉⲃⲟⲗ ⲑⲱⲛ *(Revelation 7:13)*

c) ⲣⲁⲃⲃⲓ ⲉ̀ⲧⲁⲕⲓ̀ ⲉ̀ⲙⲛⲁⲓ ⲛ̀ⲑⲛⲁⲩ *(John 6:25)*

d) ⲁⲥⲛⲁⲓ̀ ⲛ̀ⲑⲛⲁⲩ ⲛ̀ϫⲉ ϯⲙⲉⲧⲟⲩⲣⲟ ⲛⲧⲉ Ⲫϯ *(Luke 17:20)*

e) ϫⲉ ϯⲥⲱⲟⲩⲛ ϫⲉ ⲁⲕϣⲟⲡ ⲑⲱⲛ ⲡⲓⲙⲁ ⲉ̀ⲧⲉ ⲡⲓⲑ̀ⲣⲟⲛⲟⲥ ⲙ̀ⲡⲥⲁⲧⲁⲛⲁⲥ ⲭⲏ ⲙ̀ⲙⲟϥ *(Revelation 2:13)*

f) ⲁⲣⲉ ⲡⲟⲗⲉⲙⲟⲥ ⲛⲏⲟⲩ ⲉ̀ⲃⲟⲗ ⲑⲱⲛ *(James 4:1)*

g) ⲁⲣⲉ Ⲫⲣⲏ ⲛⲁϩⲱⲧⲡ ⲛ̀ⲑⲛⲁⲩ ϩⲓⲛⲁ ⲛ̀ⲧⲁⲙ̀ⲧⲟⲛ ⲙ̀ⲙⲟⲓ ⲉ̀ⲃⲟⲗ ϧⲉⲛ ⲛⲁϧⲓⲥⲓ ⲛⲉⲙ ⲛⲁⲙ̀ⲕⲁϩ ⲛ̀ϩⲏⲧ *(Job 2:6)*

h) ⲡⲉϫⲉ ⲛⲓⲙⲁⲑⲏⲧⲏⲥ ϫⲉ ⲁⲛⲛⲁϫⲉⲙ ⲧⲁⲓⲏⲡⲓ ⲛ̀ⲱⲓⲕ ⲑⲱⲛ ϩⲓ ⲡⲁⲓⲙⲁⲛ̀ϣⲁϥⲉ *(Matthew 15:33)*

Practice text 17
Jonah 1:8-9
Jonah's drawing of the lot set off a barrage of questions from his fellow sailors, in some ways it could even be thought of as an interrogation, hence providing the perfect opportunity to practice the interrogative.

ⲟⲩⲟϩ ⲡⲉϫⲱⲟⲩ ⲛⲁϥ ϫⲉ ⲉⲑⲃⲉ ⲟⲩ ⲧⲁⲓⲕⲁⲕⲓⲁ ϣⲟⲡ ⲛϧⲏⲧⲕ ⲟⲩⲟϩ ⲟⲩ ⲧⲉ ⲧⲉⲕⲓⲟⲡⲏ ⲟⲩⲟϩ ⲁⲕⲛⲏⲟⲩ ⲉⲃⲟⲗ ⲑⲱⲛ ⲟⲩⲟϩ ⲛⲑⲟⲕ ⲟⲩ ⲉⲃⲟⲗϧⲉⲛ ⲁϣ ⲛⲭⲱⲣⲁ ⲛⲑⲟⲕ ⲟⲩⲟϩ ⲉⲃⲟⲗϧⲉⲛ ⲁϣ ⲛⲡⲟⲗⲓⲥ. ⲟⲩⲟϩ ⲡⲉϫⲁϥ ⲛⲱⲟⲩ ϫⲉ ⲁⲛⲟⲕ ⲟⲩⲃⲱⲕ ⲛⲧⲉ Π̅ⲟ̅ⲥ̅ ⲁⲛⲟⲕ^.

Vocab			
ⲓⲟⲡⲏ	occupation (f)	**ⲟϩⲓ ⲉⲣⲁⲧ⸗**	to stand (vi,rfx)
ⲕⲁⲕⲓⲁ	evil, malice (f)	**ⲣⲱϥ**	(his) mouth (poss.noun) **(15.4)**
ⲟⲩⲧⲉ ⲟⲩⲧⲱ⸗	between, among (prep)		

---

^ Does the ⲁⲛⲟⲕ look out of place? Take another look at confusion corner **page 64**

14. MAKING CONVERSATION

14.1. Getting acquainted

Meeting someone for the first time always seems to involve the same questions. Some of these are presented here so you'll have something to say next time you start a conversation with somebody new in Coptic.

The first step is to introduce yourself. For simplicity, let's assume your name is Ⲙⲁⲣⲕⲟⲥ. Now you'll need to give your name using the nominal sentence structure from **(3.1)**.

ⲁⲛⲟⲕ Ⲙⲁⲣⲕⲟⲥ

Next, you'll want to ask the other person's name

ⲛⲓⲙ ⲡⲉ ⲡⲉⲕⲣⲁⲛ *(Luke 8:30)*

literally *"who is your name"* or *"what's you name?"*

An alternative is to ask:

ⲛⲑⲟⲕ ⲛⲓⲙ *(John 8:25)*

Which literally means *"you who"*, but is understood to mean "who are you?"

When there is real importance to the question, another ⲛⲑⲟⲕ is added to the end. This construction is used for added emphasis, in the sense of asking "who do you think you are?".

I.e. ⲛⲑⲟⲕ ⲛⲓⲙ ⲛⲑⲟⲕ

ⲛⲑⲟⲕ ⲛⲓⲙ ⲛⲑⲟⲕ ⲫⲏ ⲉⲧϯϩⲁⲡ ⲉⲟⲩⲃⲱⲕ ⲛϣⲉⲙⲙⲟ *(Romans 14:4)*
"who are you to be the one who judges a slave of a stranger"

ⲡⲉϫⲉ Ⲓⲥⲁⲁⲕ ⲡⲉϥⲓⲱⲧ ⲛⲁϥ ϫⲉ ⲛⲑⲟⲕ ⲛⲓⲙ ⲛⲑⲟⲕ, ⲛⲑⲟϥ ⲇⲉ ⲡⲉϫⲁϥ ϫⲉ ⲁⲛⲟⲕ ⲡⲉ ⲡⲉⲕϣⲏⲣⲓ ⲡⲉⲕϣⲟⲣⲡ ⲙⲙⲓⲥⲓ Ⲏⲥⲁⲩ *(Genesis 27:32)*
"Isaac his father said to him "who are you" and he said to him "I am your son, your first born Esau."

Another question which may come up later in conversation is:

ⲕⲭⲏ ϧⲉⲛ ⲟⲩⲏⲣ ⲛⲣⲟⲙⲡⲓ *(Ambal pg 2)*

Literally "you exist how many years" or "how old are you"
Alternatively,

So You want to Learn Coptic?

ⲟⲩⲏⲣ ⲛⲉ ⲛⲓⲣⲟⲙⲡⲓ ⲛ̀ⲉ̀ϩⲟⲟⲩ ⲛ̀ⲧⲉ ⲡⲉⲕⲱⲛϧ *(Genesis 47:8)*
"how many are the years of days of your life"

14.1.i.   Jobs for the boys

Now it's time to get a better idea of the person you've just met. A very useful question here is:

ⲟⲩ ⲧⲉ ⲧⲉⲕⲓⲟⲡⲏ *(AmBal pg2)*

"what is your occupation?"

Who knows? Your new found friend could be any one of these:

Vocab			
ⲟⲓⲕⲟⲛⲟⲙⲟⲥ	manager, steward, administrator (Gk, m)	ⲣⲉϥϯϩⲁⲡ	judge (m)
ⲙⲁⲧⲟⲓ	soldier (m)	ⲥⲁϧ	teacher, lawyer (m)
ⲙⲟⲩⲥⲓⲕⲟⲥ	musician (m)	ⲥⲏⲓⲛⲓ	doctor (m)
ⲟⲩⲣⲱⲙⲓ ⲛ̀ⲟⲩⲱⲓ	farmer (m)	ϩⲁⲙϣⲉ	carpenter (m)

E.g. ⲁⲛⲟⲕ ⲟⲩⲙⲁⲧⲟⲓ *(AmBal pg2)*

"I am a soldier"

14.1.ii.   What have you been doing?

After becoming a little more familiar, you may be interested to know what your new acquaintance did the day before. For this, we turn to the interrogative particle ⲟⲩ **(13.3)**.

ⲟⲩ is combined with the copula to form ⲟⲩ ⲡⲉ   "what is it?" This happens to be the form you would use to enquire about an event that's happened. For example, to ask 'what did you do?',

You would start with the ⲟⲩ ⲡⲉ.

You would then add the pronominal form **(5.3.i)** of the verb ⲓⲣⲓ *"to do"* which is ⲁⲓ⧸:

ⲟⲩ ⲡⲉ _ⲁⲓⲁⲓ⧸

Assuming you're talking to a male, you'd then add the prefix for the second person masculine singular past perfect **(5.2)**:

ⲟⲩ ⲡⲉ ⲁⲕⲁⲓ⧸

In the deep recesses of your mind, you may remember a little device called the resumptive morph **(pg.106)**. In this case, it takes the form of ϥ which is added to the ⲁⲓ⸌ and refers back to the 'it' in 'what is it' which is represented by ⲟⲩ ⲡⲉ.

ⲟⲩ ⲡⲉ ⲁⲕⲁⲓϥ

That still only gives you "what is it you did", something is still missing, which is the word for 'which', so add in the relative article ⲉⲧ **(5.4)** and you get:

ⲟⲩ ⲡⲉ ⲉⲧⲁⲕⲁⲓϥ
"what is it which you did ?".

The ⲡⲉ and the ⲉⲧ are then contracted to form ⲡⲉⲧ (note that this looks the same but is different in meaning to the the relative substantive on **(pg90)**.) So the combination now becomes ⲟⲩ ⲡⲉⲧⲁⲕⲁⲓϥ

E.g. ⲟⲩⲟϩ ⲡⲉϫⲉ ⲡ϶ⲟⲓⲥ ⲫⲛⲟⲩϯ ϫⲉ ⲟⲩ ⲡⲉⲧⲁⲕⲁⲓϥ *(Genesis 4:10)*
"and the Lord God said "what did you do"

Finally, we'll take the word for yesterday from our list of adverbs **(9.1.i)** to give:

ⲟⲩ ⲡⲉⲧⲁⲕⲁⲓϥ ⲛ̀ⲥⲁϥ
"what did you do yesterday ?".

There are many options here are just a few:
He might have done something with friends:

ⲁⲓϣⲗⲏⲗ ⲛⲉⲙ ⲛⲁϣ̀ⲫⲏⲣ
"I prayed with my friends"

ⲁⲓϫⲉⲣϫⲉⲣ ⲛⲉⲙ ⲛⲁϣⲏⲣⲓ
"I played with my children"

Or he might have gone somewhere:

ⲁⲓϣⲉ ⲛⲏⲓ ⲉϧⲟⲩⲛ ⲉ̀ϯⲉⲕⲕⲗⲏⲥⲁ
"I went to the church"

ⲁⲛϣⲉ ⲛⲁⲛ ⲉ̀ⲛⲉⲛⲥ̀ⲫⲟⲧⲟⲩ ⲙ̀ⲫⲓⲟⲙ
"We went to the beach"

You may be interested to find out what he'll do the next day. This time, we'll use the ⲟⲩ ⲡⲉ with the relative first future **(5.9.ii)**.

E.g. **ⲟⲩ ⲡⲉ ⲉⲧⲉⲕⲛⲁⲁⲓϥ ⲛ̀ⲣⲁⲥϯ**
"what will you do tomorrow"

You might consider inviting him to your house, where you'd use the imperative of the verb **ⲓ̀ (p195)**, whether he be on his own:

E.g. **ⲁⲙⲟⲩ ⲉ̀ϧⲟⲩⲛ ⲉ̀ⲡⲁⲏⲓ**
"come (inside) to my house"

...or with his friends, as the Apostles were when they were invited by Lydia

ⲁⲙⲱⲓⲛⲓ ⲉ̀ϧⲟⲩⲛ ⲉ̀ⲡⲁⲏⲓ *(Acts 16:15)*
"come (inside) to my house"

You can then be a bit more specific and use the subjunctive **(6.2)** to say why you're inviting him;

E.g. ...**ⲛ̀ⲧⲉⲕ ⲟⲩⲱⲙ ⲛⲉⲙⲏⲓ**
"...so that you eat with me"

Eventually, it will come time to say 'goodbye', for which you would finally say:

ⲟⲩϫⲁⲓ ϧⲉⲛ Ⲡ̀ϭⲟⲓⲥ, which literally means:
"health in the Lord"

14.2. Interjections

From the words we've seen in this book so far, we've noticed that a word said on its own won't make any sense, it has to appear as part of a sentence with at least a minimum of basic parts.

For example, if I were to just say the word 'road' to you, you'd wonder if you'd missed something I said. Saying the word 'road' on it's own might sound cute if it was said by a baby, but it wouldn't make much sense if said by an adult.

There is however a special class of words which in fact do just that, that is, they appear on their own and still make perfect sense. We use these words every day. For example, words like 'yes', 'no' and 'behold', these special kind of words are called 'interjections.'

There are two basic categories of interjections. Those which change their ending *'inflected interjections'* and those which don't *'non inflected'*. Some of these interjections could be classed under other categories, and some will be familiar from other sections already, but they also deserve a special place here with the other interjections.

14.2.i. Non inflected interjections

ⲁⲙⲏⲛ	amen, may it be
ⲁϩⲁ	yes
ⲓⲥ, ϩⲏⲡⲡⲉ	behold! (these two are often used together)
ⲙ̀ⲙⲟⲛ	no
ⲙ̀ⲫⲱⲣ	no, don't
ⲥⲉ	yes
ⲭⲉⲣⲉ	hail (note that there is also an inflected form below)

14.2.ii. Inflected interjections

ⲁϩⲟ⸌	what!, why?, what is the matter with...?
ⲙⲓⲟ⸌	thank you
ⲛⲁⲓⲁⲧ⸌	blessed is
ⲟⲩⲟⲓ ⲛ⸌	woe unto
ⲭⲉⲣⲉ ⲛ⸌	hail to

You'll remember ⲁϩⲟ⸌ from not so long ago where it was used as an interrogative pronoun **(13.3)**. It can also be used as a rhetorical interjection, where it's asked in the form of a question but an answer isn't really expected. It was used by the parents of St.Pachomious when they were worried that he'd offended their gods:

E.g. ⲁϩⲟⲕ ⲛ̀ⲑⲟⲕ ⲉⲣⲉⲛⲓⲛⲟⲩϯ ϫⲟⲛⲧ ⲉ̀ⲣⲟⲕ *(S.Pachomii vita. pg.2)*
"what is the matter with you! The gods will be angry with you"

So You want to Learn Coptic?

Vocab			
ⲁⲥⲡⲁⲥⲙⲟⲥ	greeting (Gk,m)	ⲥⲱϥ ⲥⲉϥ- ⲥⲟϥ⳯ ⲥⲟϥ	to defile, pollute (v.t)
ⲁⲅⲟⲣⲁ	market place (Gk,f)	ⲧⲁⲓⲟ ⲧⲁⲓⲏⲟⲩⲧ	to honour (v.i), to be honoured (q)
Ⲉⲗⲓⲁⲥ	Elijah (prop noun)	ϣⲓⲛⲓ ϣⲉⲛ- ϣⲉⲛ⳯	to ask, to question (v.t)
ⲉⲛⲭⲁⲓ	thing, (m) possession	ϩⲩⲡⲉⲣⲉⲧⲏⲥ	servant, attendant (Gk, m)
ⲙⲁⲛϩⲉⲙⲥⲓ	seat (place of sitting) (m)	ϭⲱϧⲉⲙ ϭⲁϧⲉⲙ- ϭⲁϧⲙ⳯ ϭⲁϧⲉⲙ	to defile, pollute (v.t)
ⲟⲩⲱⲙ ⲟⲩⲉⲙ- ⲟⲩⲟⲙ⳯	to eat (v.t)		

Exercise 14:1

a) ⲡⲉⲧⲣⲟⲥ ⲇⲉ ⲡⲉϫⲁϥ ϫⲉ ⲙ̀ⲫⲱⲣ Ⲡ̅ⲟ̅ⲥ̅ ϫⲉ ⲙ̀ⲡⲓⲟⲩⲉⲙ ϩ̀ⲗⲓ ⲛ̀ⲉⲛⲭⲁⲓ ⲉⲛⲉϩ ⲉϥϭⲁϧⲉⲙ ⲓⲉ ⲉϥⲥⲟϥ (*Acts 10:14*)

b) Ⲟⲩⲟϩ ⲁⲩⲱϣ ⲉ̀ⲡ̀ϣⲱⲓ ϩⲁ Ⲡ̅ⲟ̅ⲥ̅ ⲟⲩⲟϩ ⲡⲉϫⲱⲟⲩ ϫⲉ ⲙ̀ⲫⲱⲣ Ⲡ̅ⲟ̅ⲥ̅ ⲙ̀ⲡⲉⲛⲑ̀ⲣⲉⲛⲧⲁⲕⲟ ⲉⲑⲃⲉ ϯⲯⲩⲭⲏ ⲛ̀ⲧⲉ ⲡⲁⲓⲣⲱⲙⲓ (*Jonah 1:14*)

c) ⲟⲩⲟϩ ⲛⲁⲩⲛⲏⲟⲩ ϩⲁⲣⲟϥ ⲡⲉ ⲉⲩϫⲱ ⲙ̀ⲙⲟⲥ ϫⲉ ⲭⲉⲣⲉ ⲡ̀ⲟⲩⲣⲟ ⲛ̀ⲧⲉ ⲛⲓⲓⲟⲩⲇⲁⲓ (*John 19:3*)

d) ⲙ̀ⲓⲱⲧⲉⲛ ⲛ̀ⲁϩⲩⲡⲉⲣⲉⲧⲏⲥ ⲉⲧⲧⲁⲓⲏⲟⲩⲧ (*hom vat ii pg.87*)

e) ⲡⲉϫⲁϥ ⲛⲁϥ ϫⲉ ⲁϫⲟⲥ ⲛⲏⲓ ϫⲉ ⲛ̀ⲑⲟⲕ ⲟⲩⲣⲱⲙⲉⲟⲥ ⲛ̀ⲑⲟϥ ⲇⲉ ⲡⲉϫⲁϥ ϫⲉ ⲁϩⲁ (*Acts 22:27*)

f) ⲟⲩⲟϩ ⲁⲩϣⲉⲛϥ ϫⲉ ⲛ̀ⲑⲟⲕ ⲡⲉ Ⲏⲗⲓⲁⲥ ⲡⲉϫⲁϥ ϫⲉ ⲙ̀ⲙⲟⲛ ⲛ̀ⲑⲟⲕ ⲡⲉ ⲡⲓⲡⲣⲟⲫⲏⲧⲏⲥ ⲁϥⲉⲣⲟⲩⲱ ϫⲉ ⲙ̀ⲙⲟⲛ (*John 1:21*)

Making conversation

g) ⲟⲩⲟⲓ ⲛⲱⲧⲉⲛ ⲛⲓⲫⲁⲣⲓⲥⲉⲟⲥ ϫⲉ ⲧⲉⲧⲉⲛⲙⲉⲓ ⲙ̀ⲛⲓϣⲟⲣⲡ ⲙ̀ⲙⲁⲛ̀ϩⲉⲙⲥⲓ ϧⲉⲛ ⲛⲓⲥⲩⲛⲁⲅⲱⲅⲏ ⲛⲉⲙ ⲛⲓⲁⲥⲡⲁⲥⲙⲟⲥ ϧⲉⲛ ⲛⲓⲁⲅⲟⲣⲁ (*Luke* 11:43)

h) ⲟⲩⲟϩ ⲡⲉϫⲉ I̅H̅C̅ ⲛⲱⲟⲩ ϫⲉ ⲧⲉⲧⲉⲛⲛⲁϯ ϫⲉ ⲟⲩⲟⲛ ϣ̀ϫⲟⲙ ⲙ̀ⲙⲟⲓ ⲉ̀ⲉⲣ ⲫⲁⲓ ⲡⲉϫⲱⲟⲩ ⲛⲁϥ ϫⲉ ⲥⲉ ⲡⲉⲛⲟ̅ⲥ̅ (*Matthew* 9:28)

i) ⲟⲩⲟϩ ϩⲏⲡⲡⲉ ⲓⲥ ⲟⲩⲁⲅⲅⲉⲗⲟⲥ ⲛ̀ⲧⲉ Π̅Ⲟ̅Ⲥ̅ ⲁϥⲓ̀ (*Acts* 12:7)

j) ⲁⲙⲏⲛ ϯϫⲱ ⲙ̀ⲙⲟⲥ ⲛⲱⲧⲉⲛ (*Luke* 4:24)

241

So You want to Learn Coptic?

15. DIFFERENT WAYS OF HAVING THINGS

Throughout the book we've met different ways of 'belonging', that is indicating when something belongs to another, or when someone has 'possession' of something. Grammatically, this is called the *possessive*. Though we have already come across some ways of expressing the possessive, there are some more which we shall discuss in this the final chapter.

15.1. Possessive articles

These are the words like 'my', 'yours' and 'his' which we met way back in **(2.1.iii)**. The possessive articles actually also provide us with an opportunity to talk about *sharing* or *reciprocating*. You see, things aren't always just owned by one person, or even by just a group of people, but are often shared with "one another". As we've seen over and over again, we find that there are often complicated sounding grammatical terms for innocent words that we use everyday without a fuss. And true to form, the term for "one another" is the *reciprocating pronoun*. It's represented in Coptic by -ⲉⲣⲏⲟⲩ, which attaches to any of the plural possessive articles as in the table below:

ⲛⲉⲛⲉⲣⲏⲟⲩ	one another (of ourselves)
ⲛⲉⲧⲉⲛⲉⲣⲏⲟⲩ	one another (of yourselves)
ⲛⲟⲩⲉⲣⲏⲟⲩ	one another (of themselves)

E.g. ⲁⲗⲗⲁ ⲉⲃⲟⲗϩⲓⲧⲉⲛ ϯⲁⲅⲁⲡⲏ ⲁⲣⲓⲃⲱⲕ ⲛ̀ⲛⲉⲧⲉⲛⲉⲣⲏⲟⲩ (*Galatians 5:13*)
"*but through love serve one another*"

15.2. Possessive construction

We first met the possessive construction in **(2.4.ii)** where we learnt about the ⲙ̀/ⲛ̀ or ⲛ̀ⲧⲉ (attributive) construction.

E.g. ϯⲙⲉⲧⲟⲩⲣⲟ ⲛ̀ⲛⲓⲫⲏⲟⲩⲓ
"*The kingdom of the Heavens*"

What wasn't mentioned at that time however, was that there is also a special pronominal form of ⲛ̀ⲧⲉ which indicates possession towards a pronoun as opposed to a noun, as for example, when you would want to say 'the bread of him' as opposed to the "bread of Simon."

It uses the stem ⲛ̀ⲧ⳿ linked to different personal suffixes **(5.3.i)** as shown in the table below:

of me	ⲛ̀ⲧⲏⲓ
of you (m)	ⲛ̀ⲧⲁⲕ
of you (f)	ⲛ̀ⲧⲉ
of him	ⲛ̀ⲧⲁϥ
of her	ⲛ̀ⲧⲁⲥ
of us	ⲛ̀ⲧⲁⲛ
of you (pl)	ⲛ̀ⲧⲱⲧⲉⲛ
of them	ⲛ̀ⲧⲱⲟⲩ

E.g. ⲡⲓⲱⲓⲕ ⲛ̀ⲧⲁϥ
"the bread of him", or 'his bread'

15.3. Using the existential ⲟⲩⲟⲛ

We first met the existential verb **ⲟⲩⲟⲛ** in (8.2.ii) which we learnt could be translated as "there is." The existential may be combined with the pronominal form of the possessive construction above **(15.2)** to give the forms in the table below, which have the meaning of "there is to (pronoun)", e.g. "there is to me" or "there is to him." There are both complete and abbreviated forms of this combination, as shown in the table below:

	complete form	abbreviated form
there is to me or "I have"	ⲟⲩⲟⲛ ⲛ̀ⲧⲏⲓ	ⲟⲩⲟⲛϯ
You have (masculine)	ⲟⲩⲟⲛ ⲛ̀ⲧⲁⲕ	ⲟⲩⲟⲛⲧⲉⲕ
You have (feminine)	ⲟⲩⲟⲛ ⲛ̀ⲧⲉ	ⲟⲩⲟⲛⲧⲉ
He has	ⲟⲩⲟⲛ ⲛ̀ⲧⲁϥ	ⲟⲩⲟⲛⲧⲉϥ
She has	ⲟⲩⲟⲛ ⲛ̀ⲧⲁⲥ	ⲟⲩⲟⲛⲧⲉⲥ

Different ways of having things

We have	ⲟⲩⲟⲛ ⲛ̄ⲧⲁⲛ	ⲟⲩⲟⲛⲧⲉⲛ
You have (plural)	ⲟⲩⲟⲛ ⲛ̄ⲧⲱⲧⲉⲛ	ⲟⲩⲟⲛⲧⲉⲧⲉⲛ
They have	ⲟⲩⲟⲛ ⲛ̄ⲧⲱⲟⲩ	ⲟⲩⲟⲛⲧⲟⲩ

An object marker comes between the complete construction and whatever is being possessed;

E.g. **ⲟⲩⲟⲛ ⲛ̄ⲧⲏⲓ ⲛ̄ⲟⲩⲛⲓϣϯ ⲛ̄ⲗⲁⲟⲥ ϧⲉⲛ ⲧⲁⲓⲡⲟⲗⲓⲥ** *(Acts 18:10)*
"I have a great (number) of people in this city"

However, no object marker is used after the abbreviated construction.

E.g. **ⲟⲩⲟⲛϯ ⲛⲁϩϯ ⲙ̄ⲙⲁⲩ** *(James 2:14)*
"I have faith"

Notice the **ⲙ̄ⲙⲁⲩ** at the end of the sentence? The existential possessive construction can have this thrown in after the object of possession. Now we saw in (**9.1**) that **ⲙ̄ⲙⲁⲩ** means 'there', but when used with the existential possessive construction, it's really left untranslated.

E.g. **ⲟⲩⲟⲛ ⲛ̄ⲧⲁⲕ ⲛ̄ⲟⲩⲣⲁⲛ ⲙ̄ⲙⲁⲩ** *(Revelation 3:1)*
"you have a name"

The negative existential **ⲙ̄ⲙⲟⲛ** "there is no", can also be used to tell when somebody does *not* have something. As with **ⲟⲩⲟⲛ**, the **ⲙ̄ⲙⲟⲛ** possessive construction may have an optional **ⲙ̄ⲙⲁⲩ** after the object. Unlike **ⲟⲩⲟⲛ** however, **ⲙ̄ⲙⲟⲛ** doesn't take an object marker.

E.g. **ⲙ̄ⲙⲟⲛϯ ϩⲁⲓ ⲙ̄ⲙⲁⲩ** *(John 4:17)*
"I have no husband"

	complete form	abbreviated form
I do not have	ⲙ̄ⲙⲟⲛ ⲛ̄ⲧⲏⲓ	ⲙ̄ⲙⲟⲛϯ
you do not have (masculine)	ⲙ̄ⲙⲟⲛ ⲛ̄ⲧⲁⲕ	ⲙ̄ⲙⲟⲛⲧⲉⲕ

So You want to Learn Coptic?

you do not have (feminine)	ⲙⲙⲟⲛ ⲛ̀ⲧⲉ	ⲙⲙⲟⲛⲧⲉ
He does not have	ⲙⲙⲟⲛ ⲛ̀ⲧⲁϥ	ⲙⲙⲟⲛⲧⲉϥ
She does not have	ⲙⲙⲟⲛ ⲛ̀ⲧⲁⲥ	ⲙⲙⲟⲛⲧⲉⲥ
We do not have	ⲙⲙⲟⲛ ⲛ̀ⲧⲁⲛ	ⲙⲙⲟⲛⲧⲉⲛ
You do not have (plural)	ⲙⲙⲟⲛ ⲛ̀ⲧⲱⲧⲉⲛ	ⲙⲙⲟⲛⲧⲉⲧⲉⲛ
They do not have	ⲙⲙⲟⲛ ⲛ̀ⲧⲱⲟⲩ	ⲙⲙⲟⲛⲧⲟⲩ

Vocab			
ⲡⲁⲣⲣⲏⲥⲓⲁ	boldness, (Gk, f) openness, frankness, confidence, courage	ⲣⲉⲙⲛ̀ⲏⲓ	family, household (m)
ⲕⲗⲏⲣⲟⲛⲟⲙⲓⲁ	inheritance (Gk, f)	ⲉⲣϣⲓϣⲓ	authority, power (m)
ⲡⲁⲛⲧⲟⲕⲣⲁⲧⲱⲣ	Almighty (Gk,m)	ⲧⲉⲃⲛⲏ	animal, beast (m)

Exercise 15.1

a) ⲉ̀ϫⲉⲛ Ⲥⲓⲱⲛ ⲡⲓⲧⲱⲟⲩ ⲉⲑⲟⲩⲁⲃ ⲛ̀ⲧⲁϥ (Psalm 2:4 2:6)

b) ⲙⲙⲟⲛ ⲛ̀ⲧⲁⲛ ⲛ̀ⲟⲩⲡⲁⲣⲣⲏⲥⲓⲁ (Adam Aspacmos, Divine Liturgy)

c) ⲟⲩⲟⲛⲧⲏⲓ ⲙ̀ⲙⲁⲩ ⲛ̀ⲟⲩϣⲟⲩϣⲟⲩ ϧⲉⲛ Ⲡ̅ⲭ̅ⲥ̅ Ⲓⲏⲥ̅ (Romans 15:17)

d) ⲁⲃⲣⲁⲁⲙ ⲡⲉⲧⲉⲛⲓⲱⲧ ⲛⲁϥⲑⲉⲗⲏⲗ ⲡⲉ ⲉϥⲟⲩⲱϣ ⲉ̀ⲛⲁⲩ ⲉ̀ⲟⲩⲉ̀ϩⲟⲟⲩ ⲛ̀ⲧⲏⲓ ⲟⲩⲟϩ ⲁϥⲛⲁⲩ ⲁϥⲣⲁϣⲓ (John 8:56)

e) ⲙⲏ ⲙⲙⲟⲛⲧⲉⲛ ⲉⲣϣⲓϣⲓ ⲉ̀ⲟⲩⲱⲙ ⲛⲉⲙ ⲉ̀ⲥⲱ (1 Corinthians 9:4)

f) ⲟⲩⲟⲛ ⲛ̀ⲧⲁⲛ ⲙ̀ⲙⲁⲩ ⲙ̀ⲡⲉⲛⲛⲟⲩϯ ϧⲉⲛ ⲛⲓⲫⲏⲟⲩⲓ Ⲫϯ ⲡⲓⲡⲁⲛⲧⲟⲕⲣⲁⲧⲱⲣ (hom vatt ii pg.81)

g) ⲁϥⲣⲓⲙⲓ ⲉ̀ϩⲣⲏⲓ ⲉ̀ϫⲱⲟⲩ ⲙ̀ⲫⲣⲏϯ ⲛ̀ϩⲁⲛϣⲏⲣⲓ ⲙ̀ⲙⲉⲛⲣⲓⲧ ⲛ̀ⲧⲁϥ
(hom vat ii pg.89)

Different ways of having things

h) ⲉϣⲱⲡ ⲇⲉ ⲙ̅ⲙⲟⲛⲧⲉϥ ⲥⲟⲛ ⲙ̅ⲙⲁⲩ ⲉⲣⲉⲧⲉⲛⲉϯ ⲛ̅ⲧⲉϥⲕⲗⲏⲣⲟⲛⲟⲙⲓⲁ ⲛ̅ⲟⲩⲣⲉⲙⲛ̅ⲏⲓ ⲛ̅ⲧⲁϥ *(Numbers 27:11)*

i) ⲛⲉⲕⲁⲗⲱⲟⲩⲓ ⲟⲩⲟⲛⲧⲟⲩ ⲧⲉⲃⲛⲏ ⲙ̅ⲙⲁⲩ *(Numbers 32:4)*

15.4. Possessive pronouns

The Coptic possessive pronoun is the equivalent of saying words like 'yours' and 'mine' in English. One form of this may be familiar to you from the Paschal praise

ⲑⲱⲕ ⲧⲉ ϯϫⲟⲙ

"to you is the power"

The other forms based on person, number and gender are shown in the table below:

	single masculine	single feminine	plural
to me (mine)	ⲫⲱⲓ	ⲑⲱⲓ	ⲛⲟⲩⲓ
to you (male)	ⲫⲱⲕ	ⲑⲱⲕ	ⲛⲟⲩⲕ
to you (feminine)	ⲫⲱ	ⲑⲱ	ⲛⲟⲩ
to him	ⲫⲱϥ	ⲑⲱϥ	ⲛⲟⲩϥ
to her	ⲫⲱⲥ	ⲑⲱⲥ	ⲛⲟⲩⲥ
to us	ⲫⲱⲛ	ⲑⲱⲛ	ⲛⲟⲩⲛ
to you (plural)	ⲫⲱⲧⲉⲛ	ⲑⲱⲧⲉⲛ	ⲛⲟⲩⲧⲉⲛ
to them (theirs)	ⲫⲱⲟⲩ	ⲑⲱⲟⲩ	ⲛⲱⲟⲩ

For example, ϫⲟⲙ means power and is a feminine word. Hence, to say "to You is the power" (or "the power is Yours") we looked under "to you" in the single feminine column and picked ⲑⲱⲕ. Note that this choice doesn't depend on the gender of "you". To finish off the sentence, you use the feminine copula:

E.g. ⲑⲱⲕ ⲧⲉ ϯϫⲟⲙ

So You want to Learn Coptic?

For another example, we'll use ⲧⲟⲧⲥ which means 'chair' and is a masculine word, so this time to say "mine is the chair" you would pick from the masculine singular column and write: ⲫⲱⲓ ⲡⲉ ⲡⲓⲧⲟⲧⲥ

The possessive pronoun also has a prenominal form (i.e a form which precedes the noun without the need for a pronominal suffix), as shown in the table below:

masculine (s)	feminine (s)	plural
ⲫⲁ	ⲑⲁ	ⲛⲁ

Here the possessive pronoun is translated as 'of' as in 'the one of.'

E.g. ⲁⲃⲃⲁ Ⲡⲁϩⲱⲙ ⲫⲁ ϯⲕⲟⲓⲛⲱⲛⲓⲁ

"Saint Pachom of the Community"

Vocab			
ⲁⲃⲃⲁ	father (Gk,m)	ⲣⲏ	sun (m)
ⲓⲟϩ	moon (m)	ⲭⲣⲟⲛⲟⲥ	period of time, season, (Gk, m)

Exercise 15.2

a) ⲛ̀ⲑⲱⲧⲉⲛ ⲫⲱⲧⲉⲛ ⲁⲛ   *(1 Corinthians 6:19)*

b) ⲑⲱⲟⲩ ⲧⲉ ϯⲙⲉⲧⲟⲩⲣⲟ ⲛ̀ⲧⲉ ⲛⲓⲫⲏⲟⲩⲓ   *(Matthew 5:3)*

c) ⲫⲱϥ ⲡⲉ ⲡⲓⲱⲟⲩ ϣⲁ ⲉⲛⲉϩ ⲛ̀ⲧⲉ ⲛⲓⲉ̀ⲛⲉϩ ⲁⲙⲏⲛ   *(1 Philippians 4:20)*

d) ⲁⲩⲟⲩⲱⲧ ⲛ̀ϫⲉ ⲛⲁ ϯⲃⲁⲕⲓ ⲧⲏⲣⲟⲩ   *(hom vatt ii pg.85)*

e) ⲡⲓⲥⲁϫⲓ ⲉ̀ⲧⲉⲧⲉⲛⲥⲱⲧⲉⲙ ⲉ̀ⲣⲟϥ ⲫⲱⲓ ⲁⲛ ⲡⲉ ⲁⲗⲗⲁ ⲫⲁ ⲫⲓⲱⲧ ⲡⲉ ⲉ̀ⲧⲁϥⲧⲁⲟⲩⲟⲓ   *(John 14:24)*

f) ⲫⲱⲧⲉⲛ ⲁⲛ ⲡⲉ ⲉ̀ⲉ̀ⲙⲓ ⲉϩⲁⲛⲭⲣⲟⲛⲟⲥ ⲓⲉ ϩⲁⲛⲥⲏⲟⲩ   *(Acts 1:7)*

g) ⲛⲁⲓ̀ⲥⲕⲉⲩⲟⲥ ⲛⲁⲓ ⲛⲟⲩⲓ̀ ⲛⲉ   *(hom vatt ii pg.73)*

h) ⲫⲱⲕ ⲡⲉ ⲡⲓⲉϩⲟⲟⲩ ⲫⲱⲕ ⲟⲛ ⲡⲉ ⲡⲓⲉϫⲱⲣϩ ⲛ̀ⲑⲟⲕ ⲁⲕⲥⲟⲃϯ ⲙ̀ⲡⲓⲣⲏ ⲛⲉⲙ ⲡⲓⲓⲟϩ   *(Psalm 73:14 74:16)*

i) Ⲙⲓⲭⲁⲏⲗ ⲡ̀ⲁⲣⲭⲱⲛ ⲛⲁ ⲛⲓⲫⲏⲟⲩⲓ

j) ϫⲙⲉⲩⲓ ⲁⲛ ⲉ̀ⲛⲁⲫϯ ⲁⲗⲗⲁ ⲛⲁ ⲛⲓⲣⲱⲙⲓ   *(Mark 8:33)*

15.5. The Possessed nouns

Relax! These nouns are not demon possessed, but they are possessed in the innocent sense of the word. These nouns are different in that they are designed to take personal suffix at the end to indicate who they belong to. Most of these nouns are actually body parts.

For example, let's take the Coptic word for mouth.

The normal word for this is **ro**.

Ro, being one of these special nouns, has an inflected form which can changes its endings. This inflected form is **rω⁄**

The endings to this word to indicate possession are as follows:

ⲣⲱⲓ	my mouth
ⲣⲱⲕ	your mouth (masculine)
ⲣⲱ	your mouth (feminine)
ⲣⲱϥ	his mouth
ⲣⲱⲥ	her mouth
ⲣⲱⲛ	our mouth
ⲣⲱⲧⲉⲛ	your mouth (plural)
ⲣⲱⲟⲩ	their mouth

So, to say "my mouth" using this special form, you would use **ⲣⲱⲓ**.

Some other possessed nouns are listed below. As it turns out, only a few have a non inflected form.

Many of the possessed pronouns form the core of the compound prepositions which were first introduced in **(5.1.iii)** and are further explained in **(Appendix 3)**.

Inflected form		non inflected form
ϫⲱ⁄	head	—
ⲧⲟⲧ⁄, ⲧⲉⲛ–	hand	ⲧⲱⲣⲓ

249

So You want to Learn Coptic?

ϧⲏⲧ⳿	belly	—
ⲣⲁⲧ⳿	foot	—
ⲑⲟⲩⲱ⳿	bosom, chest	—
ϩⲏ⳿	chest or heart	ϩⲏⲧ
ϩⲣ⳿	face	ϩⲟ
ⲕⲉⲛ⳿	bosom	—
ⲓⲁⲧ⳿	eye	—
ⲥⲁ⳿	back	—
ⲁⲧⲣⲏϫ⳿	end	—

Vocab			
ⲟⲩⲏⲓ	indeed (adv)		

Exercise 15.3

a) ⲧⲟⲧⲉ ⲣⲱⲛ ⲁϥⲙⲟϩ ⲛ̀ⲣⲁϣⲓ (*Psalm 125:2* **126:2**)

b) ϫⲉ ϥ̀ⲥⲙⲁⲣⲱⲟⲩⲧ ⲛ̀ϫⲉ Ⲡ⳪ Ⲫϯ ⲙ̀ⲡⲓⲥⲗ ϥ̀ⲥⲙⲁⲣⲱⲟⲩⲧ ⲛ̀ϫⲉ Ⲡ⳪ Ⲫϯ ⲛ̀ⲥⲉⲇⲣⲁⲕ ⲙⲓⲥⲁⲕ ⲁⲃⲇⲉⲛⲁⲅⲱ ⲫⲏ ⲉⲧⲁϥⲟⲩⲱⲣⲡ ⲙ̀ⲡⲉϥⲁⲅⲅⲉⲗⲟⲥ ⲁϥⲛⲟϩⲉⲙ ⲛ̀ⲛⲉϥⲉ̀ⲃⲓⲁⲓⲕ ϫⲉ ⲟⲩⲏⲓ ⲛⲁⲣⲉ ϩⲑⲛⲟⲩ ϫⲏ ⲉ̀ⲣⲟϥ (*Daniel 3:28 hom vatt ii pg. 85*)

c) Ⲫⲛⲟⲩϯ ⲥⲱⲧⲉⲙ ⲉ̀ⲧⲁⲡⲣⲟⲥⲉⲩⲭⲏ ϭⲓⲥⲙⲏ ⲉ̀ⲛⲓⲥⲁϫⲓ ⲛ̀ⲧⲉ ⲣⲱⲓ (*Psalm* **53:2** *54:2*)

d) ⲉⲧⲁϥⲟⲩⲱⲛ ⲛ̀ⲣⲱϥ (*Matthew 5:2*)

e) ⲡⲉϫⲉ ⲡϭⲟⲓⲥ ⲇⲉ ⲛⲁϥ ⲟⲛ ϫⲉ ϩⲓ ⲧⲉⲕϫⲓϫ ⲉ̀ϧⲟⲩⲛ ϧⲁ ⲑⲟⲩⲱⲕ ⲟⲩⲟϩ ⲁϥϩⲓ ⲧⲉϥϫⲓϫ ⲉ̀ϧⲟⲩⲛ ϧⲁ ⲑⲟⲩⲱϥ (*Exodus 4:6*)

Practice text 18

Well done, you're almost there. Now there's just one more practice text to tie everything together and to show you just how much you've learnt. Enjoy.
Numbers 21:1-9

ⲟⲩⲟϩ ⲁϥⲥⲱⲧⲉⲙ ⲛ̀ϫⲉ ⲡⲓⲭⲁⲛⲁⲛⲉⲟⲥ ⲡ̀ⲟⲩⲣⲟ ⲛ̀ⲁⲣⲁⲇ ⲫⲏ ⲉⲧϣⲟⲡ ϩⲓ ⲡ̀ϣⲁϥⲉ ϫⲉ ⲁϥⲓ̀ ⲛ̀ϫⲉ ⲡⲓⲥⲣⲁⲏⲗ ⲉ̀ⲫⲙⲱⲓⲧ ⲛ̀ⲁⲑⲁⲣⲓⲛ ⲟⲩⲟϩ ⲁϥⲃⲱⲧⲥ ⲉ̀ⲡⲓⲥⲣⲁⲏⲗ ⲟⲩⲟϩ ⲁⲩⲱⲗⲓ ⲛ̀ⲟⲩⲉⲭⲙⲁⲗⲱⲥⲓⲁ ⲛ̀ϧⲏⲧⲟⲩ ⲟⲩⲟϩ ⲁϥⲧⲱⲃϩ ⲛ̀ϫⲉ ⲡⲓⲥⲣⲁⲏⲗ ⲛ̀ⲟⲩⲉⲩⲭⲏ ⲙ̀ⲡ̀ϭⲟⲓⲥ ⲟⲩⲟϩ ⲡⲉϫⲁϥ ϫⲉ ⲉ̀ϣⲱⲡ ⲁⲕϣⲁⲛϯ ⲙ̀ⲡⲁⲓⲗⲁⲟⲥ ⲉ̀ϧⲣⲏⲓ ⲉ̀ⲛⲁϫⲓϫ ϯⲛⲁⲉⲣⲁⲛⲁⲑⲉⲙⲁⲧⲓⲍⲓⲛ ⲙ̀ⲙⲟϥ ⲛⲉⲙ ⲛⲉϥⲃⲁⲕⲓ ⲟⲩⲟϩ ⲁϥⲥⲱⲧⲉⲙ ⲛ̀ϫⲉ ⲡ̀ϭⲟⲓⲥ ⲉ̀ⲧ̀ⲥ̀ⲙⲏ ⲙ̀ⲡⲓⲥⲣⲁⲏⲗ ⲟⲩⲟϩ ⲁϥϯⲙ̀ⲡⲓⲗⲁⲟⲥ ⲛ̀ⲭⲁⲛⲁⲛⲉⲟⲥ ⲉ̀ϧⲣⲏⲓ ⲉ̀ⲧⲟⲧϥ ⲟⲩⲟϩ ⲁϥⲉⲣⲁⲛⲁⲑⲉⲙⲁⲧⲓⲍⲓⲛ ⲙ̀ⲙⲟϥ ⲛⲉⲙ ⲛⲉϥⲃⲁⲕⲓ ⲟⲩⲟϩ ⲁⲩϯⲣⲉⲛ ⲫ̀ⲣⲁⲛ ⲙ̀ⲡⲓⲙⲁ ⲉⲧⲉⲙⲙⲁⲩ ϫⲉ ⲡⲓⲁⲛⲁⲑⲉⲙⲁ ⲟⲩⲟϩ ⲉⲧⲁⲩⲟⲩⲱⲧⲉⲃ ⲉⲃⲟⲗ ϧⲉⲛ ⲱⲣ ⲡⲓⲧⲱⲟⲩ ⲉϫⲉⲛ ⲫ̀ⲙⲱⲓⲧ ⲙ̀ⲫ̀ⲓⲟⲙ ⲛ̀ϣⲁⲣⲓ ⲁⲩⲕⲱⲧ ⲉ̀ⲡⲓⲕⲁϩⲓ ⲛ̀ⲉⲇⲱⲙ ⲟⲩⲟϩ ⲁϥⲉⲣⲕⲟⲩϫⲓ ⲛ̀ϩⲏⲧ ⲛ̀ϫⲉ ⲡⲓⲗⲁⲟⲥ ϩⲓ ⲫ̀ⲙⲱⲓⲧ ⲟⲩⲟϩ ⲁ ⲡⲓⲗⲁⲟⲥ ⲥⲁϫⲓ ⲛ̀ⲥⲁ ⲫ̀ⲛⲟⲩϯ ⲛⲉⲙ ⲙⲱⲩⲥⲏⲥ ⲉⲩϫⲱ ⲙ̀ⲙⲟⲥ ϫⲉ ⲉⲑⲃⲉⲟⲩ ⲁⲕⲉⲛⲧⲉⲛ ⲉ̀ⲃⲟⲗ ϧⲉⲛ ⲡ̀ⲕⲁϩⲓ ⲛ̀ⲭⲏⲙⲓ ⲉ̀ϧⲟⲑⲃⲉⲛ ϩⲓ ⲡ̀ϣⲁϥⲉ ϫⲉ ⲙ̀ⲙⲟⲛ ⲱⲓⲕ ⲟⲩⲇⲉ ⲙⲱⲟⲩ. ⲧⲉⲛⲯⲩⲭⲏ ⲇⲉ ⲁⲥⲉ̀ϩⲣⲟϣ ⲉ̀ⲡⲁⲓⲱⲓⲕ ⲉⲧϣⲟⲩⲱⲟⲩ ⲟⲩⲟϩ ⲁ ⲡ̀ϭⲟⲓⲥ ⲟⲩⲱⲣⲡ ⲛ̀ⲛⲓϩⲟϥ ⲉ̀ϧⲟⲩⲛ ⲉ̀ⲡⲓⲗⲁⲟⲥ ⲉϣⲁⲩϭⲱⲧⲉⲃ ⲟⲩⲟϩ ⲛⲁⲩϭⲓ ⲗⲁⲡⲥⲓ ⲛ̀ⲥⲁ ⲡⲓⲗⲁⲟⲥ ⲡⲉ ⲟⲩⲟϩ ⲁϥⲙⲟⲩ ⲛ̀ϫⲉ ⲟⲩⲛⲓϣϯ ⲙ̀ⲙⲏϣ ⲛ̀ⲧⲉ ⲛⲉⲛϣⲏⲣⲓ ⲙ̀ⲡⲓⲥⲣⲁⲏⲗ ⲟⲩⲟϩ

ⲁ ⲡⲓⲗⲁⲟⲥ ⲓ ϩⲁ ⲙⲱⲧⲥⲏⲥ ⲉⲩϫⲱ ⲙ̀ⲙⲟⲥ ϫⲉ ⲁⲛⲉⲣⲛⲟⲃⲓ
ⲁⲛⲥⲁϫⲓ ⲛ̀ⲥⲁ ⲫⲛⲟⲩϯ ⲛⲉⲙ ⲛ̀ⲥⲱⲕ ⲧⲱⲃϩ ⲟⲩⲛ ⲙ̀ⲡϭⲟⲓⲥ ⲟⲩⲟϩ
ⲙⲁⲣⲉϥⲱⲗⲓ ⲛ̀ⲛⲁⲓϩⲟϥ ⲉⲃⲟⲗ ϩⲁⲣⲟⲛ ⲟⲩⲟϩ ⲁ ⲙⲱⲧⲥⲏⲥ ⲧⲱⲃϩ
ⲙ̀ⲡϭⲟⲓⲥ ⲉⲑⲃⲉ ⲡⲓⲗⲁⲟⲥ ⲟⲩⲟϩ ⲡⲉϫⲉ ⲡϭⲟⲓⲥ ⲙ̀ⲙⲱⲧⲥⲏⲥ ϫⲉ
ⲙⲁⲑⲁⲙⲓⲟ ⲛⲁⲕ ⲛ̀ⲟⲩϩⲟϥ ⲛ̀ϩⲟⲙⲧ ⲟⲩⲟϩ ⲭⲁϥ ϩⲓ ⲟⲩⲙⲏⲓⲛⲓ
ⲟⲩⲟϩ ⲉⲥⲉϣⲱⲡⲓ ⲁⲣⲉϣⲁⲛ ⲡⲓϩⲟϥ ϭⲓ ⲗⲁⲡⲥⲓ ⲉⲟⲩⲣⲱⲙⲓ ⲟⲩⲟϩ
ⲉϥⲉϫⲟⲩϣⲧ ⲉ̀ⲡⲓϩⲟϥ ⲛ̀ϩⲟⲙⲧ ⲟⲩⲟϩ ⲉϥⲉⲱⲛϧ ⲟⲩⲟϩ ⲁϥⲑⲁⲙⲓⲟ
ⲛ̀ϫⲉ ⲙⲱⲧⲥⲏⲥ ⲙ̀ⲡⲓϩⲟϥ ⲛ̀ϩⲟⲙⲧ ⲟⲩⲟϩ ⲁϥⲧⲁϩⲟϥ ϩⲓ ⲟⲩⲙⲏⲓⲛⲓ
ⲟⲩⲟϩ ⲁⲥϣⲱⲡⲓ ϩⲟⲧⲁⲛ ⲁⲣⲉϣⲁⲛ ⲟⲩϩⲟϥ ϭⲓ ⲗⲁⲡⲥⲓ ⲛ̀ⲥⲁ
ⲟⲩⲣⲱⲙⲓ ⲟⲩⲟϩ ⲛ̀ⲧⲉϥϫⲟⲩϣⲧ ⲉ̀ⲡⲓϩⲟϥ ⲛ̀ϩⲟⲙⲧ ϣⲁϥⲱⲛϧ

Vocab

ⲭⲁⲛⲁⲛⲉⲟⲥ	Canaanite (prop noun)	ⲁⲣⲁⲇ	Arad prop noun)
ⲁⲑⲁⲣⲓⲛ	Atharin (prop noun)	ⲉⲭⲙⲁⲗⲱⲥⲓⲁ	captivity (f)
ϩⲣⲟϣ, ϩⲟⲣϣ (q)	to be cold, heavy (v.i)	ϩⲟⲙⲧ	bronze (m)
ⲃⲱⲧⲥ ⲃⲟⲧⲥ⸗	to fight, battle (v.t)	ⲉ̀ⲧⲟⲧϥ	to the hand of **(Appendix 3)**
ⲗⲁⲡⲥⲓ	bite, sting, morsel (m)	ⲱⲣ	Hor (prop noun)
ⲁⲛⲁⲑⲉⲙⲁ	devotion, curse (m)	ⲟⲩⲱⲧⲉⲃ	to depart, change (v.i)
ϯⲣⲉⲛ	to name, call (v.i)	ϣⲁⲣⲓ	red (adj)
ⲉⲣⲁⲛⲁⲑⲉⲙⲁⲧⲓⲍⲓⲛ	to devote, curse (v.t)		

Where do we go from here?

Congratulations! If you're reading this, it means one of two things. Either you've laboured through the lessons, ploughed through the exercises, sweated over the practice texts, referred constantly to the glossary, and finally made your way to the end of the book, or you've skipped to the end to see what's at the back.

If it's the first case, then you may be wondering where you can go from here. This may be time to reveal a secret which I've kept hidden up till now, and that's that you never really stop learning Coptic, as no matter how much you learn, there'll always be things you don't know. But don't be discouraged, because that's part of the fun! The best way to consolidate is to practice, practice, and practice again. Following the Coptic text in Midnight praises is an excellent way of become more fluent in your reading of Coptic text, as well as giving you a way of learning new words. To further consolidate your grammar and vocabulary, you should then start to read some literary Coptic texts.

Technological advances have made access to these much easier than even 10 years ago. The Remenkimi web site at www.coptic.org/language is maintained by a dedicated group of Coptic lovers who have provided a treasure trove of Coptic texts. There you can find most of the available texts of the Bible, as well as other literary works. The Bible is a good place to start, as you can easily compare your translation with a modern English translation. Just remember though that you'll need to download the right fonts first.

Actually, the Coptic fonts themselves have undergone a bit of a revolution. In the olden days (i.e. 2 years ago), most of the different fonts had different keyboard layout maps, which meant that you couldn't change the font of a Coptic text without changing the letters around and ending up with garble. The work of several dedicated Coptic computer lovers has resulted in the Coptic Standard fonts, which is a new standard for pre existing fonts to all now using the same keyboard layout map. A link to these can be found in the Remenkimi site. Some older texts have not yet been converted to the CS standard, so it's still useful to have some of the older fonts. At the time of writing, the site http://coptic-software.8m.net/ featured a program which would automatically install the fonts for you.

You'll also need a proper dictionary when approaching most of these texts I recommend the dictionary produced by the St.Shenouda society (www.stsheounda.com) which is available on their CD-ROM and also on the "Christian Orthodox e-Reference library" CD (coepa@netspace.net.au). Another very good dictionary is "The abbreviated Coptic Dictionary" by Adeeb Makar, which at time of writing was available from www.orthodox-bookstore.org. A particular advantage of the St.Shenouda society CD-ROM is that it also includes the Coptic New Testament.

The Remenkimi site also maintains a newsgroup where members write messages to each other in Coptic, as well as a Paltalk chat room, where members can speak to each other in Coptic over the internet.

So You want to Learn Coptic?

If you're really serious about learning Coptic, you may be interested to learn that there is Masters in Arts in Coptic studies degree which is at Maquarie University, Sydney. This degree offers courses in many aspects of Coptic culture, including a course in Sahidic as well as the other major dialects. For further information, go to www.coptic.org.au/modules/coptic_studies/.

As you can see, there are many opportunities opening up for the revival of Coptic, but it will require the hard work and dedication of people like yourself to keep the flame burning. A whole new world of possibilities awaits, and who knows? Maybe we'll look back ten years from now and marvel as to how many people didn't know Coptic.

16. APPENDICIES
Appendix 1 : Verb tables

Present	First (5.1)	Habitual (10.1)	Negative habitual (10.1.i)
1ˢᵗ P (s)	ϯ-	ϣⲁⲓ-	ⲙⲡⲁⲓ-
2ⁿᵈ P (m)	ⲕ (ⲭ)-	ϣⲁⲕ-	ⲙⲡⲁⲕ-
2ⁿᵈ P (f)	ⲧⲉ-	ϣⲁⲣⲉ-	ⲙⲡⲁⲣⲉ-
3ʳᵈ P (m)	ϥ-	ϣⲁϥ-	ⲙⲡⲁϥ-
3ʳᵈ P (f)	ⲥ-	ϣⲁⲥ-	ⲙⲡⲁⲥ-
1ˢᵗ P (pl)	ⲧⲉⲛ-	ϣⲁⲛ-	ⲙⲡⲁⲛ-
2ⁿᵈ P (pl)	ⲧⲉⲧⲉⲛ-	ϣⲁⲣⲉⲧⲉⲛ-	ⲙⲡⲁⲣⲉⲧⲉⲛ-
3ʳᵈ P (pl)	ⲥⲉ-	ϣⲁⲩ-	ⲙⲡⲁⲩ-
Pre subject form	-	ϣⲁⲣⲉ	ⲙⲡⲁⲣⲉ
Negative	(ⲛ)...ⲁⲛ		-

Future	First (5.9)	Emphatic (10.2)	Negative emph. (10.2.i)
1ˢᵗ P (s)	ϯⲛⲁ-	ⲉⲓⲉ-	ⲛⲛⲁ-
2ⁿᵈ P (m)	ⲭⲛⲁ-	ⲉⲕⲉ-	ⲛⲛⲉⲕ-
2ⁿᵈ P (f)	ⲧⲉⲛⲁ(ⲣⲁ)-	ⲉⲣⲉ-	ⲛⲛⲉ-
3ʳᵈ P (m)	ϥⲛⲁ-	ⲉϥⲉ-	ⲛⲛⲉϥ-
3ʳᵈ P (f)	ⲥⲛⲁ-	ⲉⲥⲉ-	ⲛⲛⲉⲥ-
1ˢᵗ P (pl)	ⲧⲉⲛⲛⲁ-	ⲉⲛⲉ-	ⲛⲛⲉⲛ-
2ⁿᵈ P (pl)	ⲧⲉⲧⲉⲛⲛⲁ-	ⲉⲣⲉⲧⲉⲛⲉ-	ⲛⲛⲉⲧⲉⲛ-
3ʳᵈ P (pl)	ⲥⲉⲛⲁ-	ⲉⲩⲉ-	ⲛⲛⲟⲩ-
Pre subject form	-	ⲉⲣⲉ	ⲛⲛⲉ
Negative	(ⲛ)...ⲁⲛ		

Future	Imperfect (10.3)	conditional (10.5)	neg. conditional (10.5.i)	Optative (10.4.iv)
1st P (s)	ⲛⲁⲓⲛⲁ−...(ⲡⲉ)	ⲁⲓϣⲁⲛ−	ⲁⲓ̇ϣⲧⲉⲙ−	ⲙⲁⲣⲓ−
2nd P (m)	ⲛⲁⲕⲛⲁ−...(ⲡⲉ)	ⲁⲕϣⲁⲛ−	ⲁⲕϣ̇ⲧⲉⲙ−	−
2nd P (f)	ⲛⲁⲣⲉⲛⲁ...(ⲡⲉ)	ⲁⲣⲉϣⲁⲛ−	ⲁⲣⲉϣ̇ⲧⲉⲙ−	−
3rd P (m)	ⲛⲁϥⲛⲁ−...(ⲡⲉ)	ⲁϥϣⲁⲛ−	ⲁϥϣ̇ⲧⲉⲙ−	ⲙⲁⲣⲉϥ−
3rd P (f)	ⲛⲁⲥⲛⲁ−...(ⲡⲉ)	ⲁⲥϣⲁⲛ−	ⲁⲥϣ̇ⲧⲉⲙ−	ⲙⲁⲣⲉⲥ−
1st P (pl)	ⲛⲁⲛⲛⲁ−...(ⲡⲉ)	ⲁⲛϣⲁⲛ−	ⲁⲛϣ̇ⲧⲉⲙ−	ⲙⲁⲣⲉⲛ−
2nd P (pl)	ⲛⲁⲣⲉⲧⲉⲛⲛⲁ−...(ⲡⲉ)	ⲁⲣⲉⲧⲉⲛϣⲁⲛ−	ⲁⲣⲉⲧⲉⲛϣ̇ⲧⲉⲙ−	−
3rd P (pl)	ⲛⲁⲩⲛⲁ−...(ⲡⲉ)	ⲁⲩϣⲁⲛ−	ⲁⲩϣ̇ⲧⲉⲙ−	ⲙⲁⲣⲟⲩ−
Pre subject form	ⲛⲁⲣⲉ... ...(ⲡⲉ)	ⲁⲣⲉϣⲁⲛ−	ⲁⲣⲉϣ̇ⲧⲉⲙ−	ⲙⲁⲣⲉ−

Past	First (5.2)	Imperfect (7.1)	Imperfect negative	Plu perfect (7.1.i)
1st P (s)	ⲁⲓ−	ⲛⲁⲓ−...(ⲡⲉ)	ⲛⲁⲓ...ⲁⲛ	ⲛⲉ...ⲁⲓ
2nd P (m)	ⲁⲕ−	ⲛⲁⲕ−...(ⲡⲉ)	ⲛⲁⲕ...ⲁⲛ	ⲛⲉ...ⲁⲕ
2nd P (f)	ⲁⲣⲉ−	ⲛⲁⲣⲉ−...(ⲡⲉ)	ⲛⲁⲣⲉ...ⲁⲛ	ⲛⲉ...ⲁⲣⲉ
3rd P (m)	ⲁϥ−	ⲛⲁϥ−...(ⲡⲉ)	ⲛⲁϥ...ⲁⲛ	ⲛⲉ...ⲁϥ
3rd P (f)	ⲁⲥ−	ⲛⲁⲥ−...(ⲡⲉ)	ⲛⲁⲥ...ⲁⲛ	ⲛⲉ...ⲁⲥ
1st P (pl)	ⲁⲛ−	ⲛⲁⲛ−...(ⲡⲉ)	ⲛⲁⲛ...ⲁⲛ	ⲛⲉ...ⲁⲛ
2nd P (pl)	ⲁⲣⲉⲧⲉⲛ−	ⲛⲁⲣⲉⲧⲉⲛ−..(ⲡⲉ)	ⲛⲁⲣⲉⲧⲉⲛ..ⲁⲛ	ⲛⲉ..ⲁⲣⲉⲧⲉⲛ
3rd P (pl)	ⲁⲩ−	ⲛⲁⲩ−...(ⲡⲉ)	ⲛⲁⲩ...ⲁⲛ	ⲛⲉ...ⲁⲩ
Pre subject form	ⲁ	ⲛⲁⲣⲉ−...(ⲡⲉ)	ⲛⲉ...ⲁⲩ	
Negative	ⲙ̇ⲡⲉ	−	−	ⲛⲉ...ⲙ̇ⲡⲉ

Appendix 1 - verb tables

Relative	First Present (5.1.v)	Future (5.9.ii)	Past Perfect (5.4)
1st P (s)	ⲉϯ–	ⲉϯⲛⲁ	ⲉⲧⲁⲓ–
2nd P (m)	ⲉⲧⲉⲕ–	ⲉⲧⲉⲕⲛⲁ–	ⲉⲧⲁⲕ–
2nd P (f)	ⲉⲧⲉ–	ⲉⲧⲉⲣⲁ–	ⲉⲧⲁⲣⲉ–
3rd P (m)	ⲉⲧⲉϥ–	ⲉⲧⲉϥⲛⲁ–	ⲉⲧⲁϥ–
3rd P (f)	ⲉⲧⲉⲥ–	ⲉⲧⲉⲥⲛⲁ–	ⲉⲧⲁⲥ–
1st P (pl)	ⲉⲧⲉⲛ–	ⲉⲧⲉⲛⲛⲁ–	ⲉⲧⲁⲛ–
2nd P (pl)	ⲉⲧⲉⲧⲉⲛ–	ⲉⲧⲉⲧⲉⲛⲛⲁ–	ⲉⲧⲁⲣⲉⲧⲉⲛ–
3rd P (pl)	ⲉⲧⲟⲩ–	ⲉⲧⲟⲩⲛⲁ–	ⲉⲧⲁⲩ–
Pre subject form	ⲉⲧⲉ/ⲉⲣⲉ	ⲉⲧⲉ/ⲉⲣⲉ…ⲛⲁ	ⲉⲧⲁ
Negative	(ⲛ̄)…ⲁⲛ	(ⲛ̄)…ⲁⲛ	ⲉⲧⲉ..ⲙ̄ⲡⲉ (5.4.i)

Subjunctive	Affirmative (6.2)	Negative (6.2.ii)	limitative (6.2.i)
1st P (s)	ⲛ̄ⲧⲁ–	ⲛ̄ⲧⲁϣⲧⲉⲙ–	ϣⲁⲛⲧⲁ(ⲓ)/ϣⲁϯ–
2nd P (m)	ⲛ̄ⲧⲉⲕ–	ⲛ̄ⲧⲉⲕϣⲧⲉⲙ–	ϣⲁ(ⲛ)ⲧⲉⲕ–
2nd P (f)	ⲛ̄ⲧⲉ–	ⲛ̄ⲧⲉϣⲧⲉⲙ–	ϣⲁ(ⲛ)ⲧⲉ–
3rd P (m)	ⲛ̄ⲧⲉϥ–	ⲛ̄ⲧⲉϥϣⲧⲉⲙ–	ϣⲁ(ⲛ)ⲧⲉϥ–
3rd P (f)	ⲛ̄ⲧⲉⲥ–	ⲛ̄ⲧⲉⲥϣⲧⲉⲙ–	ϣⲁ(ⲛ)ⲧⲉⲥ–
1st P (pl)	ⲛ̄ⲧⲉⲛ–	ⲛ̄ⲧⲉⲛϣⲧⲉⲙ–	ϣⲁ(ⲛ)ⲧⲉⲛ–
2nd P (pl)	ⲛ̄ⲧⲉⲧⲉⲛ–	ⲛ̄ⲧⲉⲧⲉⲛϣⲧⲉⲙ–	ϣⲁ(ⲛ)ⲧⲉⲧⲉⲛ–
3rd P (pl)	ⲛ̄ⲧⲟⲩ–/ⲛ̄ⲥⲉ–	ⲛ̄ⲧⲟⲩϣⲧⲉⲙ–	ϣⲁ(ⲛ)ⲧⲟⲩ–
Pre subject form	ⲛ̄ⲧⲉ	ⲛ̄ⲧⲉ ϣⲧⲉⲙ	ϣⲁ(ⲛ)ⲧⲉ

So You want to Learn Coptic?

Second tense	Present (12.1)	Future (12.2)	Past (12.3)
1ˢᵗ P (s)	ⲁⲓ–	ⲁⲓⲛⲁ–	ⲉⲧⲁⲓ–
2ⁿᵈ P (m)	ⲁⲕ–	ⲁⲕⲛⲁ–	ⲉⲧⲁⲕ–
2ⁿᵈ P (f)	ⲁⲣⲉ–	ⲁⲣⲉⲛⲁ–	ⲉⲧⲁⲣⲉ–
3ʳᵈ P (m)	ⲁϥ–	ⲁϥⲛⲁ–	ⲉⲧⲁϥ–
3ʳᵈ P (f)	ⲁⲥ–	ⲁⲥⲛⲁ–	ⲉⲧⲁⲥ–
1ˢᵗ P (pl)	ⲁⲛ–	ⲁⲛⲛⲁ–	ⲉⲧⲁⲛ–
2ⁿᵈ P (pl)	ⲁⲣⲉⲧⲉⲛ–	ⲁⲣⲉⲧⲉⲛⲛⲁ–	ⲉⲧⲁⲣⲉⲧⲉⲛ–
3ʳᵈ P (pl)	ⲁⲩ–	ⲁⲩⲛⲁ–	ⲉⲧⲁⲩ–
Pre subject form	ⲁⲣⲉ	ⲁⲣⲉ ⲛⲁ–	ⲉⲧⲁ

Appendix 2 : Useful prefixes

Prefixes are little groups of letters that are attached to certain pre existing words to add a new meaning. We've actually come across some of these prefixes as parts of words we've already met. The more common prefixes are shown below:

ⲁⲛ–	collection of	ⲙⲉⲧ–/ ⲙⲉⲑ–	forms an abstract noun
ⲁⲧ/ⲁⲑ–	without	ⲣⲉϥ–	comes before the verb to indicate the one who is performing the action
ⲉ–	profession	ⲥⲁⲛ–	profession
ⲗⲁ–	abundance	ϣⲟⲩ–	"worthy of"
ⲣⲉⲙ–	belonging to	ϫⲓⲛ–	forms a noun of a verb

Let's start with the prefix ⲁⲛ. Firstly, it is important to note that the ⲁⲛ used as a prefix has nothing to do with the ⲁⲛ we met way back in **(5.1.i)** which indicates the negative.

Now consider the word ϣⲁϣϥ. It means '7.'

Add ⲁⲛ to ϣⲁϣϥ and you get ⲁⲛϣⲁϣϥ , which means 'group of 7.'
Now what could 'group of 7' possibly mean?
Why it means 'a week' of course! Here are some more examples

ϣⲁⲛϣ	nourishment, rearing (m)	ⲁⲛϣⲁⲛϣ	livestock (m)
ⲥⲁϫⲓ	word (m)	ⲁⲛⲥⲁϫⲓ	dictionary

ⲁⲧ (ⲁⲑ)

ⲁⲧ (ⲁⲑ) means 'without', it attaches to the pre existing word to essentially cancel out its meaning. Some examples:

ⲥⲙⲏ	voice	ⲁⲧⲥⲙⲏ	without voice, mute (adj)
ⲉⲙⲓ	knowledge	ⲁⲧⲉⲙⲓ	ignorant (adj)
ⲑⲱⲗⲉⲃ	defilement	ⲁⲧⲑⲱⲗⲉⲃ	without defilement (adj)

ⲣⲉⲙⲛ

ⲣⲉⲙⲛ/ⲣⲉⲙ changes the meaning of the word it precedes so that it describes a person who has a characteristic of that word. It is often used before the names of countries to indicate a person who belongs to that particular country.

ⲕⲁϯ	knowledge	ⲣⲉⲙⲛⲕⲁϯ	intelligent, wise (adj)
ϩⲑⲟ	horse	ⲣⲉⲙⲛϩⲑⲟ	horseman, rider (m)
ⲣⲏⲥ	south	ⲣⲉⲙⲣⲏⲥ	southerner (m)
ⲭⲏⲙⲓ	Egypt	ⲣⲉⲙⲛⲭⲏⲙⲓ	Egyptian, coptic (m)

E.g. ⲉⲩⲉⲙⲟⲩϯ ⲉⲣⲟϥ ϫⲉ ⲡⲓⲣⲉⲙⲛⲁⲍⲁⲣⲉⲑ *(Matthew 2:23)*
"He shall be called the Nazarene."

ⲗⲁ

This prefix is attached before a noun or adjective to indicate an 'abundance of' the relevant word or noun.
E.g.

ϥⲱⲓ	hair	ⲗⲁϥⲱⲓ	hairy
ⲥⲁϫⲓ	word	ⲗⲁⲥⲁϫⲓ	chatty, talkative

ⲙⲉⲧ

This prefix comes before a noun to turn it into an *abstract* noun. What exactly are abstract nouns?

When we usually talk about nouns, we mean things that we can touch and see. E.g. you can see a car or pat a dog. But how about a noun like 'happiness.' Happiness is indeed a noun, because it is the name of a thing, but it isn't something you can see. Nouns like these are called 'abstract nouns.'

Here are some examples:

ⲁⲗⲟⲩ	child	ⲙⲉⲧⲁⲗⲟⲩ	childhood (f)
ⲛⲓϣϯ	great	ⲙⲉⲧⲛⲓϣϯ	greatness (f)
ⲟⲩⲏⲃ	priest	ⲙⲉⲧⲟⲩⲏⲃ	priesthood (f)
ⲟⲩⲣⲟ	king	ⲙⲉⲧⲟⲩⲣⲟ	kingdom (f)

ⲣⲉϥ

As with ⲡⲉⲙ, ⲣⲉϥ is used to describe a person. The difference however is that ⲣⲉϥ always comes before a verb and creates a noun of the person doing the action.

ⲥⲱⲛⲧ	to create	ⲣⲉϥⲥⲱⲛⲧ	creator
ϣⲱⲛⲓ	to be sick	ⲣⲉϥϣⲱⲛⲓ	sick person
ⲉⲣⲛⲟⲃⲓ	to sin	ⲣⲉϥⲉⲣⲛⲟⲃⲓ	sinner

ⲥⲁ ⲛ̅

The names of some professions are made by attaching this prefix to a noun related to the profession.

| ⲁϥ | meat | ⲥⲁ ⲛ̅ⲁϥ | butcher |
| ⲱⲓⲕ | bread | ⲥⲁ ⲛ̅ⲱⲓⲕ | baker |

So You want to Learn Coptic?

Appendix 3 : Where do compound prepositions come from?

Earlier in the book in **(5.1.iii)**, we gave some examples of what were called "compound prepositions." What wasn't explained was how they were derived. They're basically formed by combining the simple prepositions with the 'body parts' which we met with the possessed nouns **(15.5)**, with the combinations providing the compound prepositions. The results are words which are meant to give a meaning relating to the combination of the simple preposition and the body part, though to be honest it's often hard to understand the connection. The more common derivations are shown below.

Compounds with ⲉ̀

ⲉ̀ + ⲭⲱ forms ⲉ̀ⲭⲉⲛ

literally *"to the head of"* or *"upon"*

Compound prepositions naturally also have a pronoun form. The pronoun form for **ⲉⲭⲉⲛ** is **ⲉⲭⲱ⸗**.

These use the same pronoun endings that were used for the verbs **(5.3.i)**.

Thus **ⲉⲭⲱⲓ** is *"upon me."*

E.g. **ⲥⲉϩⲱⲟⲩⲓ ⲉ̀ⲭⲱⲟⲩ ⲛ̀ⲛⲟⲩϭⲁⲗⲁⲩϫ** *(Matthew 7:6)*
"they will crush upon them (to their heads) with their feet"

ⲟⲩⲟϩ ϯⲛⲁⲭⲱ ⲛ̀ⲧⲁⲯⲩⲭⲏ ⲉ̀ⲭⲉⲛ ⲛⲁⲉⲥⲱⲟⲩ *(John 10:15)*
"and I will place my soul upon my sheep"

ⲉ̀ + ⲣⲟ = ⲉ̀ⲣⲉⲛ

"to the mouth of"- "to the opening of", 'facing', "in front of"

pronoun form **ⲉ̀ⲣⲱ⸗**

ⲉ̀ + ⲣⲁⲧ = ⲉ̀ⲣⲁⲧ⸗

"to the foot of", "to"

ⲉ̀ + ϩⲟ = ⲉ̀ϩⲣⲉⲛ, ⲉ̀ϩⲣⲁ⸗

"toward face of", "to", "among"

So You want to Learn Coptic?

Compounds with ⲛ̀-

ⲛ̀ + ⲥⲁ = ⲛ̀ⲥⲁ "to the back of" or 'behind', 'after'

pronoun form ⲛ̀ⲥⲱ⸗

E.g. ⲧⲉⲛⲥⲱⲧⲉⲙ ⲛ̀ⲥⲁ ⲛⲉⲕⲉⲛⲧⲟⲗⲏ
"we obey (after) your commandments"

ⲛ̀ + ⲧⲟⲧ⸗ = "through the hands of" or "by means of, through"

E.g. ϯϣⲉⲡ ϩ̀ⲙⲟⲧ ⲛ̀ⲧⲟⲧϥ ⲙ̀Ⲫⲛⲟⲩϯ
"I accept grace through the hands of God" or "I thank God"
This compound preposition is special because unlike the others it has a pronominal form: ⲉ̀ⲧⲉⲛ–

E.g. ⲁϥϩⲟⲛϩⲉⲛ ⲉ̀ⲧⲉⲛ ⲛⲉϥⲙⲁⲑⲏⲧⲏⲥ *(Matthew 16:20)*
"he commanded (to the hands of) his disciples"

ⲛ̀ + ϩⲣ⸗ = ⲛⲁϩⲣⲉⲛ (literally 'to the face of') or 'before.'

Pronoun form is ⲉ̀ϩⲣ⸗

Compounds with ϩⲓ

ϩⲓ + ϫⲱ = ϩⲓϫⲉⲛ, ϩⲓϫⲱ⸗
"upon"

ϩⲓ + ⲣⲟ = ϩⲓⲣⲉⲛ, ϩⲓⲣⲱ⸗
"at the mouth of" or "at the entrance"

ϩⲓ + ⲧⲟⲧ⸗ = ϩⲓⲧⲉⲛ, ϩⲓⲧⲟⲧ⸗
"lit. through, by from"

E.g. ϩⲓⲧⲉⲛ ⲛⲓⲡⲣⲉⲥⲃⲓⲁ ⲛ̀ⲧⲉ ϯⲑⲉⲟⲧⲟⲕⲟⲥ *(Hymn from Liturgy of the word))*
"through the prayers of the mother of God."

Compounds with ϧⲁ

ϧⲁ + ⲧⲉⲛ = ϧⲁⲧⲉⲛ
"under the hand of" or *"beside"*, *"under"*, *"at"*

E.g. ⲟⲩⲟϩ ⲁϥϣⲱⲡⲓ ϧⲁⲧⲉⲛ ⲡⲓϣϣⲏⲛ ⲛ̀ⲧⲉ Ⲙⲁⲙⲃⲣⲉ *(Genesis 13:18)*
"and he dwelt before the tree of Mambre"

ⲁϥⲓ̀ ⲉ̀ⲃⲏⲑⲫⲁⲅⲏ ϧⲁⲧⲉⲛ ⲡⲓⲧⲱⲟⲩ ⲛ̀ⲧⲉ ⲛⲓϫⲱⲓⲧ *(Matthew 21:1)*
"and he came to Bethpage before the mountain of the olives"

ϧⲁ + ⲣⲁⲧ = ϧⲁⲣⲁⲧ
"under the foot of" or *"under"*

Pronoun form ϧⲁⲣⲁⲧ⸗

E.g. ⲁⲓⲛⲁⲩ ⲉ̀ⲣⲟⲕ ϧⲁⲣⲁⲧⲥ ⲛ̀ϯⲃⲱ ⲛ̀ⲕⲉⲛⲧⲉ *(John 1:51)*
"I saw you under the tree of dates"

So You want to Learn Coptic?

Appendix 4 -:variations in the pronominal suffix[16]

Life would be so much simpler if things were consistent. Take the personal suffixes we first met in **(5.3.i)**, which are those little letters that come at the end of the verb. We looked at two verbs as examples and saw how the suffixes differed between them. Unfortunately, they're not the only variations, and in fact there is a rather complex set of rules which determines when to use a particular ending. The good news is that you will quickly recognise the different letters that are used for a particular person and number when you're translating from Coptic to English, the bad news is that you will have to refer to these rules if you want to work out what the ending should be when translating into Coptic from English. It is these endings which will be the subject of this appendix:

First person singular

- For the first person singular, pronominal forms which end with **o** or **ⲱ** take **ⲓ**, those which end with **ⲁ**, **ⲓ** or a consonant take **ⲧ**.

- When the construct form already ends with **ⲧ**, it can either be left like that or it can take another **ⲧ** as well. For example, the pronominal form of the verb **ϥⲁⲓ** (to carry) is **ϥⲓⲧ⸗**. The first person singular form can therefore be either **ϥⲓⲧ** or **ϥⲓⲧⲧ**.

First person plural

- The first person plural takes **−ⲛ** after a vowel. After a consonant, it either takes **−ⲧⲉⲛ** or **−ⲉⲛ**. Stems ending in **ⲓ** which take **ⲧ** in the first person singular keep the **ⲧ** and add an **ⲉⲛ** to it for the first person plural.

Second person feminine singular

- if the stem ends in **o** or **ⲱ**, there is no extra ending for the second person feminine singular

---

[16] *Ref Mallon pg.140*

- stems which end in ⲁ⸍ or ⲓ⸍ take a ϯ for the second person singular feminine E.g. the pronoun form for the verb ⲭⲱ (to place) is ⲭⲁ⸍ The second person feminine singular is therefore ⲭⲁϯ
- if the stem ends in a consonant, it takes ⲓ instead of ϯ
- Verbs whose pronominal form ends in ⲃ ⲙ or ⲛ take an extra ⲉ̀ between the stem and suffix, for all forms apart from the 2nd person feminine singular and the 2nd and 3rd person plural. For example, let's take a look at the verb ⲛⲁϩⲙⲉⲛ (to save), whose pronoun form is ⲛⲁϩⲙ⸍

1ˢᵗ person singular	ⲛⲁϩⲙ−ⲉⲧ
2ⁿᵈ person singular masculine	ⲛⲁϩⲙ−ⲉⲕ
2ⁿᵈ person singular feminine	ⲛⲁϩⲙ−ⲓ
3ʳᵈ person singular masculine	ⲛⲁϩⲙ−ⲉϥ
3ʳᵈ person singular feminine	ⲛⲁϩⲙ−ⲉⲥ
1ˢᵗ person plural	ⲛⲁϩⲙ−ⲉⲛ
2ⁿᵈ person plural	ⲛⲁϩⲉⲙ−ⲑⲏⲛⲟⲩ
3ʳᵈ person plural	ⲛⲁϩⲙ−ⲟⲩ

Second person plural
- The first thing to point out with this form is that there is always the option of making the second person plural form of the verb by adding the construct form to -ⲑⲏⲛⲟⲩ. This is the only option for verbs ending in a consonant. However, for verbs ending in a vowel, though you can still just add the construct form to ⲑⲏⲛⲟⲩ, you can alternatively add ⸍ⲱⲧⲉⲛ to the pronominal form of the verb.

Third person plural

- The third person plural always ends in 𝐨𝐮, which is contracted to 𝐮 after verbs ending in 𝐚. E.g. ⲭⲁ⳱ becomes ⲭⲁⲩ.

For stems ending in 𝐨, sometimes a 𝐓 is placed between the stem and the 𝐨𝐮.

E.g. ⲭⲟⲧⲟⲩ

Verbs ending in 𝐢 which take the 𝐓 in the first person singular keep it for the third person plural before adding the 𝐨𝐮.

E.g. ⲁⲓⲧⲟⲩ

So You want to Learn Coptic?

Appendix 5- Answers

Exercise 1.1
nan
nai
meet
pai
mav
tai
moshi
zau-on
taun

Exercise 1.2
zeelos
xiros
xilon
hoti
epsalin
khen
kha
tishouri

Exercise 1.3
haub
val
novi
ennoub
vauhem
laubsh
e-vol
niven

Exercise 1.4
thinamis
thelta
thiakonos
thithou
theemos

Exercise 1.5
eshtou-it
theos
estoi
enthok
beethle-em
thamio

Exercise 1.6
ghamos
ghongilee
genos
agiazin

Exercise 1.7
gapoji
jeek
pegaf
peje
kouji
peg-au-ou

Exercise 1.8
mikha-eel
ekraum
kharizma
eklom
keemi
ekhristianos
kharizeste

Exercise 2.1
a) the father
b) a mother
c) the son
d) the daughter
e) fathers
f) brothers

Exercise 2.2
a) my body
b) his blood
c) our father
d) our saviour
e) your (pl) head
f) your (pl) faith
g) your faith (f.)
h) your hand (f.)
i) ⲡⲉϣⲏⲣⲓ
j) ⲡⲉⲥⲓⲱⲧ
k) ⲧⲉⲧⲉⲛⲙⲁⲩ

Exercise 2.3
a) a new man
b) the old man
c) the great city
d) one God
e) the throne of God
f) many wise men and many wise women

Exercise 2.4
a) Christ also
b) the Jews only
c) you also
d) every nation
e) all Judea
f) every person
g) you also
h) all our resurrection
i) John only
j) the whole church

Exercise 3.1
a) this is my body
b) we are Christians
c) the seed is the word of God
d) I am the Christ
e) You are the Christ
f) we are Jews
g) our bodies are altars to the God of Israel
h) the judgements of the Lord are righteous judgements
i) my tongue is a pen of a scribe
j) you are my God
k) you are a beautiful woman

So You want to Learn Coptic?

l) we are children of the promise
m) you are the light of the world
n) you are the salt of the earth
o) this is the king of the Jews

Exercise 4.1
a) 165 years
b) 730 years
c) 12 brothers
d) the 24 priests
e) 12 cubits
f) 400 years
g) 43730

Exercise 5.1
a) you are crying
b) you are exalted
c) the Lord is near
d) the fear of the Lord is pure
e) the Pharisees and we fast
f) you are blessed among women and blessed is the fruit of your womb
g) (the) days are coming
h) they understand in their heart
i) the summer is near

Exercise 5.2
a) upon a rock
b) in the name of the father
c) above the whole earth
d) you rejoice over children
e) the eyes of the Lord are on the righteous
f) through the prayers of Mark the Apostle
g) five thousand people without child and woman
h) he sat on the platform
i) the Lord sits above the Cherubim
j) lift up your gates
k) the voice of the Lord is above the waters, the voice of the Lord is in power (powerful), the voice of the Lord is in great beauty
l) for the sake of Your name O Lord
m) the blood coming down upon the earth
n) without planting or watering

Exercise 5.3
a) I ask you (pl)
b) the Jews ask for signs and the Greeks seek wisdom
c) the world hates you (pl)
d) they hear the word of God
e) He teaches the way of God
f) the people glorify them
g) the heavens speak of the Glory of God
h) He does not understand it
i) he is calling you
j) they worship one God

Exercise 5.4:
a) The elders who are inside the house
b) everyone who hears these my words
c) the lord who receives the gentle
d) every tree whose fruit is inside it
e) one whose name is Titus
f) a woman whose blood gushes
g) the chief of the Island whose name is Puplius
h) whose houses are beautiful

Exercise 5.5
a) these wonders which you do
b) all the pillars which they serve
c) which are the words which we speak in teachings
d) this which you see and know
e) this is Jesus Christ, He whom I preach to you

Exercise 5.6
a) the words of the Lord are holy words
b) evil spirits
c) with defiled hands they eat the bread

Appendix 5-Answers

d) Paul the servant of Our Lord Jesus Christ the called Apostle
e) an acceptable time
f) ⲟⲩⲟⲩⲥⲓⲁ ⲉⲥϣⲏⲡ
g) ⲡⲓϣⲙⲏⲛ ⲉⲑⲣⲏⲧ
h) ⲡⲓⲙⲏϣ ⲉⲧⲟϣ

Exercise 5.7

a) the voice of one who cries in the wilderness
b) the things that you see
c) these are those who listen
d) I who am bound in the Lord
e) she who is called the Magdalene
f) this is the generation of those who seek the Lord, who seek the face of the God of Jacob

Exercise 5.8

a) Jesus sent two disciples
b) we also believed in Jesus Christ
c) darkness happened upon the whole earth
d) he robbed his house
e) he beckoned to them
f) they beckoned to their friends
g) Jerusalem killed the prophets
h) the Father looked from Heaven upon those who dwell on earth
i) He brought water from a rock, He gave His people to drink
j) the Lord visited Sarah
k) Sarah gave birth to a son
l) the righteous cried out and the Lord heard them and saved them from all their troubles

Exercise 5.9

a) we wept and you did not weep
b) the fire of His Divinity did not burn the womb of the virgin
c) those who did not know God
d) we sang to you and you did not dance we cried and you did not lament
e) they did not enter the Praetorium

Exercise 5.10

a) the devil took Him on a mountain
b) he took them upon a mountain
c) he touched her hand and the fever left her
d) he made it with glory according to the word of the Lord
e) the sea covered them
f) he created us and placed us in the paradise of joy
g) Jesus Christ, the son of God, the virgin gave birth to Him

Exercise 5.11

a) they gave fruit
b) you loved truth and hated iniquity
c) his disciples told John
d) he bowed the heaven of heavens
e) the Spirit took him to the desert
f) they also hung two thieves with him
g) he brought out two coins
h) I hated that generation
i) they took Jesus inside
j) we cast out demons

Exercise 5.12

a) the high priest is a witness
b) the axe is at the root
c) we are all witnesses
d) the beam is in your eye

Exercise 5.13

a) I saw a star which fell
b) every scribe who has learnt the Kingdom of Heaven
c) every thing which God said
d) the men whom Cornelius sent who sought the house of Simon

e) the men which you have exalted in your kingdom did not obey your commandment
f) this is the first miracle which Jesus did in Canna of Galilee
g) the words which You gave to me I gave to them
h) that which you have received of God
i) he who built his house upon the sand

Exercise 5.14
a) when he came to it he did not find anything on it
b) John the Baptist sent us to you
c) He sent me one of the Seraphim
d) It is necessary that every written thing in the law of Moses and the prophets and the psalms regarding Me be fulfilled
e) this is Josiah who the prophets prophesied about (on) the altar
f) have mercy upon us Jesus the son of David
g) a fruit whose seed is inside it
h) that which Moses wrote about in the law and the prophets

Exercise 5.15
a) they stoned them
b) I remembered your name and found comfort, O king of ages, God of gods
c) Peter remembered the word
d) when He took bread He gave thanks
e) they preached the word of God

Exercise 5.16
a) they brought him a blind man
b) we send you the hymn
c) he gave Sara his wife to him
d) He sent us the Paraclete
e) The Lord heard and had mercy on me, he turned my weeping into joy for me
f) I called you and you did not answer me

Exercise 5.17
a) Abraham hurried he went inside the tent
b) Noah went with his wife and his children and the wives of the children with him into the Ark
c) an angel of the Lord appeared to Joseph in a dream
d) then the chiefs hurried

Exercise 5.18
a) this is my God I will glorify Him the God of my father I will exalt Him
b) the Lord will save the soul of his servants
c) the Lord will scatter the councils of the nations
d) they will throw him to the fire
e) he will receive his reward
f) he will walk in the evening
g) Heaven and earth will pass
h) in a flame of fire he will give vengeance to those who did not know God

Exercise 5.19
a) he will not sit
b) it will not be undone
c) he himself will not know
d) they will not know him
e) My eyes will not have compassion nor will I have mercy on them

Exercise 5.20
a) In the measure which you will measure
b) the Lord is the one who will accept me to Him
c) every empty word which the men will say
d) that which you have commanded us (to do) will we do (it)

Appendix 5-Answers

e)   it is I who watches over you in every path which you will fly (travel) upon

Exercise 6.1
a) Peter and John
b) the Lord commanded and they were created
c) neither an arch angel or a patriarch or a prophet
d) then Moses praised
e) since it is a commandment
f) chief or judge
g) if you are the Son of God throw your self down from this (here)
h) so that you are not a slave but a son
i) the fire did not touch them nor did a hair of their head become missing
j) O Lord my heart did not exalt nor did my eyes raise themselves

Exercise 6.2
a) For I know truly that I am a sinner
b) Indeed Elijah came first
c) Indeed I baptised you in (a) water of repentance
d) but they do not fast
e) you did not tell me "she is my wife"
f) the veil is also on their heart
g) and when he came down from the mountain
h) and the apostles heard with the brothers who are in Judea that the nations also accepted the word of God
i) they do not believe (it) that he is a disciple

Exercise 6.3
a) for you build the tombs of the prophets and you adorn the caves of the righteous
b) so that you be children of your father who abides in the Heavens
c) and great multitudes gathered to him so that he mounted the boat
d) the people grew and prevailed and multiplied in Egypt till another king arose over Egypt
e) so that the remainder of the people seek the Lord with all the nations
f) he rained rain upon the face of the earth till it sprouted to give its fruit
g) he breathed against the trees till they budded
h) lest that they see (with) their eyes and hear with their ears and understand in their hearts and they return so that I heal them
i) come forth to me that I touch you for you are my son
j) lest they trample (upon) them
k) I will hope under the shadow of your wings till the iniquity passes

Exercise 6.4
a) lest it not be sufficient for us with you
b) for it is good for you for one of your members to be destroyed and not that your whole body go to Hades
c) so that the darkness does not reach you
d) and if you do not forgive the sins of the men neither will your father forgive you your trespasses
e) my children, these I write to you so that you do not sin

Exercise 7.1
a) He was speaking with them many things in parables
b) his disciples were asking Him of the parable
c) they were mocking him
d) the multitude were amazed
e) and there was a well of water of Jacob there
f) and they knew them that they were with Jesus
g) and they were all surprised

So You want to Learn Coptic?

h) I was in the city Joppa

Exercise 7.2
a) the arch priests and the Pharisees had given commandment
b) and they came out they fled from the tomb for trembling had reached them
c) Claudius had given a command
d) And the Passover had approached, the feast of the Jews

Exercise 7.3
a) the place in which Peter was
b) this who was giving much work

Exercise 7.4
a) the arch priests of the people came to him while (he was) teaching
b) the bush which Moses saw in the desert, (with) the fire burning inside it
c) he saw a man sitting
d) two blind people walked behind him crying out
e) and Jesus was visiting all the cities and the villages teaching in their synagogues and preaching the gospel of the kingdom
f) and eating with them he commanded them
g) my father has already written your name
h) I was in the city Joppa praying and I saw in a trance a vision (of) a vessel coming down
i) but his will is in the law of the Lord

Exercise 7.5
a) and when the sun was about to cease the veil of the temple split in its middle
b) the twelve, Jesus sent them when He commanded them
c) and when they were about to bring him inside to the castle
d) and it happened as Peter was about to pass through the brethren he came upon the saints in Lidda
e) and when he had gained (a) great mercy of God he became Christian
f) and when the guard of the prison awoke and when he saw the doors of the prison open he unsheathed his sword about to kill himself thinking that 'those who are bound have fled'

Exercise 8.1
a) Pilate said to them
b) he told me everything which I did
c) like which I will not but like which you will
d) he pleased God
e) Nathaniel said to him
f) you were preaching saying "indeed I baptise you in water of repentance for the forgiveness of sins"
g) these words he said (them) in the treasury
h) he said this parable to them saying:
i) you created all things and your will was done and they were created
j) and she said "the head of John the Baptist"
k) and the sweetness differs between each one
l) they said that this is Emmanuel
m) I say to you come out from these people
n) the daughter of Herodias danced in the midst and she pleased Herod
o) they did to him everything which they wanted

Exercise 8.2
a) this which it is necessary that the Heavens accept
b) and if there is one among you
c) and they preach to us other customs, these which it is not appropriate for us to accept

Appendix 5-Answers

- d) there are not a multitude of wise according to (the) flesh there is not a multitude of strong
- e) and when Paul knew that there is a part
- f) for it is necessary (appropriate) that he believes
- g) and there was a multitude gathered
- h) those which it is not appropriate to do
- i) if there is a bad thing in this man
- j) there is no woman without man nor man without woman in the Lord

Exercise 8.3

- a) bless the Lord for a psalm is good
- b) truly I say to you, that no one stood amongst those born of women who is greater than John the Baptist
- c) it is not good to take the bread of the children
- d) and the gold of that land is good
- e) blessed are the compassionate
- f) and the woman saw that the tree is good
- g) hail to you O Mary the beautiful dove

Exercise 9.1

- a) again the devil took Him on a mountain
- b) again the kingdom of Heaven is likened to a merchant man
- c) our bread of the morrow give it to us today
- d) seven times daily
- e) the anger of the Lord burned for the sake of the sins which the people did in that time
- f) immediately, the demon convulsed the woman
- g) it happened in the 30th year in the fourth month
- h) this (He) came to Jesus by night

Exercise 9.2

- a) The time (end) of every man came before me for indeed the earth has been filled with iniquity
- b) immediately, he threw him (upward) quickly
- c) I am coming quickly
- d) the brethren accepted us to themselves joyfully
- e) people, our brethren it is appropriate that we speak with you openly regarding our fore father David
- f) for truly they gathered in this city
- g) and he said to them that rightly Isaiah prophesied regarding you

Exercise 9.3

- a) she came out behind Him
- b) he came outside the city
- c) they were thinking in (amongst) themselves
- d) and all these are the beginning of pains
- e) beneath your feet
- f) then when they went inside they went up to a high place (upper room) in which were Peter and John and James and Andrew and Philip and Thomas

Exercise 9.4

- a) they became many martyrs like the stars of Heaven
- b) your glory O Mary is exalted more than Heaven
- c) a day in your courts is more good (better) than thousands
- d) you shine more than the sun you are brighter than the Cherubim
- e) and so that I do not hinder you more
- f) if we receive the witness of (the) men the witness of God is more great
- g) and He said 'truly I say to you that this poor widow cast more than all these'

Exercise 10.1
a) they cast new wine to new wineskins
b) the words of God he hears them
c) while you are a child you bind yourself
d) you know that the summer draws near
e) she calls her friends and her neighbours saying "rejoice with me for I found my drachma which was lost"
f) the sheep hear his voice and he calls his sheep according to their names and he brings them out

Exercise 10.2
a) (he) seeks for (a) place of rest and he does not find
b) we know that God does not hear sinners
c) but the thief he does not come except perhaps to steal and to kill and to destroy
d) they do not cast new wine to old wineskins
e) for the wrath of man does not work to the righteousness of God

Exercise 10.3
a) the wine and the food which the king eats from (them)
b) the gate of the temple which is called 'beautiful'
c) the mountain which is called 'that of olives'
d) those which I love I rebuke I teach them
e) like the shepherd who divides the sheep from the goats

Exercise 10.4
a) and he who does not throw himself down to kneel he will be immediately thrown into the furnace of fire
b) from your hands O king He will save us
c) for the place which your treasure is (to) your heart will also be there
d) he will meditate in His law in the day and in the night
e) and God will give you from the dew of Heaven
f) God will bring His hand upon all the adornment of Heaven and upon the kings of the earth
g) God will humiliate the chiefs of the sons of Zion
h) You have heard that it was said 'you will love your friend and you will hate your enemy'
i) and after three days he will rise
j) the queen of (the) south will rise in the judgement with this generation and she will judge it

Exercise 10.5
a) they hold the ropes and the anchors fearing that the wind will not come upon them
b) I will not fear before evil for you are with me
c) this generation will not pass away till all these happen
d) (the) Heaven and the earth will pass away but my words will not pass away
e) fruit will not come out from inside you for ever
f) and after another seven days (are) you will not see the earth
g) do not do like the hypocrites

Exercise 10.6:
a) and you say that if we were in the days of our fathers we would not have been partners (to) them in the blood of the prophets
b) for if you were desiring sacrifice I would (still) give
c) that which He was about to complete in Jerusalem
d) for if we were examining ourselves we would not be judged

Appendix 5-Answers

e) they answered saying to him if this were not an evil person we would not have given him to you

Exercise 10.7

a) fear before God and glorify Him for the time of His judgement has come
b) give the boy Shenouti to me so that he looks over the sheep with me
c) stop your tongue from (the) evil
d) and go out to the crossings of paths
e) Jesus said to her 'go, call your husband and come here'
f) then see lest that which was spoken in the prophets come upon you
g) make us gods
h) Pilate said to them take him yourselves, crucify Him
i) O the angel of this day, who flies to the highest with this hymn, make our remembrance before the Lord to forgive us from our sins. Those who are sick heal them, those who have slept O Lord repose them, our brothers who are in every hardship O my Lord help us with them

Exercise 10.8

a) my beloved do not believe every spirit
b) go, from now do not return to sinning
c) do not rejoice in this
d) do not worry about the morrow
e) do not go nor pursue
f) do not judge so that you are not judged
g) and the Lord said to Paul through a vision in the evening 'do not fear but speak and not keep silent'
h) do not love the world nor those which are in the world
i) the commandments you know them, do not kill, do not commit adultery, not steal, do not witness falsely

Exercise 10.9

a) let us praise the Lord
b) let your name be purified
c) let your kingdom come
d) let me hear your mercy
e) let all your enemies be scattered
f) let Him save Him now if He loves Him
g) you also, that which you have heard from the beginning let it dwell in you

Exercise 10.10

a) And Peter said to him even if all the others stumble but I (will) not
b) and days are coming when the bridegroom will be taken away from them then they will fast
c) when they hear they accept the word (to themselves) joyfully
d) you will receive (a) power when the Holy Spirit comes down upon you
e) and when I receive a time I will send after you
f) for there is profit in circumcision if you do the law
g) the Lord will raise him even if he has done sins they will be forgiven to him

Exercise 10.11

a) my beloved if our hearts do not condemn us
b) for if you do not believe that "I am" you will die in your sins
c) I say to you that if you do not eat the flesh of the Son of man
d) for the Pharisees and all the Jews do not eat if they do not wash many times
e) I will give her to the (sick) bed with those who fornicate with her to a great tribulation if she does not repent
f) He said to the unlawful king Diocletian "my Lord Jesus Christ lives, if you do not write about me also that you send me down to Egypt so that

my blood be poured out in that place like my father Basil and all my brothers I will remove your head

Exercise 11.1

a) they cause the city of God to rejoice
b) He causes his sun to shine upon the wicked and the righteous
c) I will cause your name to be great
d) They caused him to sit above them
e) I will cause your bodies to shine like the sun.

Exercise 11.2

a) Lord do not cause us to perish for the sake of the soul of this man
b) the time has come and behold the day has drawn near do not cause those who buy to rejoice
c) and each one of you do not cause to (him) to think evil in your heart
d) and in that time the Lord will say to Jerusalem "comfort Zion, do not cause your hands to be undone"
e) and those who are in the country do not cause them to go inside
f) do not cause the heart of the king to be disturbed

Exercise 11.3

a) when the king heard the voice of the multitude he was amazed
b) when the Lord returned the captivity of Zion we became like those who were comforted
c) and He was saying a parable to them so that they would pray at all times
d) in (the) saying 'today, if you will hear his voice'
e) when Pharaoh let the people go God did not lead before the people to the way of the Philistine
f) the Spirit took Him to the desert so the devil (could) tempt Him

Exercise 11.4

a) those who it is possible for them to teach to you of the salvation through the faith which is in Christ Jesus
b) My Lord if you wish it is possible for you to purify me
c) this said 'it is possible for me to collapse this temple of God
d) for this it was possible to deceive her according to the wish of her heart
e) this which it is possible for us to give an account about (it) regarding the disturbance

Exercise 11.5

a) it is not possible for him to see
b) it is not possible for Him to save Him
c) for it is not possible for anyone to do these miracles which you do (them) if God is not with Him
d) all those who dwell in Jerusalem (they) know, it is not possible for us to deny
e) it is not possible for you to drink from the cup of the Lord and the cup of the demons
f) it is not possible for me to do this till Eusebius my son comes from the battle

Exercise 11.6

a) for your father knows those which you need (them) before you ask Him for them
b) and it happened before I completed these words
c) but the end has not yet come
d) for my time has not yet been completed
e) for He had not yet come upon one of them
f) and now we do not yet see everything

Exercise 11.7

a) you know to examine

b) he sat to teach them
c) for I hope to see you
d) make us worthy to say
e) it is easy to deceive her

Exercise 12.1
a) if it is appropriate for me to boast (my self) I will boast (myself) *in my weakness*
b) I ask you O the good one, *have mercy on me according to your great mercy*
c) *in the measure which you measure* it will be measured to you
d) I will open my mouth in parables and *speak of those which are hidden since the foundation of the world*
e) say to him 'the teacher says that My time has drawn near I will do the Pascha *at your (house) with my disciples*
f) the girl *did not die* but she is sleeping

Exercise 12.2
a) Jesus answered and said that this voice did not happen for *my sake but for your sake*
b) They knew truly that I came *from you*
c) for I made the man *in the image of God*
d) You came here to *destroy us before our time happened*
e) I came so *that they may have life*

Exercise 13.1
a) is it possible for you to drink the cup which I will drink? They said to him 'it is possible for us'
b) does he not leave the 99 behind?
c) he gave a blow to Jesus saying 'is this the way to answer the high priest?'
d) when they called they were asking 'is Simon who is called Peter dwelling here?'
e) does she not light a lamp and sweep the house?
f) is it appropriate for me to say something to you?
g) did not my hand make all these things?

Exercise 13:2
a) how is it that you a Jew ask through (from) me to drink?
b) and he said 'how is it possible for me to know if one does not lead me
c) how many years am I (have I been) a servant to you?
d) and they cried out with a great voice saying "till when our master, the Holy, the righteous, do you not judge?"
e) what is the place which is my place of rest?
f) who is the man that you remembered?
g) (O) woman, why are you crying?
h) for why did I not die in the womb?
i) how is it (that) you do not understand?
j) what is happening my son?

Exercise 13.3
a) when he saw them walking behind him he said to them 'what are you looking for?"
b) where did they come from?
c) Rabbi, when did you come to this place?
d) When will the kingdom of God come?
e) for I know where you dwell, the place which the throne of Satan is in
f) where do battles come from?
g) when will the sun set so that I rest from my sufferings and pain of my heart
h) the disciples said where will we find this number (amount) of bread in this wilderness?

Exercise 14:1

a) and Peter said "no O Lord for I did not eat anything ever which is defiled or polluted"

b) and they cried up to the Lord and they said "no Lord, do not destroy us for the sake of the soul of this man"

c) and they were coming to him saying "hail the king of the Jews"

d) thank you my honoured servants

e) he said to him "tell me are you a Roman?" And he said 'yes'

f) and they asked him 'are you Elijah?' he said 'no' are you a prophet? he answered 'no'

g) woe to you Pharisees for you love the first seat in the synagogue and the greetings in the market place

h) and Jesus said to them "do you believe that it is possible for me to do this?" they said to Him "Yes, our Lord"

i) and behold an angel of the Lord came

j) truly, I say to you

Exercise 15.1

a) Upon Zion His Holy Mountain

b) we do not have boldness

c) I have pride in Christ Jesus

d) Abraham your father was rejoicing desiring to see my day and he saw, he rejoiced

e) do we not have the power to eat and to drink?

f) we have our God in Heaven, God the almighty

g) he cried over them like his beloved children

h) and if he does not have a brother you will give his inheritance to his household

i) your children have animals

Exercise 15.2

a) you are not yours (you are not your own)

b) theirs is the Kingdom of Heaven

c) To Him is the glory till the age of ages amen.

d) all those of the city gathered

e) the word which you hear (it) is not mine but that of the father who sent me

f) it is not yours to know seasons and times

g) these vessels, these are mine

h) to you is the day, to you also is the evening, you prepared the sun and the moon

i) Michael the Chief of the Heavenlies

j) you do not think about the things of God but (those) of man

Exercise 15.3

a) then our mouths were filled with joy

b) blessed is the Lord God of Israel, blessed is the Lord God of Sidrak, Misak, and Abdenago who has sent his angel, he saved his servants for indeed their hearts (trust) were in him

c) God, hear my prayer, receive the voice of the words of my mouth

d) when he opened his mouth

e) and the Lord also said to him 'put your hand inwards upon your chest and he placed his hands inwards upon his chest.'

Practice texts

Practice text 1

O our mother the Saint Mary the virgin. We are your children and you are our mother. We are the children of your beloved Son. He is our Lord and we are His servants. He is our father and we are His children.

Practice text 2
The first is love. The second is hope. The third is faith. The fourth is purity. The fifth is virginity. The sixth is peace. The seventh is wisdom. The eighth is righteousness. The ninth is meekness. The tenth is patience. The eleventh is long suffering. The twelfth is asceticism

Practice text 3
Sing to the Lord with a new song. Sing to the Lord all the earth. Sing to the Lord, bless His name, proclaim His salvation day by day. Speak of His glory amongst the nations and His wonders amongst all the nations, for great is the Lord and He is very blessed. He is fearful above all the gods for all the gods of the nations are demons.

Practice text 4
You are the golden, pure censer which carries the blessed coal of fire.

Practice text 5
Hail to you Mary the beautiful dove that gave birth to God the Word for us. You are truly blessed with Your good Father and the Holy Spirit for You came and saved us.

Practice text 6
The hymn of the blessed slumber, I will give to Christ my king and my God. I will hope in Him.

Practice text 7
1) You are truly great O good announcer, amongst the ranks of angels and the Heavenly hosts
2) Gabriel the announcer, the great amongst the angels and the Holy exalted ranks which carry the sword of flaming fire
3) For Daniel the prophet saw your honour and you told him about the mystery of the life giving Trinity
4) and Zachariah the priest, you announced to him (in) the birth of the forerunner, John the Baptist.
5) You also preached to the virgin "Hail O full of grace, the Lord is with you. You will give birth to the saviour of all the earth."
6) Intercede O the Holy Archangel, Gabriel the announcer

Practice text 8
Emmanuel our God is now in our midst in the Glory of His Father and the Holy Spirit, to bless us all, to purify our hearts, to heal the sicknesses of our souls and bodies.

Practice text 9
I ask you for the sake of my son, this whom I bore in my bonds, Onesimus. This who was worthless to you for a time but now he is of value to me with you. This who I sent to you.

Practice text 10
And it happened that after these things and he was walking to every city and village preaching and announcing the kingdom of God. And the 12 being with him and the other women those whom He had healed from evil spirits and sicknesses. Mary who is called 'Magdalene' from whom He cast out 7 demons, and Joanna the wife of Chuza the steward of Herod and Susanna and many others with those who were serving Him from their possessions.

Practice text 11
And there was a disciple in Damascus whose name was Ananias. And the Lord said to him in a dream 'Ananias, and he said 'behold, (it is) I Lord.'

Practice text 12
The Lord will hear you in the day of your tribulation. He will give upon you the name of the God of Jacob. He will send to you help from the Holy (Sanctuary). He will accept you to Him from Zion. He will remember all your sacrifices, your fattened burnt offerings to Him. The Lord will give

you according to your heart and all your counsel. He will perfect. We will give thanks to the Lord in Your salvation and in the name of our God we will grow. The Lord will complete all your requests.

Practice text 13
Judge O Lord those who use violence with me and fight those who fight me. Take a weapon and a shield. Arise, help me. Draw out Your sword and shut in front (block the path of) those who persecute me. Say to my soul "I am your salvation."

Practice text 14
O Lord, do not admonish me in Your anger nor in Your wrath. Do not reprove me. Have mercy upon me O Lord for I am weak, heal me O Lord for my bones are disturbed and my soul has been greatly troubled.

Practice text 15
And if your brother sins against you go and blame him between you and him only, if he hears you, you will gain your brother. And if he does not hear you take another or two with you so that from the mouth of 2 witnesses or 3 every word stands. And if he does not hear you say (it) to the Church. And if he does not hear the Church he will be to you like a heathen and a tax collector.

Practice text 16
I will write your names in the Church of the first born. I will cause it to be preached in the whole world. When I come in my appearance I will cause your bodies to shine like the sun and so that you be as wonders before all the nations

Practice text 17
And they said to him "why is this evil in you and what is your occupation and where do you come from and what district are you from and from what city" and he said to them "I am a servant of the Lord."

Practice text 18
And the Canaanite, the king Arad who dwells in the desert heard that Israel came on the way of Atharin and he fought Israel and he took prisoners (a captivity) from them and Israel prayed a prayer to the Lord and he said if you give me this nation into my hands I will destroy (curse) it and its cities and the Lord heard the voice of Israel and He gave the nation of Canaan into his hand and he destroyed (cursed) it and its cities and he named the name of that place 'anathema' and when they departed from Hor the mountain upon the way of the red sea they circled the land of Edom and the people became small of heart on the way and the children spoke against God and Moses saying " why did you bring us from the land of Egypt to kill us in the desert, for there is no bread nor water and our soul has become cold to this dry bread" and the Lord sent the serpents into the people to kill and they were biting the people and a great multitude of the people of Israel died and the people came to Moses saying "we sinned and spoke against God and against you. Pray then to the Lord and let Him remove these serpents away from us" and Moses prayed to the Lord for the people and the Lord said to Moses "make for yourself a bronze serpent and put it on a sign and it will be that if the serpent bites a man and he will look to the bronze serpent and he will live and Moses made the bronze serpent and placed it on a sign and it happened that when a serpent bit a man and he looks to the bronze serpent, he lives.

Glossary

Note: Words of grammatical significance are presented with the page number in brackets. Transitive verbs are presented in the format of infinitive, construct form, pronominal form, and qualitative form.

ⲁⲃⲟⲧ	month (m)	ⲁⲛⲁⲑⲉⲙⲁ	devotion, curse (Gk,m)
ⲁⲃⲃⲁ	father (Gk,m)	ⲁⲛⲁⲥⲧⲁⲥⲓⲥ	resurrection (Gk,f)
ⲁⲅⲁⲑⲟⲥ	good, righteous, noble (adj.Gk)	ⲁ̀ⲛⲟⲕ	I, 1st P indep p.pronoun
	good, righteous one (m)	ⲁⲛⲟⲙⲓⲁ	iniquity (f)
ⲁⲅⲁⲡⲏ	love (Gk,f)	ⲁⲛⲟⲙⲟⲥ	lawless (adj, Gk)
ⲁⲑⲁⲣⲓⲛ	Atharin (prop noun)	ⲁⲛϣⲟ	thousands
ⲁⲓⲁⲓ, ⲟⲓ (q)	to grow, multiply (vi) to be abundant, great	ⲁⲡⲁⲥ	old (adjective)
ⲁⲕⲧⲓⲛ	light, ray (Gk,m)	ⲁⲡⲟⲥⲧⲟⲗⲟⲥ	apostle, messenger, ambassador, envoy (Gk,m)
ⲁⲗⲏⲑⲱⲥ	truly (Gk)		
ⲁⲗⲏⲓ	to mount, go up (v.i)	ⲁⲣⲁⲇ	Arad (prop noun)
ⲁⲗⲗⲁ	but (conj) (123)	ⲁⲣⲉϣⲁⲛ	pre subj form conditional (201)
ⲁⲗⲟⲩ	youth (m,f)	ⲁⲣⲉϩ	to guard, to keep, to study (v.t)
ⲁⲗⲱⲟⲩⲓ	youth (pl)	ⲁⲣⲏⲟⲩ	perhaps, may be (adv) (172)
ⲁⲙⲁϩⲓ	to prevail, to rule, be in possession of (v.i)	ⲁⲣⲏⲧⲏ	Virtue (Gk,f)
ⲁⲙⲏⲛ	amen, may it be (interj) (239)	ⲁⲣⲭⲓⲉⲣⲉⲩⲥ	high priest (m) (Gk)
ⲁⲙⲟⲛⲓ	to seize, hold (v.t)	ⲁⲣⲭⲱⲛ	chief, ruler (Gk,m)
ⲁⲛ	negative particle (66)	ⲁⲥⲑⲉⲛⲏⲥ	weak, feeble, infirm, sick (Gk, adj)
	interrogative particle (227)	ⲁⲥⲕⲟⲥ	wineskin, leather bag (m)
	Collective numeral prefix (259)	ⲁⲥⲡⲁⲥⲙⲟⲥ	greeting (Gk,m)

So You want to Learn Coptic?

ⲁⲧ/ⲁⲑ-	negative prefix (259)	ⲃⲏⲃ	cave (m)
ⲁⲧⲑⲱⲗⲉⲃ	without defilement, pure (adj)	ⲃⲏⲑⲫⲁⲅⲏ	Bethpage (prop noun)
ⲁⲧⲥⲙⲏ	without voice, mute (adj)	ⲃⲟⲏⲑⲓⲁ	help, aid, cure (Gk,f)
ⲁⲧⲉⲙⲓ	ignorant (adj)	ⲃⲟⲏⲑⲓⲛ	to help, support (Gk,v.t)
ⲁⲧϣⲁⲩ	worthless (adj.)	ⲃⲱ	tree (f)
ⲁⲩϫⲁⲗ	ship anchor (m)	ⲃⲟⲗ	the outside
ⲁ̀ⲫⲉ	head (f)	ⲃⲱⲕ	servant, slave (m)
ⲁⲫⲟⲧ	cup, chalice (m)	ⲉⲃⲓⲁⲓⲕ (pl)	servants, slaves (pl)
ⲁϣⲁⲓ, ⲟϣ(q)	to become many, multiply to be abundant (v.i)	ⲃⲱⲗ ⲃⲉⲗ- ⲃⲟⲗ⸗ ⲃⲏⲗ ⲉ̀ⲃⲟⲗ	to loosen, untie, melt, undo, collapse
ⲁϭⲟ⸗	why? (interrog.part) (229), what? infl. interjec. (239)	ⲃⲱⲧⲥ	to fight, battle (v.t)
			fight, battle (m)
ⲁϩⲁ	yes (injerjec.) (239)	ⲅⲁⲍⲟⲫⲩⲗⲁⲕⲓⲟⲛ	treasury (Gk,m)
ⲁϩⲟ	treasure (m)	ⲅⲉⲉⲛⲛⲁ	Gehana, Hades (Gk,f)
ⲁϫⲡ	hour (f)	ⲅⲉⲛⲉⲁ	race, type, generation (f)
ⲃⲁⲉⲙⲡⲓ	goat (f)	ⲇⲉⲙⲱⲛ	demon (Gk,m)
ⲃⲁⲕⲓ	city (f)	ⲇⲏⲛⲁⲣⲓⲟⲛ	denarius (roman coin) m
ⲃⲁⲗ	eye (m)	ⲇⲓⲁⲃⲟⲗⲟⲥ	devil (m)
ⲃⲁⲥⲓⲗⲓⲧⲏⲥ	Basil (prop noun)	ⲇⲓⲟⲕⲗⲏⲧⲓⲁⲛⲟⲥ	Diocletian (prop noun)
ⲃⲁⲧⲟⲥ	bush (Gk,m)	ⲇⲓⲕⲏⲟⲥⲩⲛⲏ	righteousness (Gk,f)
ⲃⲉⲗⲗⲉ	blind person (m)	ⲇⲓⲁⲕⲓⲟⲥⲩⲛⲏ	
ⲃⲉⲣⲓ	new (adjective)	ⲉ̀	obj. marker (75), to (prep.) (70)
ⲃⲉⲭⲉ	reward (m)		

Glossary

	ⲉⲣⲟ⸗	pronom. form (75)	ⲉⲛⲁⲣⲉ	
		as a conjunction (219)	ⲉⲛⲉϩ	eternally (adv.)
ⲉ̀		relative converter non verbal sentence (83)		age, eternity (m)
			ⲉⲛⲕⲁⲓ	see ⲉⲛⲭⲁⲓ
		relative converter past tense for indefinite antecedent (104)	ⲉⲛⲕⲟⲧ	to sleep, lay down, pass away (v.i)
			ⲉⲛⲧⲟⲗⲏ	commandment (Gk,f)
ⲉⲃⲓⲁⲓⲕ		slaves, servants see ⲃⲱⲕ	ⲉⲛⲭⲁⲓ	thing, possesion (m)
ⲉⲃⲟ		mute person (m)	ⲉⲡⲁⲅⲅⲉⲗⲓⲁ	promise (Gk,f)
ⲉ̀ⲃⲟⲗ		away, out (comp. prep) (173)	ⲉ̀ⲡⲉⲥⲏⲧ	(adv.) downward, down to, beneath
ⲉⲅⲕⲣⲁⲧⲓⲁ		asceticisim (Gk,f)	ⲉⲡⲓⲇⲏ	since, after, that (Gk, conj.) (123)
ⲉⲑⲃⲉ		for the sake of, because (prep) (70) conj (124)	ⲉⲡⲓⲧⲣⲟⲡⲟⲥ	steward (Gk,m)
ⲉⲑⲛⲟⲥ		nation (Gk,m)	ⲉ̀ⲡϣⲱⲓ	upwards (adv)
ⲉⲑⲣⲉ		pre subj form causative (ⲑ̀ⲣⲉ)	ⲉ̀ⲡϫⲓⲛⲧ⸗	in order to (verbal substantive pronom form) (212)
ⲉⲕⲕⲗⲏⲥⲓⲁ		church (Gk,f)	ⲉ̀ⲡϫⲓⲛⲧⲁ-	when (verbal substantive) pre subj form (212)
ⲉⲗⲓⲁⲥ		Elijah (prop noun)		
ⲉⲙⲁϣⲱ		very (adverb)	ⲉⲣⲁⲅⲓⲁⲍⲓⲛ	to sanctify (Gk,vi)
ⲉ̀ⲙⲓ		to know, understand (v.i)	ⲉⲣⲁⲛⲁⲑⲉⲙⲁⲧⲓⲍⲓⲛ	to devote, curse (v.t)
ⲉⲙⲛⲁⲓ		here (adv)	ⲉ̀ⲣⲁⲧ⸗	to the foot of, to (comp prep) (263)
ⲉⲙⲡϣⲁ		to be worthy (v.i)	ⲉⲣⲇⲓⲁⲕⲣⲓⲛⲓⲛ	to examine (v.t)
ⲉ̀ⲛⲁⲣⲉ		pre subj form imperfect future (ⲉⲛⲁⲣⲉ 191)	ⲉⲣⲇⲟⲕⲓⲙⲁⲍⲓⲛ	to test, try, examine (v.t)
ⲉ̀ⲛⲉ		shortened form of	ⲉ̀ⲣⲉ	pre subj form relative converter (81)

287

	pre subj form circumstantial (145)		(v.i)
	pre subj form emphatic future (184)	ⲉⲣⲟⲩⲱⲓⲛⲓ	to shine (v.i)
ⲉⲣⲉⲧⲓⲛ	to ask (Gk, v.t)	ⲉ̀ⲣⲟϥ	(prep) 3rd person m singular object indicator, to him
-ⲉⲣⲏⲟⲩ	one another (reciprocating pnoun) (243)	ⲉⲣⲡⲓⲣⲁⲍⲓⲛ	to tempt (Gk,v.t)
ⲉⲣⲕⲁⲧⲁϫⲓⲛⲱⲥⲕⲓⲛ	to condemn (Gk,v.t)	ⲉⲣⲡⲣⲉⲥⲃⲉⲩⲓⲛ	to intercede
ⲉⲣⲙⲉⲗⲉⲧⲁⲛ	to meditate (Gk v.i)	ⲉⲣⲡⲣⲟⲥⲉⲩⲭⲉⲥⲑⲉ	to pray
ⲉⲣⲙⲉⲧⲁⲛⲟⲓⲛ	to repent (Gk, v.i)	ⲉⲣⲡⲣⲟⲫⲏⲧⲉⲩⲓⲛ	to prophesy (v.t)
ⲉⲣⲛⲏⲥⲧⲉⲩⲓⲛ	to fast (Gk, v.i)	ⲉⲣⲥⲟⲃⲧ	to make a wall around, protect (v.t)
ⲉⲣⲛⲓϣϯ	to be great (v)	ⲉⲣⲫⲁϧⲣⲓ	to heal (v.t)
ⲉⲣⲛⲟⲃⲓ	to sin (v)	ⲉⲣⲫⲉⲓ	sanctuary, temple, altar (m)
ⲉⲣⲛⲟϥⲣⲓ	to be good	ⲉⲣⲫⲙⲉⲩⲓ	to remember
ⲉⲣⲛⲱⲓⲕ	to fornicate, commit adultery (v.i)	ⲉⲣϣⲓϣⲓ	authority, power (m)
ⲉ̀ⲣⲟⲩⲱ	to answer (v)	ⲉⲣϣⲫⲏⲣⲓ	to be amazed (v.i)
ⲉ̀ⲣⲟ	(prep) 2nd person f singular object indicator, to you (f,s)	ⲉⲣϩⲁⲗ	to deceive (v.t)
		ⲉⲣϩⲉⲗⲡⲓⲥ	to hope (v)
ⲉ̀ⲣⲟⲓ	(prep) 1st person singular object indicator, to me	ⲉ̀ⲣϩⲙⲟⲧ	to grant, bestow
		ⲉⲣϩⲟⲩⲟ̀	to increase (v)
		ⲉⲣϩⲱⲃ	to work, labour (v.i)
ⲉ̀ⲣⲟⲕ	(prep) 2nd person m singular object indicator, to you (m,s)	ⲉⲥⲱⲟⲩ	sheep (m)
		ⲉⲧ-	relative converter (79)
ⲉ̀ⲣⲟⲥ	(prep) 3rd person f singular object indicator, to her	ⲉ̀ⲧⲉ	Relative converter (5.1.v)
		ⲉ̀ⲧⲉ ⲙ̀ⲙⲁⲩ	That (far dem. art) (34)
ⲉ̀ⲣⲟⲩⲱ	to answer, reply		

ⲉⲧⲉⲛ-	construct form of ⲛ̀ⲧⲟⲧ⸝ (264)	ϯ	f definite art (28)
ⲉⲧⲏⲙⲁ	request, demand (Gk,m)	ⲑⲁ	f pre subj form poss p.noun (248)
ⲉ̀ⲧⲓ	after, during, and (conj, Gk) (124)	ⲑⲁⲓ	feminine demonstrative pronoun
ⲉ̀ⲧϩⲏ	forward, ahead (adv)	ⲑⲁⲙⲓⲟ ⲑⲁⲙⲓⲉ- ⲑⲁⲙⲓⲟ⸝ ⲑⲁⲙⲓⲏⲟⲩⲧ	to make, create (v.t)
ⲉⲩⲁⲅⲅⲉⲗⲓⲟⲛ	Gospel (Gk,m)		
ⲉⲩⲥⲉⲃⲓⲟⲥ	Eusebius (prop.noun)	ⲑⲉⲃⲓⲟ ⲑⲉⲃⲓⲉ- ⲑⲉⲃⲓⲟ⸝ ⲑⲉⲃⲓⲏⲟⲩⲧ	to be humble to humiliate (v.t)
ⲉⲩⲭⲏ	prayer (Gk,f)		
ⲉ̀ⲫⲁϩⲟⲩ	backwards (adv)		
ⲉⲭⲙⲁⲗⲱⲥⲓⲁ	captivity (Gk, f)	Ⲑⲉⲟⲧⲟⲕⲟⲥ	Mother of God (f) (Gk) (llt: bearer of God)
ⲉ̀ϣⲱⲡ	if, when (conditional) (130) (202)	ⲑⲉϣⲉ	neighbour, borderer (m.f)
ⲉ̀ϧⲟⲩⲛ	inside (compound prep) (70)	ⲑⲉϣⲉⲩ	neighbours (pl)
ⲉ̀ϩⲟⲟⲩ	day (m)	ⲑⲏⲟⲩ	wind, breath (m)
ⲉ̀ϩⲣⲉⲛ	facing, in front of (comp prep) (263)	ⲑ̀ⲙⲏⲓ	righteousness, truth (f)
ⲉ̀ϩⲣⲏⲓ	downwards (adv)	ⲑ̀ⲣⲉ	pre subj form causative (207)
ⲉ̀ϫⲉⲛ	upon (com prep) (263)	ⲑ̀ⲣⲟⲛⲟⲥ	throne (Gk,m)
ⲉϫⲱ⸝	pronom form	ⲑⲩⲥⲓⲁ	offering (Gk,f)
ⲉϫⲱⲣϩ	evening (m)	ⲑⲱⲕⲉⲙ	to draw out (knife or sword) v.t
ⲏⲓ	house (m)	ⲑⲱⲟⲩϯ ⲑⲟⲩⲉⲧ- ⲑⲟⲩⲱⲧ⸝ ⲑⲟⲩⲏⲧ	to gather (v.t)
ⲏⲡⲓ	number (f)		
ⲏⲣⲡ	wine (m)		
Ⲏⲥⲁⲩ	Esau (prop. noun)	ⲑⲱϩⲉⲙ ⲑⲁϩⲉⲙ- ⲑⲁϩⲙ⸝ ⲑⲁϩⲉⲙ	to knock, summon, to invite, to be invited (q)

So You want to Learn Coptic?

(ⲓ)

ⲓ, ⲛⲏⲟⲩ (q)	to come (v.i), to be coming	ⲕⲁⲛ	even if (124)
ⲓⲃⲓ, ⲟⲃⲓ (q)	to thirst, to be thirsty (q)	ⲕⲁⲥ	bone (m)
ⲓⲉ	or (conj) (124)	ⲕⲁⲧⲁⲃⲟⲗⲏ	foundation, establishment (Gk,f)
ⲓⲏⲥ ⲙⲙⲟ⸗	to hasten (v,r)	ⲕⲁⲧⲁⲡⲉⲧⲁⲥⲙⲁ	veil (Gk,m)
ⲓⲛⲓ ⲉⲛ- ⲉⲛ⸗	to bring (v.t)	ⲕⲁϣ	reed, pen (m)
ⲓⲟⲩⲇⲁⲓ	Jew (m)	ⲕⲁϩⲓ	world, land, earth (m)
Ἰⲟⲩⲇⲉⲁ	Judah (f)	ⲕⲁϩⲥ	custom, habit (f)
ⲓⲟϩ	moon (m)	ⲕⲁϯ, ⲉ̀	to understand
ⲓⲣⲓ ⲉⲣ- ⲁⲓ⸗ ⲟⲓ	to do, make (v.t)	ⲕⲉ	other, also (art) (44)
ⲓⲥ	behold (interj)	ⲕⲉⲗⲉⲃⲓⲛ	axe (m)
ⲓⲥϫⲉ	if (conj) (124)	ⲕⲉⲛⲓ	to fatten (v.t)
ⲓⲥϫⲉⲛ	since (simple preposition) (70)	ⲕⲉⲛⲓⲱⲟⲩⲧ	to be fattened (qual)
Ἰⲱⲁⲛⲛⲏⲥ	John (prop.noun)	ⲕⲉⲛⲧⲉ	date (m)
ⲓⲱⲡⲡⲏ	Joppa (prop.noun)	ⲕⲏⲛ	To cease, already (v.i) (145)
ⲓⲱⲧ	father (m)	ⲕⲟⲥⲙⲟⲥ	world (Gk,m)
ⲓⲟϯ	fathers, parents (pl)	ⲕⲟⲓ	field (f)
ⲓⲱϯ	dew (f)	ⲕⲟⲩⲣ	slap, blow (m)
ⲓϣⲓ ⲉϣ-ⲁϣ⸗ ⲁϣⲓ	to hang, suspend, crucify	ⲕⲟⲩϫⲓ	little (m) small (adj)
ⲕⲁⲕⲓⲁ	evil, malice (Gk,f)	ⲕⲣⲓⲥⲓⲥ	judgment (Gk,f)
ⲕⲁⲗⲩⲙⲙⲁ	veil (Gk,m)	ⲕⲩⲃⲱⲧⲟⲥ	ark (f)
ⲕⲁⲗⲱⲥ	good, beautiful, fair, righteously, truly (adv)	ⲕⲩⲑⲁⲣⲁ	harp (Gk,f)
		ⲕⲱⲧ ⲕⲉⲧ	to build (v.t)

ⲕⲟⲧ⳱			ⲙⲁⲛϣⲁϥⲉ	desert (m)
ⲕⲱϯ		to turn, go around, to go about seeking (v.i)	ⲙⲁⲛϩⲉⲙⲥⲓ	place of sitting, seat (m)
	ⲙ̀ⲙⲟ⳱	to turn, self, return	ⲙⲁⲑⲏⲧⲏⲥ	disciple
	ⲛ̀ⲥⲁ	to seek	ⲙⲁⲣⲉ	pre. subj. form optative (199,256)
		Repeat of action (116)	ⲙⲁⲥⲓ	calf (m)
ⲗⲁⲙⲡⲣⲟⲥ		brilliant, bright (adj)	ⲙⲁⲧⲟⲓ	soldier (m)
ⲗⲁⲡⲥⲓ		bite, sting, morsel (m)	ⲙⲁⲩ	mother (f)
ⲗⲁⲥ		tongue (m)	ⲙⲁ	place (m)
ⲗⲁⲥⲁϫⲓ		chatty, talkative (adj)	ⲙⲁϩⲓ	cubit (m)
ⲗⲁⲟⲥ		nation, people (Gk,m)	ⲙ̀ⲃⲟⲛ	wrath (m)
ⲗⲁϥⲱⲓ		hairy (adj)	ⲙⲉⲑⲙⲏⲓ	rigtheousness, truth (f)
ⲗⲉⲡⲧⲟⲛ		mite (Gk)	ⲙⲉⲑⲛⲟⲩϯ	Divinity (f)
ⲗⲟⲅⲟⲥ		word (Gk,m)	ⲙⲉⲑⲣⲉ	witness, testimony (f)
ⲗⲩⲇⲇⲁ		Lidda (prop noun)	ⲙⲉⲧⲙⲉⲑⲣⲉ	witness (m)
ⲙ̀		for ⲛ̀ before ⲙ ⲡ	ⲙⲉⲓ ⲙⲉⲛⲣⲉ-	to love (v.t)
		ⲃ ⲫ ⲯ (39)	ⲙⲉⲛⲣⲓⲧ⳱ ⲙⲁⲓ- (p.c)	
ⲙⲁϩ		place (m)	ⲙⲉⲗⲟⲥ	share, limb, member (Gk)
ⲙⲁⲕⲁⲣⲓⲟⲥ		blessed one (Gk,m)	ⲙⲉⲛⲉⲛⲥⲁ	after (prep) (70)
ⲙⲁⲙ̀ⲃⲣⲉ		Mamre (prop. Noun)	ⲙⲉⲛⲣⲏⲧ	beloved (m)
ⲙⲁⲛ̀ⲉⲣϣⲱⲟⲩϣⲓ		place of sacrifice, altar (m)	ⲙⲉⲛⲣⲁϯ	beloved (pl)
ⲙⲁⲛⲉⲥⲱⲟⲩ		shepherd (m)	ⲙⲉⲣⲟⲥ	share, portion (Gk,m)
ⲙⲁⲛⲙ̀ⲧⲟⲛ		place of rest (m)	ⲙⲉⲧⲁⲗⲟⲩ	childhood (f)
			ⲙⲉⲧⲁⲛⲟⲓⲁ	repentance (f)

ⲙⲉⲧⲛⲓϣϯ	greatness (f)
ⲙⲉⲧⲟⲩⲏⲃ	priesthood (f)
ⲙⲉⲧⲟⲩⲣⲟ	kingdom (f)
ⲙⲉⲧⲣⲉⲙⲣⲁⲩϣ	meekness (f)
ⲙⲉⲧⲣⲉϥϯⲥⲃⲱ	Teaching (f)
ⲙⲉⲧⲥⲁⲓⲉ	Beauty (f)
ⲙⲉⲩⲓ	to think, suppose (v.i)
	thought, remembrance (m)
ⲙⲏ	interrogative particle (228)
ⲙⲏⲓ	truth, verity, justice (f)
ⲙⲏⲓⲛⲓ	sign, wonder (m)
ⲙⲏⲡⲟⲧⲉ	lest, perhaps (Gk,conj.) (124)
ⲙⲏⲡⲱⲥ	lest, perhaps (Gk,conj.)
ⲙⲏϣ	multitude (m)
ⲙⲏϯ	midst, middle (f)
ⲙⲓⲥⲓ ⲙⲉⲥ- ⲙⲁⲥ⸌	to give birth to (v.t)
ⲙⲟⲥⲓ	
ⲙⲓⲥⲓ	birth
ⲙ̀ⲕⲁϩ	pain, suffering (m)
ⲙ̀ⲙⲁⲩ	there (adv)
ⲉⲧⲉ ⲙ̀ⲙⲁⲩ	
ⲙ̀ⲙⲁⲩⲁⲧ⸌	alone, only (inflected adj.) (42)
ⲙ̀ⲙⲁϣⲱ	very, greatly (adv.)
ⲙ̀ⲙⲏⲓⲛⲓ	every day, daily (adv.)
ⲙ̀ⲙⲓⲛ ⲙ̀ⲙⲟ⸌	own (inflected adj.) (44)
ⲙ̀ⲛⲁⲓ	here (Adv)
ⲙⲟⲕⲙⲉⲕ	to think, ponder, meditate (v.i)
ⲙⲟⲥϯ ⲙⲉⲥⲧⲉ- ⲙⲉⲥⲧⲱ⸌	to hate (v.t)
ⲙⲟⲩ, ⲙⲱⲟⲩⲧ	to die, to be dead (v.i)
	death (m)
ⲙⲟⲩⲱ	spring (f)
ⲙⲟⲩⲛ ⲉ̀ⲃⲟⲗ	to continue, to endure (v.i)
ⲙⲟⲩⲛⲕ	to cease, perish (v.i)
ⲙⲟⲩⲛϩⲱⲟⲩ	rain (m)
ⲙⲟⲩⲣ ⲙⲉⲣ- ⲙⲟⲣ⸌ ⲙⲏⲣ	to bind (v.t)
ⲙⲟⲩⲥⲓⲕⲟⲥ	musician (m)
ⲙⲟⲩϯ	to call, pronounce (v.t)
ⲙⲟϣⲓ	to walk
ⲙⲟϩ, ⲙⲉϩ	to fill, burn (v.t)
ⲙ̀ⲡⲁⲓⲣⲏϯ	in this manner, in this way
ⲙ̀ⲡⲁⲣⲉ	pre subj form negative habitual (181)
ⲙ̀ⲡⲉ	pre subj form past perfect (95)
ⲙ̀ⲡⲉⲙⲑⲟ	before, in front of, facing

ⲙ̀ⲡⲓⲥⲏⲟⲩ	at that time (adv.)		pnoun, pl. demonstrative art)
ⲙ̀ⲡⲓⲉϩⲟⲟⲩ	by day (adv.)		mercy, pity (m)
ⲙ̀ⲡϣⲱⲓ	above (adv)		to have mercy (v.t)
ⲙ̀ⲧⲟⲛ	to rest, repose (v.i)	ⲛⲁⲓⲁⲧ⸗	to be blessed (adj. vb) (164)
ⲙⲩⲥⲧⲏⲣⲓⲟⲛ	sacrament, mystery (Gk,m)	ⲛⲁⲕϩⲓ	pain, birth pain (f)
ⲙ̀ⲫⲟⲟⲩ	today (adv.)	ⲛⲁⲛⲉ- ⲛⲁⲛⲉ⸗	to be good, fair (adj vb) (162)
ⲙ̀ⲫⲣⲏϯ	like, as (adv) (176)	ⲛⲁⲩ	to look, behold (v.t)
ⲙ̀ⲫⲱⲣ	no! (interj) (239)		time (m)
ⲙⲱⲓⲧ	path, way (m)	ⲛⲁϣⲉ- ⲛⲁϣⲱ⸗	to be numerous (adj. vb) (164)
ⲙⲱⲟⲩ	water (m)	ⲛⲁϩⲙⲉⲛ	to save (v.t)
ⲛ̀	attributive construction (38)	ⲛⲁϩⲣⲉⲛ	before (comp prep) (264)
	possessive construction (39)	ⲉ̀ϩⲣ⸗	pronom form
	as a conjunction (218)	ⲛⲁϩϯ	to believe, have faith (v.t)
			faith (m)
ⲛ̀ (ⲙ̀ⲙⲟ⸗)	object marker (73)	ⲛⲉⲕ	your (2ⁿᵈ P pl , m subject) (32)
ⲛ̀...ⲁⲛ	negative particle (66)	ⲛⲉⲙ	with, and (conj) (70)
ⲛⲁ	My (1ˢᵗ P pl obj poss art) (32)	ⲛⲉⲛ	our (1ˢᵗ P pl. subj poss art) (32)
	pl. pre subj form poss. pnoun (248)		pl definite art (29)
		ⲛⲉⲥ	her (3ʳᵈ P f pl obj poss art) (32)
ⲛⲁⲁ ⲛⲁⲁ⸗	to be great (adj. vb) (164)	ⲛⲉⲥⲉ- ⲛⲉⲥⲱ⸗	to be beautiful (adj vb) (164)
ⲛⲁⲏⲧ	compassionate person (m)	ⲛⲉⲧⲉⲛ	your (second person plural)
ⲛⲁⲓ	these (pl demonstrative	ⲛⲉϥ	his (third person masc plural)

293

ⲛⲉϩⲡⲓ	weeping (m)
ⲛⲉϩⲥⲓ	to awaken (v.i)
ⲛⲉϫⲓ	womb (f)
ⲛⲏⲃ	master, lord (m)
ⲛⲓ	pl definite art (29)
ⲛⲓⲃⲉⲛ	every
ⲛⲓϣϯ	great (adj.)
ⲛ̀ⲕⲟⲧ	to rest, repose (v.i)
ⲛ̀ⲑⲙⲏϯ	in the midst, middle (adv.)
ⲛ̀ⲑⲟ	you (f 3rd P indep. pers. pnoun) (35)
ⲛ̀ⲑⲟⲕ	you (2nd P m indep. pers. pnoun) (35)
ⲛ̀ⲑⲟⲥ	she (3rd P f indep. pers. pnoun) (35)
ⲛ̀ⲑⲟϥ	he (3rd P m indep. pers. pnoun) (35)
ⲛ̀ⲑⲱⲟⲩ	they (3rd P pl indep. pers. pnoun) (35)
ⲛ̀ⲑⲱⲧⲉⲛ	you (2nd P pl indep. pers. pnoun (35)
ⲛ̀ⲕⲉⲥⲟⲡ	again (adv.)
ⲛⲟⲙⲟⲥ	law (m)
ⲛⲟⲙϯ	strength, comfort (f)
ⲛⲟϩⲉⲙ	to save (v.t)
ⲛⲟⲩⲃ	gold, money (m)
ⲛⲟⲩⲛⲓ	root (f)
ⲛⲟⲩϫ	untrue, false (adj)
ⲛⲟϩ	rope, cord (m)
ⲛⲟϩⲉⲙ ⲛⲟϩⲉⲙ- ⲛⲁϩⲉⲙ- ⲛⲁϩⲙ⸗ ⲛⲟϩⲉⲙ	to save, deliver (v.t)
ⲛ̀ⲣⲁⲥϯ	tomorrow (adv.)
ⲛ̀ⲥⲁ	behind, after, against (comp prep) (264)
ⲛ̀ⲥⲁϥ	yesterday (adv.)
ⲛ̀ⲧⲉ	possessive construction (40)
ⲛ̀ⲧⲟⲧ⸗	through the hands of, agency (264)
ⲛ̀ⲭⲱⲗⲉⲙ	quickly (adv.)
ⲛ̀ϣⲱⲣⲡ	early (adv.)
ⲛ̀ϧⲣⲏⲓ	below, from below (adv) (174)
ⲛ̀ϩⲣⲏⲓ	upward, above (adv)
ⲛ̀ϫⲉ	post poned subject indicator, "which is" (65)
ⲛ̀ϯⲟⲩⲛⲟⲩ	immediately (adv.)
ⲟⲓ (q)	to be (v. ipi)
ⲟⲛ	again, also, still, further (adv)
ⲟⲩⲁⲓ	(number) one
ⲟⲩⲁϩⲥⲁϩⲛⲓ	To order, command (v.i)
ⲟⲩⲃⲁϣ ⲟⲩⲟⲃϣ (q)	to become white (vi), to be white
ⲟⲩⲇⲉ	nor (conj.) (123)

ⲟⲩⲉⲓⲛⲓⲛ	Greek person (m)	ⲟⲩⲱⲙ ⲟⲩⲱⲙ- ⲟⲩⲉⲙ- ⲟⲩⲟⲙ⸗	to eat (v.t)
ⲟⲩⲏⲃ	priest (m)		
ⲟⲩⲏⲓ	indeed (adv.)	ⲟⲩⲱⲛ, ⲟⲩⲏⲛ (q)	to open, to be opened (q)
ⲟⲩⲓⲛⲁⲙ	right hand (f)	ⲟⲩⲱⲛϩ, ⲟⲩⲟⲛϩ⸗	to reveal, announce, appear
ⲟⲓⲕⲟⲛⲟⲙⲟⲥ	manager, steward, administrator (Gk,m)	ⲟⲩⲱⲛϩ ⲉⲃⲟⲗ	to reveal, give thanks (v.i)
ⲟⲩⲛⲟⲩ	hour, time (f)	ⲟⲩⲱⲣⲡ ⲟⲩⲉⲣⲡ- ⲟⲩⲟⲣⲡ⸗	to send (v.t)
ⲛ̀ⲧⲟⲩⲛⲟⲩ	instantly, at once (adv)		
ϧⲉⲛ ϯⲟⲩⲛⲟⲩ	instantly, at once (adv)	ⲟⲩⲱⲧ	(adj.) unique, one, single
ⲟⲩⲛⲟϥ	delight, joy (m)	ⲟⲩⲱⲧⲉⲃ	to depart, change (v.i)
ⲟⲩⲛⲟϥ ⲙⲙⲟ⸗	to rejoice (v.r)	ⲟⲩⲱϣ ⲟⲩⲁϣ⸗ ⲟⲩⲁϣ- ⲟⲩⲉϣ-	to desire, to love (v.t)
ⲟⲩⲟⲃϣ (q) v. ⲟⲩⲃⲁϣ	to be white		
			wish, desire (m)
ⲟⲩⲟⲛ	someone, something (pron.)	ⲟⲩϫⲁⲓ	salvation, health (m)
ⲟⲩⲟⲛ ⲟⲩⲟⲛⲧⲉ- ⲟⲩⲟⲛⲧⲁ⸗	to be, to have (existential.vb)	ⲟϩⲓ ⲉⲣⲁⲧ⸗	to stand up
ⲟⲩⲟⲡ, ⲟⲩⲁⲃ (q)	to become holy, to be holy (q)	ⲡ̀	m definite art (28)
ⲟⲩⲟϩ	and (conj) (124)	ⲡⲁ-	My (masc obj.), 1st P sing. possessive article (32)
ⲟⲩⲣⲟ	king (m)		
ⲟⲩⲣⲱⲟⲩ	kings (pl)	ⲡⲁⲓ	this, (m s demonstrative art) (36)
ⲟⲩⲣⲱ	queen (f)		
ⲟⲩⲧⲁϩ	fruit (m)	ⲡⲁⲗⲓⲛ	again, once more (adv. Gk)
ⲟⲩⲧⲉ	between, among (prep) (70)	ⲡⲁⲗⲓⲛ ⲟⲛ	
		ⲡⲁⲛⲧⲟⲕⲣⲁⲧⲱⲣ	Almighty (Gk,m)
		ⲡⲁⲣⲁⲃⲟⲗⲏ	parable (Gk,f)
ⲟⲩⲱⲓⲛⲓ	light (m)	ⲡⲁⲣⲁⲇⲓⲥⲟⲥ	paradise (Gk,m)

ⲡⲁⲣⲁⲕⲗⲧⲟⲛ	comforter (Gk,m)
ⲡⲁⲣⲁⲡⲧⲱⲙⲁ	trespass (Gk,m)
ⲡⲁⲣⲉⲙⲃⲟⲗⲏ	barrack (Gk,f)
ⲡⲁⲣⲑⲉⲛⲓⲁ	virginity (Gk,f)
ⲡⲁⲣⲑⲉⲛⲟⲥ	(Gk,f) virgin
ⲡⲁⲣⲣⲏⲥⲓⲁ	boldness, openness, frankness, confidence, courage (Gk,f)
ⲡⲁⲥⲭⲁ	Passover (Gk,m)
ⲡⲁⲧⲣⲓⲁⲣⲏⲭⲥ	patriarch (Gk,m)
ⲡⲁⲧϣⲉⲗⲉⲧ	bridegroom (m)
ⲡⲉ	is (m copula) (47)
ⲡⲉ-	your (fem obj, 2nd P poss art) (32)
ⲡⲉⲑⲟⲩⲁⲃ	the Holy one, saint, sanctuary (m)
ⲡⲉⲕ-	your (masc obj,) 2nd P poss article (32)
ⲡⲉⲛ	our (masc obj. 1st P plural poss article) (32)
ⲡⲉⲥ	her (third person fem singular) (32)
ⲡⲉⲧⲉⲛ-	your (masc obect, 2nd P plu poss article) (32)
ⲡⲉⲧⲣⲁ	rock (Gk,f)
ⲡⲉϥ	his (3rd P m poss art) (32)
ⲡⲉϫⲉ	said (past inf of ϫⲱ) (154)
ⲡⲓ	m definite art (28)
ⲡⲓⲥⲧⲟⲥ	faithful (Gk,m)
ⲡⲟⲗⲉⲙⲟⲥ	war, fight, battle (Gk,m)
ⲡⲣⲉⲥⲃⲩⲧⲉⲣⲟⲥ	Priest (Gk,m)
ⲡⲣⲉⲧⲱⲣⲓⲟⲛ	Praetorium (Gk,m)
ⲡⲣⲟⲥⲉⲩⲭⲏ	prayer (Gk,m)
ⲡⲣⲟⲫⲏⲧⲏⲥ	prophet (Gk,m)
ⲡⲩⲗⲏ	gate (Gk,f)
ⲡ̅ϣⲱⲓ	that which is high, above
ⲣⲁⲃⲃⲓ	Rabbi (prop. Noun)
ⲣⲁⲥⲟⲩⲓ	dream (f)
ⲣⲁⲥϯ	morrow (m)
ⲣⲁϣⲓ	to rejoice (v.i) joy, gladness (m)
ⲣⲉⲙⲛ̀ⲕⲁϯ	intelligent, wise (adj)
ⲣⲉⲙⲛ̀ⲭⲏⲙⲓ	Egyptian, Coptic (adj.)
ⲣⲉⲙⲣⲁⲩϣ	gentle person
ⲣⲉⲙⲛ̀ⲣⲏⲥ	southerner (m)
ⲣⲉⲙⲛ̀ϩⲑⲟ	horseman, rider (m)
ⲣⲉⲙϩⲉ	free person (m)
ⲣⲉϥⲧⲁⲛϧⲟ	life giver (m)
ⲣⲉϥϭⲓⲟⲩⲓ	thief (m)
ⲣⲉϥϯⲥⲃⲱ	teacher (m)

ⲡⲉϥϯϩⲁⲡ	judge (m)	ⲥⲁⲃⲟⲗ	outside (adv)
ⲣⲏ	sun (m)	ⲥⲁⲓⲉ	beauty (adj.)
ⲣⲏⲥ	south (m)	ⲥⲁⲓⲏ	beautiful person, thing (f)
ⲣⲏϯ	manner, condition (m)	ⲥⲁⲙⲡⲉⲑⲛⲁⲛⲉϥ	beneficent, good (n)
ⲣⲓⲕⲓ ⲣⲉⲕ- ⲣⲁⲕⲓ (q)	to bend, lean, tilt (v.t)	ⲥⲁⲙⲡⲉⲧϩⲱⲟⲩ	evil doer, sinner (n)
ⲣⲓⲕⲓ ⲙ̀ⲃⲁⲗ	twinkling of an eye, moment, second (m)	ⲥⲁⲡⲉⲥⲏⲧ	beneath (adv)
		ⲥⲁⲡϣⲱⲓ	above
ⲣⲓⲙⲓ	to cry (v.i)	ⲥⲁⲣⲏⲥ	southern side, south
ⲣⲟ	mouth (m)		
ⲣⲱⲟⲩ	mouths (pl)	ⲥⲁⲣⲝ	flesh (Gk,f)
ⲣⲟⲙⲡⲓ	year (f)	ⲥⲁⲧⲁⲛⲁⲥ	Satan (prop noun)
ⲣⲟⲩϩⲓ	evening (m)	ⲥⲁⲫⲁϩⲟⲩ	behind, after (adv)
	at the time of evening (adv.)	ⲥⲁϧ	scribe, teacher, lawyer (m)
ⲣⲱⲟⲩϣ	to have care, be intent on (v.t)	ⲥⲁϧⲟⲩⲛ	inside (adv)
ⲣⲱⲕϩ ⲣⲉⲕϩ- ⲣⲟⲕϩ⳱ ⲣⲟⲕϩ (q)	to burn (v.t)	ⲥⲁϩⲛⲓ	command
		ⲥⲁϩⲟⲩⲓ ⲥϩⲟⲩⲉⲣ- ⲥϩⲟⲩⲱⲣ⳱ ⲥϩⲟⲩⲟⲣⲧ (q)	to rebuke, curse (v.t)
ⲣⲱⲙⲏ	Rome (prop noun)		
ⲣⲱⲙⲓ	person, man (m)	ⲥⲁϫⲓ	to speak (v.t)
ⲣⲱⲧ ⲣⲉⲧ- ⲣⲟⲧ⳱ ⲣⲏⲧ (q)	to bud, plant, to be planted (q)	ⲉ̀	to speak, talk to
		ⲛⲉⲙ	to speak with
ⲣⲱϣⲓ ⲣⲁϣ- ⲣⲁϣⲓ (q)	to be sufficient, enough (v.t)	ⲉ̀ ⲉⲑⲃⲉ ϧⲁ	to speak about
		ⲛ̀ⲥⲁ ⲟⲩⲃⲏ ⲟⲩⲃⲉ	to speak against
ⲣⲱϭⲧ ⲣⲉϭⲧ- ⲣⲁϭⲧ⳱ ⲣⲁϭⲧ (q)	to strike, convulse (v.t)		word (m)
		ⲥⲉⲃⲓ	circumcision (m)

ⲥⲉⲛϯ	foundation (f)		consider (v.i)
ⲥⲏⲓⲛⲓ	doctor (m,f)	ⲥⲟⲛ	brother (m)
ⲥⲏⲟⲩ	time (m)	ⲥ̀ⲛⲏⲟⲩ	brothers (pl)
ⲥⲏϥⲓ	sword (f)	ⲥⲟⲛⲓ	thief (m)
ⲥⲓⲛⲓ	to pass by, pass away (v.i)	ⲥⲟⲡ	time, occasion (m)
ⲥⲓⲟⲩ	star (m)	ⲥⲟⲩⲥⲟⲩ	minute, very short time (m)
ⲥⲓⲱⲛ	Zion (prop. Noun)	ⲥⲱⲟⲩⲉⲛ ⲥⲟⲩⲉⲛ- ⲥⲟⲩⲱⲛ⳱	to know (v.t)
ⲥ̀ⲕⲉⲩⲟⲥ	vessel (Gk,m)		
ⲥⲕⲩⲛⲏ	tabernacle, tent, dome (Gk,f)	ⲥⲱⲟⲩⲧⲉⲛ ⲥⲟⲩⲧⲉⲛ- ⲥⲟⲩⲧⲱⲛ- ⲥⲟⲩⲧⲱⲛ⳱	to stretch (v.t)
ⲥ̀ⲙⲏ	Voice (f)		
ⲥ̀ⲙⲟⲩ, ⲥ̀ⲙⲁⲣⲱⲟⲩⲧ (q)	to praise/ bless, to be blessed (v.i)		
		ⲥⲟⲫⲓⲁ	wisdom (Gk,f)
ⲥ̀ⲛⲁⲩ	two (no.) (m)	ⲥⲟϩⲓ ⲥⲁϩⲱ⳱	to reprove, correct, admonish (v.t)
ⲥ̀ⲛⲁⲩ	bond (m)	ⲥⲟϭⲛⲓ	counsel, design (m)
ⲥ̀ⲛⲟⲩϯ	two (no.) (f)		
ⲥ̀ⲛⲟϥ	blood (m)	ⲥⲧⲩⲗⲏ	column, pillar (Gk,m)
ⲥⲟⲃϯ ⲥⲉⲃⲧⲉ- ⲥⲉⲃⲧⲱⲧ⳱ ⲥⲉⲃⲧⲱⲧ (q)	to prepare, to be ready (q)	ⲥⲩⲛⲁⲅⲱⲅⲏ	synagogue (f)
		ⲥ̀ⲫⲟⲧⲟⲩ ⲙ̀ⲫⲓⲱⲙ	seashore, beach (lit. lips of the sea)
ⲥⲟⲓ	wooden beam (m,f)	ⲥⲱ ⲥⲉ- ⲥⲟ⳱ ⲥⲁⲩ (p.c)	to drink (v.t)
ⲥⲟⲗⲥⲉⲗ ⲥⲉⲗⲥⲉⲗ- ⲥⲉⲗⲥⲱⲗ⳱	to adorn, comfort (v.t)	ⲥⲱⲃⲓ	to laugh, deride (v.t)
ⲥⲟⲗⲥⲉⲗ	adornment (m)	ⲥⲱⲙⲁ	body (Gk,m)
ⲥⲟⲙⲥ ⲉ̀	to behold, look,	ⲥⲱⲛⲓ	sister (f,pl)

Glossary

ⲥⲱⲛⲧ ⲥⲉⲛⲧ- ⲥⲟⲛⲧ⸗	to create, to renew (v.t)
ⲥⲱⲛϩ, ⲥⲟⲛϩ (q)	to bind, to be bound (v.t)
ⲥⲱⲟⲩⲛ ⲥⲟⲩⲉⲛ- ⲥⲟⲩⲱⲛ⸗	to know (v.t)
ⲥⲱⲣϩ, ⲥⲁⲣϩ-	to sweep (v.t)
ⲥⲱⲧⲉⲙ ⲥⲟⲧⲙ⸗	
ⲉ ⲉⲣⲟ⸗	to listen (v.t)
ⲛ̀ ⲙⲙⲟ⸗	to obey (v.t)
ⲥⲱϥ ⲥⲉϥ- ⲥⲟϥ⸗ ⲥⲟϥ	to defile, pollute (v.t)
ⲥⲱⲧ ⲥⲉⲧ- ⲥⲟⲧ⸗	to save (v.t)
ⲥ̀ϩⲓⲙⲓ	woman (f)
ϩⲓⲟⲩⲙⲓ	women (pl)
ⲧ̀	the, (f definite art) (28)
ⲧⲁ	my (f obj, 1st P sing. poss art) (32)
ⲧⲁⲅⲙⲁ	core, division (Gk,m)
ⲧⲁⲓ	this (f s demonstrative art) (34)
ⲧⲁⲟⲓ ⲧⲁⲓⲉ- ⲧⲁⲓⲟ⸗ ⲧⲁⲓⲏⲟⲩⲧ	to honour
	honour, respect, praise, gift (m)
ⲧⲁⲕⲟ	to destroy, lose (v.t)
ⲧⲁⲗⲟ ⲧⲁⲗⲉ- ⲧⲁⲗⲟ⸗ ⲧⲁⲗⲏⲟⲩⲧ	to lift up, mount (v.t)
ⲧⲁⲗϭⲟ ⲧⲁⲗϭⲉ- ⲧⲁⲗϭⲟ⸗	to heal (v.t)
	healing (m)
ⲧⲁⲙⲟ ⲧⲁⲙⲉ- ⲧⲁⲙⲟ⸗	to inform, tell (vb, trans)
ⲧⲁⲡⲁⲛⲏ	food (m)
ⲧⲁⲥⲑⲟ ⲧⲁⲥⲑⲉ- ⲧⲁⲥⲑⲟ⸗ ⲧⲁⲥⲑⲏⲟⲩⲧ	to return, bring back (v.t)
ⲧⲁⲫⲙⲏ	truth (m)
	truly (adv)
ⲧⲁϩⲛⲟ ⲧⲁϩⲛⲉ- ⲧⲁϩⲛⲟ⸗	to hinder, hamper (v.t)
ⲧⲁϩⲟ ⲧⲁϩⲉ- ⲧⲁϩⲟ⸗ ⲧⲁϩⲏⲟⲩⲧ	to reach, attain (v.t)
ⲉ̀ⲣⲁⲧ⸗	to make to stand (v.t)
ⲧⲁϫⲣⲟ ⲧⲁϫⲣⲉ- ⲧⲁϫⲣⲟ⸗ ⲧⲁϫⲣⲏⲟⲩⲧ	to make firm, strong (v.t)
ⲧⲉⲃⲛⲏ	animal, beast (m)
ⲧⲉⲃⲛⲱⲟⲩⲓ	animals (pl)
ⲧⲉⲛ	our (f 1st P poss art) (32)

299

So You want to Learn Coptic?

ⲧⲉⲛϩ	wing (m)	ⲧ̀ⲣⲓⲁⲥ	Trinity (Gk,f)
ⲧⲉⲛϩⲟⲩⲧ	to believe, to trust (v.t)	ⲧ̀ⲥⲟ ⲧⲥⲉ- ⲧⲥⲟ⸍	to give to drink
ⲧⲉⲛϩⲉⲧ-		ⲧⲩⲡⲟⲥ	type, symbol (Gk,m)
ⲧⲉⲛϩⲟⲩⲧ⸍		ⲧⲱⲙⲧ	to be amazed, stunned (v.i)
ⲧⲉⲥ-	her (3rd P f s poss art) (32)		trance, amazement (m)
ⲧⲉⲕ-	your (2nd P f s poss art) (32)	ⲧⲱⲟⲛ ⲧⲉⲛ-	to raise, rise
ⲧⲉⲧⲉⲛ-	your (2nd P f pl poss art) (32)	ⲧⲱⲛ⸍	
ⲧⲏⲣ⸍	all (inflected adjective) (43)	ⲧⲱⲟⲩ	mountain (m)
ⲧⲟⲛⲟⲩ, ⲧⲟⲛⲱ	very, greatly (adv.)	ⲫ̀	m def art (28)
ⲧⲟⲧⲥ	chair (m,n)	ⲫⲁⲓ	m demonstrative p.noun
ⲧⲟⲧⲉ	then (conj) (124)	ⲫⲁⲣⲓⲥⲉⲟⲥ	Pharisee (Gk,m)
ⲧⲟⲩ	their (3rd P f s object poss art) (32)	ⲫⲉ	heaven (f)
		ⲫⲏⲟⲩⲓ	heavens (pl)
ⲧⲟⲩⲃⲟ ⲧⲟⲩⲃⲉ- ⲧⲟⲩⲃⲟ⸍	to purify, to be pure (q)	ⲫⲏ	that, m far demonstrative pronoun
ⲧⲟⲩⲃⲏⲟⲩⲧ (q)		ⲫⲟⲩⲁⲓ ⲫⲟⲩⲁⲓ	each one
ⲧⲟⲩⲃⲟ	purity (m)	ⲫⲟϩ	to reach (v.i)
ⲧⲟⲩⲛⲟⲥ	to raise, arouse (v.t)	ⲫⲱⲛϩ, ⲫⲉⲛϩ- ⲫⲟⲛϩ⸍ ⲫⲟⲛϩ	to turn (v.t)
ⲧⲟⲩⲛⲟⲥ-			
ⲧⲟⲩⲛⲉⲥ-		ⲫⲱⲣϫ ⲫⲉⲣϫ- ⲫⲟⲣϫ⸍ ⲫⲟⲣϫ	to divide, separate (v.t)
ⲧⲟⲩⲛⲟⲥ⸍			
ⲧⲟⲩϫⲟ ⲧⲟⲩϫⲉ- ⲧⲟⲩϫⲟ⸍	to make whole, save (v.t)	ⲫⲱⲧ, ⲫⲏⲧ (q)	to run, flee
		ϣⲁ	to run, flee to
ⲧⲟⲩϫⲏⲟⲩⲧ		ⲛ̀ⲥⲁ	to pursue
ⲧⲣⲁⲡⲉⲍⲁ	table (Gk,f)		

ⲫⲱϧ ⲫⲉϧ- ⲫⲁϧ⸌ ⲫⲏϧ	to rip, tear apart (v.t)	ϩⲱⲣ	Hor (prop noun)
ⲭⲁⲕⲓ	darkness (n)	ⲱⲟⲩ	glory (m)
ⲭⲁⲣⲱ⸌	to be silent (v.i)	ⲱⲟⲩⲛⲓⲁⲧ⸌	to be blessed (adj vb) (164)
ⲭⲉⲣⲟⲩⲃⲓⲙ	Cherubim (m)	ⲱϣ	
ⲭⲏⲙⲓ	Egypt (m)	ⲉ̀	to cry, read
ⲭⲏⲣⲁ	widow (f)	ⲉ̀ⲃⲟⲗ	to cry out, proclaim
ⲭⲣⲏⲥⲧⲓⲁⲛⲟⲥ	Christian (Gk,m)	ϣⲁ	(prep) to, towards, till (70)
ⲭ̀ⲣⲓⲥⲧⲟⲥ	Christ, anointed one (Gk,m)	ϣⲁⲛⲧⲉ	till (pre subj form of limitative) (132)
ⲭⲣⲟⲛⲟⲥ	period of time, season (Gk,m)	ϣⲁⲡⲓ	red (adj)
ⲭ̀ⲣⲱⲙ	fire (m)	ϣⲁⲧⲉ	till (pre subj form of limitative) (6.2.i)
ⲭⲱ ⲭⲁ- ⲭⲁ⸌ ⲭⲏ (q)	to place, (q) to exist	ϣⲁⲩ	of value (adj.)
ⲉ̀ⲃⲟⲗ	to let go, to forgive	ϣⲁϣⲛⲓ	to win, gain (v.t)
ⲛ̀ⲥⲁ	to leave behind	ϣⲁϩ	flame, fire (m,n)
ⲭⲱⲗⲉⲙ ⲙⲙⲟ⸌	to hasten (v,r)	ϣⲁϥⲉ	wilderness, desert (m)
ⲭⲱⲡ	to hide (v.i)	ϣⲉⲃϣⲓ	shield (f)
ⲭⲱⲣⲁ	district, country (Gk,f)	ϣⲉⲡϭⲓⲥⲓ	to suffer (v)
ⲯⲁⲗⲙⲟⲥ	psalm (m)	ϣⲉⲡϩⲙⲟⲧ	to accept grace, to thank (v)
ⲯⲩⲭⲏ	soul (Gk,f)	ϣⲉⲣⲓ	daughter (f)
ⲱⲓⲕ	bread (m)	ϣⲏⲣⲓ	son (m)
ⲱⲗⲓ ⲉⲗ- ⲟⲗ⸌ ⲟⲗ (q)	to hold, take	ϣⲑⲁⲙ	to close, shut (v.t)
ⲱⲙⲥ ⲉⲙⲥ- ⲟⲙⲥ⸌	to baptise (v.t)	ϣⲟⲉϩ	street (m)
		ϣⲟⲟⲣⲧⲉⲣ	to disturb, to be disturbed (q)
		ϣⲑⲉⲣⲧⲉⲣ-	

ϣⲧⲉⲣⲱⲣ⸗		ϣⲫⲏⲣⲓ	wonder, amazement (f)
ϣⲧⲉⲣⲱⲣ		ϣⲱⲙ	summer (m)
ϣⲑⲟⲣⲧⲉⲣ	disturbance (m)	ϣⲱⲛⲓ	to be sick (v.i)
ϣⲓ	measure (m)		sick person (m)
	to measure (v.t)	ϣⲱⲛϩ, ϣⲟⲛϩ⸗	to deprive (v.t)
ϣⲓⲛⲓ ϣⲉⲛ- ϣⲉⲛ⸗	to ask, seek	ϣⲱⲟⲩⲓ, ϣⲟⲩⲱⲟⲩ (q)	to dry, to be dried, withered (q)
ὲ	to visit	ϣⲱⲡ ϣⲉⲡ- ϣⲟⲡ⸗ ϣⲏⲡ	to receive, accept, buy (v.t)
ⲛ̀ⲥⲁ	to inquire for, seek after		
ϣⲗⲏⲗ	to pray (v.i)	ϣⲱⲡⲓ	to happen, become (v.t)
ϣⲛⲉ	net (m)	ϣⲱⲣⲡ	morning (m)
ϣⲛⲏⲟⲩ	nets (pl)		to be early (v.i)
ϣⲟⲃⲓ	hypocrite (m)	ϣⲱⲧ ϣⲉⲧ- ϣⲁⲧ⸗ ϣⲏⲧ	to cut, slaughter, slay (v.t)
ϣⲟⲩⲓⲧ	vain		
ϣⲟⲩ-	worthy of (pfx)	ϣⲱⲧ	merchant, trader (m)
ϣⲟⲩⲟ, ϣⲟⲩⲓⲧ	to empty out, to flow, to be empty (q)	ϣϣⲏⲛ	tree (m)
		ϥⲁⲓ ϥⲓ- ϥⲓⲧ⸗	to lift, carry (v.t)
ϣⲟⲩⲣⲏ	censor (f)	ϥⲁⲓϣⲉⲛⲛⲟⲩϥⲓ	announcer (n)
ϣⲟⲩϣⲟⲩ	to boast, be proud (v.t)	ϥⲓⲣⲱⲟⲩϣ	to worry, take care of (v.i)
ϣⲟⲩϣⲱⲟⲩϣⲓ	sacrifice (m)	ϥⲱⲓ	hair (m)
ϣⲧⲉⲙ	form for neg subjunctive (135)	ϧⲁ	under (prep)
	form for neg condtional (203)		towards direction of (prep)
ϣⲫⲉⲣⲓ	friend (f)		used in apposition
ϣⲫⲏⲣ	friend, companion (m)		for the sake of (prep)

	against (prep) is also used un translated with some verbs e.g. ϥⲁⲓ ϧⲁ- to carry	ϩⲁ	to, under (prep) (70)
		ϩⲁⲓ	husband (m)
		ϩⲁⲗⲁϯ	birds (n.pl)
ϧⲁ ⲉ	last	ϩⲁⲗⲏⲧ	bird, flying creature (m)
ϧⲁⲧϩⲏ	before, in front of (prep)	ϩⲁⲙϣⲉ	carpenter (m)
ϧⲁϫⲉⲛ	before (prep)	ϩⲁⲛⲁⲣⲟⲩϩⲓ	evening (m) see ⲣⲟⲩϩⲓ
ϧⲁϫⲱ⸌	before (pronoun form)	ϩⲁⲛⲟⲩⲟⲛ	some
ϧⲉⲛ	in (prep) (70)	ϩⲁⲡ	judgment (m)
ⲛ̀ϧⲏⲧ⸌	pronom form	ϩⲉⲓ, ϩⲓⲱⲟⲩⲧ (q)	to fall, to be fallen (q)
ϧⲉⲛ ⲡ̀ϫⲓⲛⲑ̀ⲣⲉ⸌	when (verbal substantive) (212)	ϩⲉⲗⲡⲓⲥ	hope (Gk,f)
ϧⲉⲛ ⲡ̀ϫⲓⲛⲧ⸌	when (verbal substantive) (212)	ϩⲉⲙⲥⲓ	to sit (v.i)
ϧⲏⲃⲥ	lamp (m)	ϩⲏ	beginning (m)
ϧⲏⲃⲓ	shadow (f)	ϩⲏⲃⲓ	to weep, lament (v.i)
ϧⲓⲥⲓ, ϧⲟⲥⲓ (q)	to toil, to be wearied, suffering	ϩⲏⲅⲉⲙⲱⲛ	governor (Gk,m)
ϧⲓⲥⲓ	weariness, suffering (m)	ϩⲏⲕⲓ	poor, needy (m)
ϧⲙⲟⲙ	fever, heat (m)	ϩⲏⲡⲡⲉ	behold! (interj) (239)
ϧⲟⲩⲛ	inward part (m)	ϩⲏⲧ	heart (m)
ϧⲣⲏⲓ	down, lower part (m)	ϩⲏⲟⲩ	profit, gain (m)
ϧⲣⲱⲟⲩ	voice (m)	ϩⲓ	on (prep) (70)
ϧⲱⲛⲧ, ϧⲉⲛⲧ (q)	to draw near, to be near (q)	ϩⲓⲕⲱⲛ	image, icon, likeness (Gk,f)
ϧⲱⲧⲉⲃ ϧⲁⲧⲉⲃ- ϧⲟⲑⲃ⸌	to kill (v.t)	ϩⲓⲛⲁ	so that (Gk,conj.) (124)
		ϩⲓⲛⲓ ϩⲉⲛ- ϩⲉⲛ⸌	to move self forwards, backwards

ϩⲓⲟⲩⲓ ϩⲓ- ϩⲓⲧ⸗ ϩⲱⲟⲩⲓ	to strike, cast, lay (v.t)
ⲉ̀ϧⲣⲏⲓ	throw down
ϩⲓⲣⲉⲛ	at the mouth of, at the entrance of (com prep) (47)
ϩⲓⲣⲱ⸗	pronom form
ϩⲓⲣⲏⲛⲏ	peace (Gk,f)
ϩⲓⲧⲉⲛ	through (comp prep)
ϩⲓⲧⲟⲧ⸗	pronom form
ϩⲓⲱⲓϣ	to preach (v.i)
ϩⲓϣⲉⲛⲛⲟⲩϥⲓ ⲙ̀ⲙⲟ⸗	to preach, proclaim, announce
ϩⲓϫⲉⲛ	above (prep)
ϩ̀ⲕⲟ, ϩⲟⲕⲉⲣ (q)	to hunger, to be hungry (q)
ϩ̀ⲗⲓ	anything, nothing, someone, no one (pro.noun) at all (adv.)
ϩ̀ⲙⲟⲧ	grace (m)
ϩ̀ⲙⲟⲩ	salt (m)
ϩⲟ	face (m)
ϩⲟⲗⲓ	moth (f)
ϩⲟⲙⲧ	bronze (m)
ϩⲟⲛϩⲉⲛ	to command (v.t)
	commandment (m)
ϩⲟⲡⲗⲟⲛ	weapon (Gk,m)
ϩⲟⲡⲱⲥ	so that (Gk,conj) (124)
ϩⲟⲣⲁⲙⲁ	vision (Gk,m)
ϩⲟⲧⲁⲛ	that (Gk,conj)
ϩⲟⲩⲓⲧ	first, chief (m)
ϩⲟϥ	serpent (m)
ϩⲟϫϩⲉϫ	trouble, tribulation (m)
ϩⲟϯ	fear (f)
	to fear (v.i)
ϩ̀ⲣⲏⲓ	upper part (m)
ϩ̀ⲣⲟϣ, ϩⲟⲣϣ (q)	to be cold, heavy (v.i)
ϩ̀ⲣⲱ	furnace (f)
ϩⲩⲙⲛⲟⲥ	hymn (m)
ϩⲩⲛⲓⲙ	slumber (m)
ϩⲩⲡⲁⲣⲭⲟⲛⲧⲁ	possessions, property (Gk,m)
ϩⲩⲡⲉⲣⲧⲏⲥ	servant, attendant (Gk,m)
ϩⲩⲡⲟⲙⲟⲛⲏ	(Gk,f) patience
ϩⲱ⸗	also (inflected adjective) (43)
ϩⲱⲃ	thing, work, matter (m)
ϩ̀ⲃⲏⲟⲩⲓ	things, works (pl)
ϩⲱⲗ ϩⲏⲗ (q)	to fly, to be flying (q)
ϩⲱⲗⲉⲙ ϩⲉⲗⲉⲙ- ϩⲟⲗⲙ⸗	to rob (v.t)
ϩⲱⲙⲓ ϩⲉⲙ-	to tread, trample (v.t)

Glossary

ϩⲟⲩ⸗ ϩⲟⲩ		ϫⲓϫ	hand (f)
ϩⲱⲛ	command (m)	ϫⲣⲟϫ	seed (m)
ϩⲱⲟⲩ	to rain (v.i)	ϫⲟⲓ	ship, boat (m)
ϩⲱⲟⲩ	to be bad, evil (q)	ϫⲟⲙ	power (f)
ϩⲱⲟⲩⲧ	male, husband (m)	ϫⲟⲙϫⲉⲙ	to touch, grope (v.t)
ϩⲱⲡ ϩⲉⲡ- ϩⲟⲡ⸗ ϩⲏⲡ	to hide (v.t)	ϫⲟⲥ	half (m)
		ϫⲟⲩϣⲧ	to look, see (v.t)
ϩⲱⲥ ⲉ̀	to sing (v.i)	ϫⲫⲟ ϫⲫⲉ- ϫⲫⲟ⸗	to beget, give birth to (v.t)
	like, as (adverb)		
ϩⲱⲥⲧⲉ	so that (conj. Gk) (124)	ϫⲱ ϫⲉ- ϫⲟ⸗ ϫⲟⲧ⸗	to speak, say (v.t) (153)
ϩⲱⲧⲡ	to set, sink (v.i)		
ϩⲱϯ	It is necessary (impersonal vb) (161)	ϫⲱⲓⲗⲓ ϫⲁⲗⲏⲟⲩⲧ	to dwell, to be dwelling (q)
ϫⲁϫⲓ	enemy (m)	ϫⲱⲕ ϫⲉⲕ- ϫⲟⲕ⸗ ϫⲏⲕ ⲉⲃⲟⲗ	to complete, perfect (v.t)
ϫⲉ ⲟⲩⲏⲓ	indeed (adv.)		
ϫⲉⲃⲥ	coal (m,f)		
ϫⲉ	for, because, used to introduce direct and indirect speech (125)	ϫⲱⲗ ⲉⲃⲟⲗ	to deny (v.i)
		ϫⲱⲙ	book (m)
		ϫⲱⲛⲧ	anger, wrath (m)
ϫⲉⲙⲛⲟⲩϯ	to find comfort, comfort	ϫⲱⲟⲩ	generation (m)
ϫⲉⲙϯⲡⲓ	to taste (v.t)	ϫⲱⲣ ϫⲉⲣ- ϫⲟⲣ⸗ ϫⲏⲣ ⲉ̀ⲃⲟⲗ	to scatter, disperse (v.t)
ϫⲉⲥⲕⲓϯ	drachma (unit of currency) (f)		
ϫⲉⲕⲁⲥ	so that, although (conj) (124)		
ϫⲓⲙⲓ ϫⲉⲙ- ϫⲉⲙ⸗	to find (v.t)	ϫⲱⲣⲓ	strong, bold (adj.)
		ϭⲁⲗⲟϫ	foot, knee (f)

305

ϭⲁⲗⲁⲩϫ	feet (pl)	ϭⲟϫⲓ	to run, (v.i)
ϭⲱϩⲉⲙ ϭⲁϩⲉⲙ- ϭⲁϩⲙ⸗ ϭⲁϩⲉⲙ	to defile, pollute (v.t)	ⲛⲥⲁ	to run after, persecute
ϭⲉⲣⲟ ϭⲉⲣⲉ- ϭⲉⲣⲟ- ϭⲉⲣⲛⲟⲩⲧ	to light up, burn, kindle (v.t)	†	f def art (28)
ϭⲓ ϭⲓ- ϭⲓⲧ⸗ ϭⲏⲩ	to receive, take	† †- ⲧⲏⲓ⸗ ⲧⲟⲓ (q)	
		ⲛ- ⲙⲙⲟ⸗	to give
ⲛ	to take, receive	ⲉⲃⲟⲗ	to sell (v.t)
ⲛⲉⲙ	to touch	ϯⲁⲥⲟ	to be compassionate (v.t)
ϭⲓⲥⲁⲣⲝ	to take flesh, incarnate	ϯⲗⲟⲅⲟⲥ	give account (v.i)
ϭⲓⲥⲃⲱ	to learn (v.t)	ϯⲙⲓ	village, town (m)
ϭⲓⲥⲓ ϭⲁⲥ- ϭⲉⲥ- ϭⲁⲥ⸗, ϭⲟⲥⲓ (q)	to exalt, to be exalted (q)	ϯⲛⲟⲙϯ	to strengthen, comfort (v.t)
		ϯⲛⲟⲩ	now (adv.) (165)
ϭⲓⲥⲓ	the height, highest (m)	ϯⲣⲉⲛ	to name, call (v.i)
ϭⲓⲙⲡϣⲓϣ	vengeance (m)	ϯⲥⲃⲱ	to teach, reprove
ϭⲓⲛϫⲟⲛⲥ	violence, oppression, iniquity (m)	ϯⲱⲙⲥ	to baptise (v.t)
		ϯⲱⲟⲩ	to glorify (v.t)
ϭⲓⲟⲩⲓ	to steal (v.t)	ϯϣⲱϣ	to hate, despise (v.t)
ϭⲓⲱⲙⲥ	to immerse, baptise (v.i)	ϯϩⲁⲡ	to judge (v.t)
ϭⲓⲙⲱⲓⲧ ϩⲁ	to lead (v.t)	ϯϩⲟ	to ask (v.t)
ϭⲗⲉⲙⲗⲱⲙ	to be busy (i)		
ϭⲗⲓⲗ	burnt offering (m)		
ϭⲟⲓⲥ	Lord (m)		
ϭⲟⲥϫⲉⲥ	to dance (v.i)		

REFERENCES

Grammatical References

Crum, WE. "A Coptic Dictionary compiled with the help of many scholars" Oxford 1939, reprinted 1972

Dawoud, Moawad. "Lessons to simplify Coptic Grammar" Dar Nafle 1973

Dawoud, Moawad "Ⲡⲓⲁⲛⲥⲁϫⲓ ⲛ̇ⲧⲁⲥⲡⲓ ⲛ̇ⲣⲉⲙⲛ̇ⲭⲏⲙⲓ", Cairo, 2000

Kosack, Wolfgang "Lehrbuch des Koptischen" Graz 1974

Lambdin, Thomas "Introduction to Sahidic Coptic" Macon 1983

Layton, Bentley "A Coptic Grammar with Chrestomathy and Glossary Sahidic Dialect", Wiesbaden 2000

Liddell, H. G., A lexicon abridged from Liddell and Scott's Greek-English lexicon, Oxford 1871

Liddel and Scott "Greek-English Lexicon" Abridged Edition Oxford University Press 1891, reprinted 2002.

Maher, Emile Ishak "Ⲥⲁϫⲓ ⲛⲉⲙⲁⲛ" Cairo 1985

Mallon, Alexis "Grammaire Copte" 4.éd., revue par Michel Malinine, Beyrouth 1956

Makkar, Adeeb "The Abbreviated Coptic-English Dictionary" St.Antonious Coptic Orthodox Church, San Francisco 2001

Mattar, Nabil "A Study in Bohairic Coptic", Pasadena 1990

Houghton, Herbert Pierrepont "The Coptic Verb Bohairic Dialect" Leiden 1959

Plumley, J.Martin "An introductory Coptic Grammar (Sahidic dialect)" London 1948

Raphael, Monir Barsoum "The Coptic Liturgy of St.Basil- Coptic language analysis, Chicago 1994

Shisha-Halevy, Ariel. "Coptic Grammatical Chrestomathy- a course for Academic and Private Study", Orientalia Lovaniensia analecta vol. 30 Leuven 1988

Takla, Hany M. 1996 *The history of the Coptic language.* Retrieved May 3, 2004 from www.stshenouda.com

Text editions consulted

Aboseif, Anthony.,ed "**Coptic Hymns a book for all occasions of the Coptic year**", Saint Antonious Coptic Orthodox Church, San Jose area, California 2000

Balestri L. and. Hyvernat,H.,ed "Acta Martyrum" Vols.1 and 2. *Corpus Scriptorum Christianorum Orientalium*, vols. 37 and 38, Paris 1907

De Vis ,Henri.,ed "Homélies Coptes de la vaticane" vol.1 and 5. Hauniae 1929

Horner, G.,ed "The Coptic Version of the New Testament Northern Dialect, otherwise called memphitic and Bohairic, with introduction, critical apparatus and literal English translation". Vols 1-4 Oxford, 1898 (reprint Osnabrück 1969)

Hyvernat, Henri.,ed "Les Actes des Martyrs de L'Egypte" Paris 1886, (reprint Hildescheim 1977)

KHS-Burmeister O.,ed "The Horologion of the Egyptian Church, Coptic and Arabic text from a mediaeval manuscript" *Studia Orientalia Christiana Aegyptiaca* Cairo 1973

Lagarde, Paul de "Der Pentateuch Koptisch" Leipzig 1867, (reprint Osnabrück 1967)

Leipoldt, Johannes and Crum W.E., eds "Sinuthii Archimandritae vita et opera omnia III." *Corpus Scriptorum Christianorum Orientalium*, vol.42 / Scriptores Coptici 2, Leipzig 1908 (reprint Louvain 1955)

Lefort.L .,ed"S.Pachomii Vita- Bohairice scripta" *Corpus Scriptorum Christianorum Orientalium* vol.89/ Scriptores Coptici 7. Paris 1925, (reprint Lovain 1945)

Peeters, M. "A critical edition of the Coptic (Bohairic) Pentateuch" vol.1 and 2 , Atlanta 1985

St.Shenouda society 1998 "Bohairic English Dictionary". Retrieved November 4,.2000 from *St.Shenouda society Coptic CD volume 1*

Tattam, Henricus. "Prophetae Maiores in dialecto linguae Aegypticae Memphitica seu Coptica", 2 vols. Oxford 1852, (reprint Hildesheim 1989)

The Coptic Liturgy of St.Basil, St.John the Beloved publishing house, Cairo 1994

INDEX

A

abbreviations 37
abstract noun .... *See* noun, abstract
adjective 38
adjective verbs 162
adjectives 38
    "other", "also" 44
    attributive construction 38
    comparisions 175
    inflected 41
adverbial phrase 211
adverbs 165
    adverbs of manner 171
    adverbs of situation 173
    adverbs of time and place 165
Alexander the Great 6
antecedent 80
Articles 27
    Definitie article 27
    Demonstrative articles 34
    indefinite article 31
    near demonstrative article 34
    Posessive articles 32
articulated relative ...... *See* relative substantive
attributive construction 38

B

Bohairic 7

C

causative 207
causative infinitive ..... *See* infinitive, causative
causitive
    negative causative 209
circumstantial conversion
    future tense 149
    past perfect 149
    present tense 144
clause 123
    dependent 144
    main 144
comparisions 175
compound verbs .... *See* verbs, compound
conditional 201
    negative of the conditional 203
conjunctions 123
    enclitic 126
consonants 14
copula 47
Crum 8

D

demonstrative 34
Demotic 6, 11
dialect 7

E

existential 160

F

Far demonstrative article: 34
Future
    emphatic future 183
    emphatic future, negative 188
    first future 118
    imperfect future 189
    relative first future 121
    second future 223

G

greeting 114
Gregorian calendar 169

H

habitual 179
Hieroglyphics 5, 11
hours 166

I

imperative 192
Imperative
    negative imperative 197
imperfect past tense .. *See* past tense, imperfect
indirect object pronoun 113
infinitive 62
    causative 207
    potential 213
    simple 207
inflected adjectives .... *See* adjectives, inflected
interjections 238
    inflected interjections 239

non inflected interjections 239
interrogative 227
    particle 227
Interrogative
    interrogative pronouns 229
intransitive verbs .... *See* verbs, intransitive

J

jenkem 16

L

limitative 132

M

Maher, Father Shenouda 11
Moftah, Erian 7
months 169

N

nominal sentence
    subject + copula + predicate 48
    subject + predicate 48
nominal sentences 47
    pronoun + copula 49
non verbal sentences .... *See* nominal sentences
noun
    abstract 261
nouns 27
    plural 29
    proper nouns 15, 17, 18
    number 29
    numbers 53

O

object 61
    direct 113
    indirect 113
object marker 73
Old Bohairic 11, 14, 16, 18, 19, 21, 22, 23
optative 199

P

parts of speech 27
past infinitive 154
past perfect .... *See* past tense, perfect
past tense
    imperfect 139
    perfect 91
    second 225

person
    first 41
    second 41
    third 41
personal pronouns
    dependent 62
    independent 35
personal suffix 96, 108
pluperfect tense 142
plus quam perfectum .... *See* plu perfect tense
Pope Cyril IV 7
Pope Shenouda III 8
possessed noun 249
possessive construction 39, 243
    pronominal form 243
postponed subject indicator 65
potential infinitive .... *See* infinitive, potential
pre subject form
    past perfect 93
predicate 47, 61
prepositional phrase 172
prepositions
    compound 70
    Greek 71
    pronominal form 107
    simple 70
present tense
    first present 61
    second present 221
    third present 145
pronouns 35
    demonstrative pronouns 36
    personal pronouns 35
    reciprocating pronouns 243

Q

qualitative 66, 68

R

reflexive verbs 115
relative converter 79
    future 121
    past 104
relative substantive 90
remenkimi site 253
resumptive morph 85, 105, 109
    past perfect 105
    used with prepositions 109

S

Sahidic 8
Shenouda, Saint 6
Stern 8
subject 47, 61
subject prefix
    first present 63
    past perfect 92
subjunctive 129
subordinate clause .... *See* dependent clause
substantive 90
    relative 90
    verbal 211
suffix pronoun .... *See* personal suffix

T

tense 61
time 166
transitive verbs .... *See* verbs, transitive

V

verbal substantive 210
verboids 162
verbs
    intransitive 61
    transitive 61
vilminor letters 28
vocative 30
Vowels 13

So You want to Learn Coptic?

ⲟⲩⲛⲁⲓ ⲙ̀ⲫⲁⲓ ⲉⲧⲥ̀ϧⲁⲓ ⲁⲙⲏⲛ

ⲟⲩϩⲓⲣⲏⲛⲏ ⲙ̀ⲫⲏ ⲉⲧⲱϣ ⲁⲙⲏⲛ

ⲟⲩⲕⲁϯ ⲙ̀ⲫⲏ ⲉⲧⲥⲱⲧⲉⲙ ⲁⲙⲏⲛ*****

***** Kosack pg. 442